CASE CLOSED™

VOLUME 77

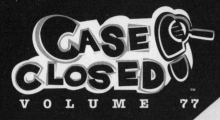

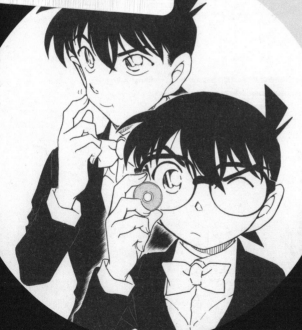

Gosho Aoyama

Case Briefing:

Subject:
Occupation:
Special Skills:
Equipment:

Jimmy Kudo, a.k.a. Conan Edogawa
High School Student/Detective
Analytical thinking and deductive reasoning, Soccer
Bow Tie Voice Transmitter, Super Sneakers,
Homing Glasses, Stretchy Suspenders

The subject is hot on the trail of a pair of suspicious men in black when he is attacked from behind and administered a strange substance which physically transforms him into a first grader. When the subject confides in the eccentric inventor Dr. Agasa, they decide to keep the subject's true identity a secret for the safety of everyone around him. Assuming the new identity of first-grader Conan Edogawa, the subject continues to assist the police force on their most baffling cases. The only problem is that most crime-solving professionals won't take a little kid's advice!

Table of Contents

CONFIDEN

CASE CLOSED
Volume 77
Shonen Sunday Edition

Story and Art by GOSHO AOYAMA

MEITANTEI CONAN Vol. 77
by Gosho AOYAMA
© 1994 Gosho AOYAMA
All rights reserved.
Original Japanese edition published by SHOGAKUKAN.
English translation rights in the United States of America, Canada, the United Kingdom,
Ireland, Australia and New Zealand arranged with SHOGAKUKAN.

Translation
Tetsuichiro Miyaki

Touch-up & Lettering
Freeman Wong

Cover & Graphic Design
Andrea Rice

Editor
Shaenon K. Garrity

Printed in the U.S.A.

Published by VIZ Media, LLC
P.O. Box 77010
San Francisco, CA 94107

10 9 8 7 6 5 4 3 2 1
First printing, January 2021

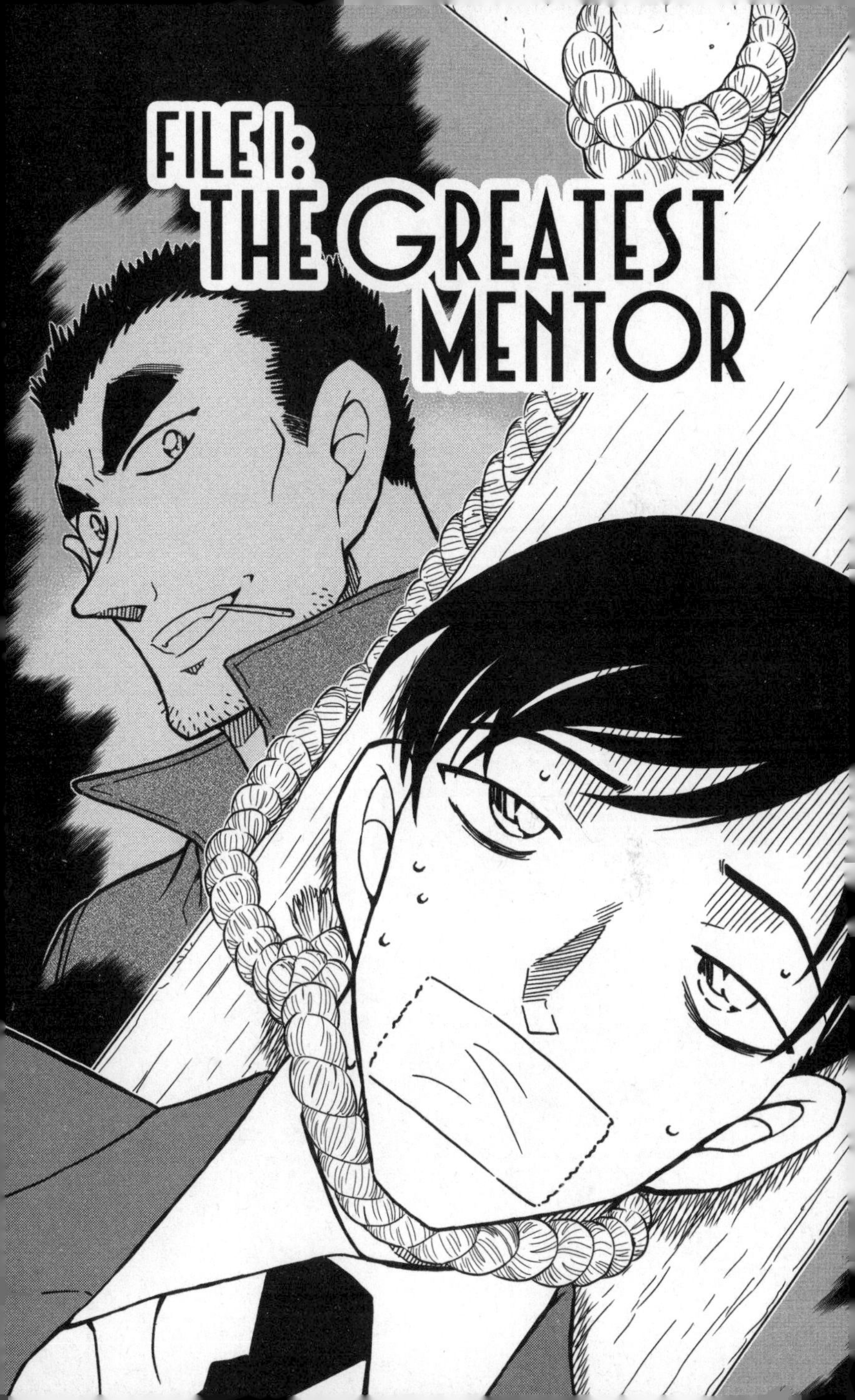
FILE 1:
THE GREATEST MENTOR

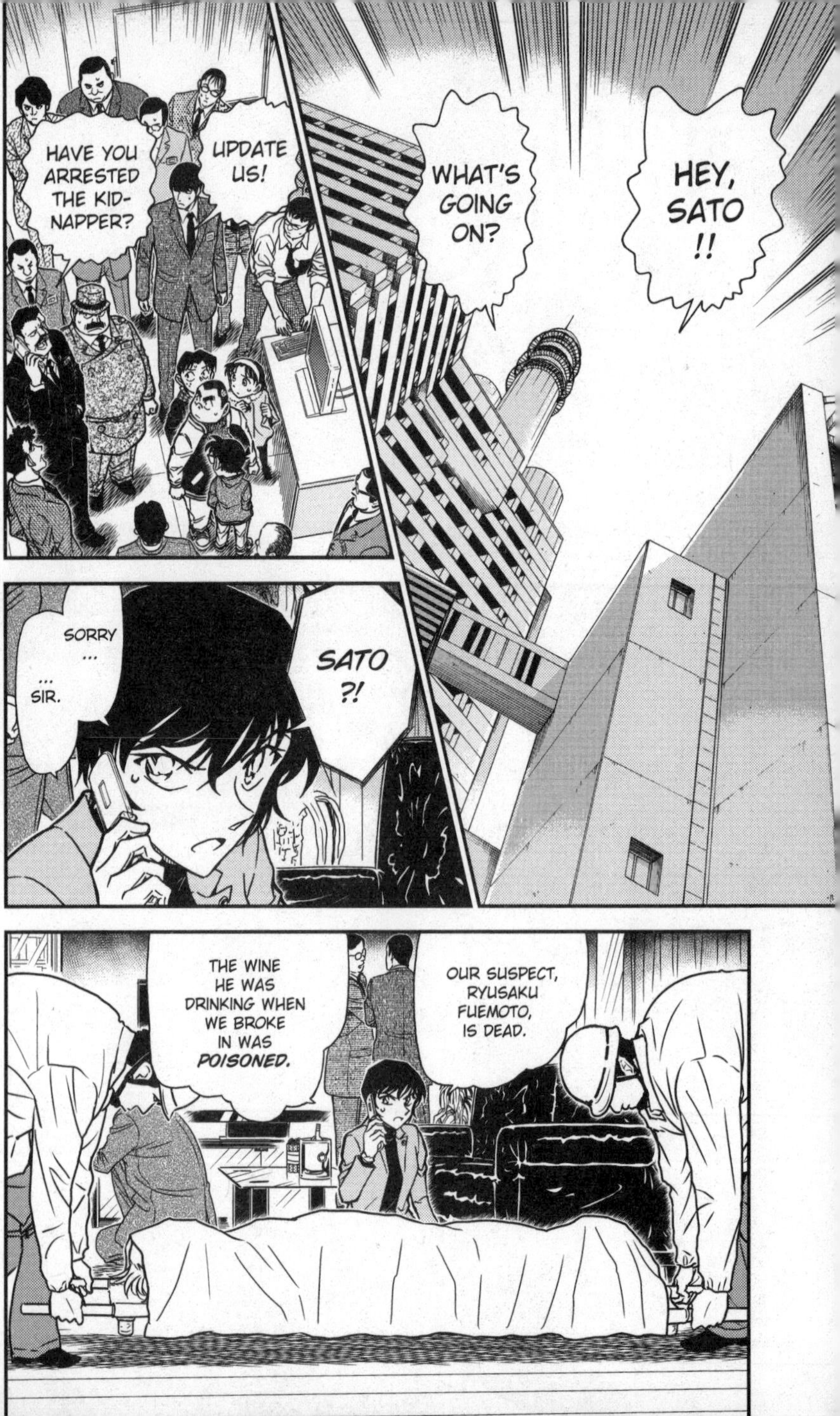
HEY, SATO!!
WHAT'S GOING ON?
UPDATE US!
HAVE YOU ARRESTED THE KID-NAPPER?
SATO?!
SORRY... ...SIR.
OUR SUSPECT, RYUSAKU FUEMOTO, IS DEAD.
THE WINE HE WAS DRINKING WHEN WE BROKE IN WAS POISONED.

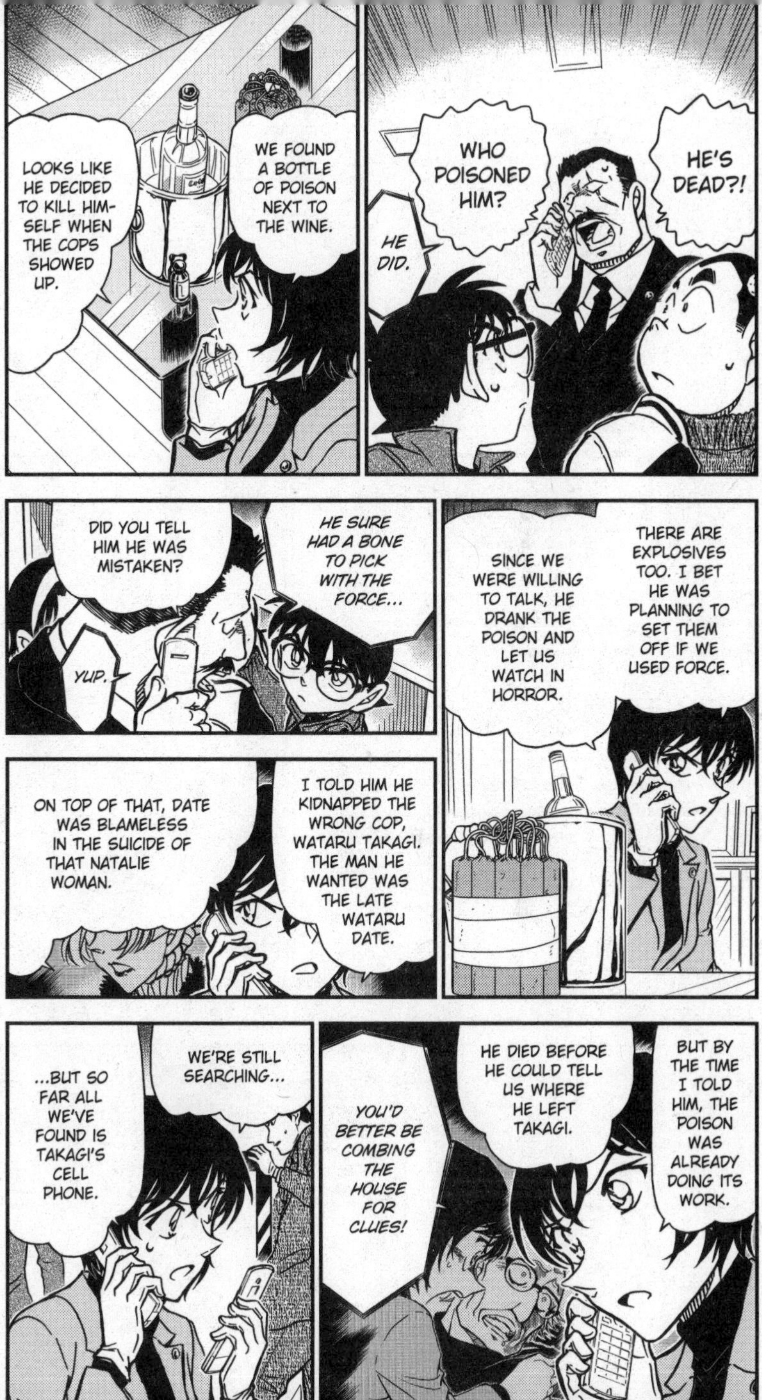
HE'S DEAD?!
WHO POISONED HIM?
HE DID.
WE FOUND A BOTTLE OF POISON NEXT TO THE WINE.
LOOKS LIKE HE DECIDED TO KILL HIM-SELF WHEN THE COPS SHOWED UP.
THERE ARE EXPLOSIVES TOO. I BET HE WAS PLANNING TO SET THEM OFF IF WE USED FORCE.
SINCE WE WERE WILLING TO TALK, HE DRANK THE POISON AND LET US WATCH IN HORROR.
HE SURE HAD A BONE TO PICK WITH THE FORCE...
DID YOU TELL HIM HE WAS MISTAKEN?
YUP.
I TOLD HIM HE KIDNAPPED THE WRONG COP, WATARU TAKAGI. THE MAN HE WANTED WAS THE LATE WATARU DATE.
ON TOP OF THAT, DATE WAS BLAMELESS IN THE SUICIDE OF THAT NATALIE WOMAN.
BUT BY THE TIME I TOLD HIM, THE POISON WAS ALREADY DOING ITS WORK.
HE DIED BEFORE HE COULD TELL US WHERE HE LEFT TAKAGI.
YOU'D BETTER BE COMBING THE HOUSE FOR CLUES!
WE'RE STILL SEARCHING...
...BUT SO FAR ALL WE'VE FOUND IS TAKAGI'S CELL PHONE.

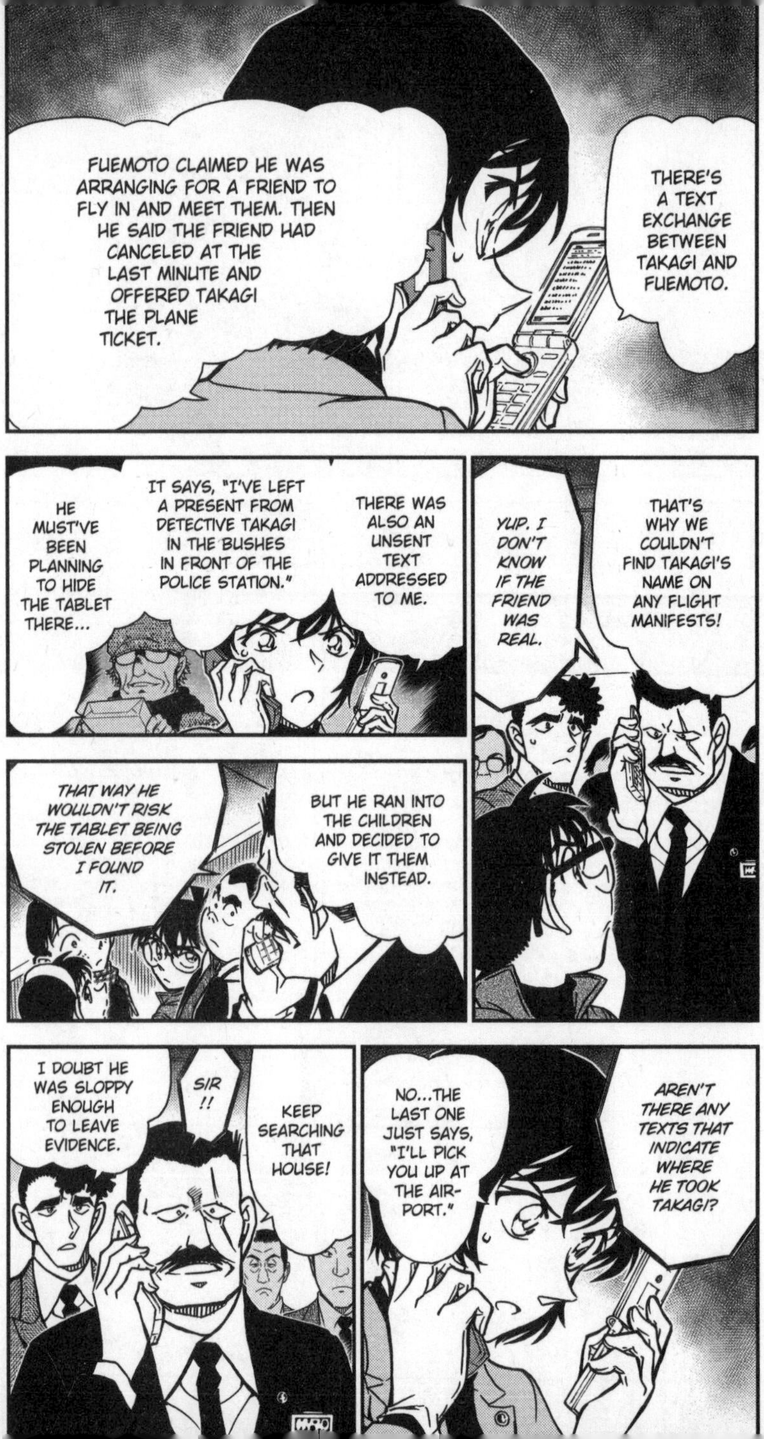
THERE'S A TEXT EXCHANGE BETWEEN TAKAGI AND FUEMOTO.
FUEMOTO CLAIMED HE WAS ARRANGING FOR A FRIEND TO FLY IN AND MEET THEM. THEN HE SAID THE FRIEND HAD CANCELED AT THE LAST MINUTE AND OFFERED TAKAGI THE PLANE TICKET.
THAT'S WHY WE COULDN'T FIND TAKAGI'S NAME ON ANY FLIGHT MANIFESTS!
YUP. I DON'T KNOW IF THE FRIEND WAS REAL.
THERE WAS ALSO AN UNSENT TEXT ADDRESSED TO ME.
IT SAYS, "I'VE LEFT A PRESENT FROM DETECTIVE TAKAGI IN THE BUSHES IN FRONT OF THE POLICE STATION."
HE MUST'VE BEEN PLANNING TO HIDE THE TABLET THERE...
BUT HE RAN INTO THE CHILDREN AND DECIDED TO GIVE IT THEM INSTEAD.
THAT WAY HE WOULDN'T RISK THE TABLET BEING STOLEN BEFORE I FOUND IT.
AREN'T THERE ANY TEXTS THAT INDICATE WHERE HE TOOK TAKAGI?
NO...THE LAST ONE JUST SAYS, "I'LL PICK YOU UP AT THE AIR-PORT."
KEEP SEARCHING THAT HOUSE!
SIR!!
I DOUBT HE WAS SLOPPY ENOUGH TO LEAVE EVIDENCE.

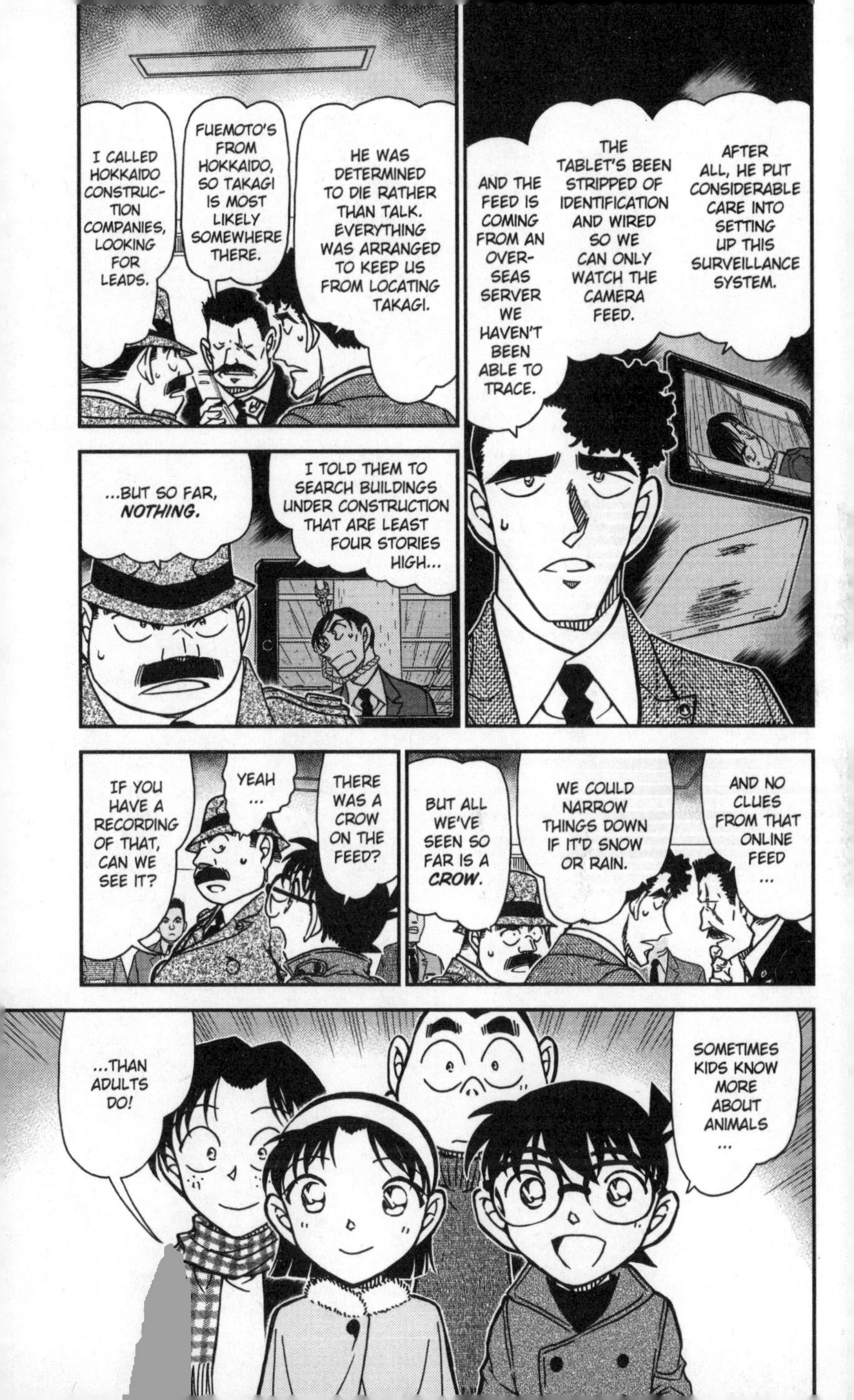
AFTER ALL, HE PUT CONSIDERABLE CARE INTO SETTING UP THIS SURVEILLANCE SYSTEM.
THE TABLET'S BEEN STRIPPED OF IDENTIFICATION AND WIRED SO WE CAN ONLY WATCH THE CAMERA FEED.
AND THE FEED IS COMING FROM AN OVER-SEAS SERVER WE HAVEN'T BEEN ABLE TO TRACE.
HE WAS DETERMINED TO DIE RATHER THAN TALK. EVERYTHING WAS ARRANGED TO KEEP US FROM LOCATING TAKAGI.
FUEMOTO'S FROM HOKKAIDO, SO TAKAGI IS MOST LIKELY SOMEWHERE THERE.
I CALLED HOKKAIDO CONSTRUC-TION COMPANIES, LOOKING FOR LEADS.
I TOLD THEM TO SEARCH BUILDINGS UNDER CONSTRUCTION THAT ARE LEAST FOUR STORIES HIGH...
...BUT SO FAR, **NOTHING.**
AND NO CLUES FROM THAT ONLINE FEED ...
WE COULD NARROW THINGS DOWN IF IT'D SNOW OR RAIN.
BUT ALL WE'VE SEEN SO FAR IS A **CROW.**
THERE WAS A CROW ON THE FEED?
YEAH ...
IF YOU HAVE A RECORDING OF THAT, CAN WE SEE IT?
SOMETIMES KIDS KNOW MORE ABOUT ANIMALS ...
...THAN ADULTS DO!

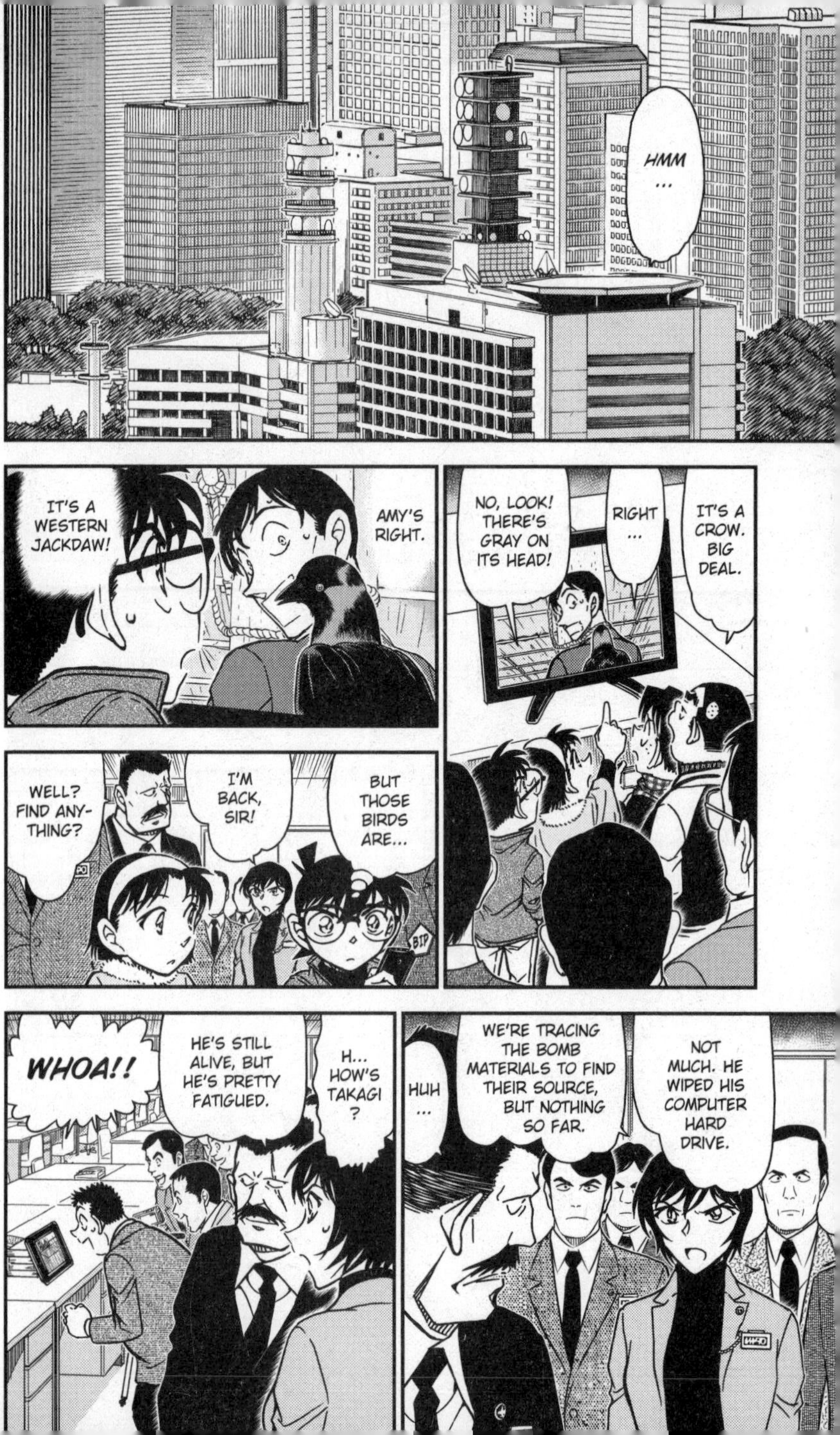
HMM ...
IT'S A CROW. BIG DEAL.
RIGHT ...
NO, LOOK! THERE'S GRAY ON ITS HEAD!
AMY'S RIGHT.
IT'S A WESTERN JACKDAW!
BUT THOSE BIRDS ARE...
I'M BACK, SIR!
WELL? FIND ANY-THING?
BIP
NOT MUCH. HE WIPED HIS COMPUTER HARD DRIVE.
WE'RE TRACING THE BOMB MATERIALS TO FIND THEIR SOURCE, BUT NOTHING SO FAR.
HUH ...
H... HOW'S TAKAGI ?
HE'S STILL ALIVE, BUT HE'S PRETTY FATIGUED.
WHOA!!

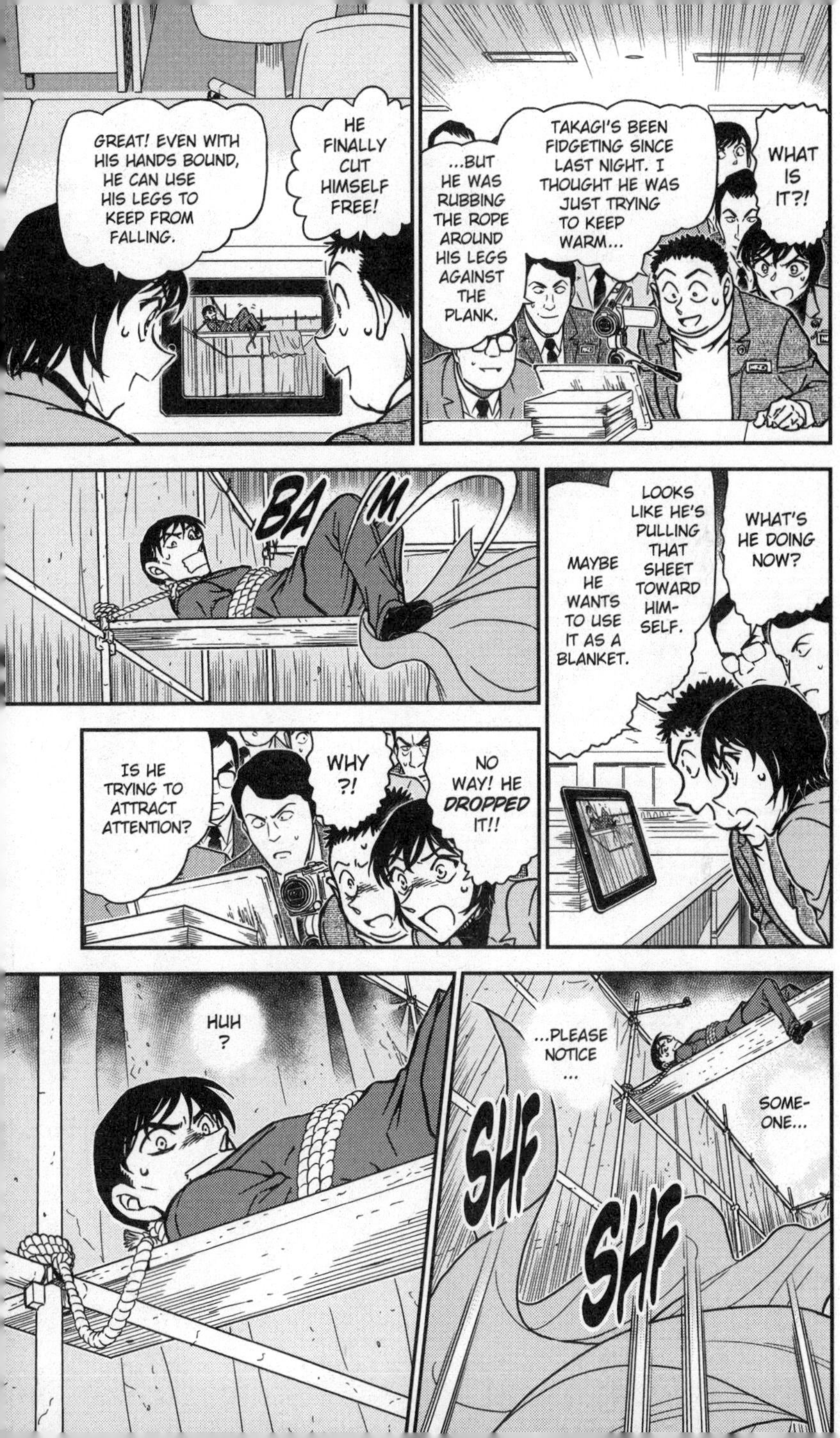
WHAT IS IT?!
TAKAGI'S BEEN FIDGETING SINCE LAST NIGHT. I THOUGHT HE WAS JUST TRYING TO KEEP WARM...
...BUT HE WAS RUBBING THE ROPE AROUND HIS LEGS AGAINST THE PLANK.
HE FINALLY CUT HIMSELF FREE!
GREAT! EVEN WITH HIS HANDS BOUND, HE CAN USE HIS LEGS TO KEEP FROM FALLING.
WHAT'S HE DOING NOW?
LOOKS LIKE HE'S PULLING THAT SHEET TOWARD HIM-SELF.
MAYBE HE WANTS TO USE IT AS A BLANKET.
BAM
NO WAY! HE *DROPPED* IT!!
WHY?!
IS HE TRYING TO ATTRACT ATTENTION?
SOME-ONE...
...PLEASE NOTICE ...
SHF
SHF
HUH?

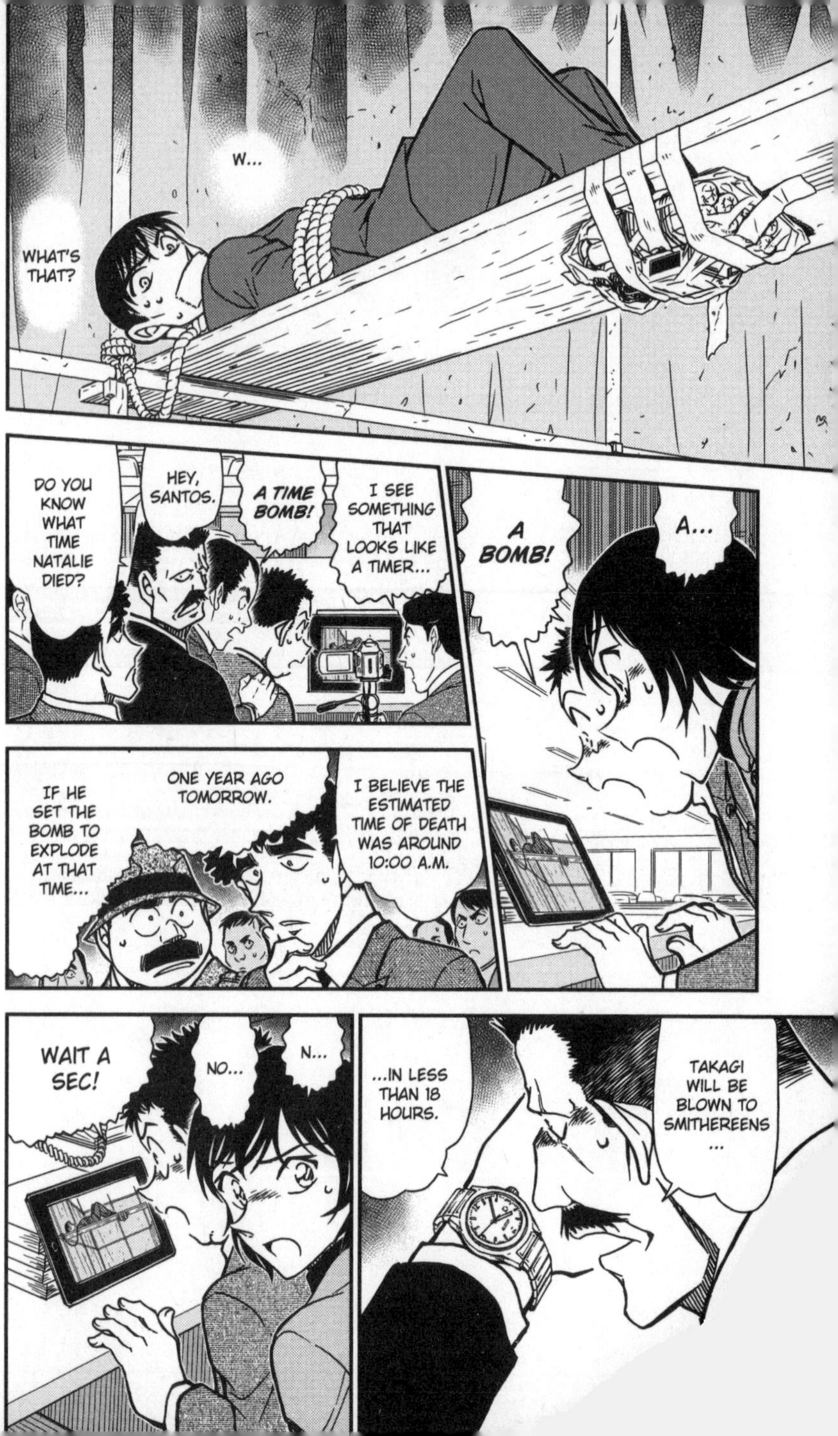
W...
WHAT'S THAT?
A...
A BOMB!
I SEE SOMETHING THAT LOOKS LIKE A TIMER...
A TIME BOMB!
HEY, SANTOS.
DO YOU KNOW WHAT TIME NATALIE DIED?
I BELIEVE THE ESTIMATED TIME OF DEATH WAS AROUND 10:00 A.M.
ONE YEAR AGO TOMORROW.
IF HE SET THE BOMB TO EXPLODE AT THAT TIME...
TAKAGI WILL BE BLOWN TO SMITHEREENS ...
...IN LESS THAN 18 HOURS.
N...
NO...
WAIT A SEC!

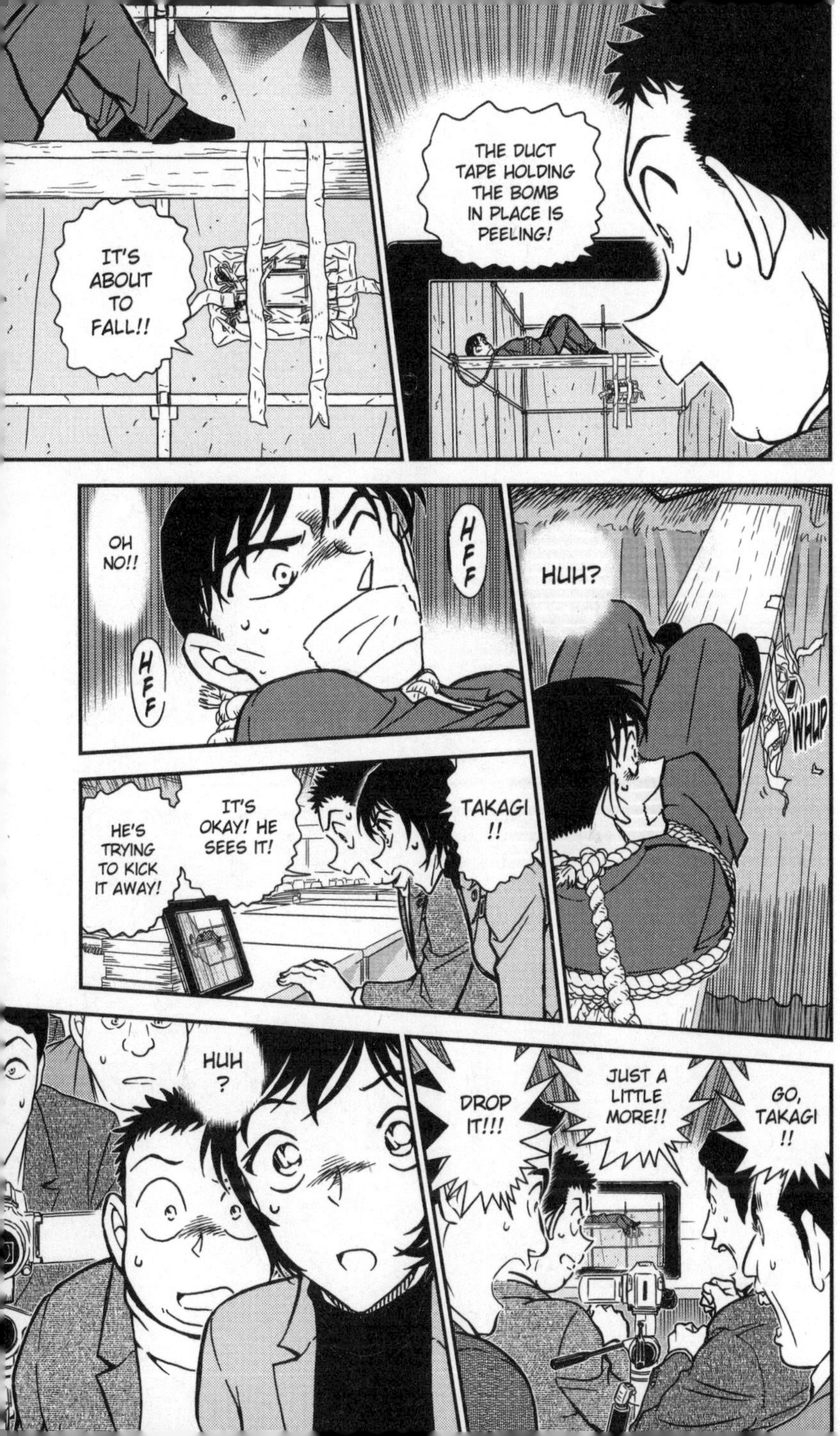
THE DUCT TAPE HOLDING THE BOMB IN PLACE IS PEELING!
IT'S ABOUT TO FALL!!
HUH?
WHUP
HFF
OH NO!!
HFF
TAKAGI!!
IT'S OKAY! HE SEES IT!
HE'S TRYING TO KICK IT AWAY!
GO, TAKAGI!!
JUST A LITTLE MORE!!
DROP IT!!!
HUH?

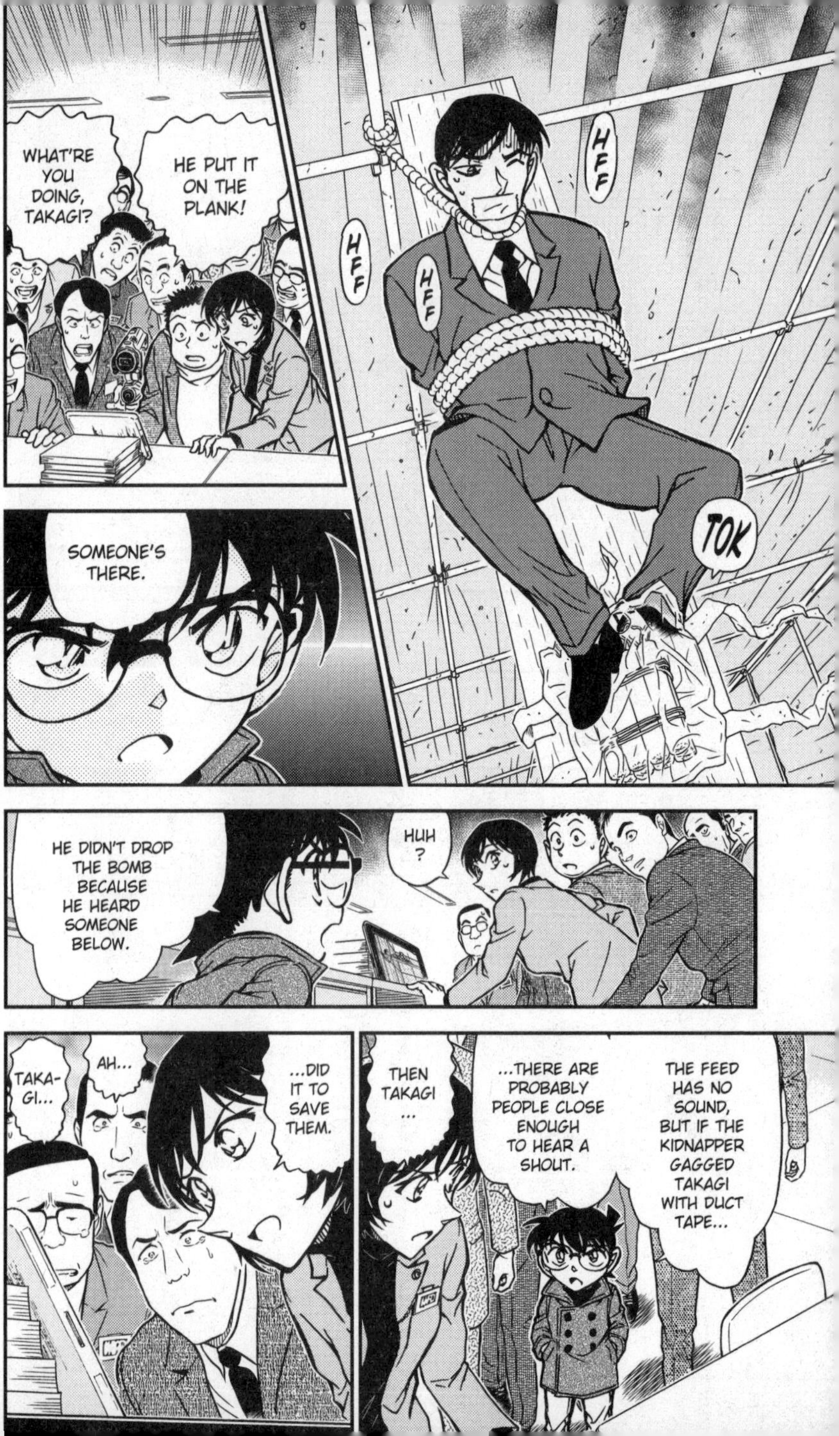
HFF
HFF
HFF
TOK
HE PUT IT ON THE PLANK!
WHAT'RE YOU DOING, TAKAGI?
SOMEONE'S THERE.
HUH?
HE DIDN'T DROP THE BOMB BECAUSE HE HEARD SOMEONE BELOW.
THE FEED HAS NO SOUND, BUT IF THE KIDNAPPER GAGGED TAKAGI WITH DUCT TAPE...
...THERE ARE PROBABLY PEOPLE CLOSE ENOUGH TO HEAR A SHOUT.
THEN TAKAGI...
...DID IT TO SAVE THEM.
AH...
TAKA-GI...

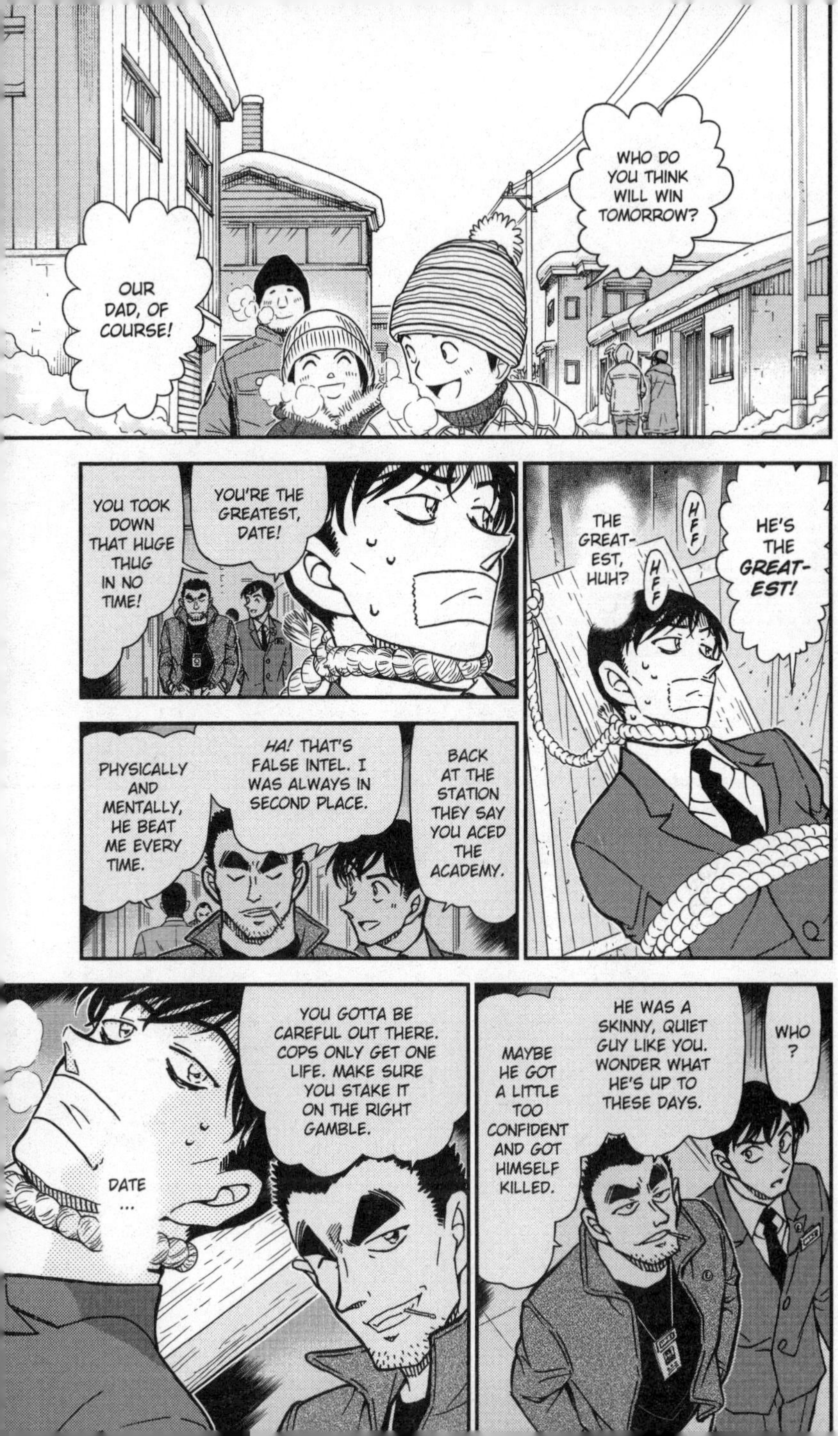
WHO DO YOU THINK WILL WIN TOMORROW?
OUR DAD, OF COURSE!
HE'S THE *GREATEST!*
HFF
HFF
THE GREATEST, HUH?
YOU'RE THE GREATEST, DATE!
YOU TOOK DOWN THAT HUGE THUG IN NO TIME!
BACK AT THE STATION THEY SAY YOU ACED THE ACADEMY.
HA! THAT'S FALSE INTEL. I WAS ALWAYS IN SECOND PLACE.
PHYSICALLY AND MENTALLY, HE BEAT ME EVERY TIME.
WHO ?
HE WAS A SKINNY, QUIET GUY LIKE YOU. WONDER WHAT HE'S UP TO THESE DAYS.
MAYBE HE GOT A LITTLE TOO CONFIDENT AND GOT HIMSELF KILLED.
YOU GOTTA BE CAREFUL OUT THERE. COPS ONLY GET ONE LIFE. MAKE SURE YOU STAKE IT ON THE RIGHT GAMBLE.
DATE ...

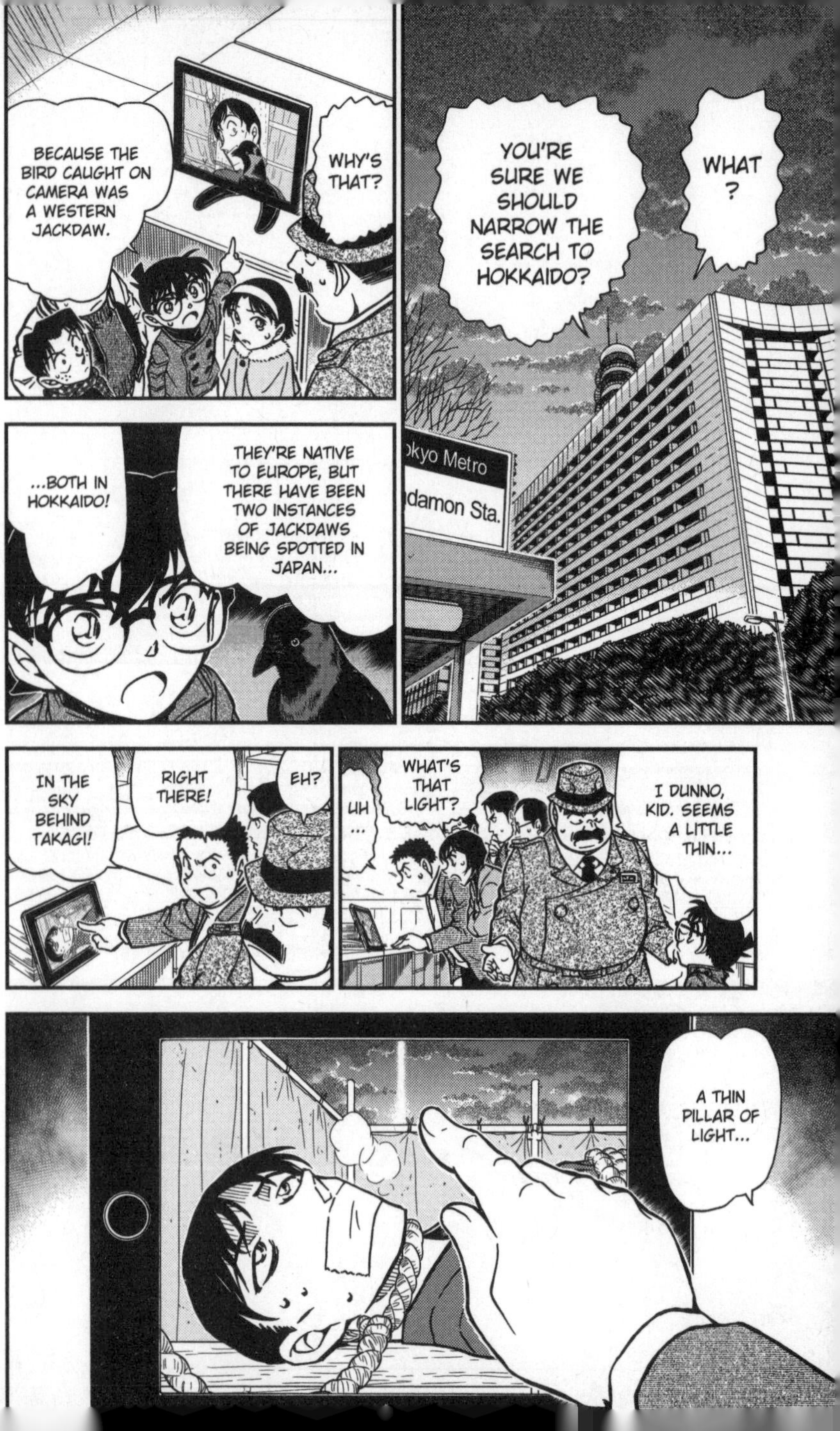
WHAT ?
YOU'RE SURE WE SHOULD NARROW THE SEARCH TO HOKKAIDO?
WHY'S THAT?
BECAUSE THE BIRD CAUGHT ON CAMERA WAS A WESTERN JACKDAW.
THEY'RE NATIVE TO EUROPE, BUT THERE HAVE BEEN TWO INSTANCES OF JACKDAWS BEING SPOTTED IN JAPAN...
...BOTH IN HOKKAIDO!
WHAT'S THAT LIGHT?
I DUNNO, KID. SEEMS A LITTLE THIN...
UH ...
EH?
RIGHT THERE!
IN THE SKY BEHIND TAKAGI!
A THIN PILLAR OF LIGHT...

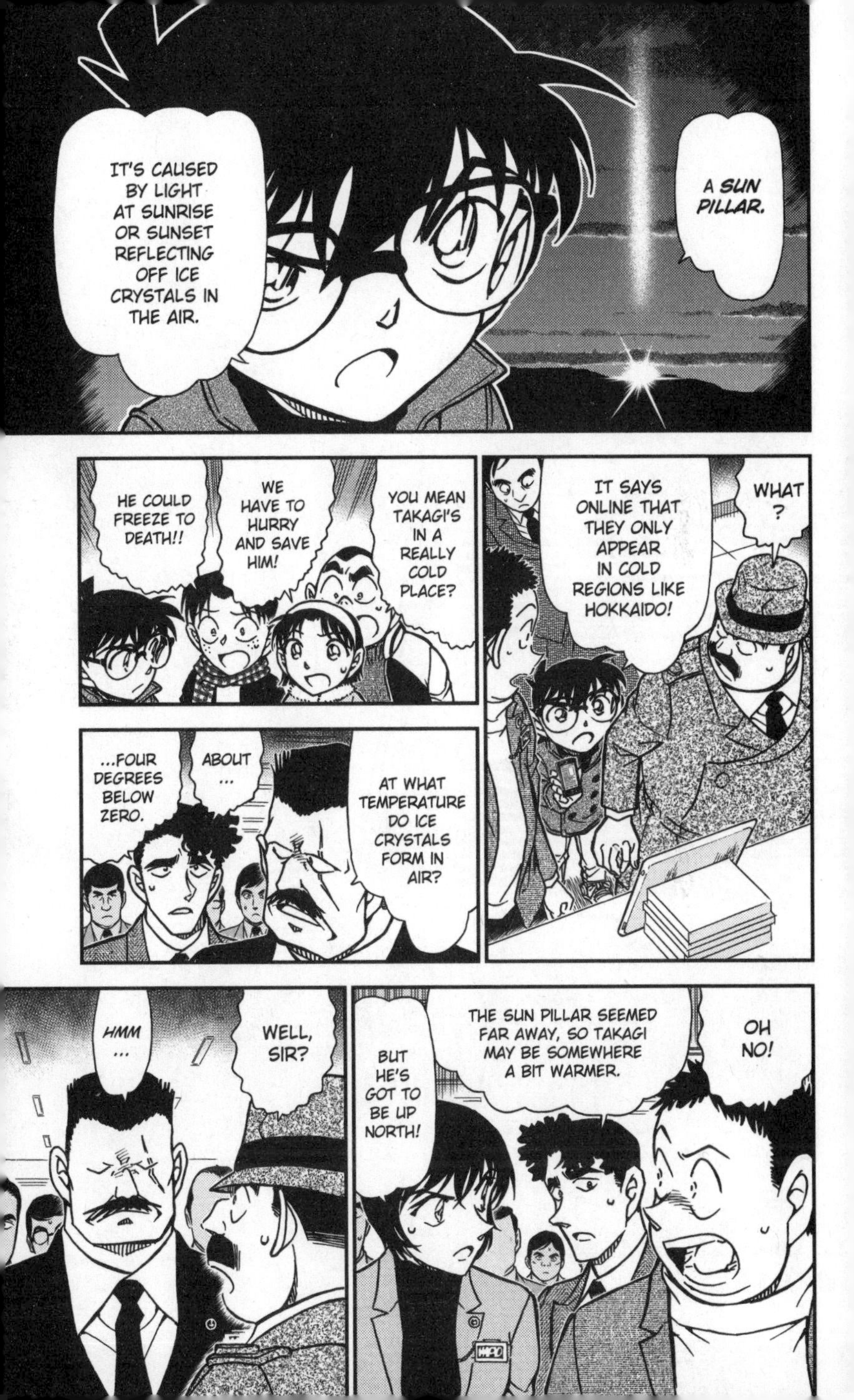
A SUN PILLAR.
IT'S CAUSED BY LIGHT AT SUNRISE OR SUNSET REFLECTING OFF ICE CRYSTALS IN THE AIR.
WHAT?
IT SAYS ONLINE THAT THEY ONLY APPEAR IN COLD REGIONS LIKE HOKKAIDO!
YOU MEAN TAKAGI'S IN A REALLY COLD PLACE?
WE HAVE TO HURRY AND SAVE HIM!
HE COULD FREEZE TO DEATH!!
AT WHAT TEMPERATURE DO ICE CRYSTALS FORM IN AIR?
ABOUT ...
...FOUR DEGREES BELOW ZERO.
OH NO!
THE SUN PILLAR SEEMED FAR AWAY, SO TAKAGI MAY BE SOMEWHERE A BIT WARMER.
BUT HE'S GOT TO BE UP NORTH!
WELL, SIR?
HMM ...

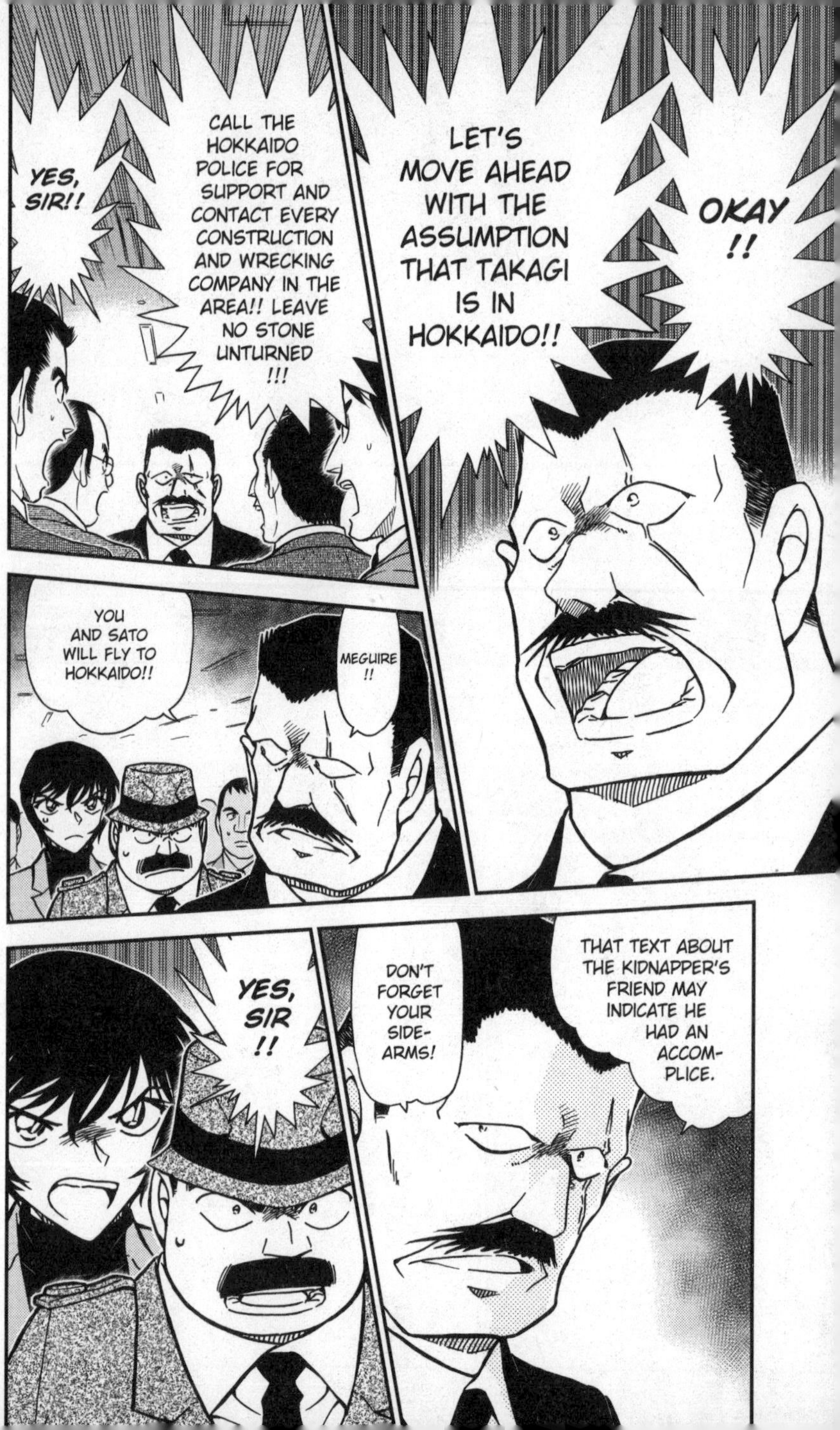
OKAY!!
LET'S MOVE AHEAD WITH THE ASSUMPTION THAT TAKAGI IS IN HOKKAIDO!!
CALL THE HOKKAIDO POLICE FOR SUPPORT AND CONTACT EVERY CONSTRUCTION AND WRECKING COMPANY IN THE AREA!! LEAVE NO STONE UNTURNED!!!
YES, SIR!!
MEGUIRE!!
YOU AND SATO WILL FLY TO HOKKAIDO!!
THAT TEXT ABOUT THE KIDNAPPER'S FRIEND MAY INDICATE HE HAD AN ACCOMPLICE.
DON'T FORGET YOUR SIDE-ARMS!
YES, SIR!!

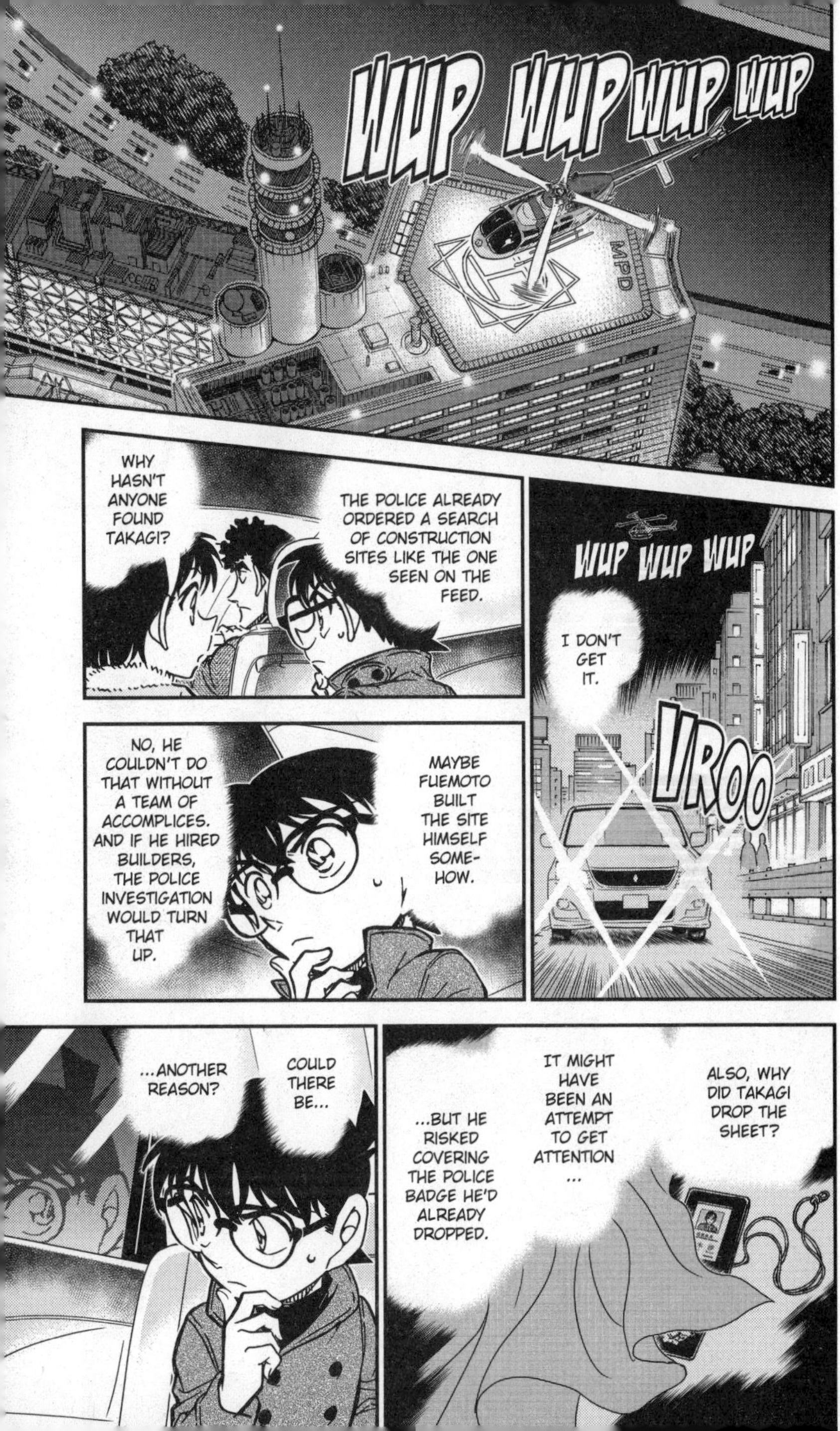
WUP WUP WUP WUP
MPD
WUP WUP WUP
I DON'T GET IT.
VROO
THE POLICE ALREADY ORDERED A SEARCH OF CONSTRUCTION SITES LIKE THE ONE SEEN ON THE FEED.
WHY HASN'T ANYONE FOUND TAKAGI?
MAYBE FUEMOTO BUILT THE SITE HIMSELF SOME-HOW.
NO, HE COULDN'T DO THAT WITHOUT A TEAM OF ACCOMPLICES. AND IF HE HIRED BUILDERS, THE POLICE INVESTIGATION WOULD TURN THAT UP.
ALSO, WHY DID TAKAGI DROP THE SHEET?
IT MIGHT HAVE BEEN AN ATTEMPT TO GET ATTENTION ...
...BUT HE RISKED COVERING THE POLICE BADGE HE'D ALREADY DROPPED.
COULD THERE BE...
...ANOTHER REASON?

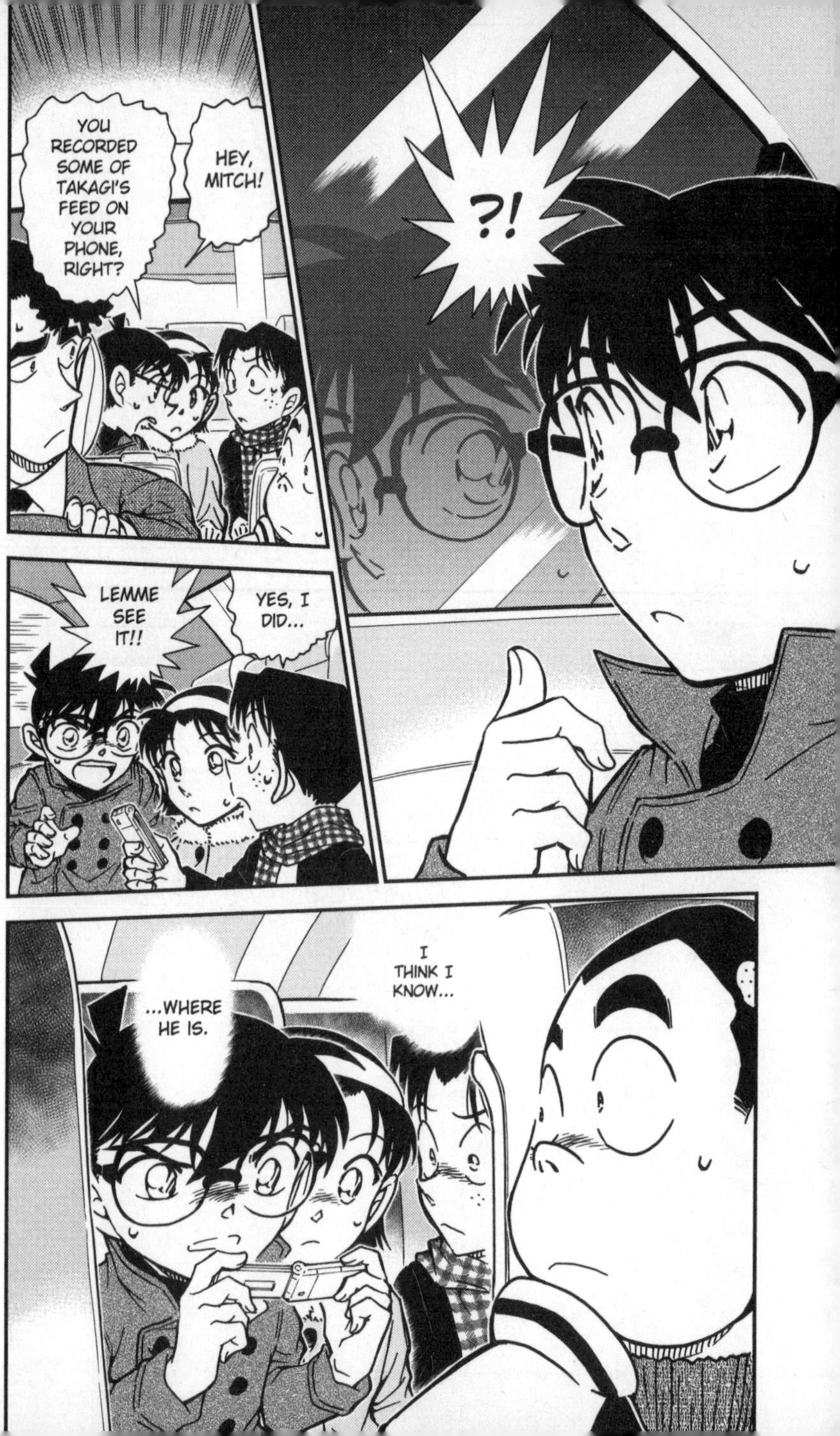
?!
HEY, MITCH!
YOU RECORDED SOME OF TAKAGI'S FEED ON YOUR PHONE, RIGHT?
YES, I DID...
LEMME SEE IT!!
I THINK I KNOW...
...WHERE HE IS.

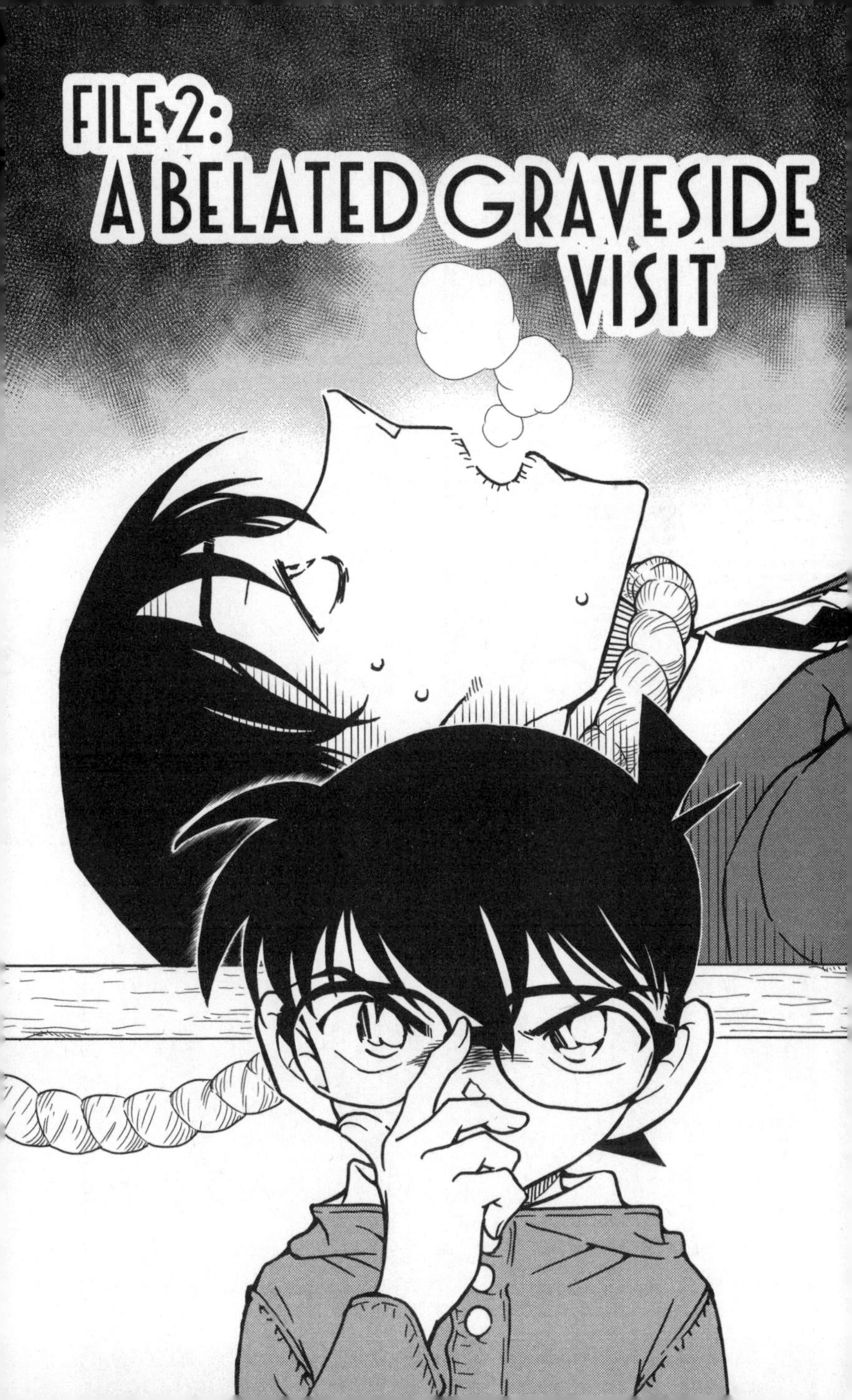
FILE 2:
A BELATED GRAVESIDE VISIT

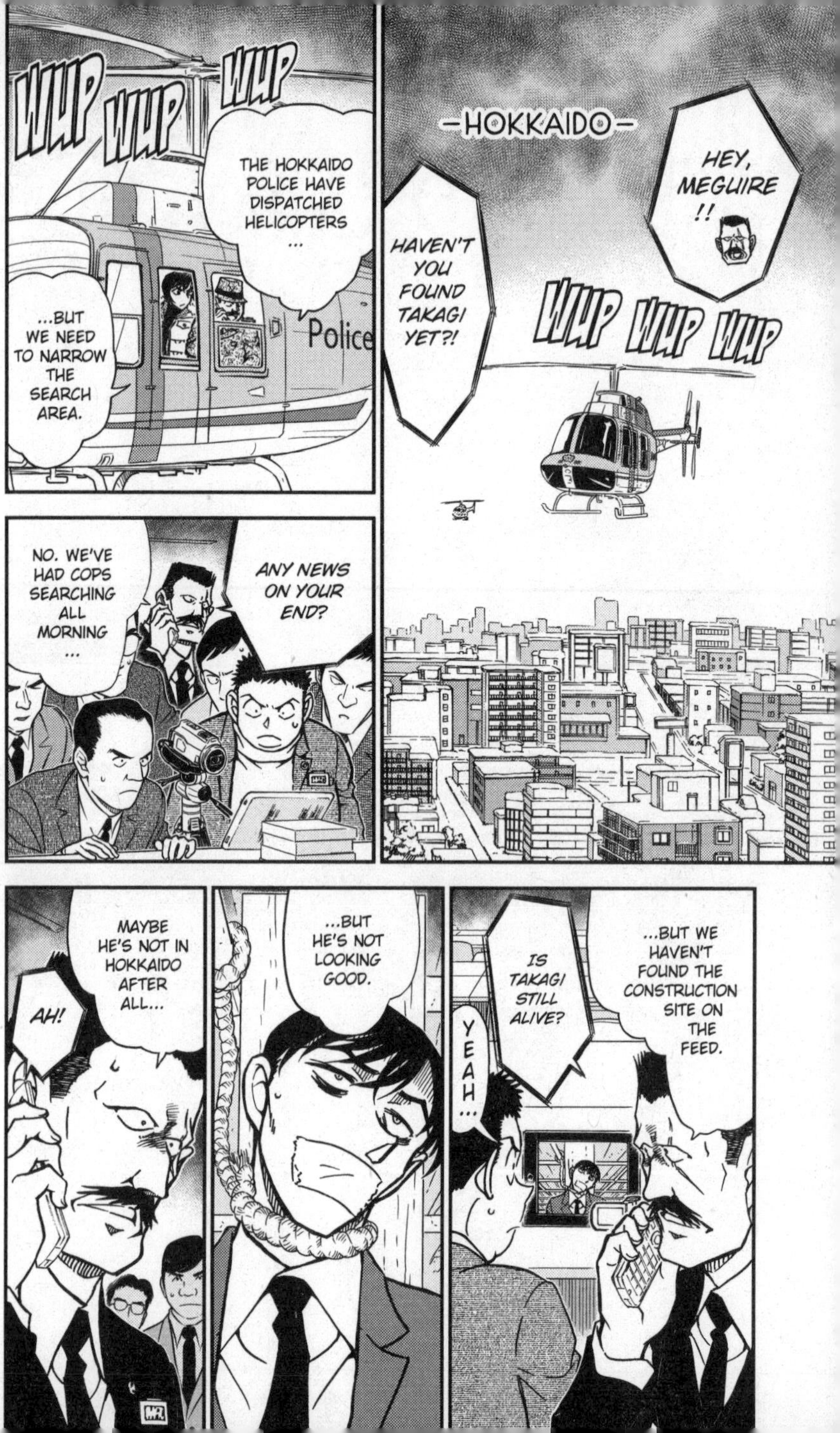
-HOKKAIDO-
HEY, MEGUIRE!!
HAVEN'T YOU FOUND TAKAGI YET?!
WUP WUP WUP
WUP WUP WUP
THE HOKKAIDO POLICE HAVE DISPATCHED HELICOPTERS...
...BUT WE NEED TO NARROW THE SEARCH AREA.
Police
ANY NEWS ON YOUR END?
NO. WE'VE HAD COPS SEARCHING ALL MORNING...
...BUT WE HAVEN'T FOUND THE CONSTRUCTION SITE ON THE FEED.
IS TAKAGI STILL ALIVE?
YEAH...
...BUT HE'S NOT LOOKING GOOD.
MAYBE HE'S NOT IN HOKKAIDO AFTER ALL...
AH!

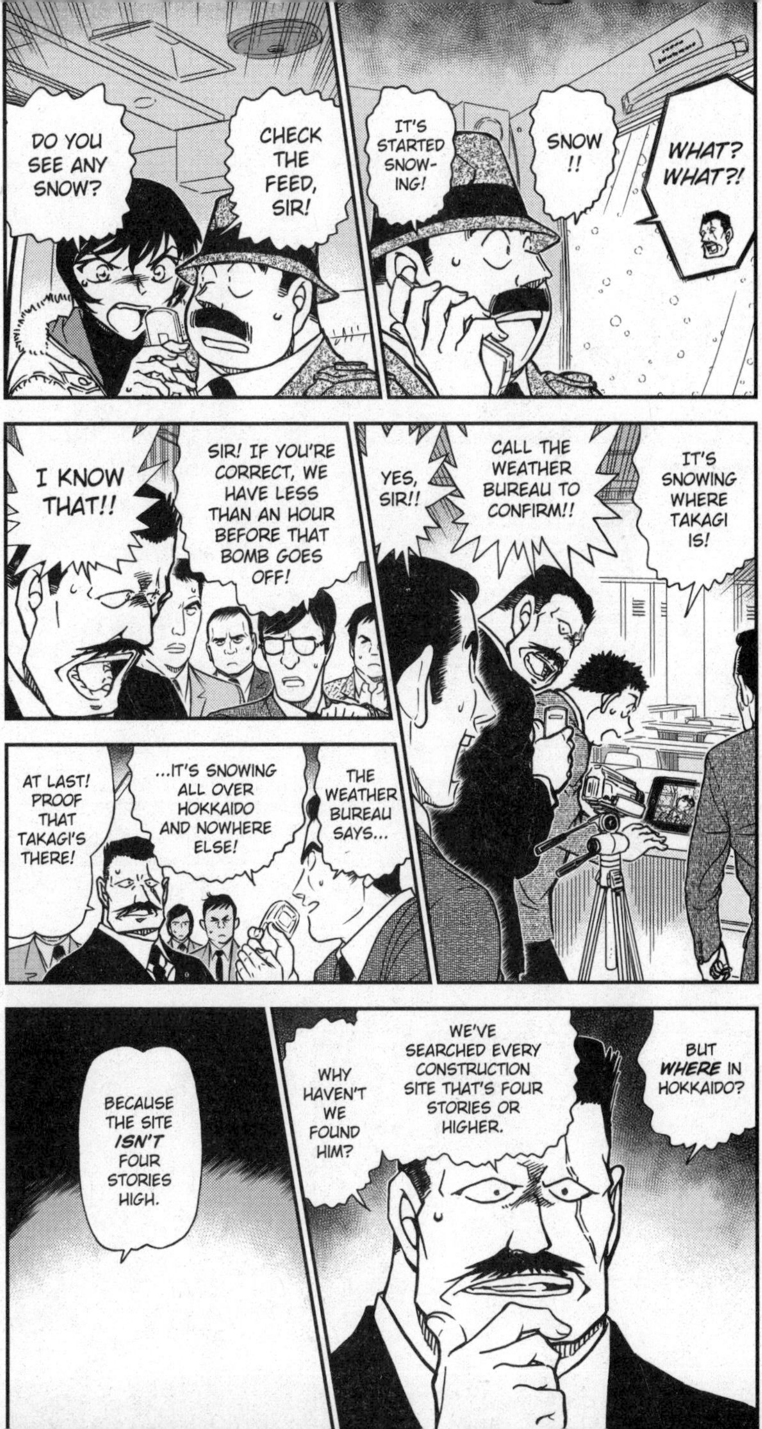

WHAT? WHAT?!
SNOW !!
IT'S STARTED SNOW-ING!
CHECK THE FEED, SIR!
DO YOU SEE ANY SNOW?
IT'S SNOWING WHERE TAKAGI IS!
CALL THE WEATHER BUREAU TO CONFIRM!!
YES, SIR!!
SIR! IF YOU'RE CORRECT, WE HAVE LESS THAN AN HOUR BEFORE THAT BOMB GOES OFF!
I KNOW THAT!!
THE WEATHER BUREAU SAYS...
...IT'S SNOWING ALL OVER HOKKAIDO AND NOWHERE ELSE!
AT LAST! PROOF THAT TAKAGI'S THERE!
BUT WHERE IN HOKKAIDO?
WE'VE SEARCHED EVERY CONSTRUCTION SITE THAT'S FOUR STORIES OR HIGHER.
WHY HAVEN'T WE FOUND HIM?
BECAUSE THE SITE ISN'T FOUR STORIES HIGH.

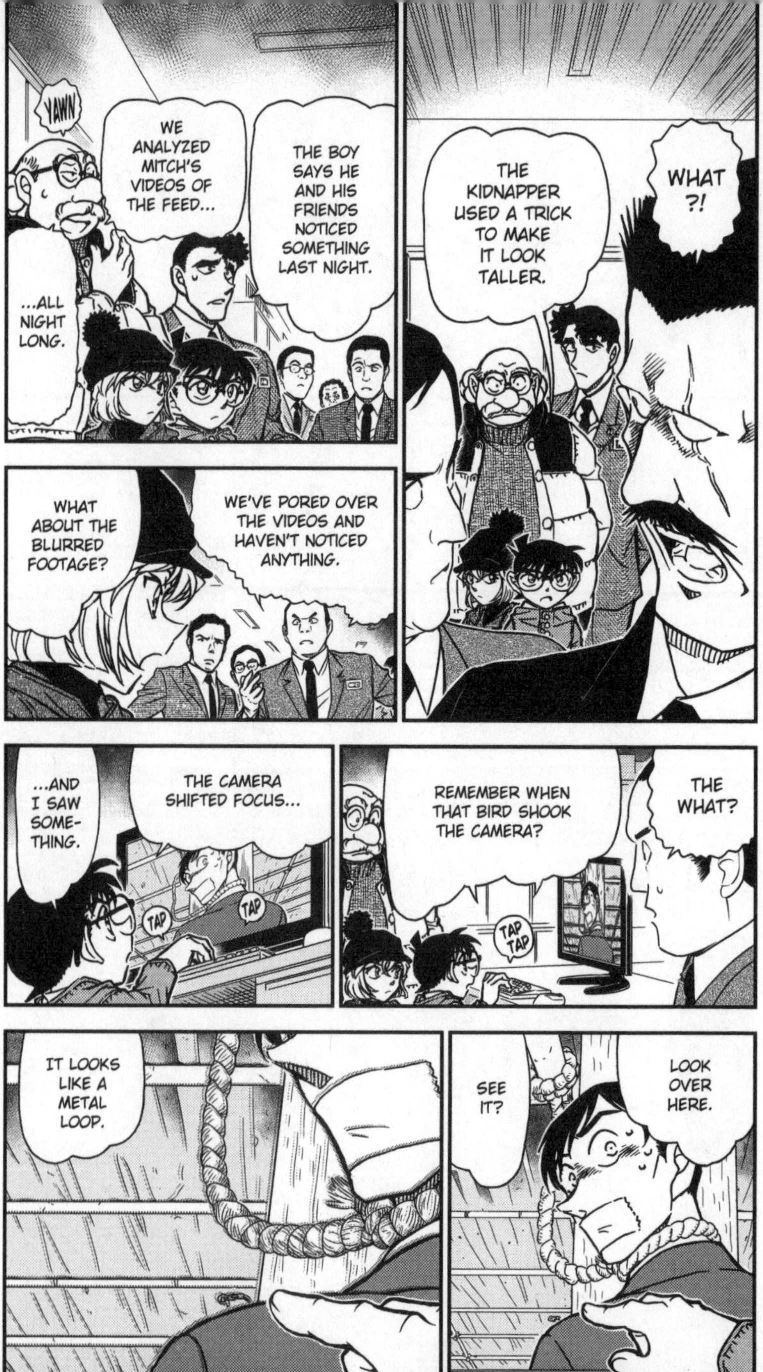
WHAT ?!
THE KIDNAPPER USED A TRICK TO MAKE IT LOOK TALLER.
THE BOY SAYS HE AND HIS FRIENDS NOTICED SOMETHING LAST NIGHT.
WE ANALYZED MITCH'S VIDEOS OF THE FEED...
YAWN
...ALL NIGHT LONG.
WE'VE PORED OVER THE VIDEOS AND HAVEN'T NOTICED ANYTHING.
WHAT ABOUT THE BLURRED FOOTAGE?
THE WHAT?
REMEMBER WHEN THAT BIRD SHOOK THE CAMERA?
TAP TAP
THE CAMERA SHIFTED FOCUS...
TAP
TAP
...AND I SAW SOME-THING.
LOOK OVER HERE.
SEE IT?
IT LOOKS LIKE A METAL LOOP.

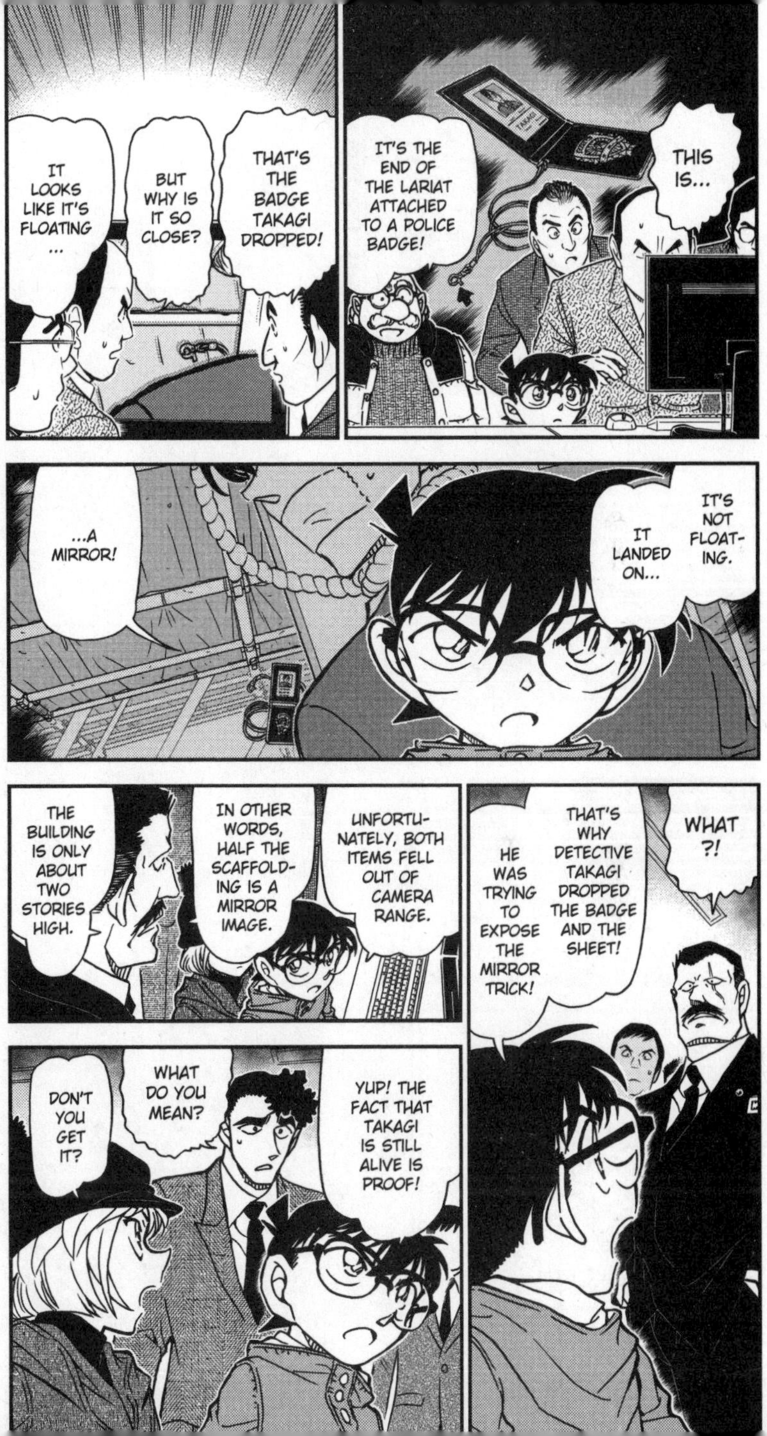
THIS IS...
IT'S THE END OF THE LARIAT ATTACHED TO A POLICE BADGE!
THAT'S THE BADGE TAKAGI DROPPED!
BUT WHY IS IT SO CLOSE?
IT LOOKS LIKE IT'S FLOATING ...
IT'S NOT FLOAT-ING.
IT LANDED ON...
...A MIRROR!
WHAT ?!
THAT'S WHY DETECTIVE TAKAGI DROPPED THE BADGE AND THE SHEET!
HE WAS TRYING TO EXPOSE THE MIRROR TRICK!
UNFORTU-NATELY, BOTH ITEMS FELL OUT OF CAMERA RANGE.
IN OTHER WORDS, HALF THE SCAFFOLD-ING IS A MIRROR IMAGE.
THE BUILDING IS ONLY ABOUT TWO STORIES HIGH.
YUP! THE FACT THAT TAKAGI IS STILL ALIVE IS PROOF!
WHAT DO YOU MEAN?
DON'T YOU GET IT?

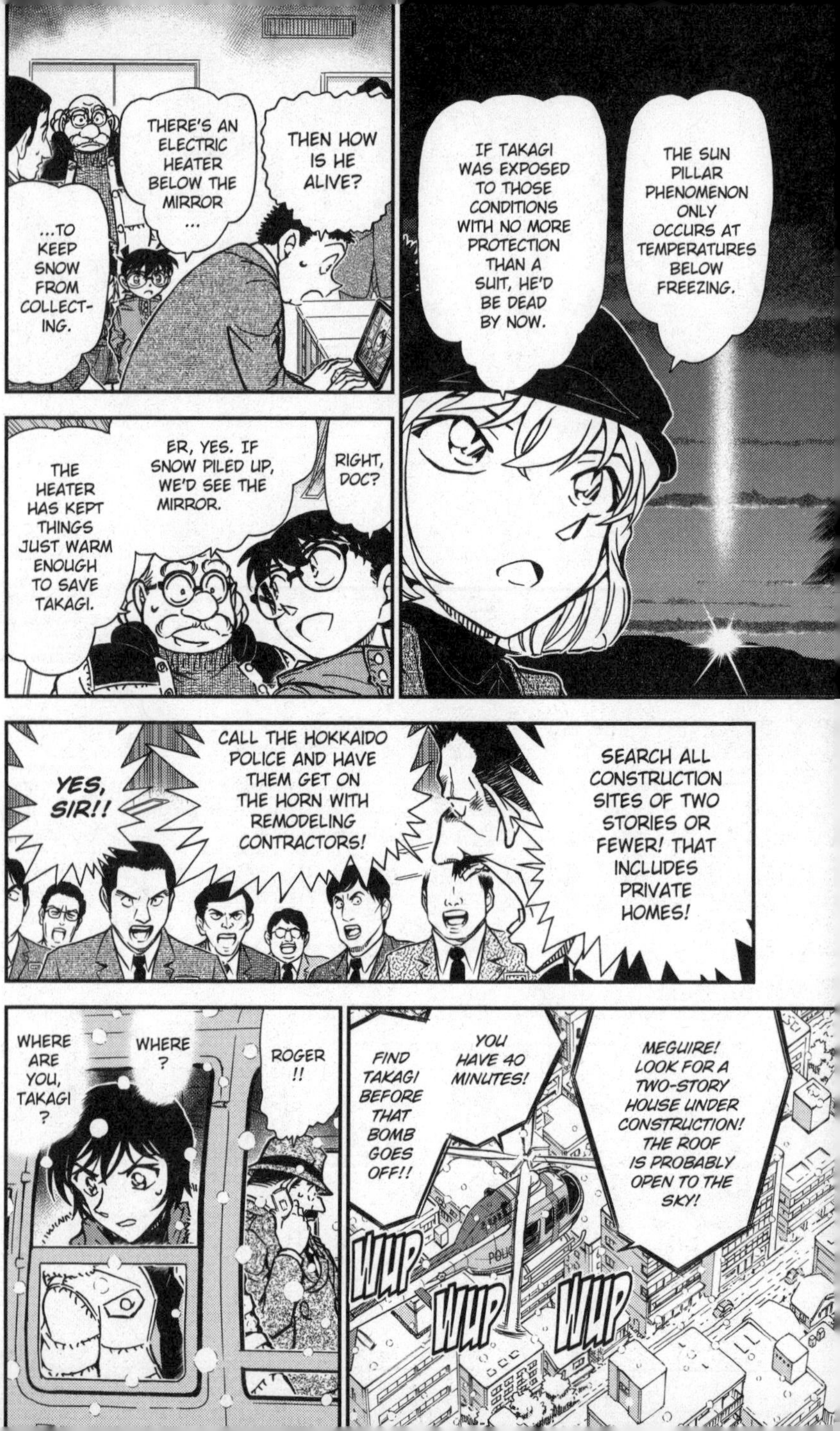
THE SUN PILLAR PHENOMENON ONLY OCCURS AT TEMPERATURES BELOW FREEZING.
IF TAKAGI WAS EXPOSED TO THOSE CONDITIONS WITH NO MORE PROTECTION THAN A SUIT, HE'D BE DEAD BY NOW.
THEN HOW IS HE ALIVE?
THERE'S AN ELECTRIC HEATER BELOW THE MIRROR...
...TO KEEP SNOW FROM COLLECT-ING.
RIGHT, DOC?
ER, YES. IF SNOW PILED UP, WE'D SEE THE MIRROR.
THE HEATER HAS KEPT THINGS JUST WARM ENOUGH TO SAVE TAKAGI.
SEARCH ALL CONSTRUCTION SITES OF TWO STORIES OR FEWER! THAT INCLUDES PRIVATE HOMES!
CALL THE HOKKAIDO POLICE AND HAVE THEM GET ON THE HORN WITH REMODELING CONTRACTORS!
YES, SIR!!
MEGUIRE! LOOK FOR A TWO-STORY HOUSE UNDER CONSTRUCTION! THE ROOF IS PROBABLY OPEN TO THE SKY!
YOU HAVE 40 MINUTES!
FIND TAKAGI BEFORE THAT BOMB GOES OFF!!
WUP
WUP
WUP
ROGER!!
WHERE?
WHERE ARE YOU, TAKAGI?

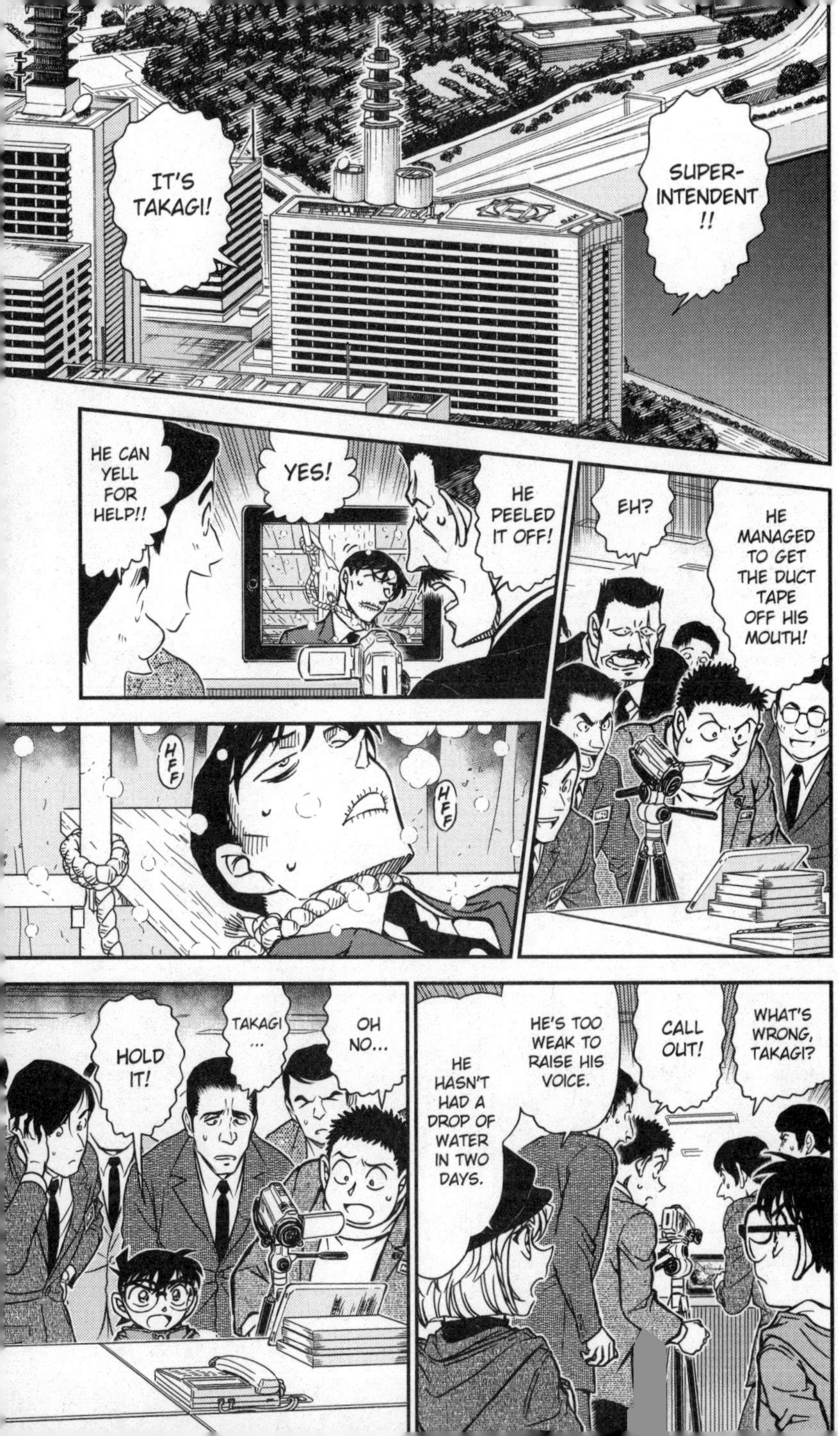
SUPER-INTENDENT!!
IT'S TAKAGI!
HE MANAGED TO GET THE DUCT TAPE OFF HIS MOUTH!
EH?
HE PEELED IT OFF!
YES!
HE CAN YELL FOR HELP!!
HFF
HFF
WHAT'S WRONG, TAKAGI?
CALL OUT!
HE'S TOO WEAK TO RAISE HIS VOICE.
HE HASN'T HAD A DROP OF WATER IN TWO DAYS.
OH NO...
TAKAGI...
HOLD IT!

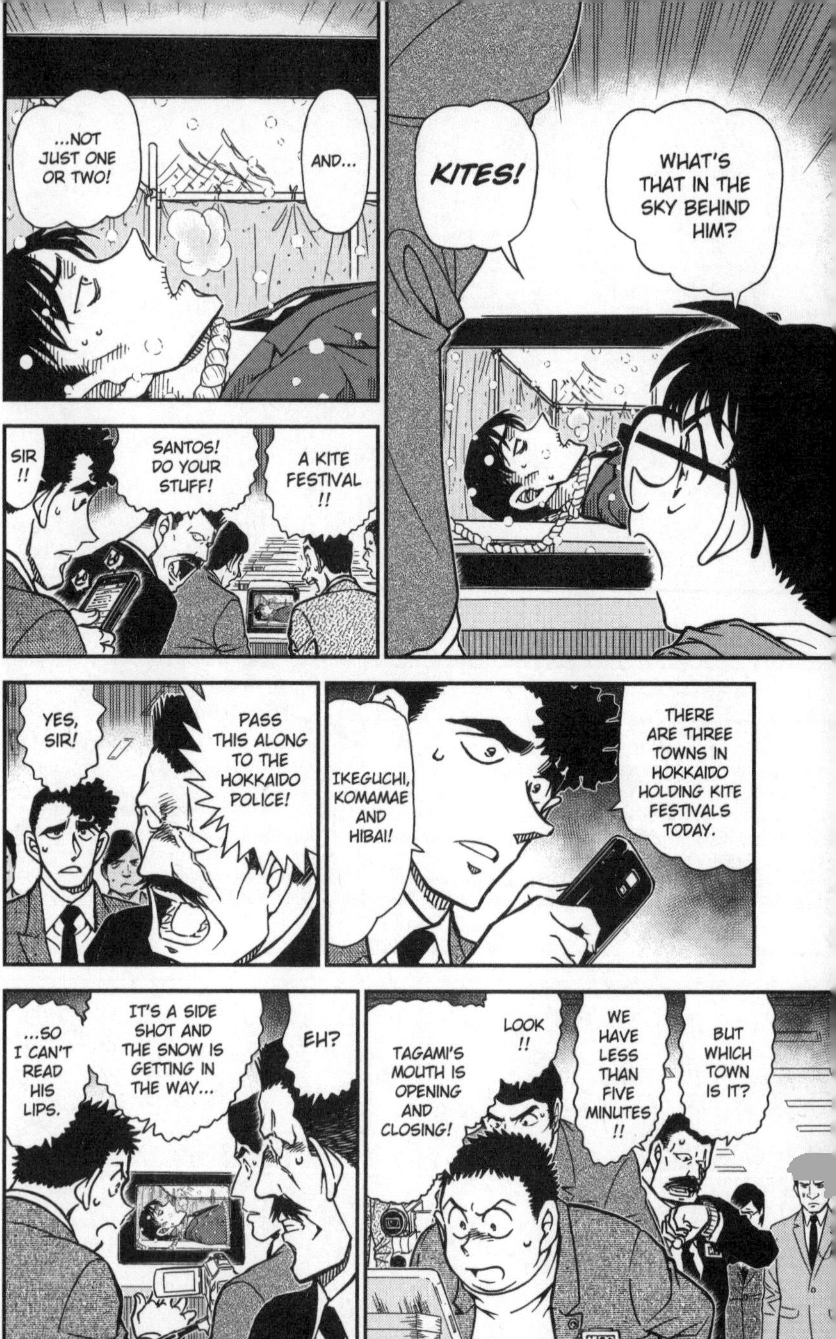
WHAT'S THAT IN THE SKY BEHIND HIM?
KITES!
AND...
...NOT JUST ONE OR TWO!
A KITE FESTIVAL !!
SANTOS! DO YOUR STUFF!
SIR !!
THERE ARE THREE TOWNS IN HOKKAIDO HOLDING KITE FESTIVALS TODAY.
IKEGUCHI, KOMAMAE AND HIBAI!
PASS THIS ALONG TO THE HOKKAIDO POLICE!
YES, SIR!
BUT WHICH TOWN IS IT?
WE HAVE LESS THAN FIVE MINUTES !!
LOOK !!
TAGAMI'S MOUTH IS OPENING AND CLOSING!
EH?
IT'S A SIDE SHOT AND THE SNOW IS GETTING IN THE WAY...
...SO I CAN'T READ HIS LIPS.

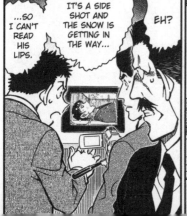

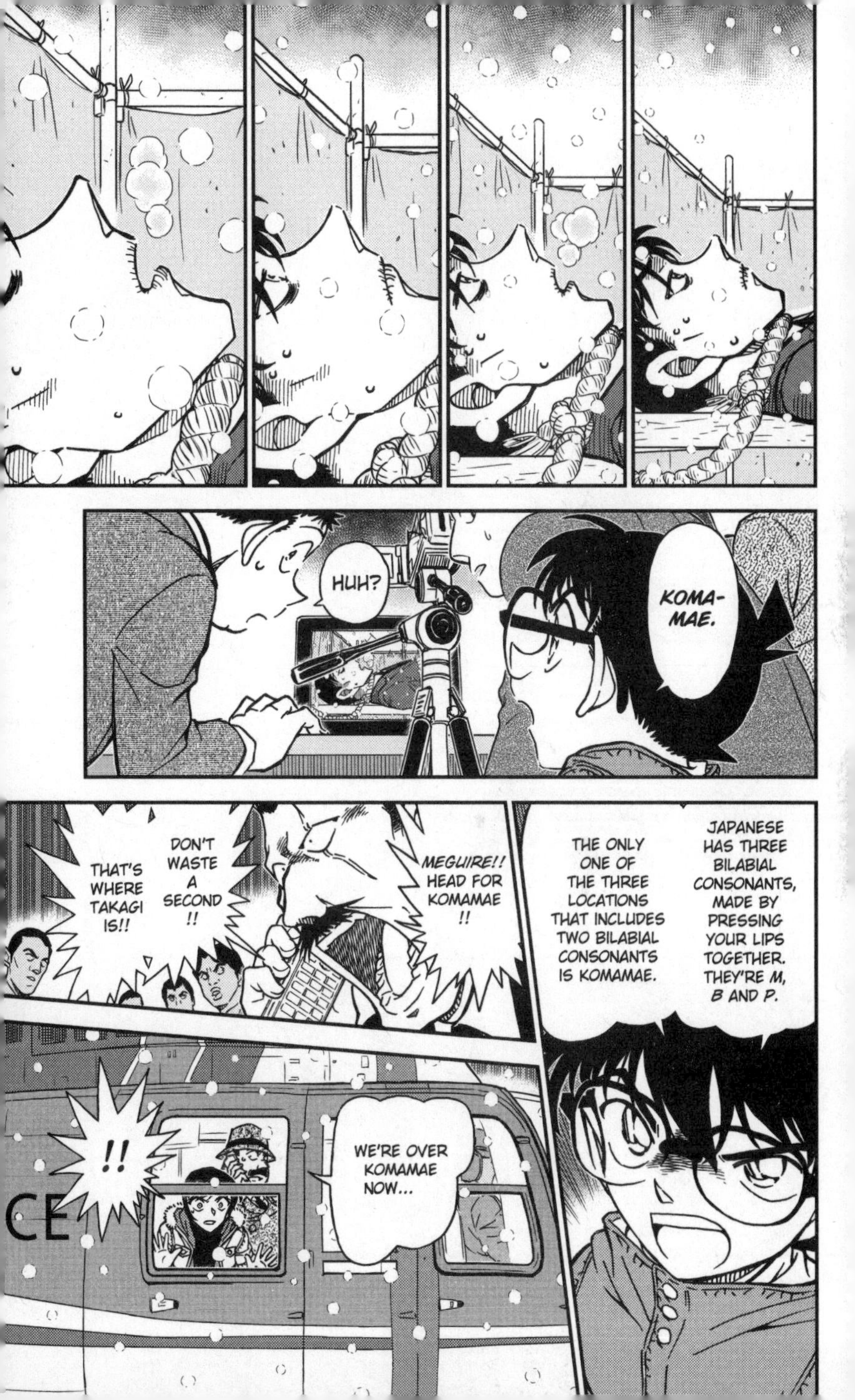

KOMA-MAE.
HUH?
JAPANESE HAS THREE BILABIAL CONSONANTS, MADE BY PRESSING YOUR LIPS TOGETHER. THEY'RE *M*, *B* AND *P*.
THE ONLY ONE OF THE THREE LOCATIONS THAT INCLUDES TWO BILABIAL CONSONANTS IS KOMAMAE.
MEGUIRE!! HEAD FOR KOMAMAE !!
DON'T WASTE A SECOND !!
THAT'S WHERE TAKAGI IS!!
WE'RE OVER KOMAMAE NOW...
!!
CE

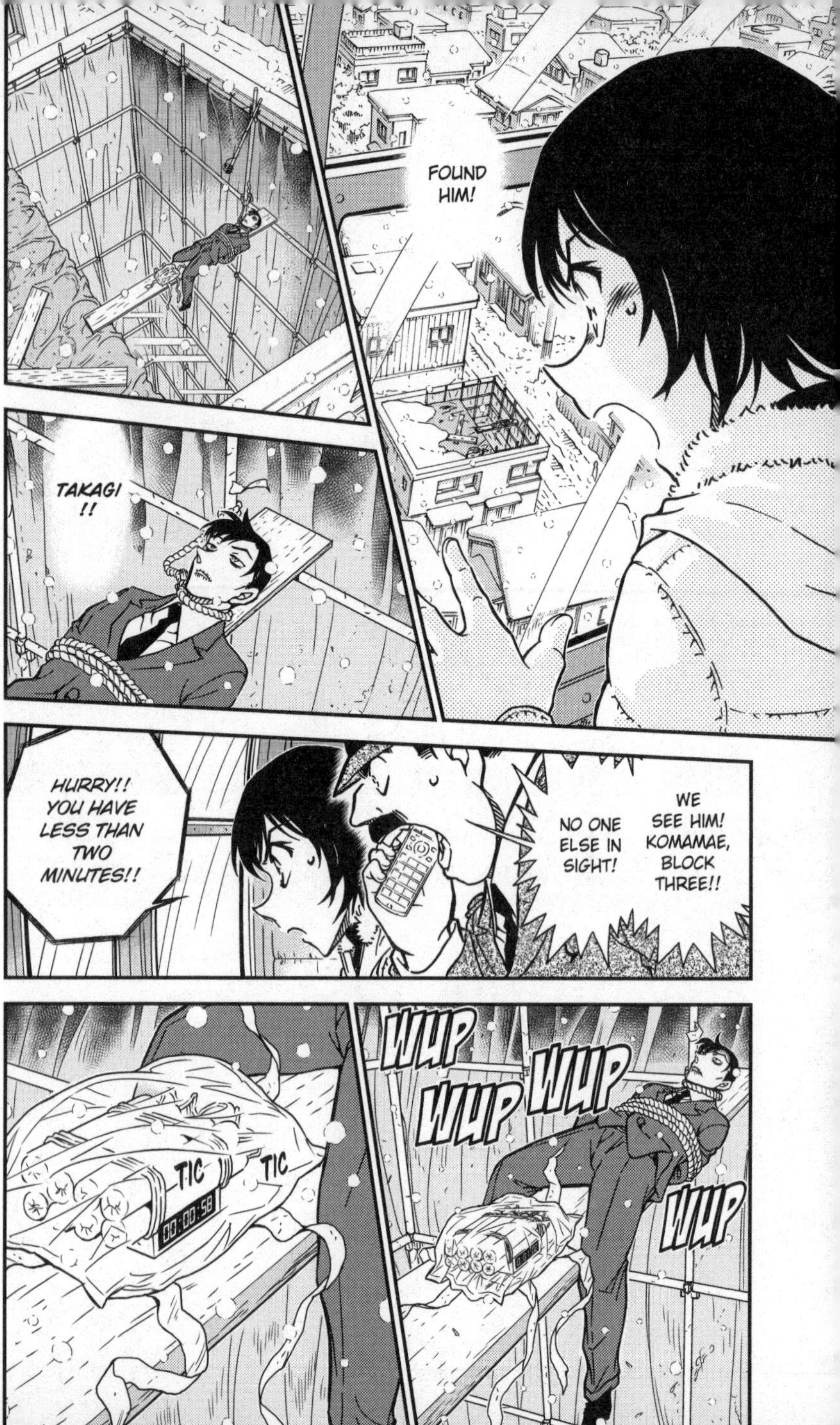
FOUND HIM!
TAKAGI !!
WE SEE HIM! KOMAMAE, BLOCK THREE!!
NO ONE ELSE IN SIGHT!
HURRY!! YOU HAVE LESS THAN TWO MINUTES!!
WUP
WUP
WUP
WUP
TIC
TIC
00:00:58

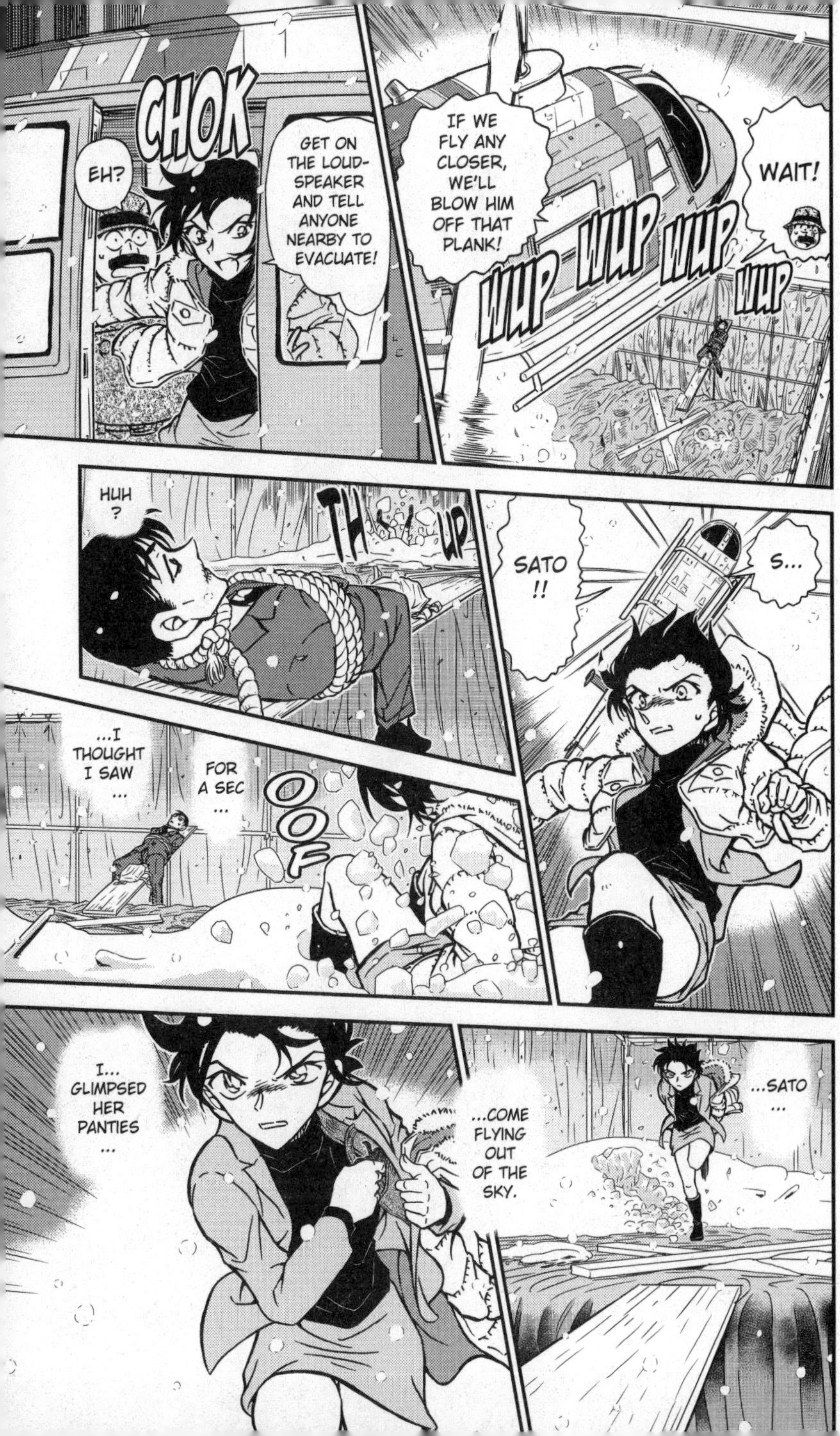
IF WE FLY ANY CLOSER, WE'LL BLOW HIM OFF THAT PLANK!
WAIT!
WUP WUP WUP WUP
CHOK
GET ON THE LOUD-SPEAKER AND TELL ANYONE NEARBY TO EVACUATE!
EH?
S...
SATO !!
THUP
HUH ?
...I THOUGHT I SAW ...
FOR A SEC ...
OOF
...SATO ...
I... GLIMPSED HER PANTIES ...
...COME FLYING OUT OF THE SKY.

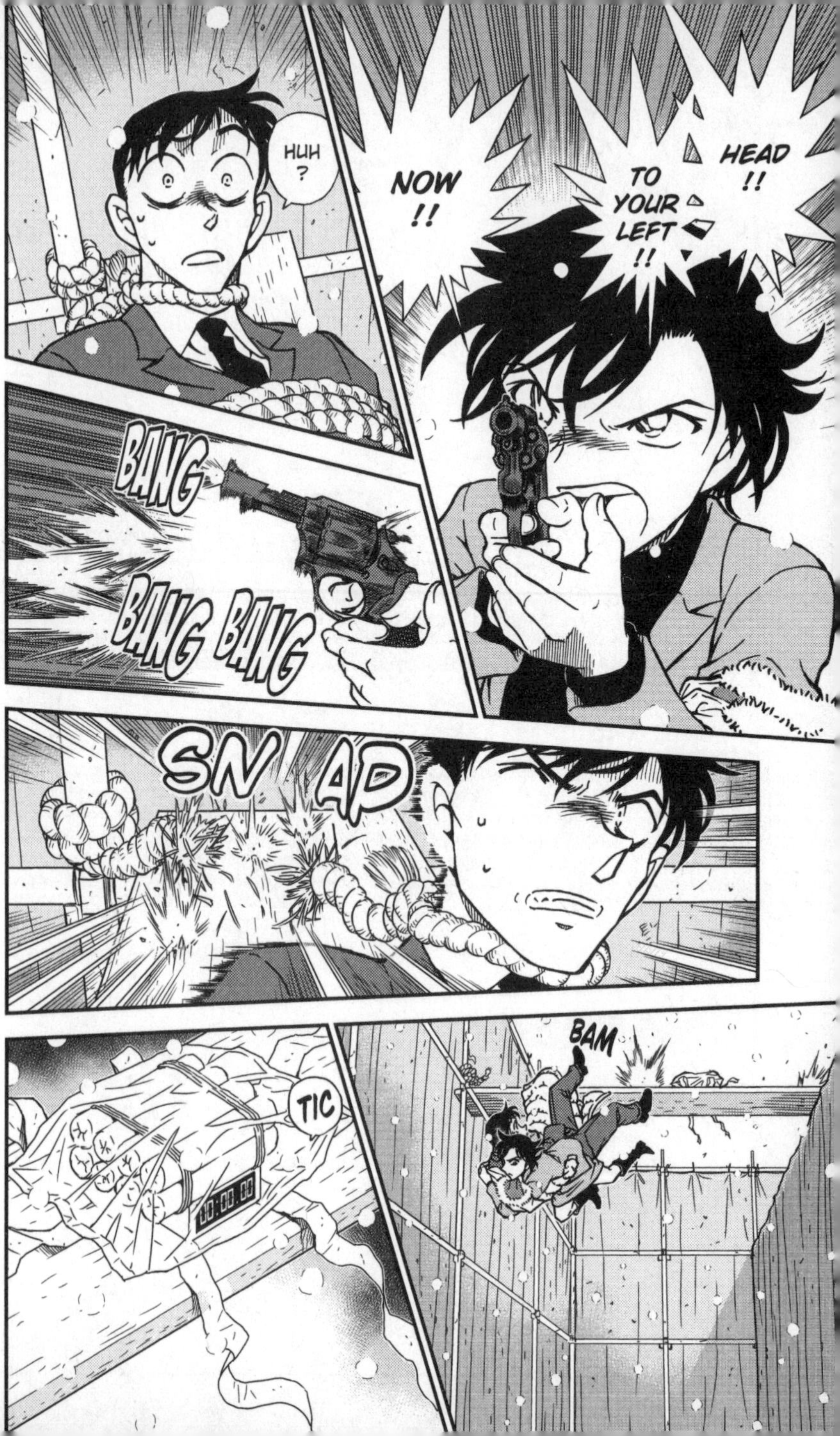
HEAD!!
TO YOUR LEFT!!
NOW!!
HUH?
BANG
BANG BANG
SN AP
BAM
TIC

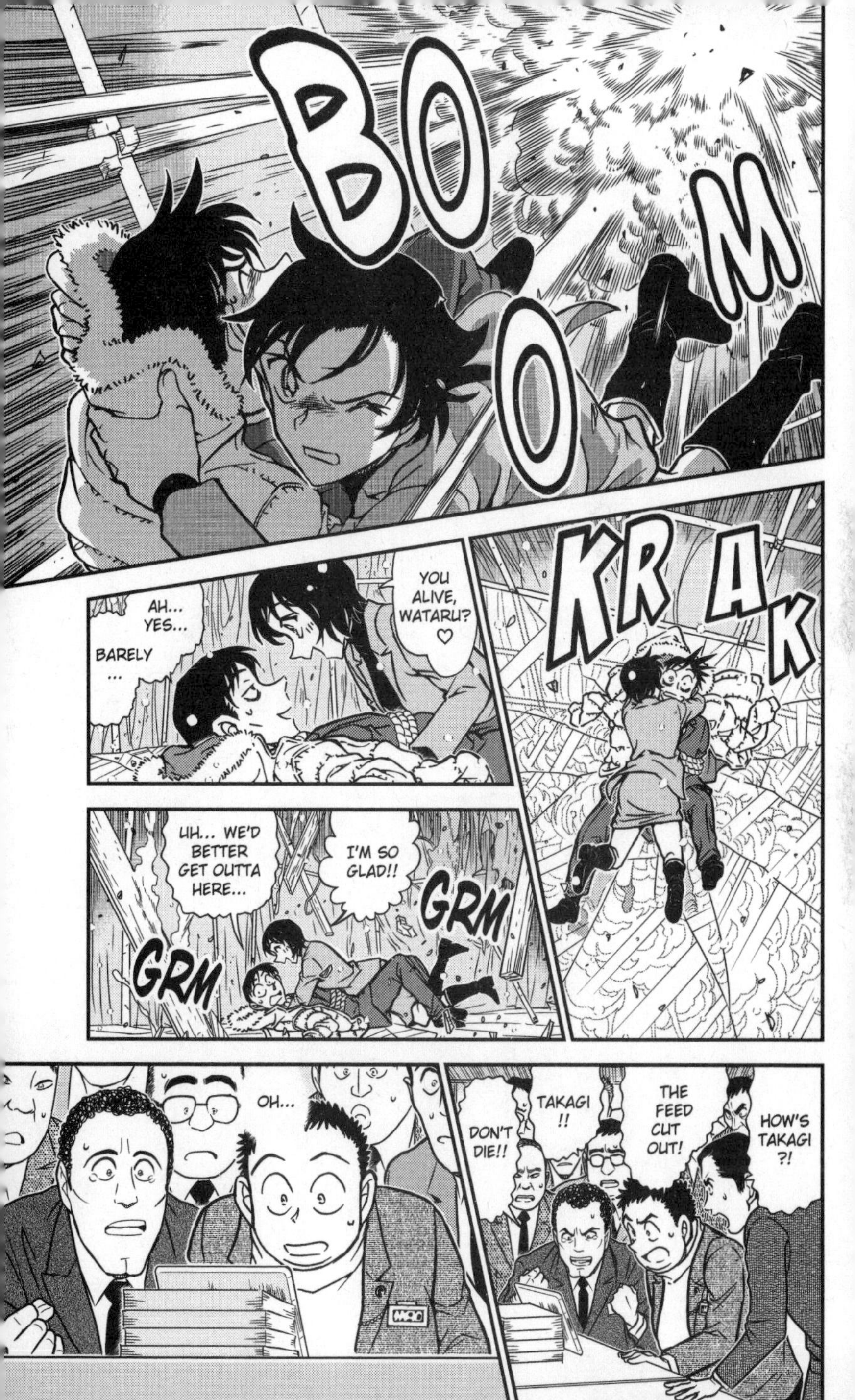
BOOM
KRAK
YOU ALIVE, WATARU? ♡
AH... YES...
BARELY...
I'M SO GLAD!!
UH... WE'D BETTER GET OUTTA HERE...
GRM
GRM
HOW'S TAKAGI?!
THE FEED CUT OUT!
TAKAGI!!
DON'T DIE!!
OH...

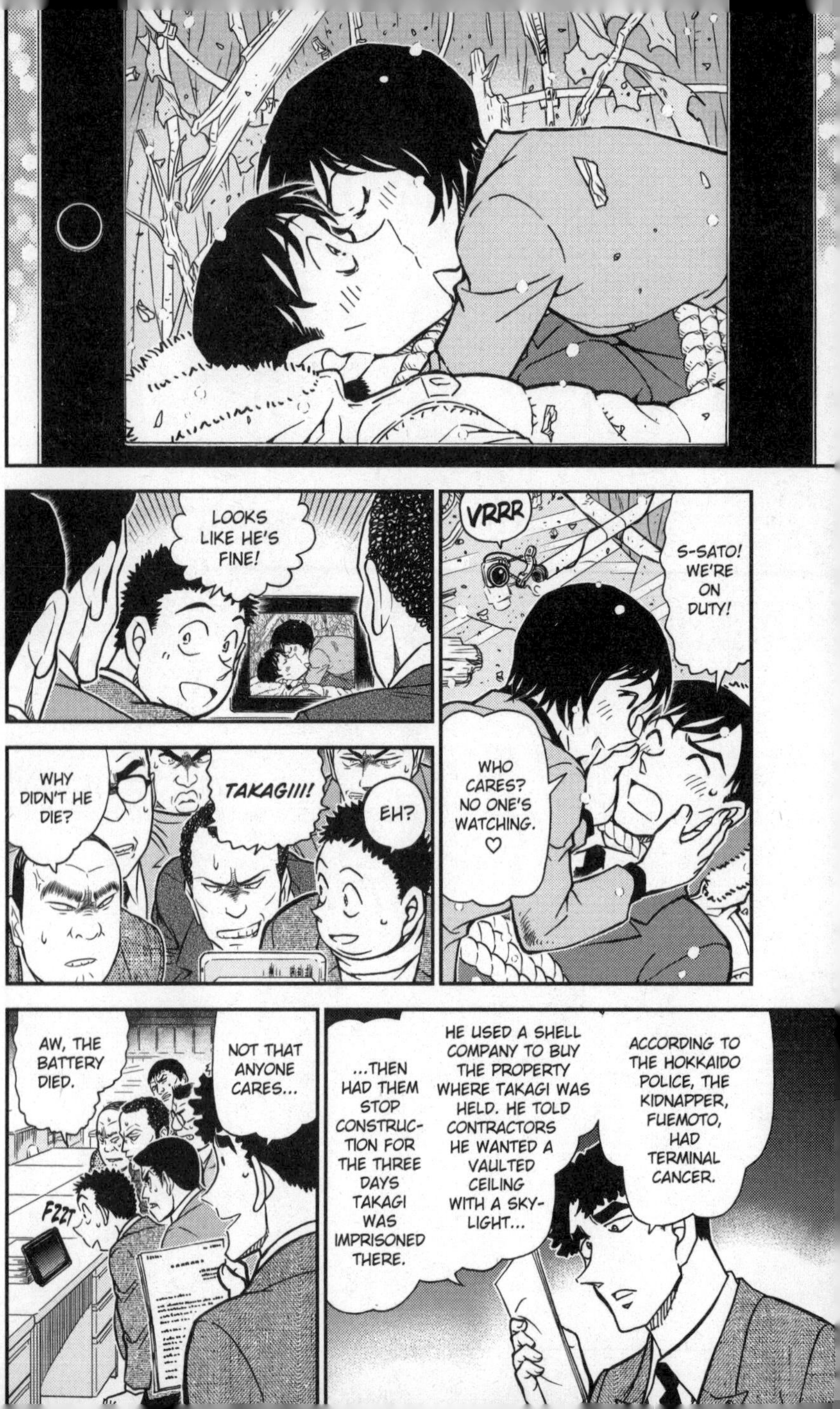
S-SATO! WE'RE ON DUTY!
VRRR
WHO CARES? NO ONE'S WATCHING. ♥
LOOKS LIKE HE'S FINE!
EH?
TAKAGIII!
WHY DIDN'T HE DIE?
ACCORDING TO THE HOKKAIDO POLICE, THE KIDNAPPER, FUEMOTO, HAD TERMINAL CANCER.
HE USED A SHELL COMPANY TO BUY THE PROPERTY WHERE TAKAGI WAS HELD. HE TOLD CONTRACTORS HE WANTED A VAULTED CEILING WITH A SKY-LIGHT...
...THEN HAD THEM STOP CONSTRUC-TION FOR THE THREE DAYS TAKAGI WAS IMPRISONED THERE.
NOT THAT ANYONE CARES...
AW, THE BATTERY DIED.
FZZT

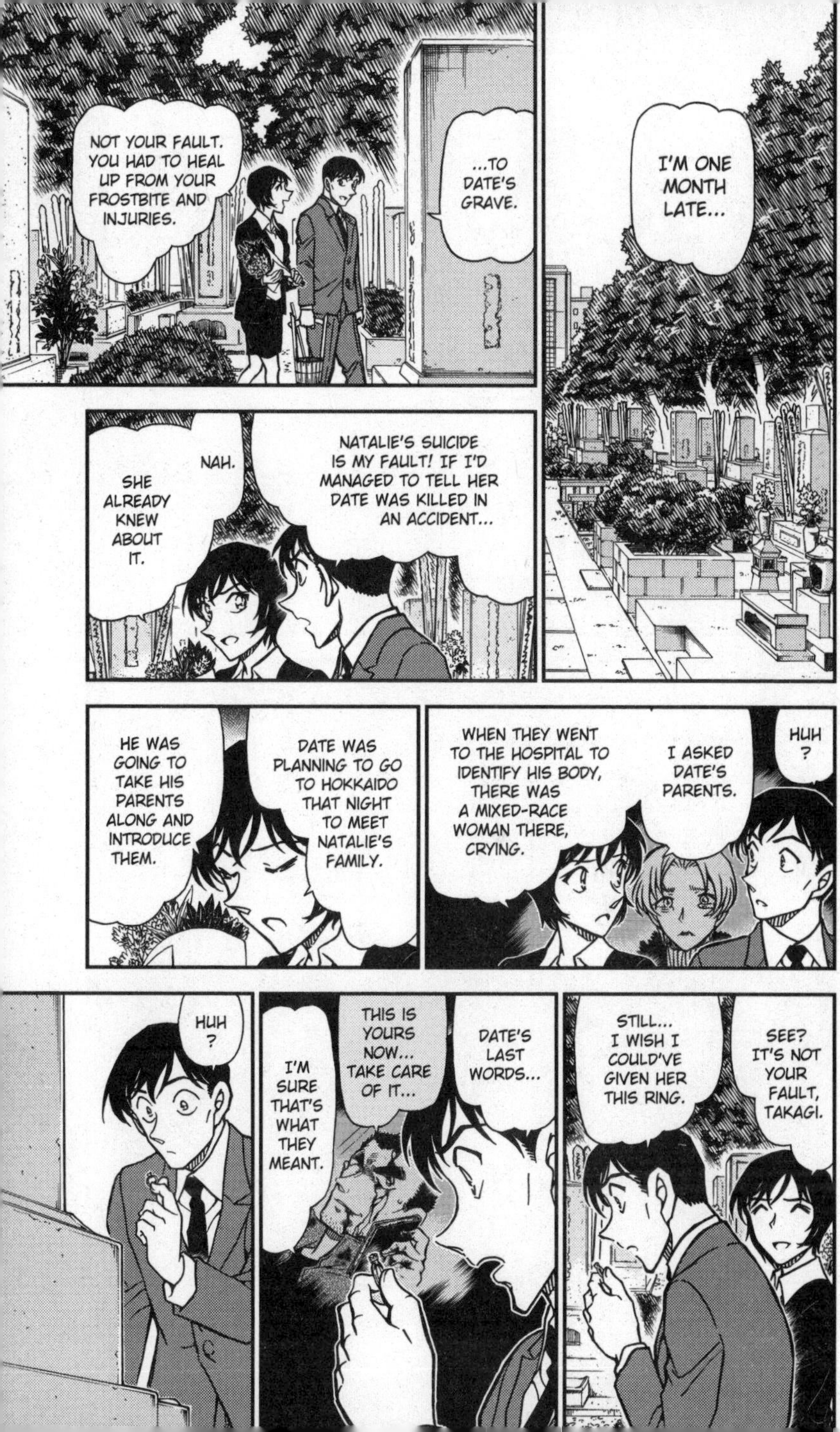
I'M ONE MONTH LATE...
...TO DATE'S GRAVE.
NOT YOUR FAULT. YOU HAD TO HEAL UP FROM YOUR FROSTBITE AND INJURIES.
NATALIE'S SUICIDE IS MY FAULT! IF I'D MANAGED TO TELL HER DATE WAS KILLED IN AN ACCIDENT...
NAH.
SHE ALREADY KNEW ABOUT IT.
HUH?
I ASKED DATE'S PARENTS.
WHEN THEY WENT TO THE HOSPITAL TO IDENTIFY HIS BODY, THERE WAS A MIXED-RACE WOMAN THERE, CRYING.
DATE WAS PLANNING TO GO TO HOKKAIDO THAT NIGHT TO MEET NATALIE'S FAMILY.
HE WAS GOING TO TAKE HIS PARENTS ALONG AND INTRODUCE THEM.
SEE? IT'S NOT YOUR FAULT, TAKAGI.
STILL... I WISH I COULD'VE GIVEN HER THIS RING.
DATE'S LAST WORDS...
THIS IS YOURS NOW... TAKE CARE OF IT...
I'M SURE THAT'S WHAT THEY MEANT.
HUH?

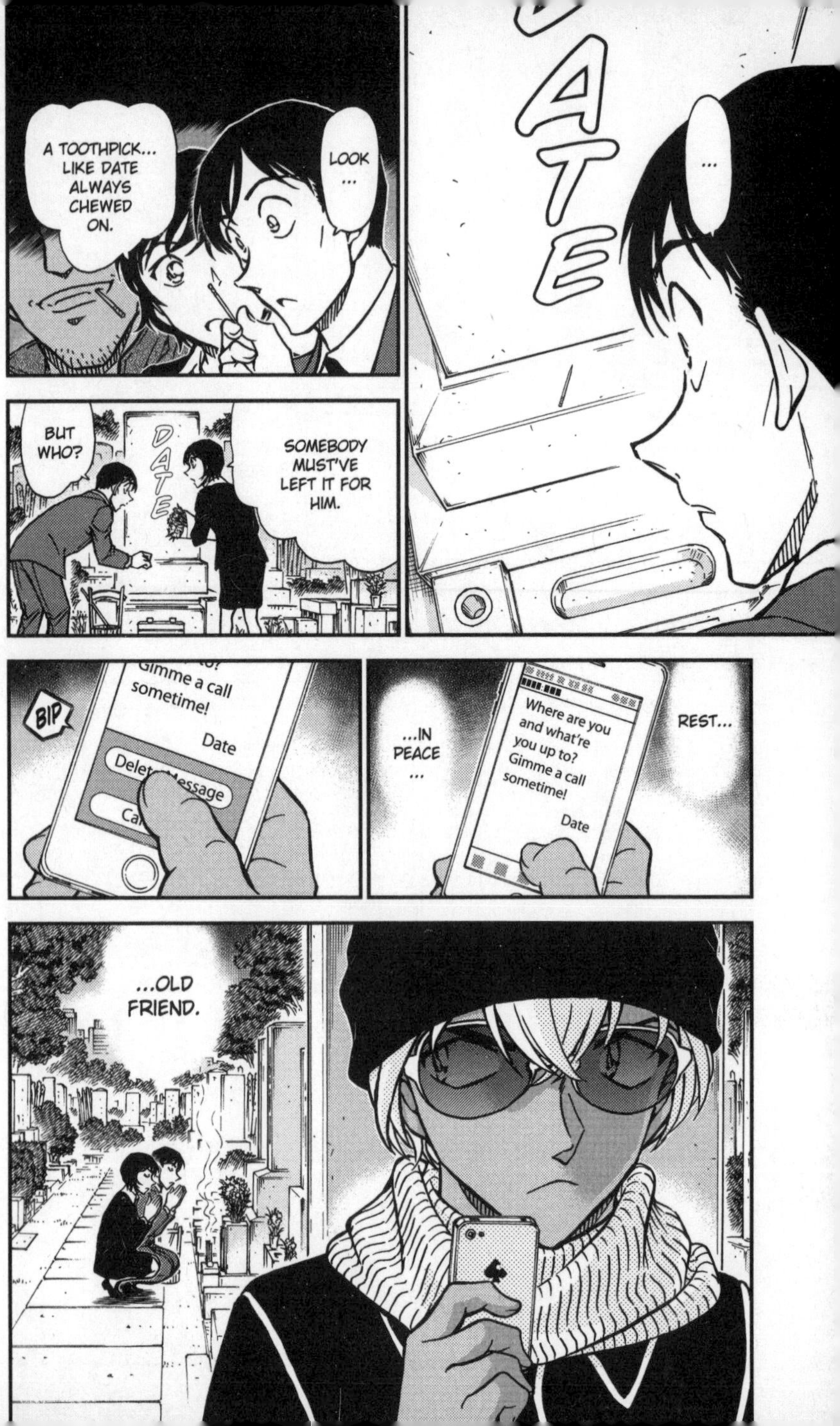
DATE
...
LOOK...
A TOOTHPICK... LIKE DATE ALWAYS CHEWED ON.
SOMEBODY MUST'VE LEFT IT FOR HIM.
DATE
BUT WHO?
REST...
Where are you and what're you up to? Gimme a call sometime!
Date
...IN PEACE...
Gimme a call sometime!
Date
BIP
...OLD FRIEND.

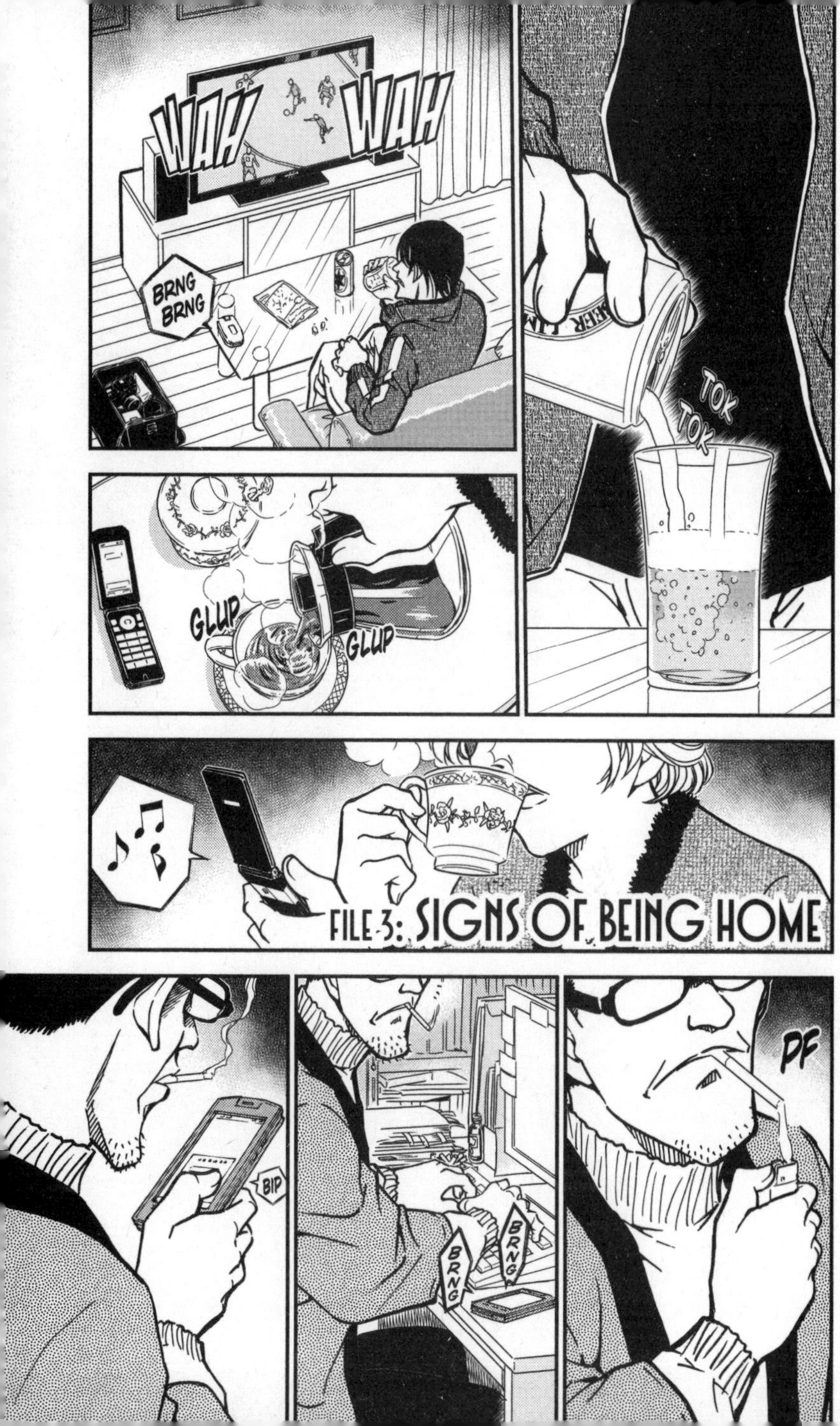
TOK TOK
WAH WAH
BRNG BRNG
GLUP GLUP
♪ ♫
FILE 3: SIGNS OF BEING HOME
PF
BRNG BRNG
BIP

FILE 3: SIGNS OF BEING HOME

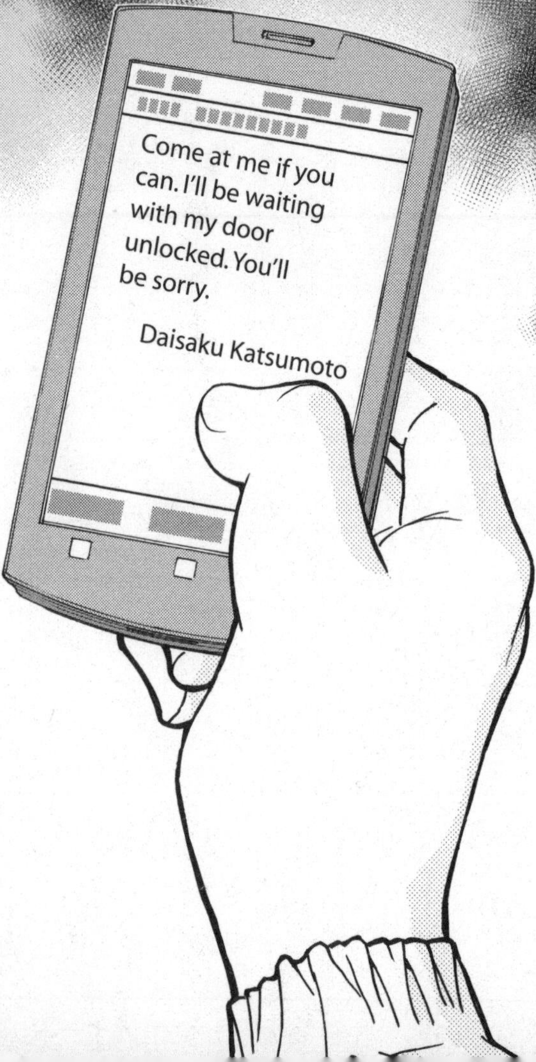
Come at me if you can. I'll be waiting with my door unlocked. You'll be sorry.
Daisaku Katsumoto

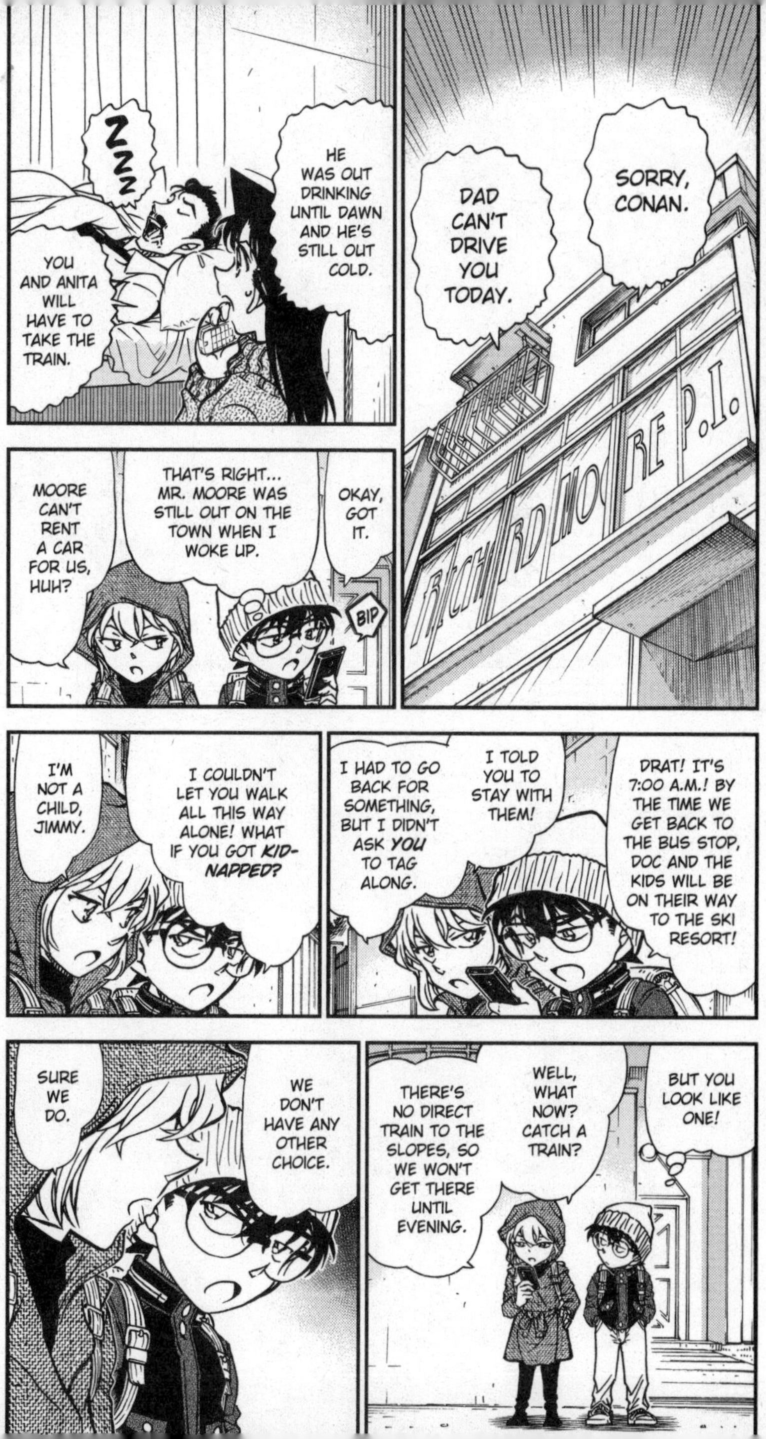
SORRY, CONAN.
DAD CAN'T DRIVE YOU TODAY.
RICHARD MOORE P.I.
HE WAS OUT DRINKING UNTIL DAWN AND HE'S STILL OUT COLD.
ZZZ
YOU AND ANITA WILL HAVE TO TAKE THE TRAIN.
OKAY, GOT IT.
BIP
THAT'S RIGHT... MR. MOORE WAS STILL OUT ON THE TOWN WHEN I WOKE UP.
MOORE CAN'T RENT A CAR FOR US, HUH?
DRAT! IT'S 7:00 A.M.! BY THE TIME WE GET BACK TO THE BUS STOP, DOC AND THE KIDS WILL BE ON THEIR WAY TO THE SKI RESORT!
I TOLD YOU TO STAY WITH THEM!
I HAD TO GO BACK FOR SOMETHING, BUT I DIDN'T ASK YOU TO TAG ALONG.
I COULDN'T LET YOU WALK ALL THIS WAY ALONE! WHAT IF YOU GOT KID-NAPPED?
I'M NOT A CHILD, JIMMY.
BUT YOU LOOK LIKE ONE!
WELL, WHAT NOW? CATCH A TRAIN?
THERE'S NO DIRECT TRAIN TO THE SLOPES, SO WE WON'T GET THERE UNTIL EVENING.
WE DON'T HAVE ANY OTHER CHOICE.
SURE WE DO.

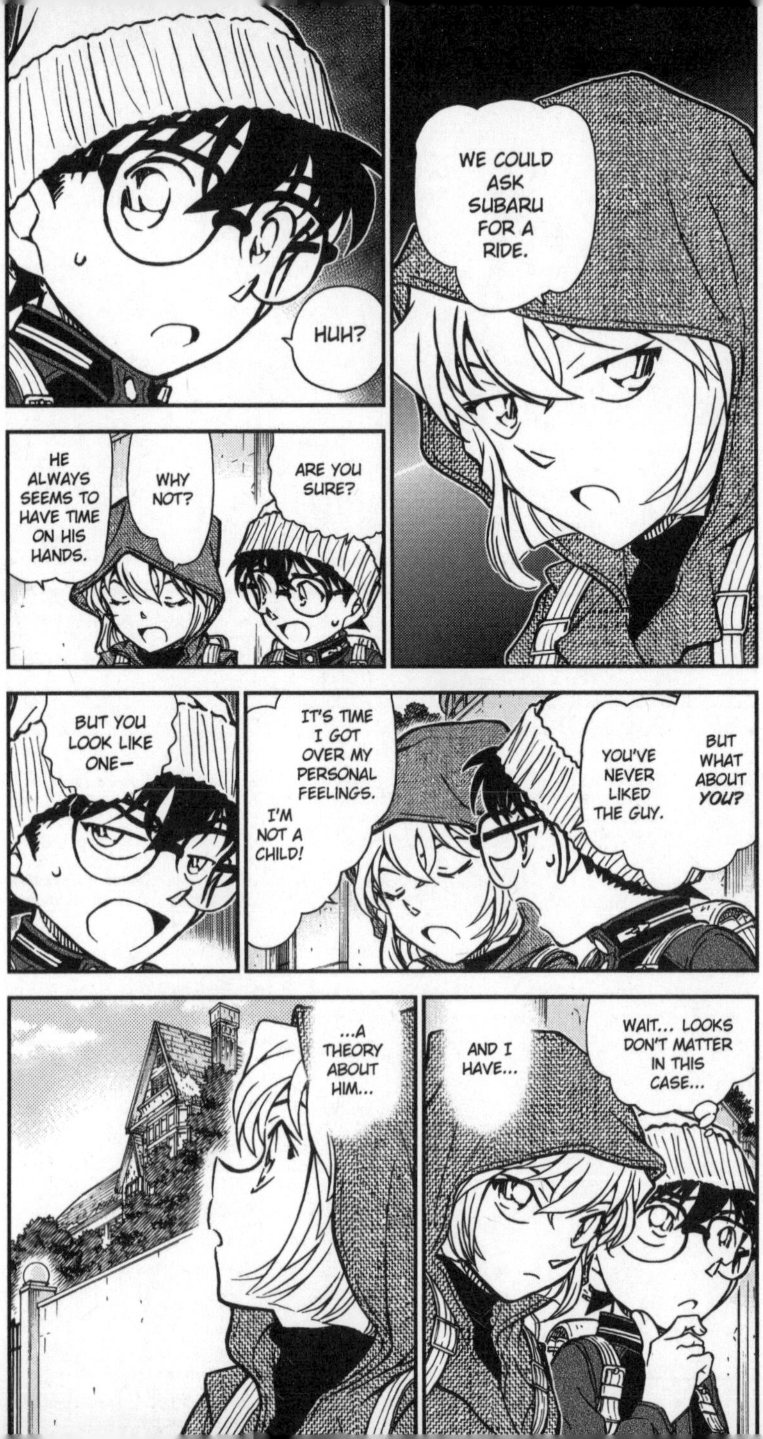
WE COULD ASK SUBARU FOR A RIDE.
HUH?
ARE YOU SURE?
WHY NOT?
HE ALWAYS SEEMS TO HAVE TIME ON HIS HANDS.
BUT WHAT ABOUT *YOU?*
YOU'VE NEVER LIKED THE GUY.
IT'S TIME I GOT OVER MY PERSONAL FEELINGS.
I'M NOT A CHILD!
BUT YOU LOOK LIKE ONE—
WAIT... LOOKS DON'T MATTER IN THIS CASE...
AND I HAVE...
...A THEORY ABOUT HIM...

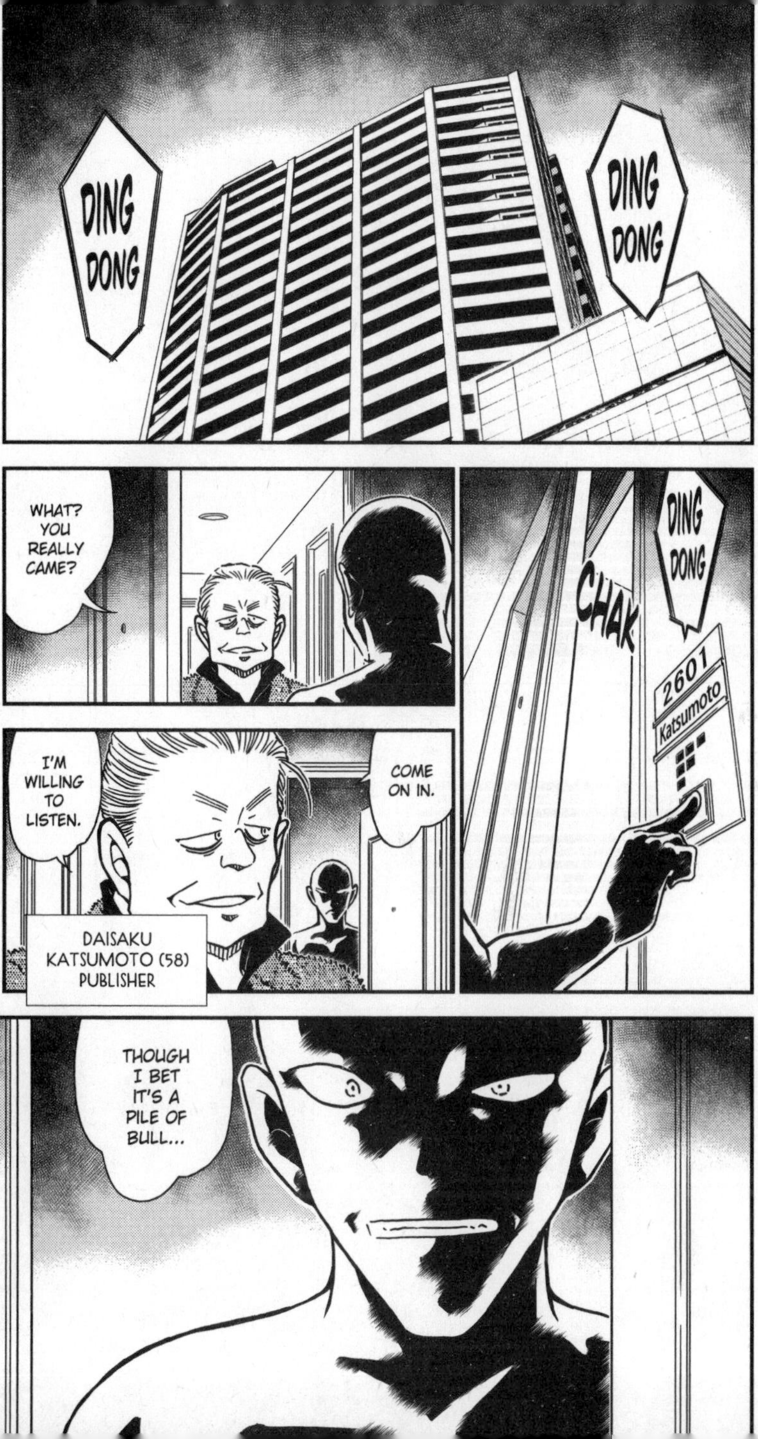
DING DONG
DING DONG
DING DONG
CHAK
2601
Katsumoto
WHAT? YOU REALLY CAME?
COME ON IN.
I'M WILLING TO LISTEN.
DAISAKU KATSUMOTO (58) PUBLISHER
THOUGH I BET IT'S A PILE OF BULL...

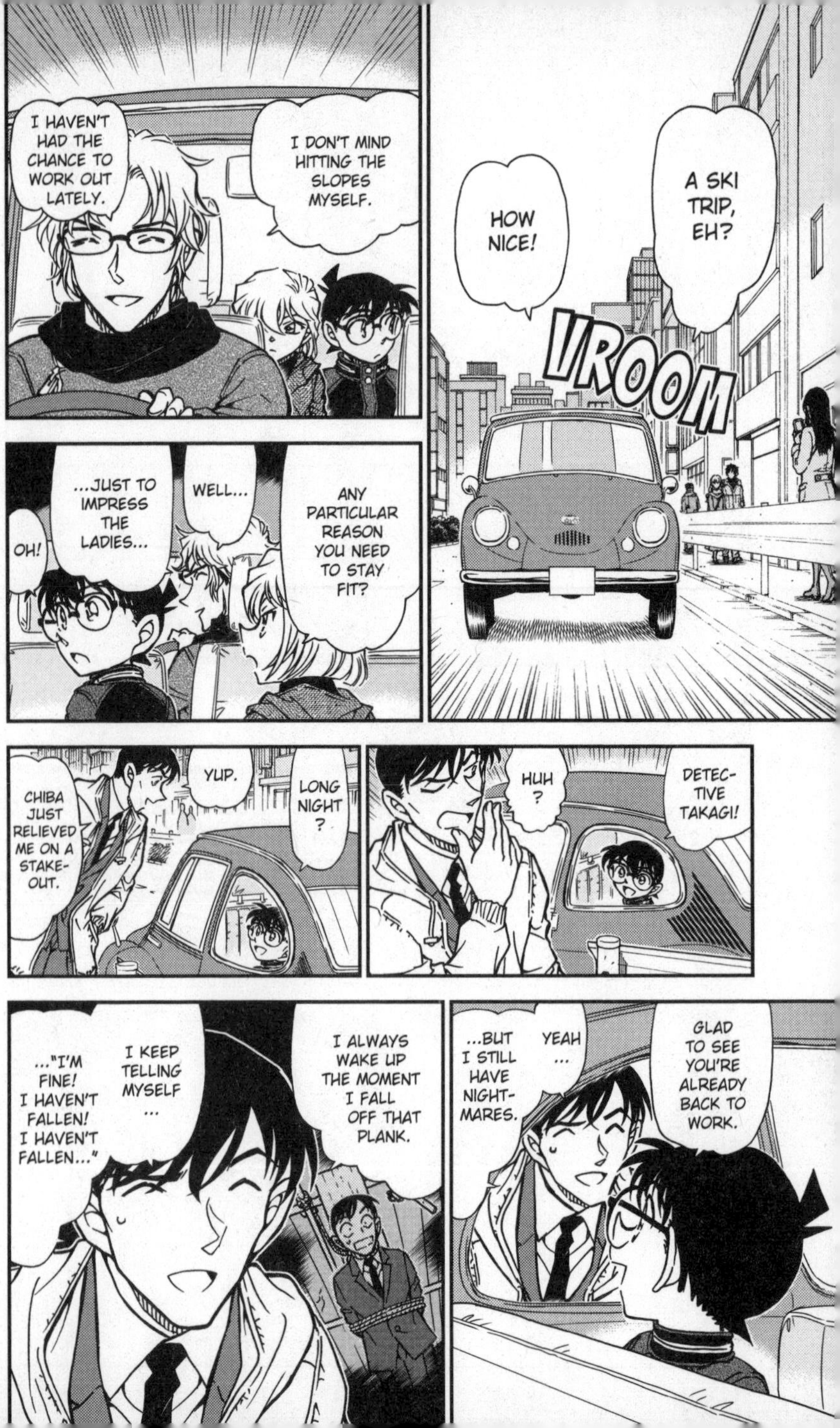
A SKI TRIP, EH?
HOW NICE!
VROOM
I DON'T MIND HITTING THE SLOPES MYSELF.
I HAVEN'T HAD THE CHANCE TO WORK OUT LATELY.
ANY PARTICULAR REASON YOU NEED TO STAY FIT?
WELL...
...JUST TO IMPRESS THE LADIES...
OH!
DETECTIVE TAKAGI!
HUH?
LONG NIGHT?
YUP.
CHIBA JUST RELIEVED ME ON A STAKEOUT.
GLAD TO SEE YOU'RE ALREADY BACK TO WORK.
YEAH...
...BUT I STILL HAVE NIGHTMARES.
I ALWAYS WAKE UP THE MOMENT I FALL OFF THAT PLANK.
I KEEP TELLING MYSELF...
..."I'M FINE! I HAVEN'T FALLEN! I HAVEN'T FALLEN..."

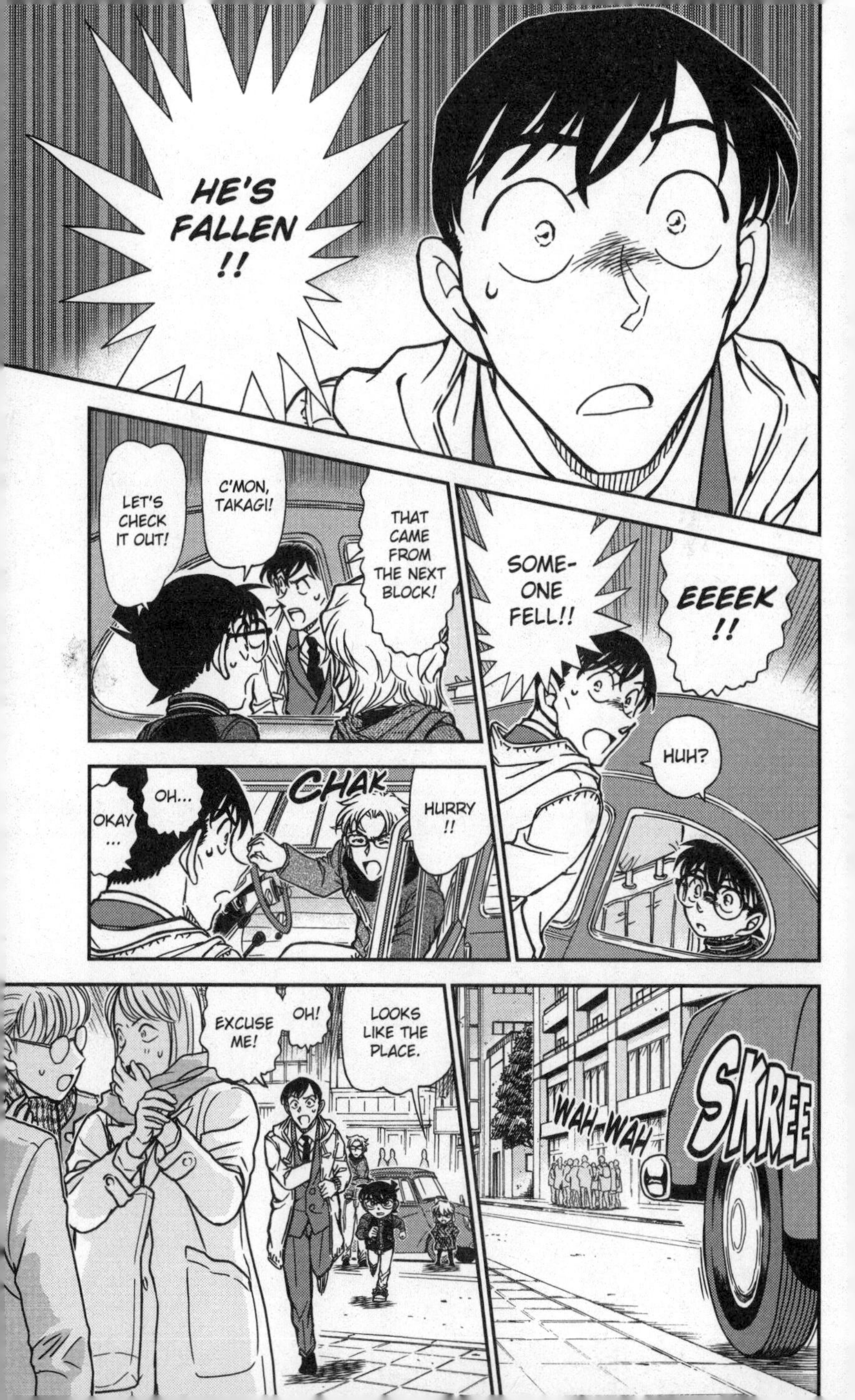
HE'S FALLEN!!
EEEEK!!
SOME-ONE FELL!!
HUH?
THAT CAME FROM THE NEXT BLOCK!
C'MON, TAKAGI!
LET'S CHECK IT OUT!
HURRY!!
CHAK
OH...
OKAY...
SKREE
WAH-WAH
LOOKS LIKE THE PLACE.
OH!
EXCUSE ME!

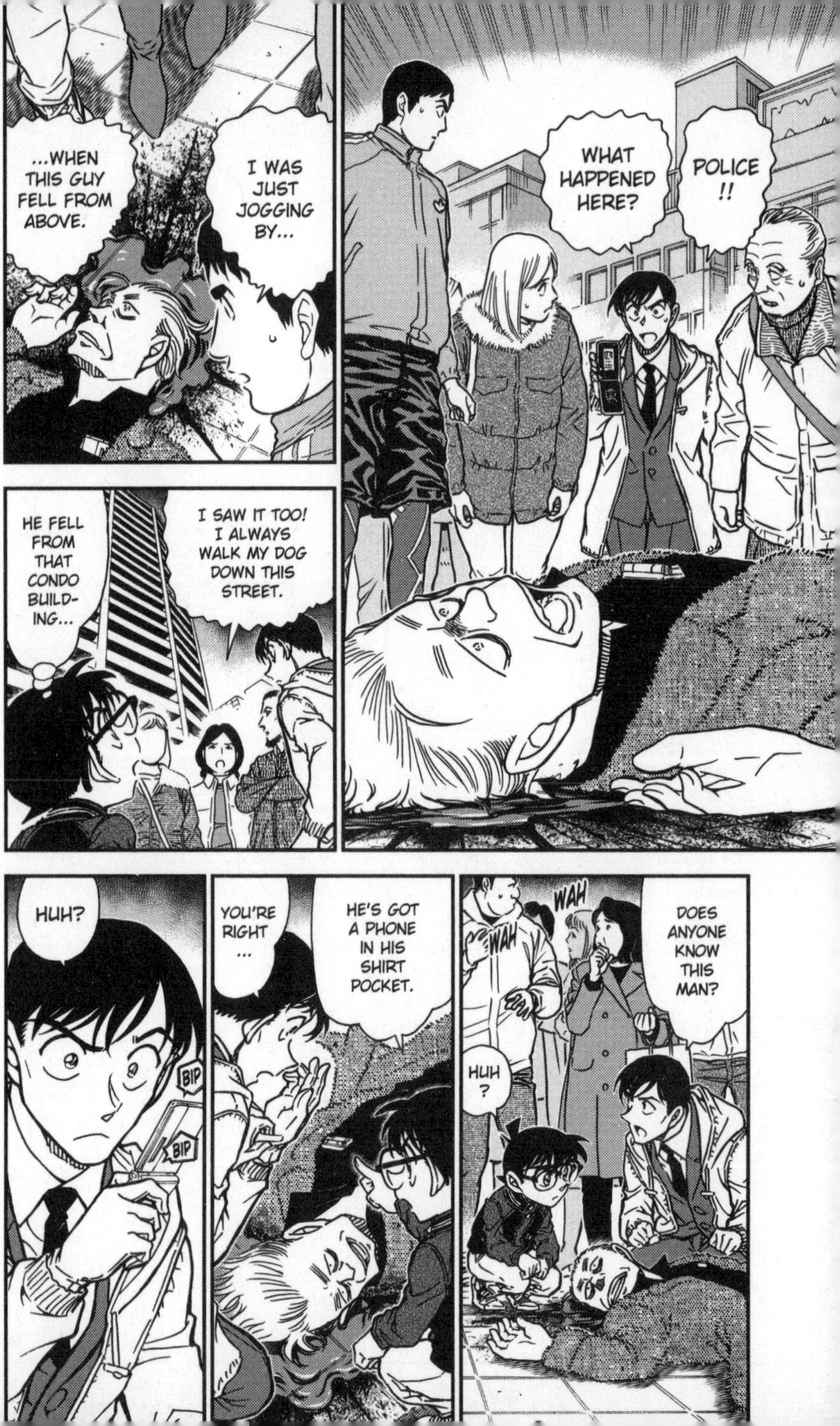
POLICE !!
WHAT HAPPENED HERE?
I WAS JUST JOGGING BY...
...WHEN THIS GUY FELL FROM ABOVE.
I SAW IT TOO! I ALWAYS WALK MY DOG DOWN THIS STREET.
HE FELL FROM THAT CONDO BUILDING-ING...
DOES ANYONE KNOW THIS MAN?
WAH
WAH
HUH ?
HE'S GOT A PHONE IN HIS SHIRT POCKET.
YOU'RE RIGHT ...
HUH?
BIP
BIP

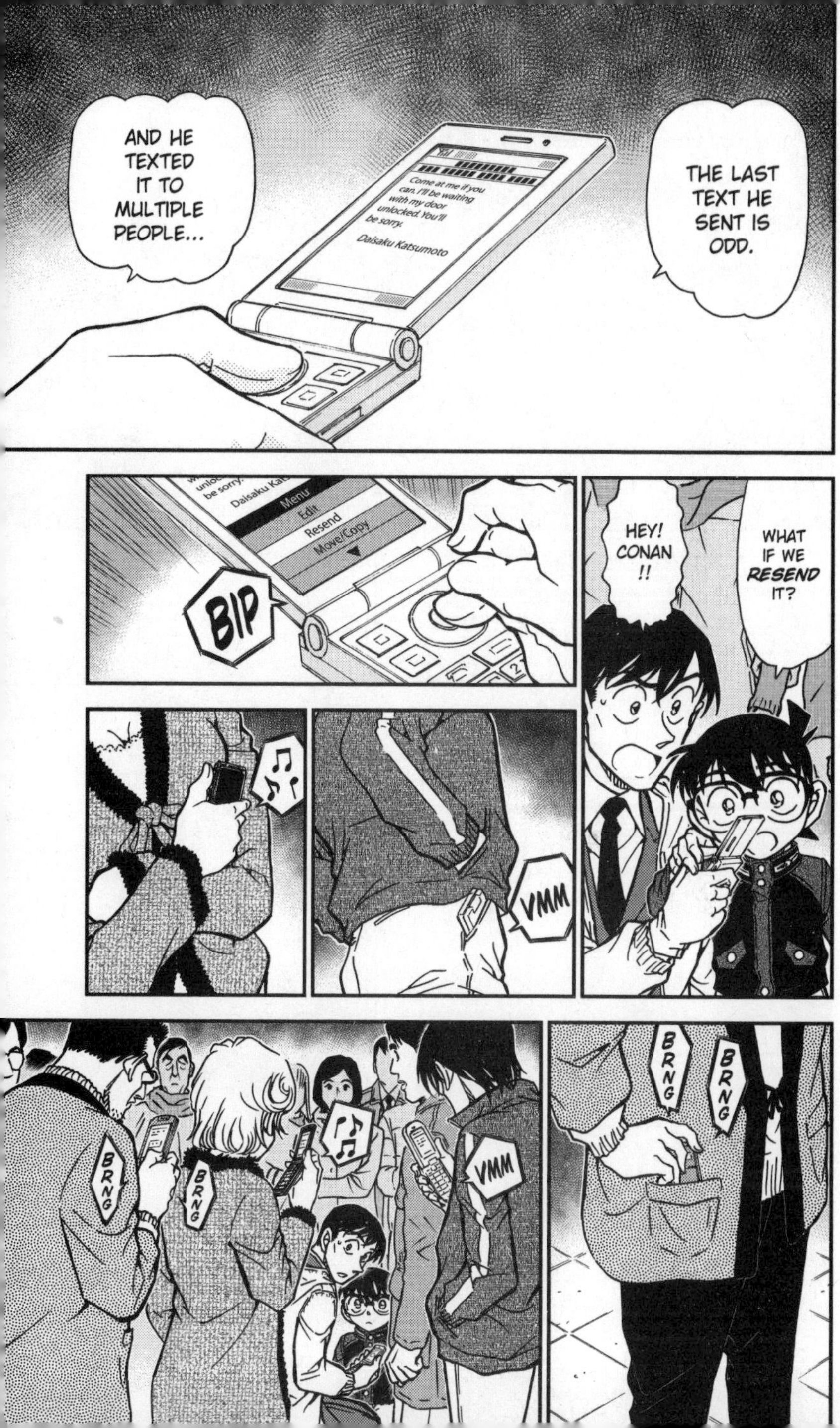
THE LAST TEXT HE SENT IS ODD.
Come at me if you can. I'll be waiting with my door unlocked. You'll be sorry.
Daisaku Katsumoto
AND HE TEXTED IT TO MULTIPLE PEOPLE...
WHAT IF WE *RESEND* IT?
HEY! CONAN!!
Menu
Edit
Resend
Move/Copy
BIP
VMM
BRNG
BRNG
VMM
BRNG
BRNG

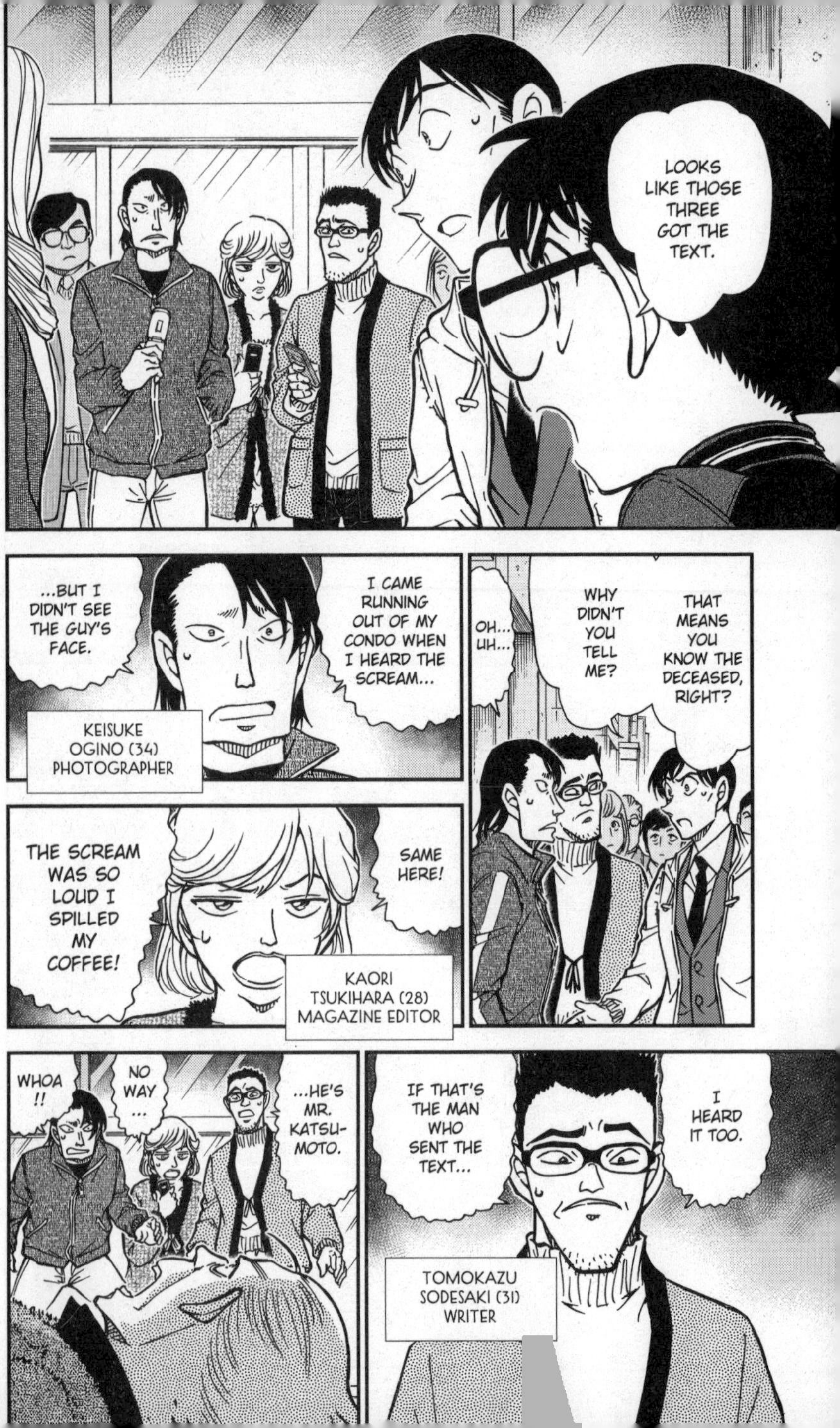
LOOKS LIKE THOSE THREE GOT THE TEXT.
THAT MEANS YOU KNOW THE DECEASED, RIGHT?
WHY DIDN'T YOU TELL ME?
OH... UH...
I CAME RUNNING OUT OF MY CONDO WHEN I HEARD THE SCREAM...
...BUT I DIDN'T SEE THE GUY'S FACE.
KEISUKE OGINO (34) PHOTOGRAPHER
SAME HERE!
THE SCREAM WAS SO LOUD I SPILLED MY COFFEE!
KAORI TSUKIHARA (28) MAGAZINE EDITOR
I HEARD IT TOO.
IF THAT'S THE MAN WHO SENT THE TEXT...
TOMOKAZU SODESAKI (31) WRITER
...HE'S MR. KATSU-MOTO.
NO WAY...
WHOA!!

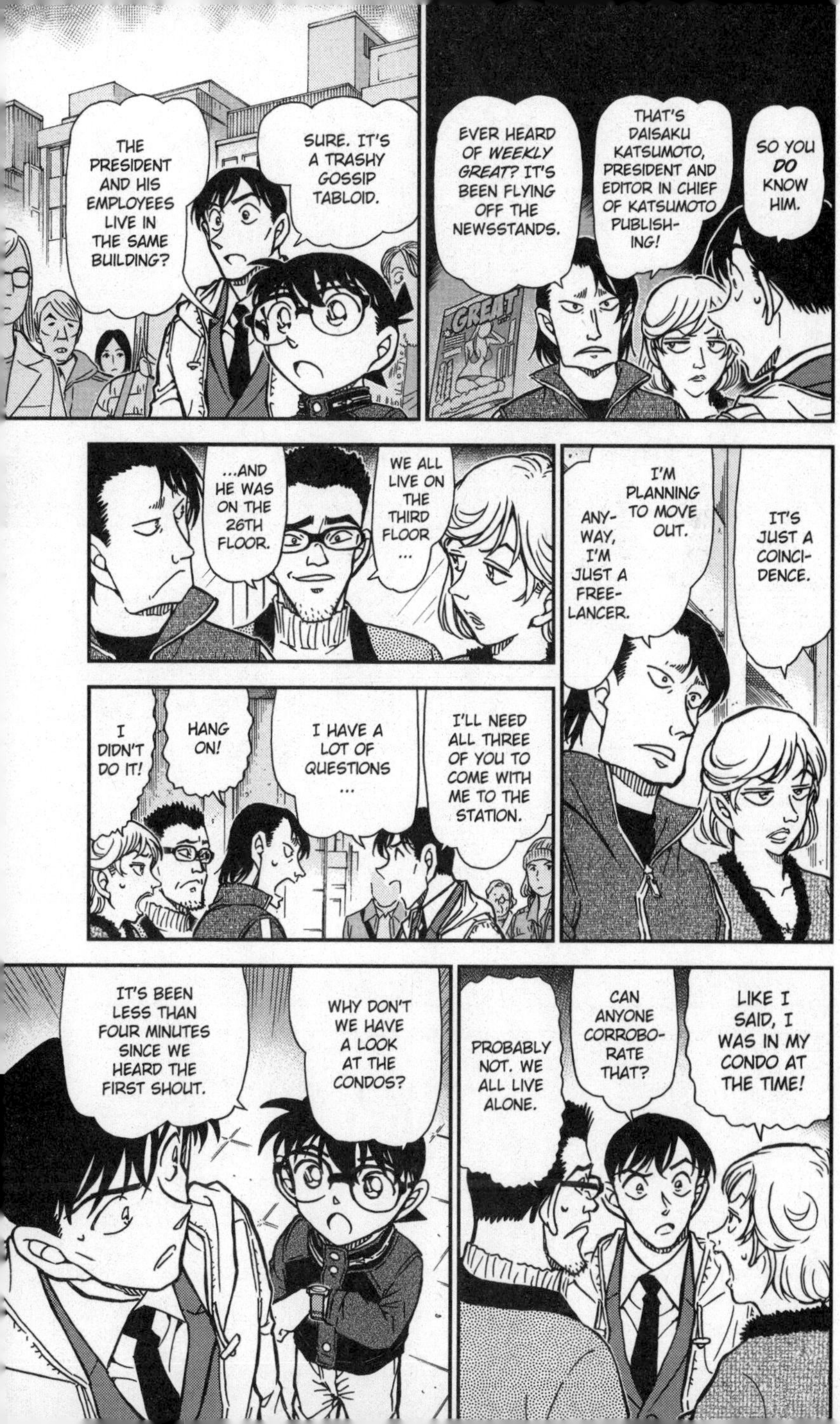
SO YOU *DO* KNOW HIM.
THAT'S DAISAKU KATSUMOTO, PRESIDENT AND EDITOR IN CHIEF OF KATSUMOTO PUBLISHING!
EVER HEARD OF *WEEKLY GREAT*? IT'S BEEN FLYING OFF THE NEWSSTANDS.
SURE. IT'S A TRASHY GOSSIP TABLOID.
THE PRESIDENT AND HIS EMPLOYEES LIVE IN THE SAME BUILDING?
IT'S JUST A COINCIDENCE.
I'M PLANNING TO MOVE OUT.
ANYWAY, I'M JUST A FREELANCER.
WE ALL LIVE ON THE THIRD FLOOR...
...AND HE WAS ON THE 26TH FLOOR.
I'LL NEED ALL THREE OF YOU TO COME WITH ME TO THE STATION.
I HAVE A LOT OF QUESTIONS...
HANG ON!
I DIDN'T DO IT!
LIKE I SAID, I WAS IN MY CONDO AT THE TIME!
CAN ANYONE CORROBORATE THAT?
PROBABLY NOT. WE ALL LIVE ALONE.
WHY DON'T WE HAVE A LOOK AT THE CONDOS?
IT'S BEEN LESS THAN FOUR MINUTES SINCE WE HEARD THE FIRST SHOUT.

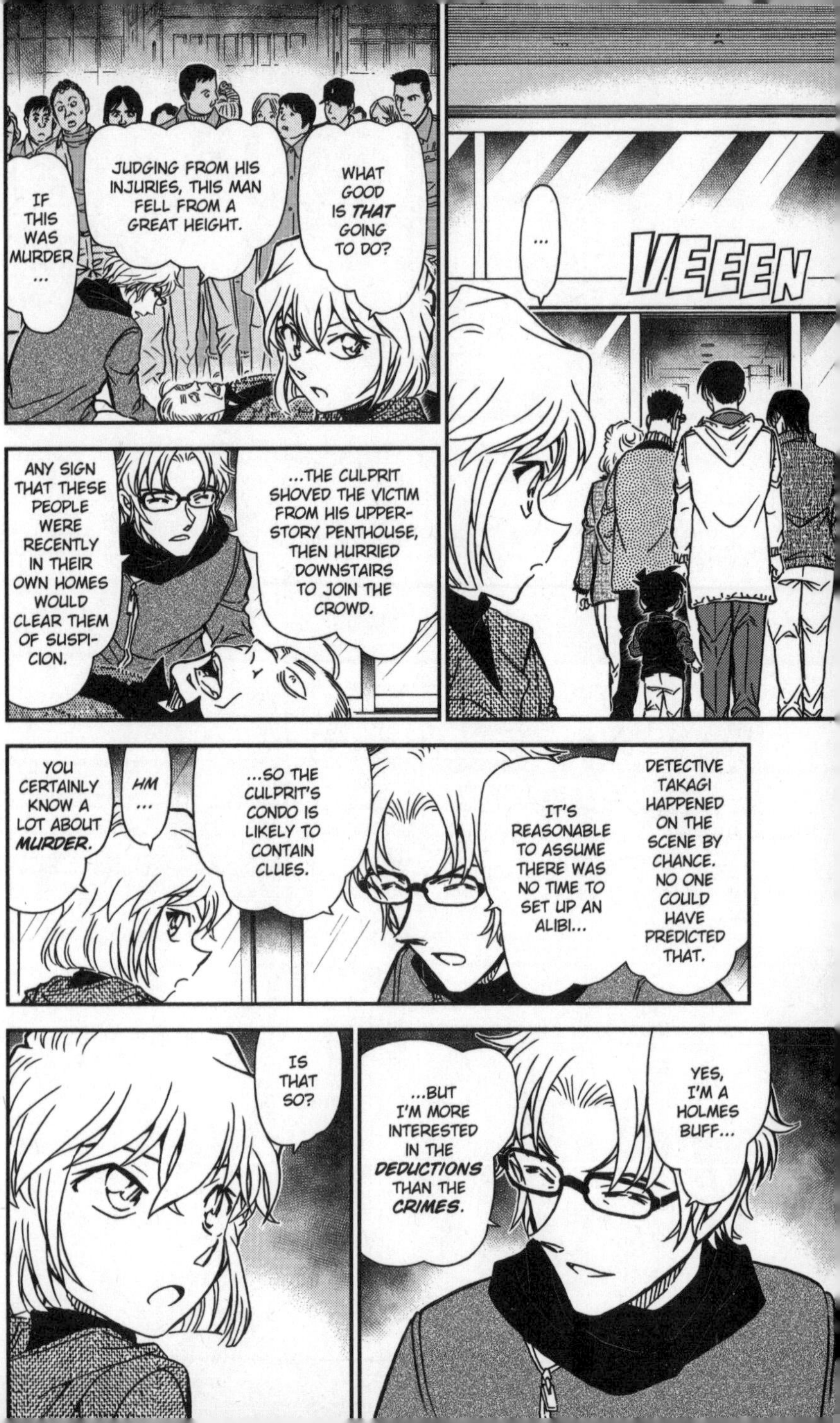
...
VEEEN
WHAT GOOD IS *THAT* GOING TO DO?
JUDGING FROM HIS INJURIES, THIS MAN FELL FROM A GREAT HEIGHT.
IF THIS WAS MURDER...
...THE CULPRIT SHOVED THE VICTIM FROM HIS UPPER-STORY PENTHOUSE, THEN HURRIED DOWNSTAIRS TO JOIN THE CROWD.
ANY SIGN THAT THESE PEOPLE WERE RECENTLY IN THEIR OWN HOMES WOULD CLEAR THEM OF SUSPICION.
DETECTIVE TAKAGI HAPPENED ON THE SCENE BY CHANCE. NO ONE COULD HAVE PREDICTED THAT.
IT'S REASONABLE TO ASSUME THERE WAS NO TIME TO SET UP AN ALIBI...
...SO THE CULPRIT'S CONDO IS LIKELY TO CONTAIN CLUES.
HM...
YOU CERTAINLY KNOW A LOT ABOUT ***MURDER***.
YES, I'M A HOLMES BUFF...
...BUT I'M MORE INTERESTED IN THE ***DEDUCTIONS*** THAN THE ***CRIMES***.
IS THAT SO?

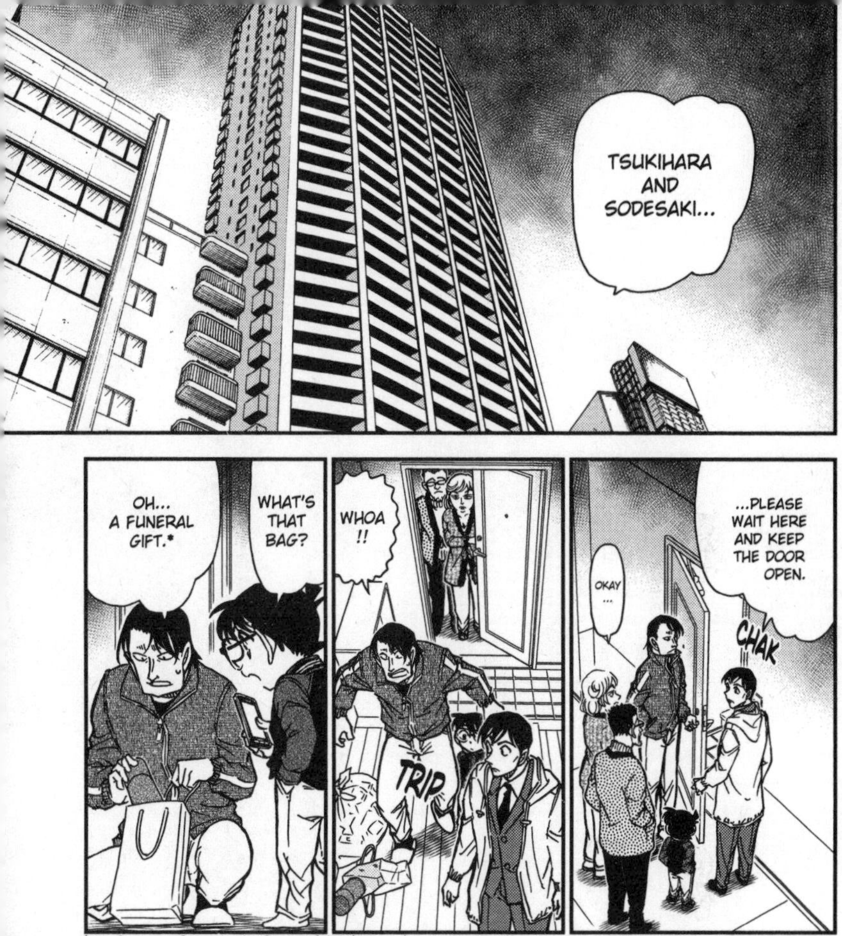
TSUKIHARA AND SODESAKI...
...PLEASE WAIT HERE AND KEEP THE DOOR OPEN.
OKAY ...
CHAK
WHOA !!
TRIP
WHAT'S THAT BAG?
OH... A FUNERAL GIFT.*

*At Japanese funerals, the family of the deceased typically gives the mourners small appreciation gifts.

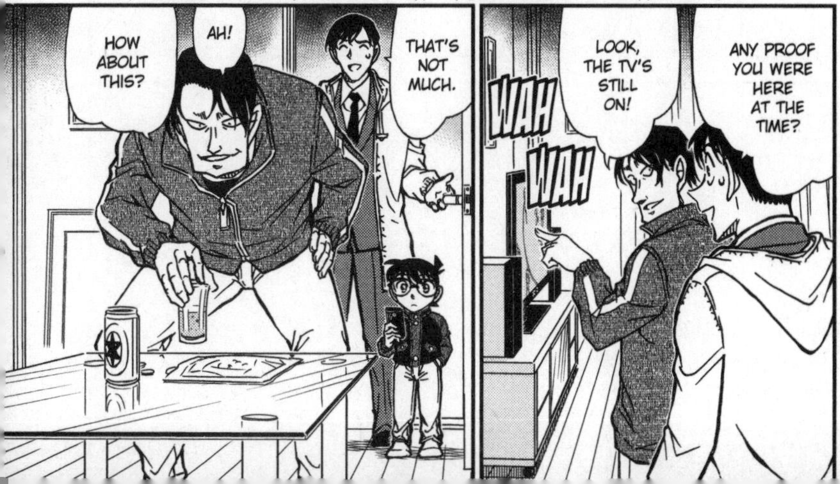
ANY PROOF YOU WERE HERE AT THE TIME?
LOOK, THE TV'S STILL ON!
WAH
WAH
THAT'S NOT MUCH.
AH!
HOW ABOUT THIS?

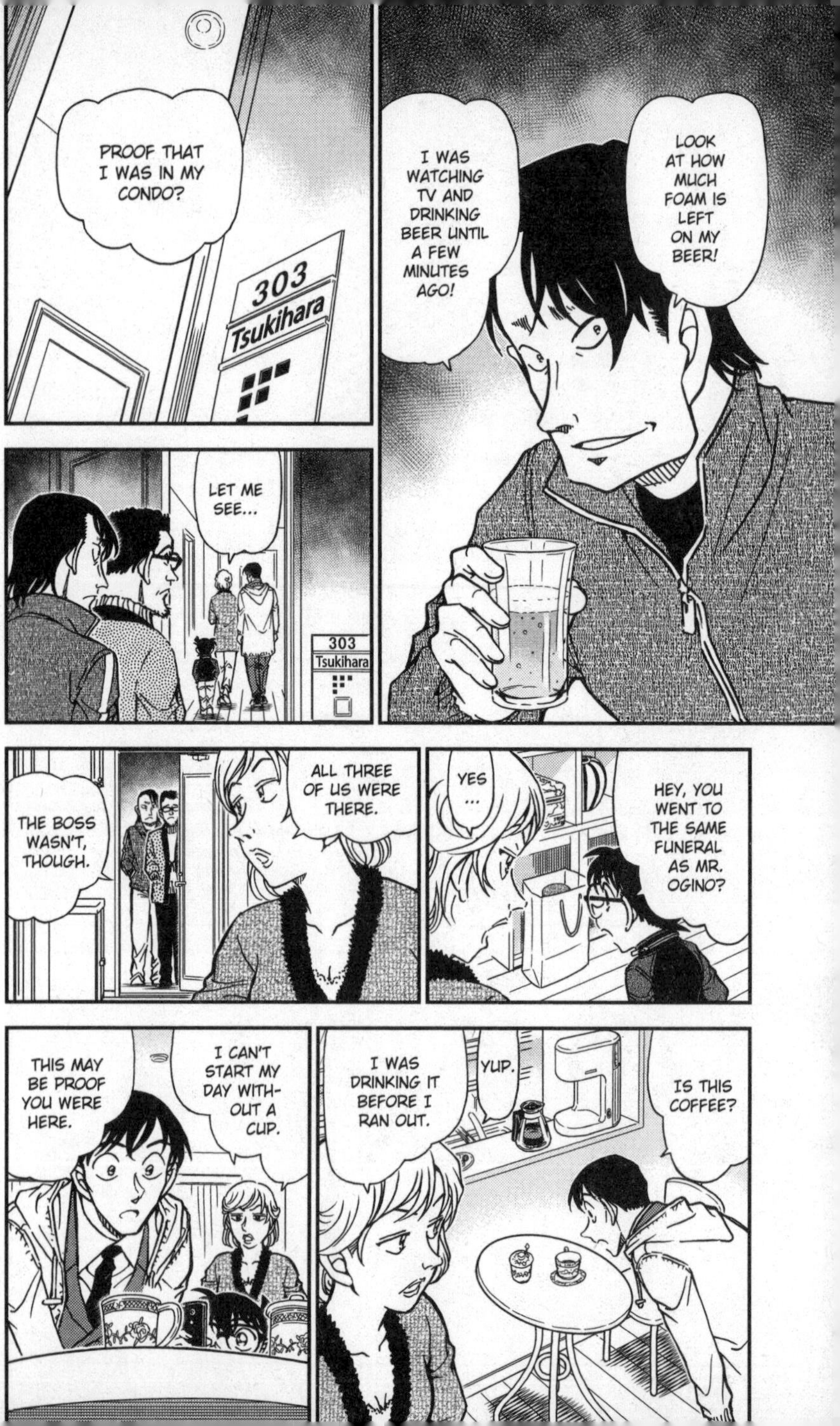
LOOK AT HOW MUCH FOAM IS LEFT ON MY BEER!
I WAS WATCHING TV AND DRINKING BEER UNTIL A FEW MINUTES AGO!
PROOF THAT I WAS IN MY CONDO?
303
Tsukihara
LET ME SEE...
303
Tsukihara
HEY, YOU WENT TO THE SAME FUNERAL AS MR. OGINO?
YES ...
ALL THREE OF US WERE THERE.
THE BOSS WASN'T, THOUGH.
IS THIS COFFEE?
YUP.
I WAS DRINKING IT BEFORE I RAN OUT.
I CAN'T START MY DAY WITH-OUT A CUP.
THIS MAY BE PROOF YOU WERE HERE.

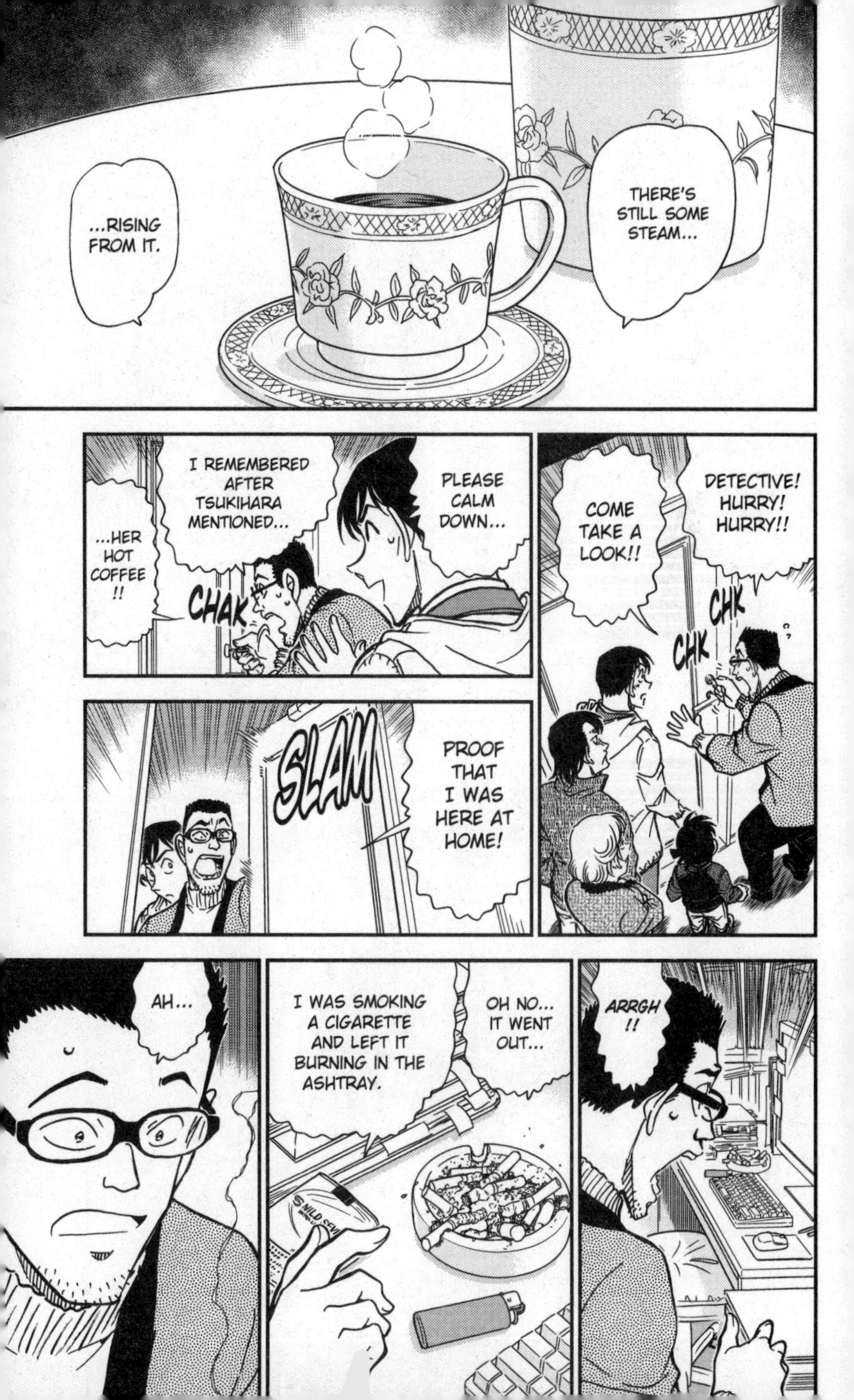
THERE'S STILL SOME STEAM...
...RISING FROM IT.
DETECTIVE! HURRY! HURRY!!
COME TAKE A LOOK!!
CHK
CHK
PLEASE CALM DOWN...
I REMEMBERED AFTER TSUKIHARA MENTIONED...
...HER HOT COFFEE!!
CHAK
PROOF THAT I WAS HERE AT HOME!
SLAM
ARRGH!!
OH NO... IT WENT OUT...
I WAS SMOKING A CIGARETTE AND LEFT IT BURNING IN THE ASHTRAY.
AH...

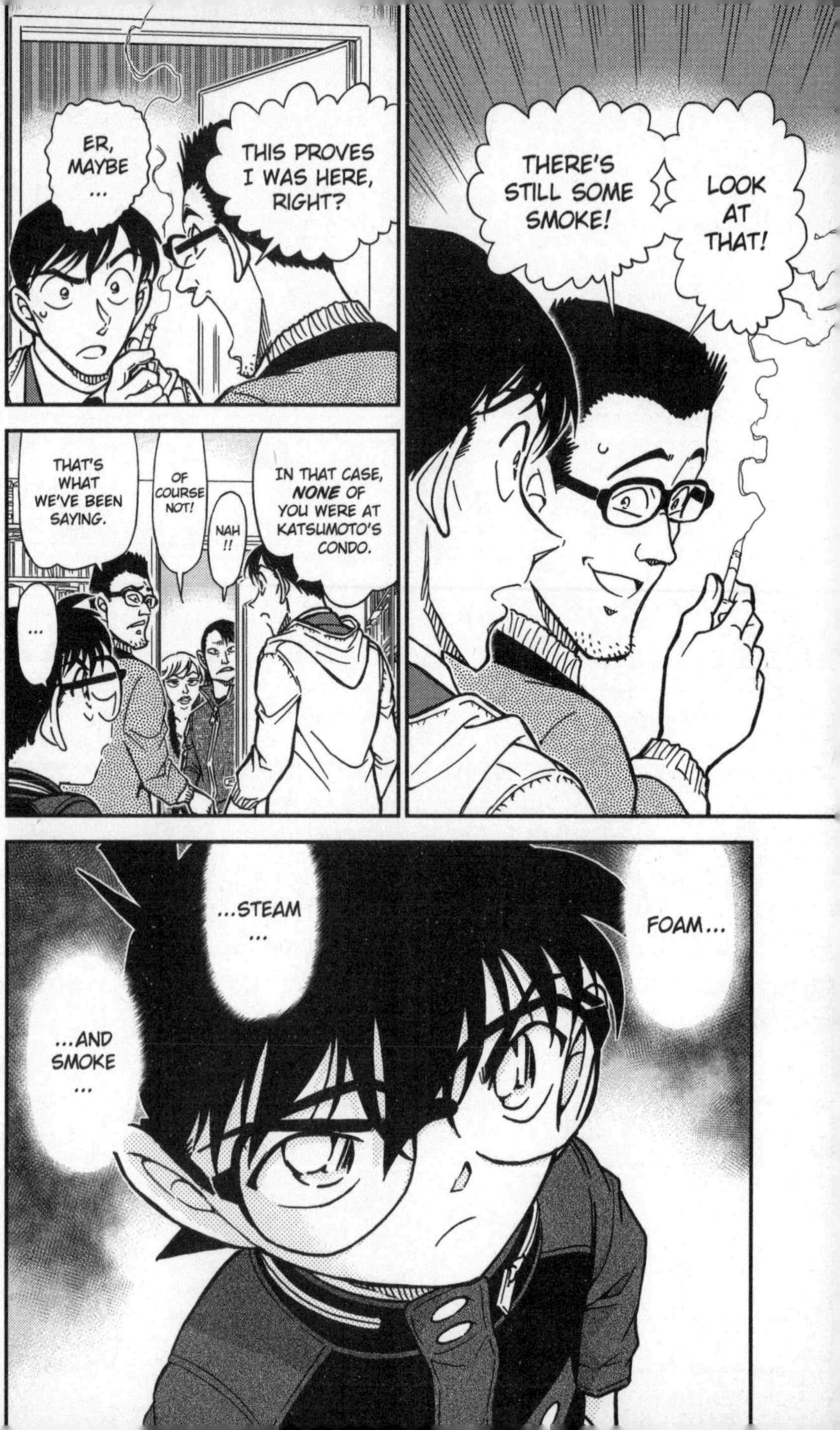
LOOK AT THAT!
THERE'S STILL SOME SMOKE!
THIS PROVES I WAS HERE, RIGHT?
ER, MAYBE ...
IN THAT CASE, NONE OF YOU WERE AT KATSUMOTO'S CONDO.
NAH !!
OF COURSE NOT!
THAT'S WHAT WE'VE BEEN SAYING.
...
FOAM...
...STEAM ...
...AND SMOKE ...

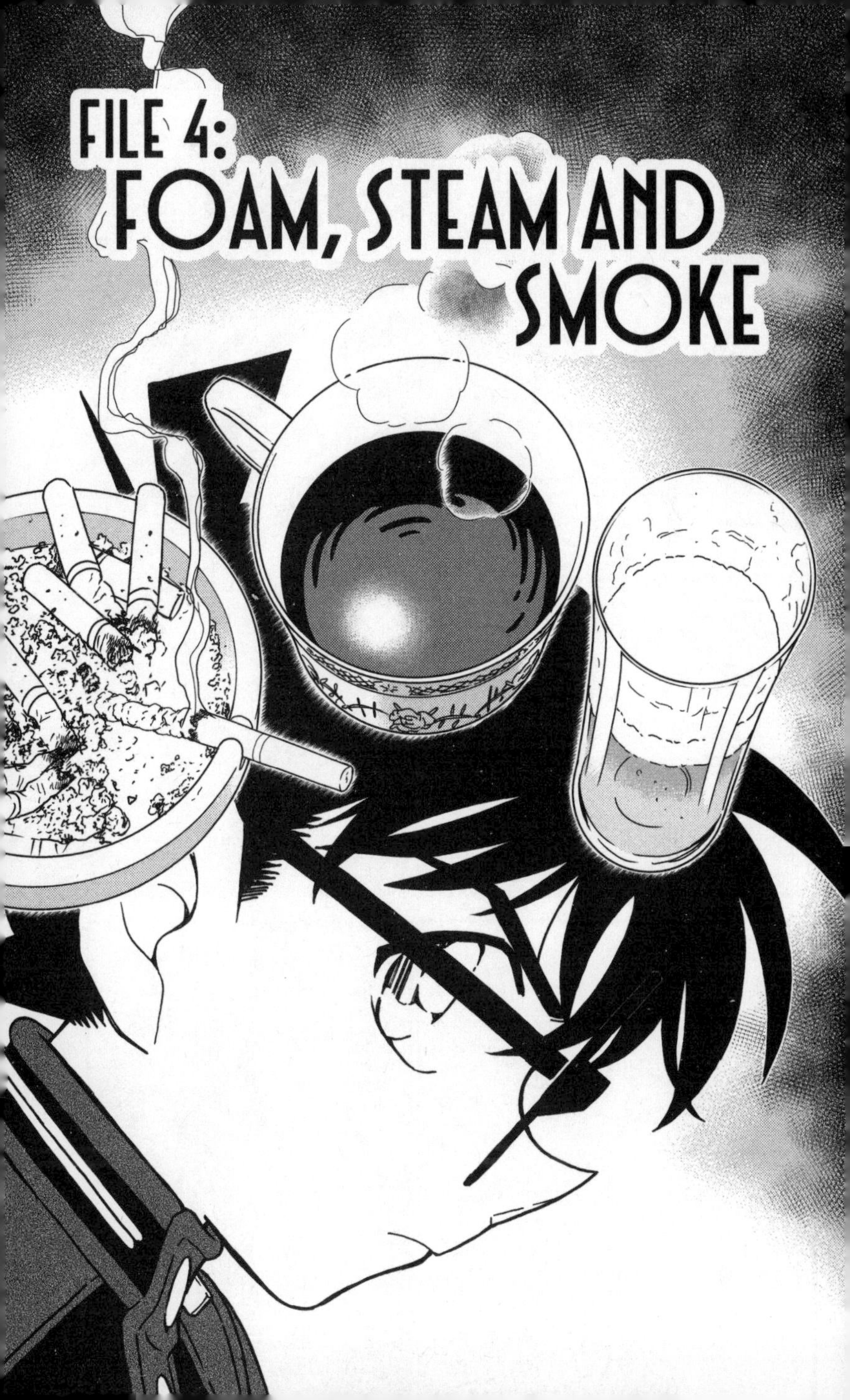
FILE 4:
FOAM, STEAM AND
SMOKE

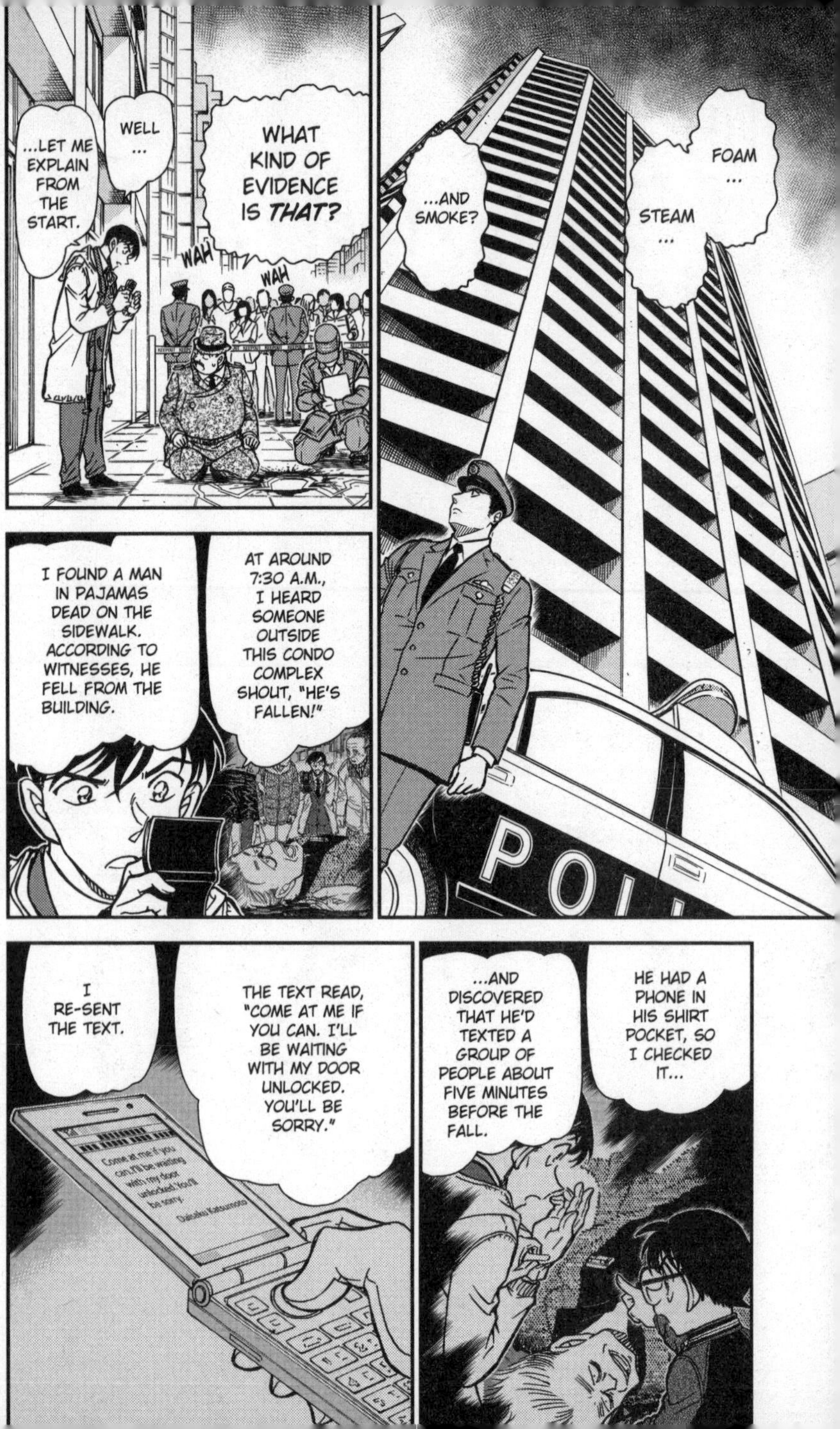
FOAM ...
STEAM ...
...AND SMOKE?
POLI
WHAT KIND OF EVIDENCE IS *THAT?*
WAH
WAH
WELL ...
...LET ME EXPLAIN FROM THE START.
AT AROUND 7:30 A.M., I HEARD SOMEONE OUTSIDE THIS CONDO COMPLEX SHOUT, "HE'S FALLEN!"
I FOUND A MAN IN PAJAMAS DEAD ON THE SIDEWALK. ACCORDING TO WITNESSES, HE FELL FROM THE BUILDING.
HE HAD A PHONE IN HIS SHIRT POCKET, SO I CHECKED IT...
...AND DISCOVERED THAT HE'D TEXTED A GROUP OF PEOPLE ABOUT FIVE MINUTES BEFORE THE FALL.
THE TEXT READ, "COME AT ME IF YOU CAN. I'LL BE WAITING WITH MY DOOR UNLOCKED. YOU'LL BE SORRY."
I RE-SENT THE TEXT.
Come at me if you can. I'll be waiting with my door unlocked. You'll be sorry.

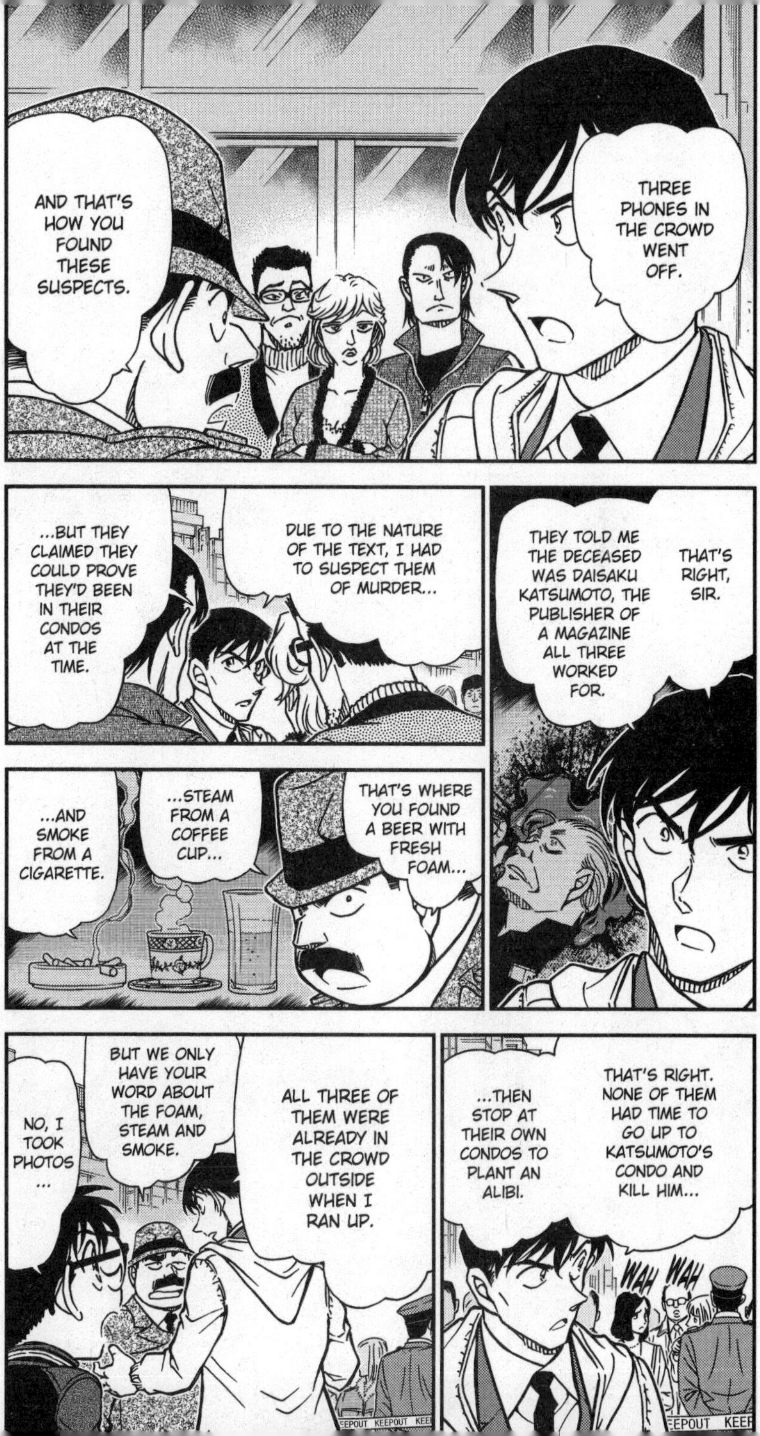
THREE PHONES IN THE CROWD WENT OFF.
AND THAT'S HOW YOU FOUND THESE SUSPECTS.
THAT'S RIGHT, SIR.
THEY TOLD ME THE DECEASED WAS DAISAKU KATSUMOTO, THE PUBLISHER OF A MAGAZINE ALL THREE WORKED FOR.
DUE TO THE NATURE OF THE TEXT, I HAD TO SUSPECT THEM OF MURDER...
...BUT THEY CLAIMED THEY COULD PROVE THEY'D BEEN IN THEIR CONDOS AT THE TIME.
THAT'S WHERE YOU FOUND A BEER WITH FRESH FOAM...
...STEAM FROM A COFFEE CUP...
...AND SMOKE FROM A CIGARETTE.
THAT'S RIGHT. NONE OF THEM HAD TIME TO GO UP TO KATSUMOTO'S CONDO AND KILL HIM...
...THEN STOP AT THEIR OWN CONDOS TO PLANT AN ALIBI.
WAH WAH
ALL THREE OF THEM WERE ALREADY IN THE CROWD OUTSIDE WHEN I RAN UP.
BUT WE ONLY HAVE YOUR WORD ABOUT THE FOAM, STEAM AND SMOKE.
NO, I TOOK PHOTOS ...

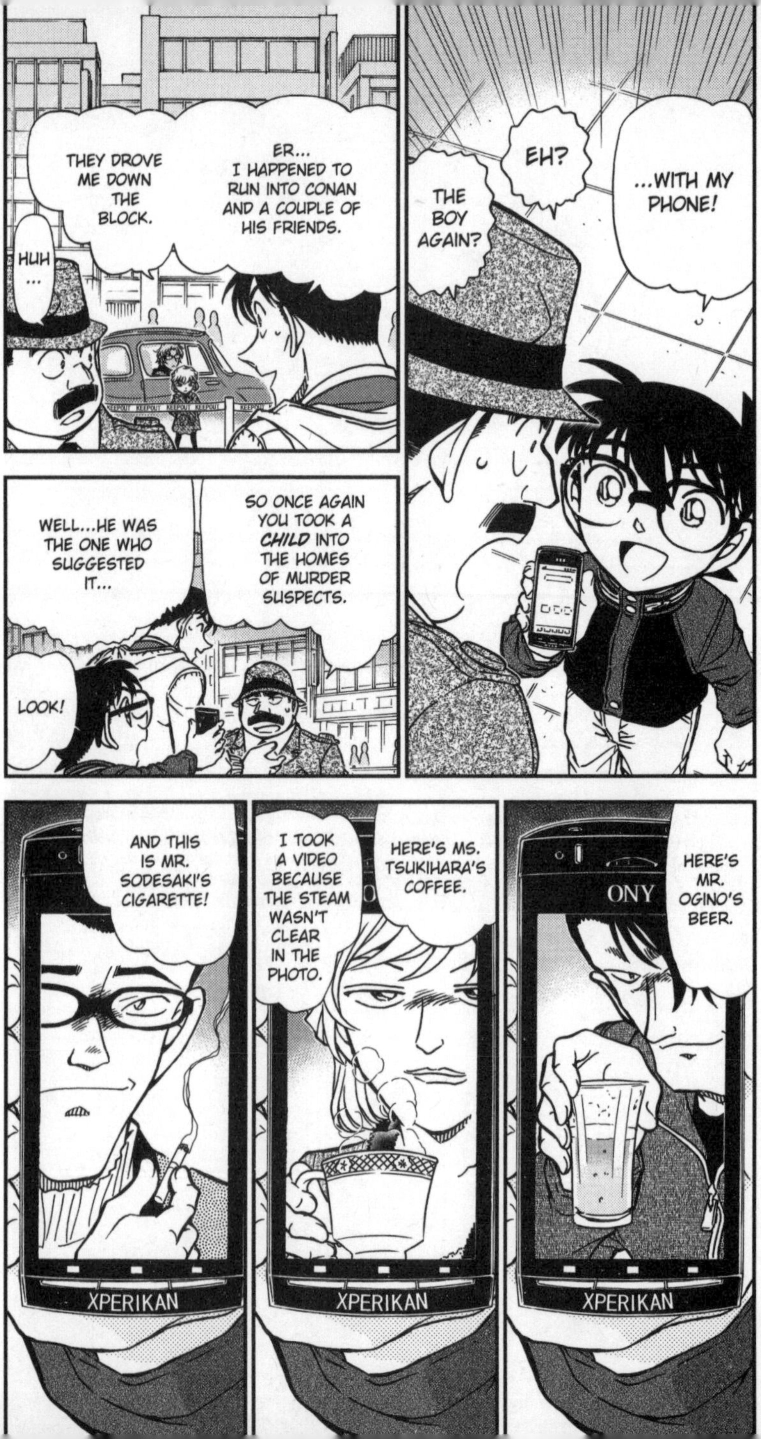
...WITH MY PHONE!
EH?
THE BOY AGAIN?
ER... I HAPPENED TO RUN INTO CONAN AND A COUPLE OF HIS FRIENDS.
THEY DROVE ME DOWN THE BLOCK.
HUH...
SO ONCE AGAIN YOU TOOK A CHILD INTO THE HOMES OF MURDER SUSPECTS.
WELL...HE WAS THE ONE WHO SUGGESTED IT...
LOOK!
HERE'S MR. OGINO'S BEER.
ONY
XPERIKAN
HERE'S MS. TSUKIHARA'S COFFEE.
I TOOK A VIDEO BECAUSE THE STEAM WASN'T CLEAR IN THE PHOTO.
XPERIKAN
AND THIS IS MR. SODESAKI'S CIGARETTE!
XPERIKAN

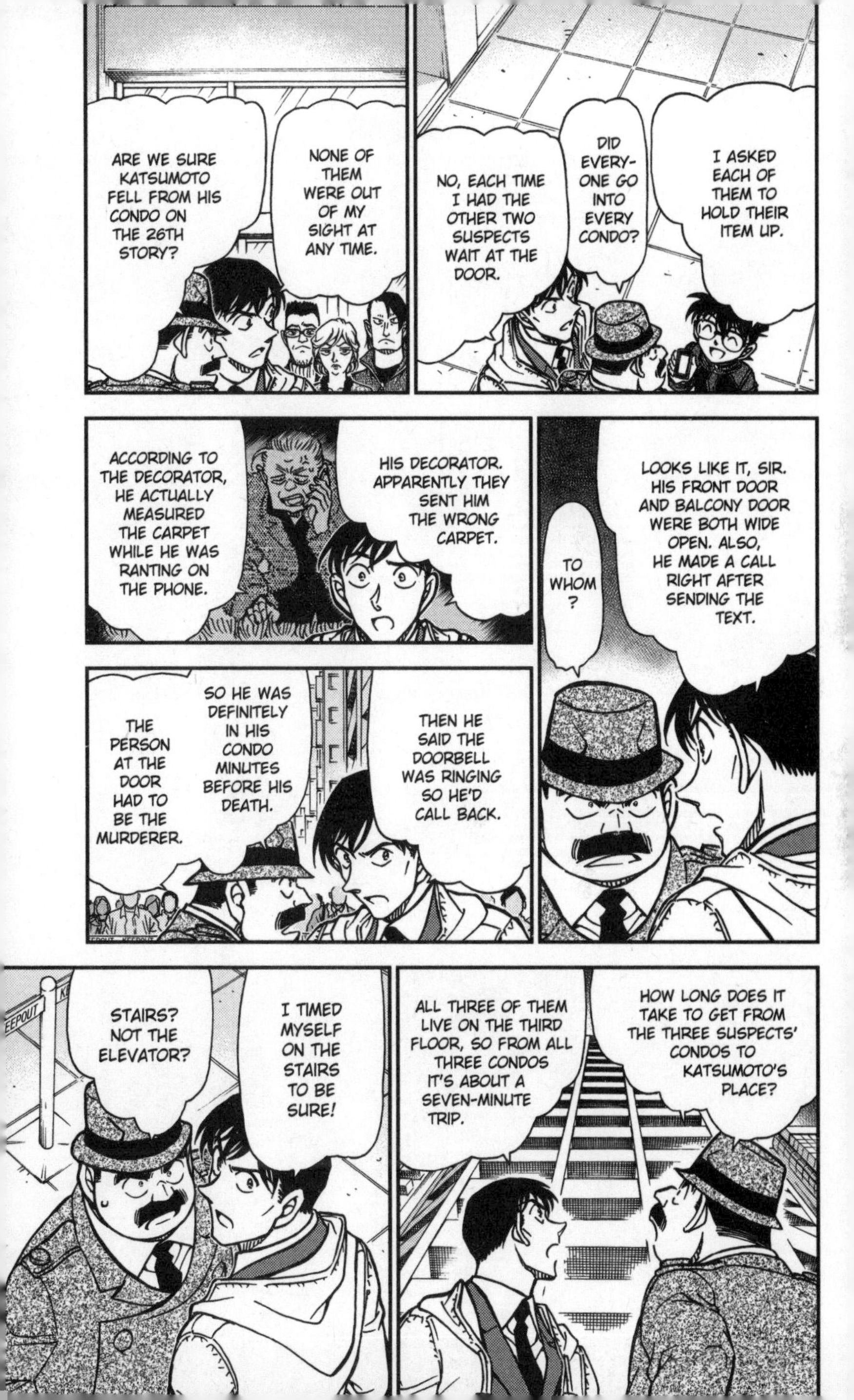
I ASKED EACH OF THEM TO HOLD THEIR ITEM UP.
DID EVERYONE GO INTO EVERY CONDO?
NO, EACH TIME I HAD THE OTHER TWO SUSPECTS WAIT AT THE DOOR.
NONE OF THEM WERE OUT OF MY SIGHT AT ANY TIME.
ARE WE SURE KATSUMOTO FELL FROM HIS CONDO ON THE 26TH STORY?
LOOKS LIKE IT, SIR. HIS FRONT DOOR AND BALCONY DOOR WERE BOTH WIDE OPEN. ALSO, HE MADE A CALL RIGHT AFTER SENDING THE TEXT.
TO WHOM?
HIS DECORATOR. APPARENTLY THEY SENT HIM THE WRONG CARPET.
ACCORDING TO THE DECORATOR, HE ACTUALLY MEASURED THE CARPET WHILE HE WAS RANTING ON THE PHONE.
THEN HE SAID THE DOORBELL WAS RINGING SO HE'D CALL BACK.
SO HE WAS DEFINITELY IN HIS CONDO MINUTES BEFORE HIS DEATH.
THE PERSON AT THE DOOR HAD TO BE THE MURDERER.
HOW LONG DOES IT TAKE TO GET FROM THE THREE SUSPECTS' CONDOS TO KATSUMOTO'S PLACE?
ALL THREE OF THEM LIVE ON THE THIRD FLOOR, SO FROM ALL THREE CONDOS IT'S ABOUT A SEVEN-MINUTE TRIP.
I TIMED MYSELF ON THE STAIRS TO BE SURE!
STAIRS? NOT THE ELEVATOR?

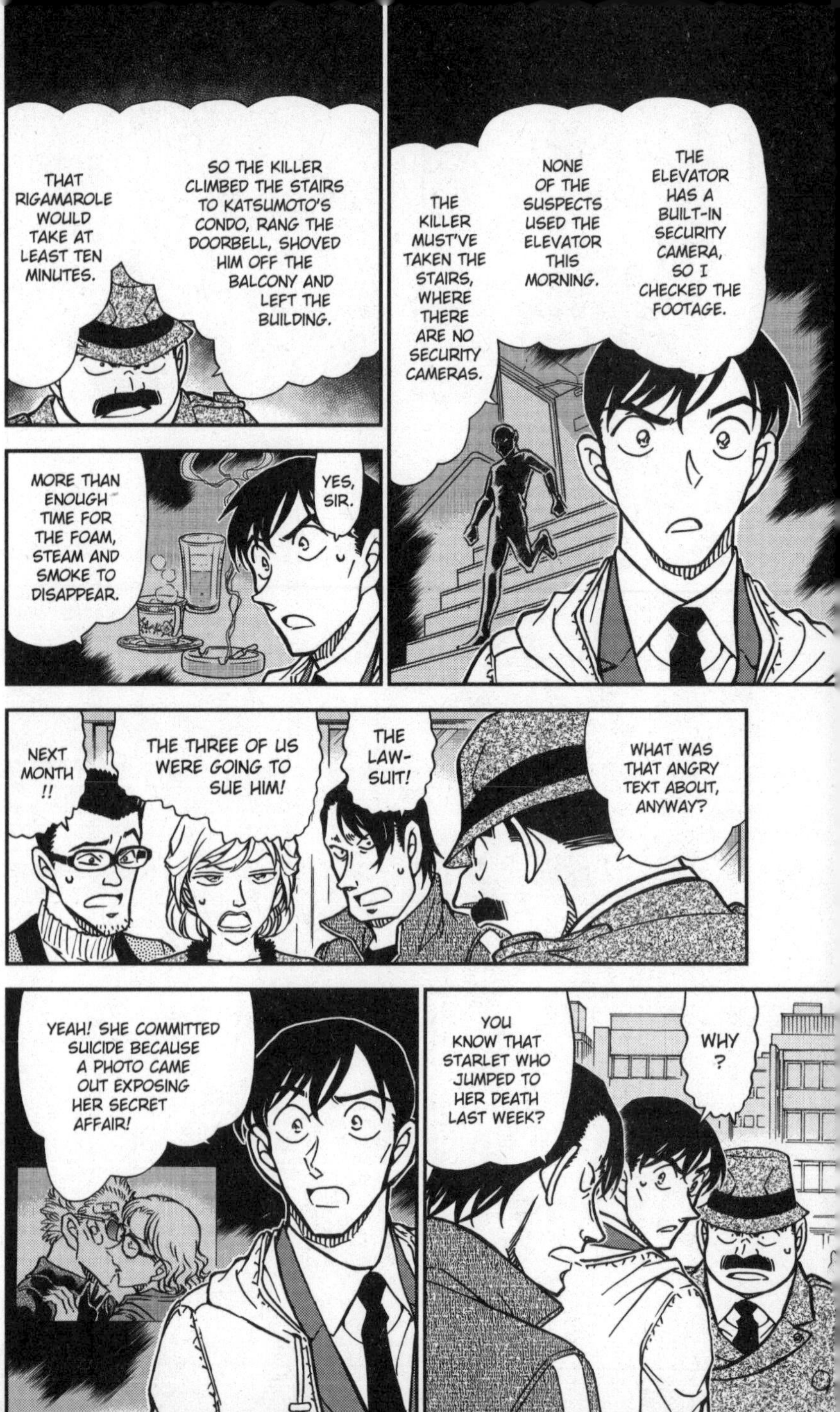
THE ELEVATOR HAS A BUILT-IN SECURITY CAMERA, SO I CHECKED THE FOOTAGE.
NONE OF THE SUSPECTS USED THE ELEVATOR THIS MORNING.
THE KILLER MUST'VE TAKEN THE STAIRS, WHERE THERE ARE NO SECURITY CAMERAS.
SO THE KILLER CLIMBED THE STAIRS TO KATSUMOTO'S CONDO, RANG THE DOORBELL, SHOVED HIM OFF THE BALCONY AND LEFT THE BUILDING.
THAT RIGAMAROLE WOULD TAKE AT LEAST TEN MINUTES.
YES, SIR.
MORE THAN ENOUGH TIME FOR THE FOAM, STEAM AND SMOKE TO DISAPPEAR.
WHAT WAS THAT ANGRY TEXT ABOUT, ANYWAY?
THE LAW-SUIT!
THE THREE OF US WERE GOING TO SUE HIM!
NEXT MONTH !!
WHY ?
YOU KNOW THAT STARLET WHO JUMPED TO HER DEATH LAST WEEK?
YEAH! SHE COMMITTED SUICIDE BECAUSE A PHOTO CAME OUT EXPOSING HER SECRET AFFAIR!

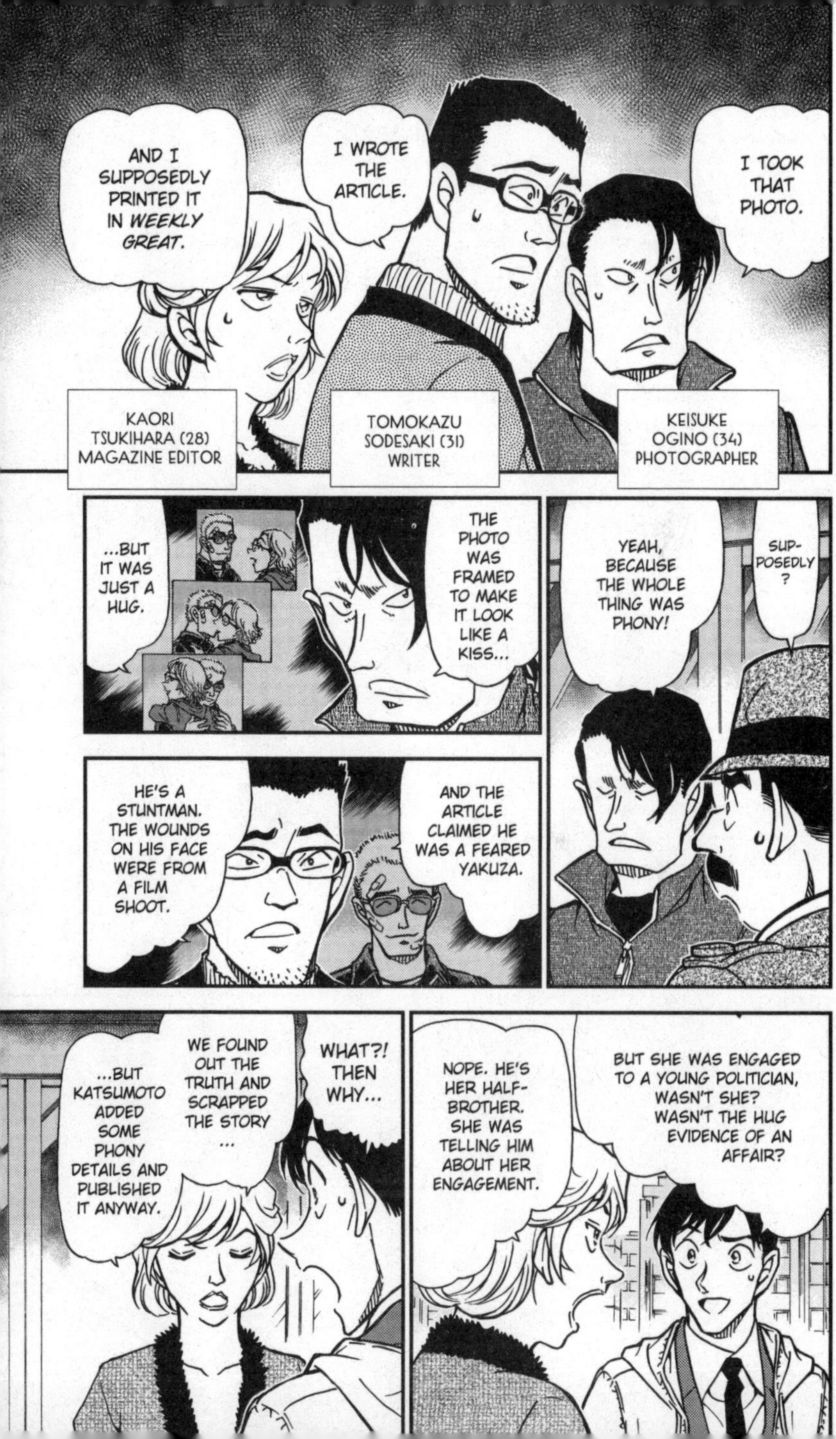
I TOOK THAT PHOTO.
I WROTE THE ARTICLE.
AND I SUPPOSEDLY PRINTED IT IN *WEEKLY GREAT*.
KEISUKE OGINO (34) PHOTOGRAPHER
TOMOKAZU SODESAKI (31) WRITER
KAORI TSUKIHARA (28) MAGAZINE EDITOR
SUP-POSEDLY?
YEAH, BECAUSE THE WHOLE THING WAS PHONY!
THE PHOTO WAS FRAMED TO MAKE IT LOOK LIKE A KISS...
...BUT IT WAS JUST A HUG.
AND THE ARTICLE CLAIMED HE WAS A FEARED YAKUZA.
HE'S A STUNTMAN. THE WOUNDS ON HIS FACE WERE FROM A FILM SHOOT.
BUT SHE WAS ENGAGED TO A YOUNG POLITICIAN, WASN'T SHE? WASN'T THE HUG EVIDENCE OF AN AFFAIR?
NOPE. HE'S HER HALF-BROTHER. SHE WAS TELLING HIM ABOUT HER ENGAGEMENT.
WHAT?! THEN WHY...
WE FOUND OUT THE TRUTH AND SCRAPPED THE STORY...
...BUT KATSUMOTO ADDED SOME PHONY DETAILS AND PUBLISHED IT ANYWAY.

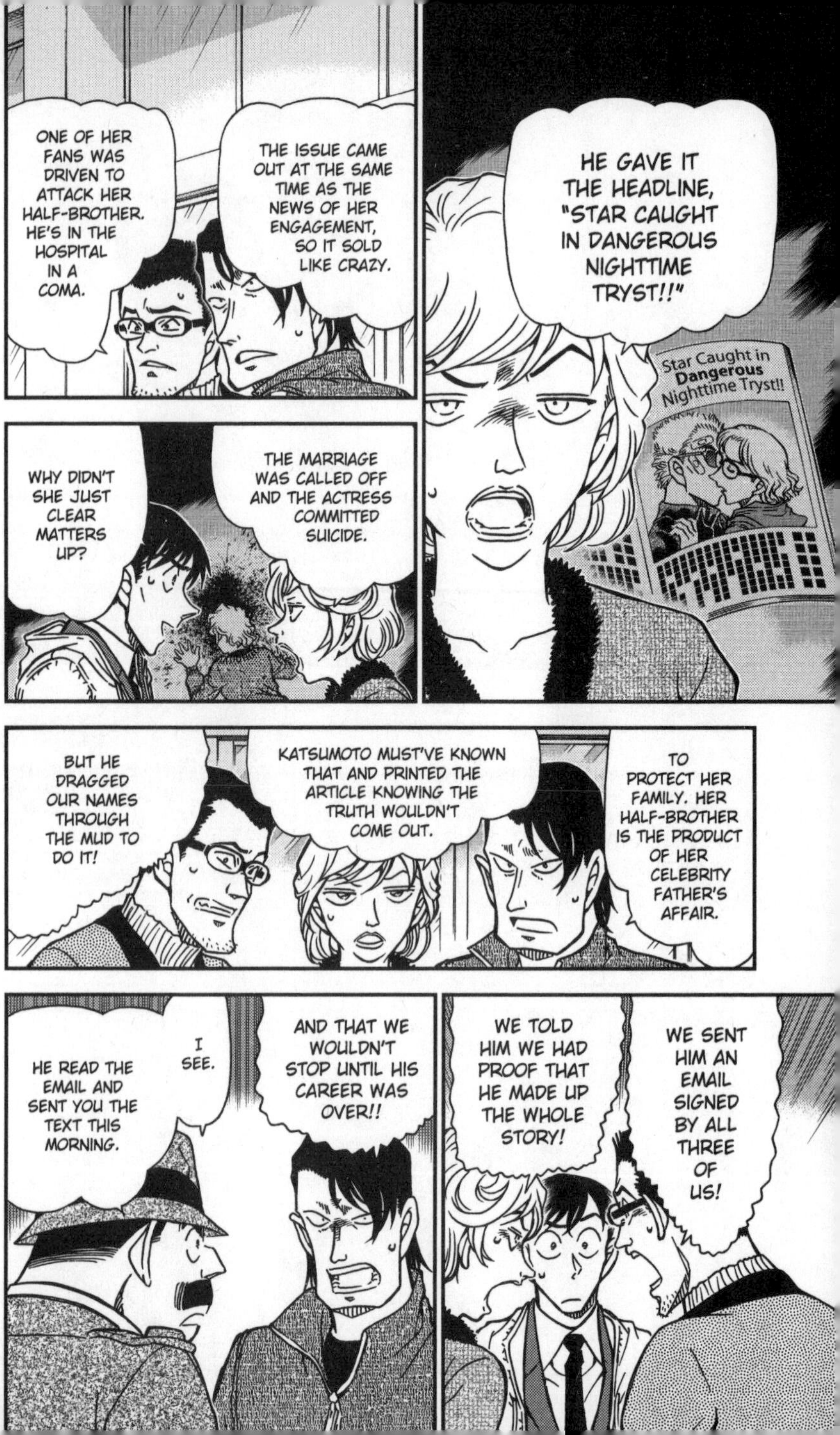

HE GAVE IT THE HEADLINE, "STAR CAUGHT IN DANGEROUS NIGHTTIME TRYST!!"
Star Caught in Dangerous Nighttime Tryst!!
THE ISSUE CAME OUT AT THE SAME TIME AS THE NEWS OF HER ENGAGEMENT, SO IT SOLD LIKE CRAZY.
ONE OF HER FANS WAS DRIVEN TO ATTACK HER HALF-BROTHER. HE'S IN THE HOSPITAL IN A COMA.
THE MARRIAGE WAS CALLED OFF AND THE ACTRESS COMMITTED SUICIDE.
WHY DIDN'T SHE JUST CLEAR MATTERS UP?
TO PROTECT HER FAMILY. HER HALF-BROTHER IS THE PRODUCT OF HER CELEBRITY FATHER'S AFFAIR.
KATSUMOTO MUST'VE KNOWN THAT AND PRINTED THE ARTICLE KNOWING THE TRUTH WOULDN'T COME OUT.
BUT HE DRAGGED OUR NAMES THROUGH THE MUD TO DO IT!
WE SENT HIM AN EMAIL SIGNED BY ALL THREE OF US!
WE TOLD HIM WE HAD PROOF THAT HE MADE UP THE WHOLE STORY!
AND THAT WE WOULDN'T STOP UNTIL HIS CAREER WAS OVER!!
I SEE.
HE READ THE EMAIL AND SENT YOU THE TEXT THIS MORNING.

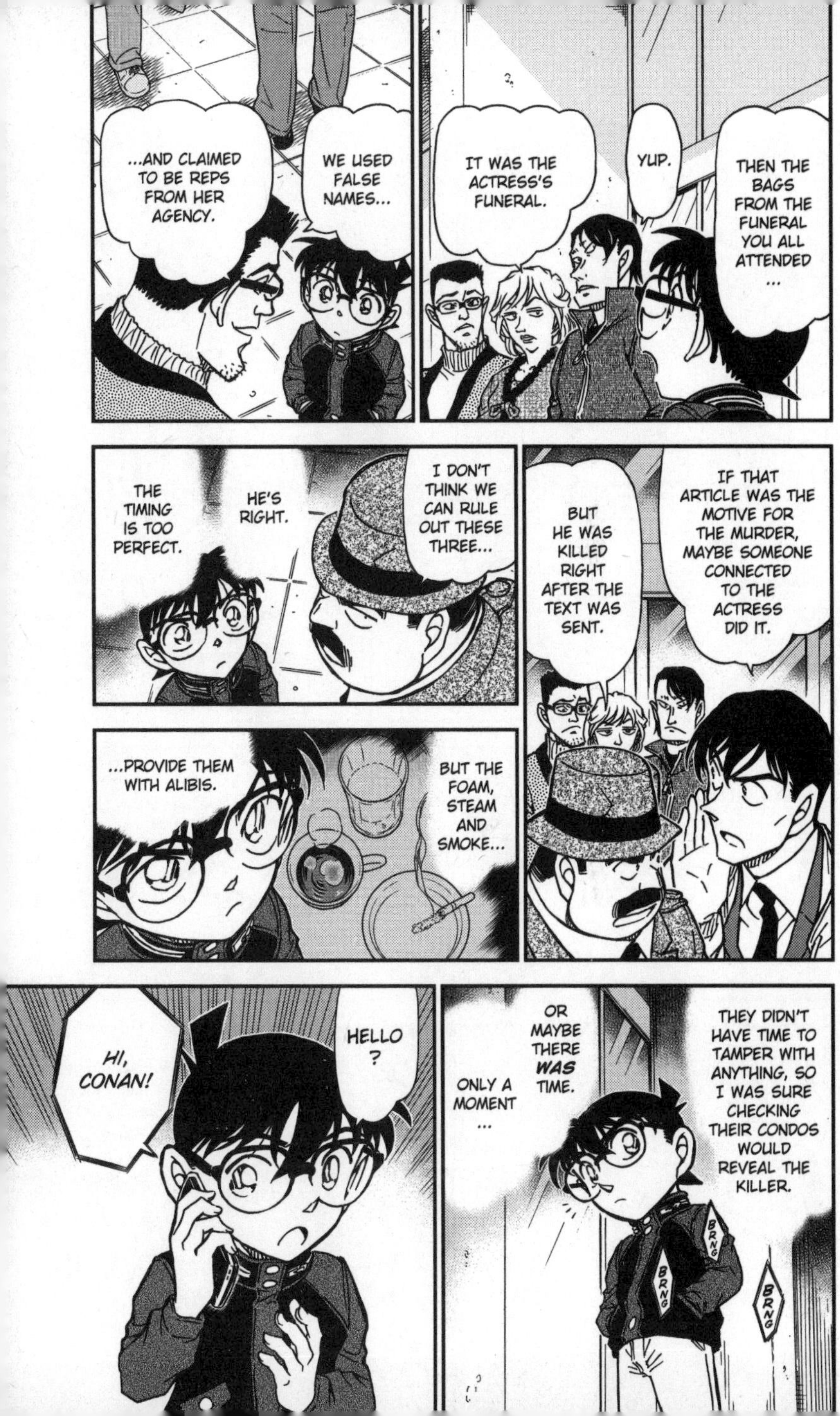
THEN THE BAGS FROM THE FUNERAL YOU ALL ATTENDED ...
YUP.
IT WAS THE ACTRESS'S FUNERAL.
WE USED FALSE NAMES...
...AND CLAIMED TO BE REPS FROM HER AGENCY.
IF THAT ARTICLE WAS THE MOTIVE FOR THE MURDER, MAYBE SOMEONE CONNECTED TO THE ACTRESS DID IT.
BUT HE WAS KILLED RIGHT AFTER THE TEXT WAS SENT.
I DON'T THINK WE CAN RULE OUT THESE THREE...
HE'S RIGHT.
THE TIMING IS TOO PERFECT.
BUT THE FOAM, STEAM AND SMOKE...
...PROVIDE THEM WITH ALIBIS.
THEY DIDN'T HAVE TIME TO TAMPER WITH ANYTHING, SO I WAS SURE CHECKING THEIR CONDOS WOULD REVEAL THE KILLER.
OR MAYBE THERE *WAS* TIME.
ONLY A MOMENT ...
BRNG
BRNG
BRNG
HELLO ?
HI, CONAN!

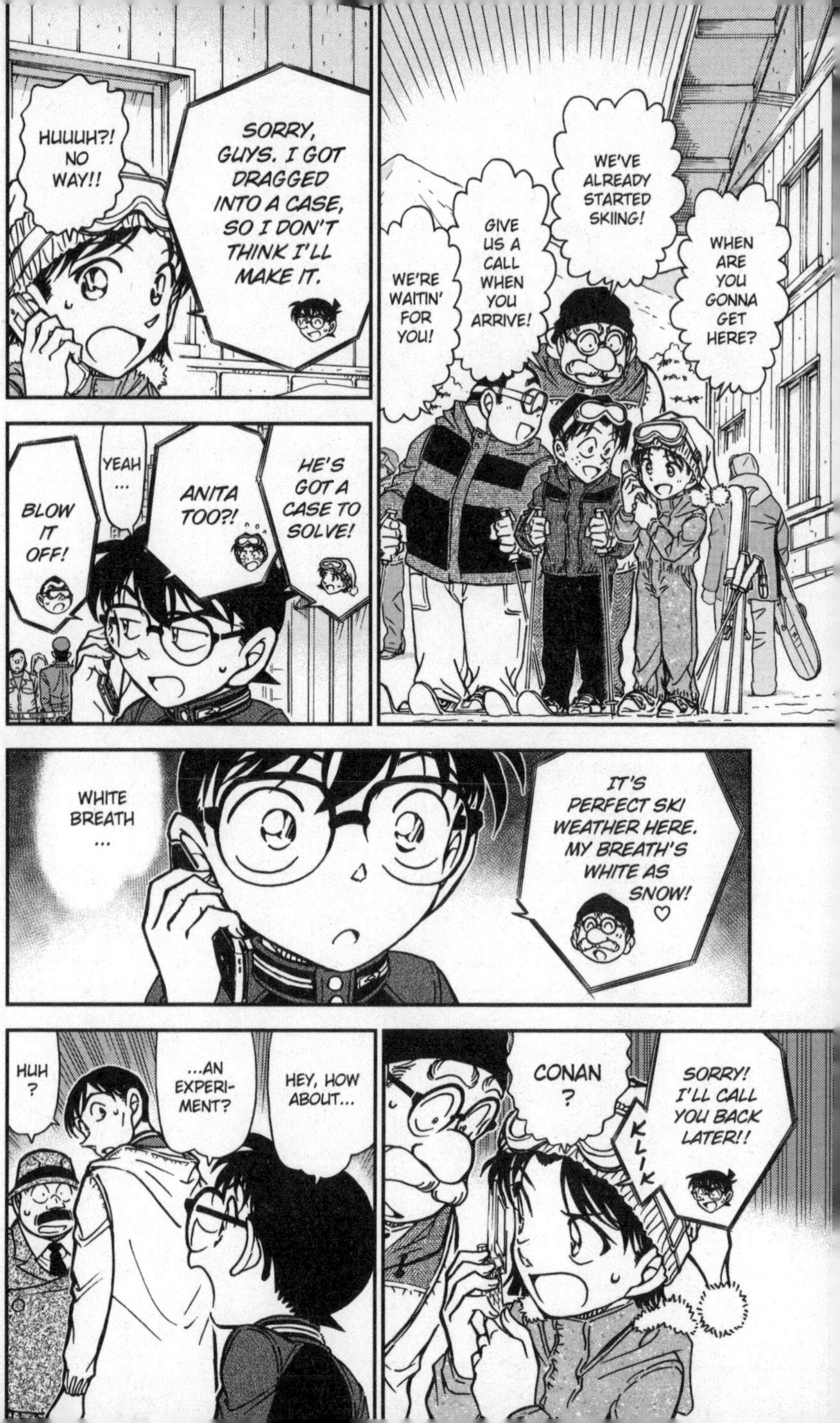
WHEN ARE YOU GONNA GET HERE?
WE'VE ALREADY STARTED SKIING!
GIVE US A CALL WHEN YOU ARRIVE!
WE'RE WAITIN' FOR YOU!
SORRY, GUYS. I GOT DRAGGED INTO A CASE, SO I DON'T THINK I'LL MAKE IT.
HUUUH?! NO WAY!!
HE'S GOT A CASE TO SOLVE!
ANITA TOO?!
YEAH ...
BLOW IT OFF!
IT'S PERFECT SKI WEATHER HERE. MY BREATH'S WHITE AS SNOW! ♡
WHITE BREATH ...
SORRY! I'LL CALL YOU BACK LATER!!
KLIK
CONAN ?
HEY, HOW ABOUT...
...AN EXPERI-MENT?
HUH ?

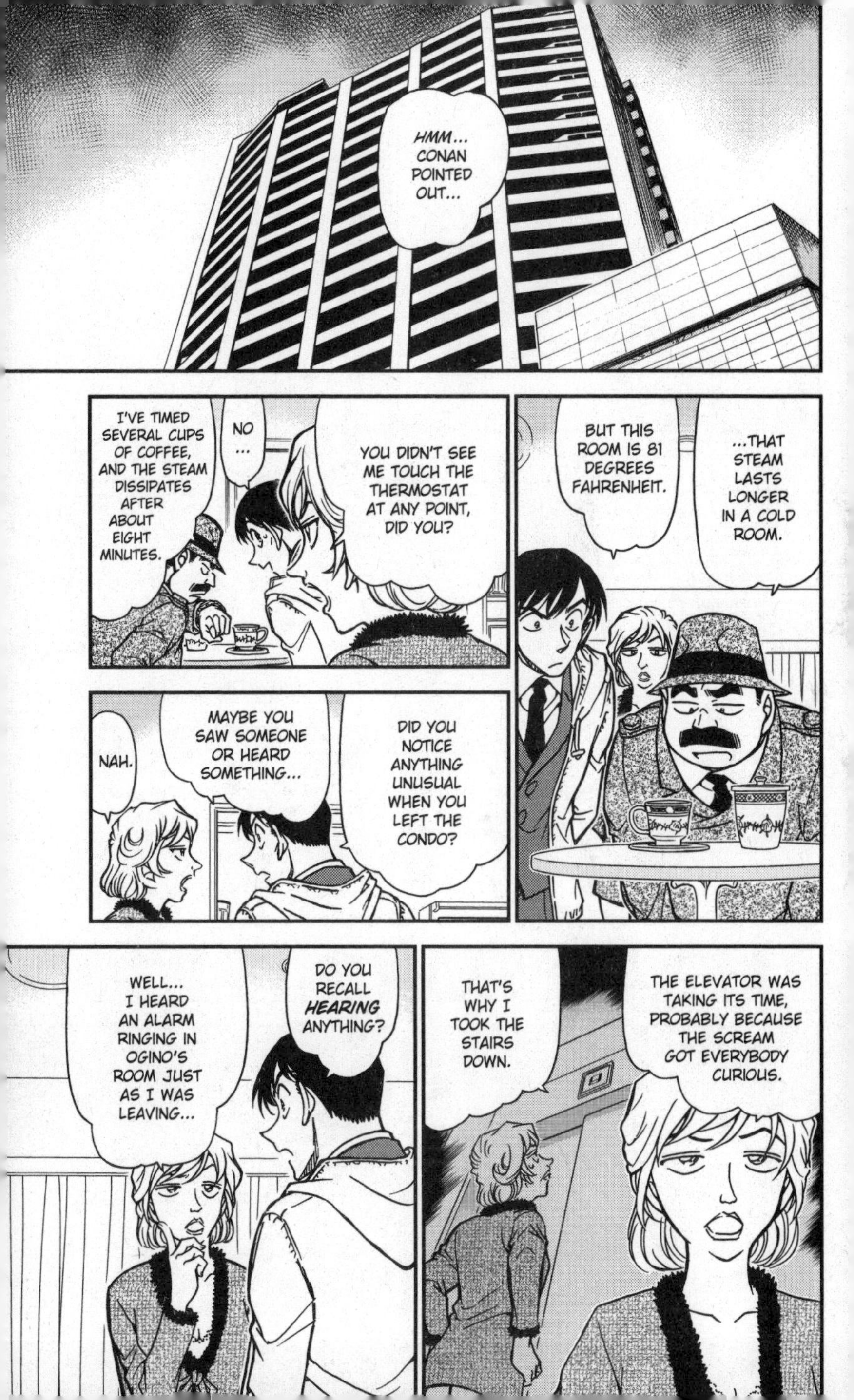
HMM... CONAN POINTED OUT...
...THAT STEAM LASTS LONGER IN A COLD ROOM.
BUT THIS ROOM IS 81 DEGREES FAHRENHEIT.
YOU DIDN'T SEE ME TOUCH THE THERMOSTAT AT ANY POINT, DID YOU?
NO...
I'VE TIMED SEVERAL CUPS OF COFFEE, AND THE STEAM DISSIPATES AFTER ABOUT EIGHT MINUTES.
DID YOU NOTICE ANYTHING UNUSUAL WHEN YOU LEFT THE CONDO?
MAYBE YOU SAW SOMEONE OR HEARD SOMETHING...
NAH.
THE ELEVATOR WAS TAKING ITS TIME, PROBABLY BECAUSE THE SCREAM GOT EVERYBODY CURIOUS.
THAT'S WHY I TOOK THE STAIRS DOWN.
DO YOU RECALL *HEARING* ANYTHING?
WELL... I HEARD AN ALARM RINGING IN OGINO'S ROOM JUST AS I WAS LEAVING...

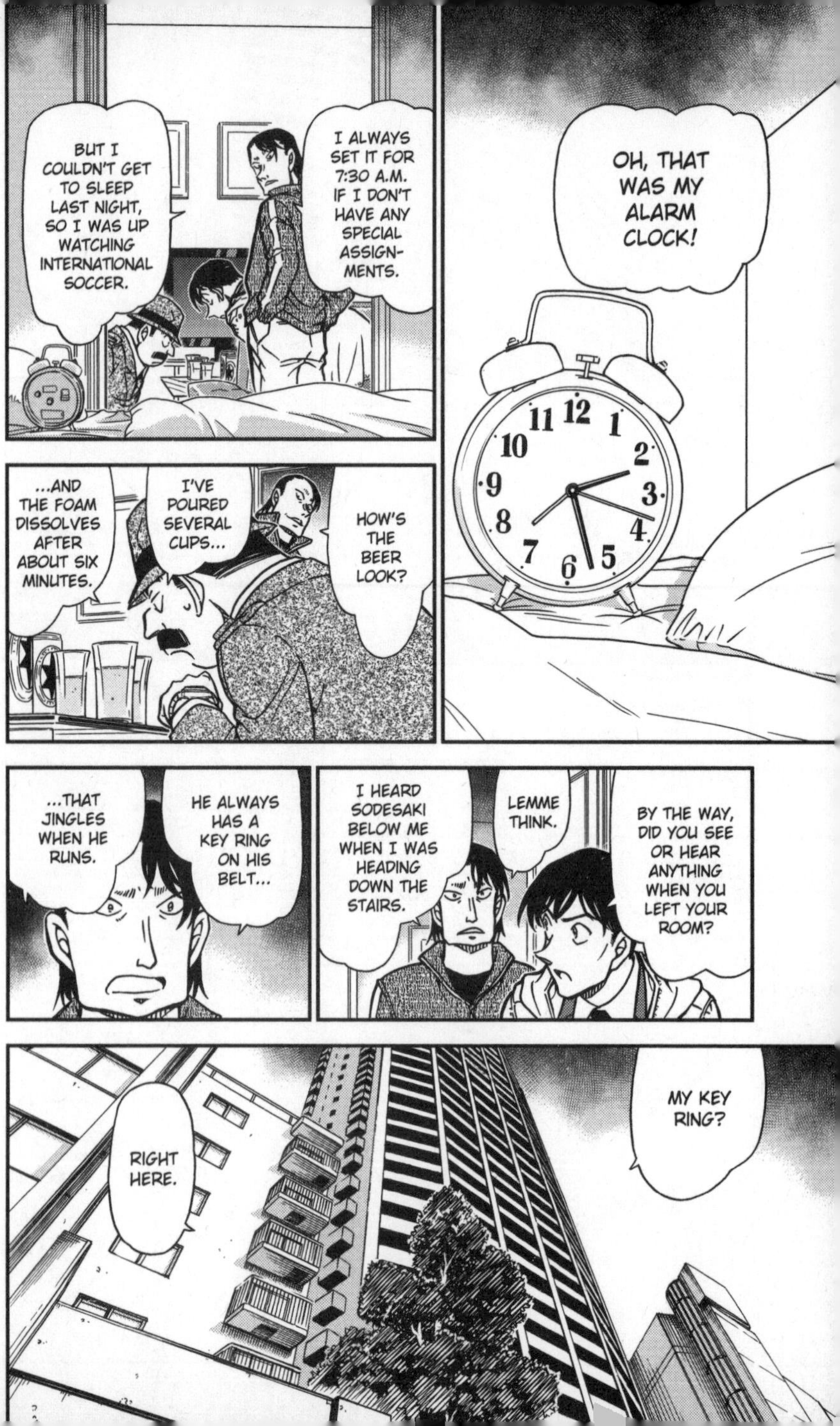
OH, THAT WAS MY ALARM CLOCK!
I ALWAYS SET IT FOR 7:30 A.M. IF I DON'T HAVE ANY SPECIAL ASSIGN-MENTS.
BUT I COULDN'T GET TO SLEEP LAST NIGHT, SO I WAS UP WATCHING INTERNATIONAL SOCCER.
HOW'S THE BEER LOOK?
I'VE POURED SEVERAL CUPS...
...AND THE FOAM DISSOLVES AFTER ABOUT SIX MINUTES.
BY THE WAY, DID YOU SEE OR HEAR ANYTHING WHEN YOU LEFT YOUR ROOM?
LEMME THINK.
I HEARD SODESAKI BELOW ME WHEN I WAS HEADING DOWN THE STAIRS.
HE ALWAYS HAS A KEY RING ON HIS BELT...
...THAT JINGLES WHEN HE RUNS.
MY KEY RING?
RIGHT HERE.

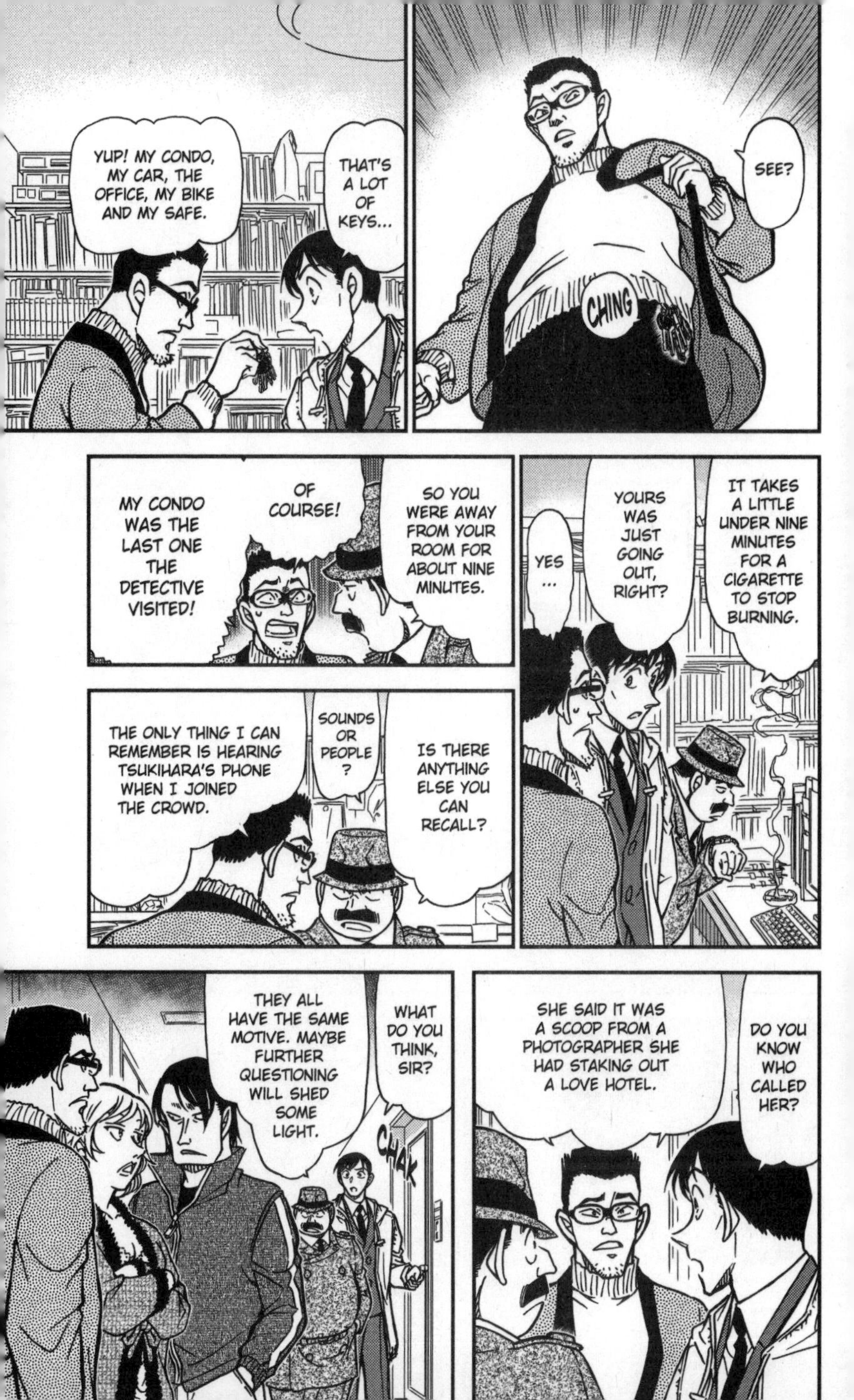
SEE?
CHING
THAT'S A LOT OF KEYS...
YUP! MY CONDO, MY CAR, THE OFFICE, MY BIKE AND MY SAFE.
IT TAKES A LITTLE UNDER NINE MINUTES FOR A CIGARETTE TO STOP BURNING.
YOURS WAS JUST GOING OUT, RIGHT?
YES ...
SO YOU WERE AWAY FROM YOUR ROOM FOR ABOUT NINE MINUTES.
OF COURSE!
MY CONDO WAS THE LAST ONE THE DETECTIVE VISITED!
IS THERE ANYTHING ELSE YOU CAN RECALL?
SOUNDS OR PEOPLE?
THE ONLY THING I CAN REMEMBER IS HEARING TSUKIHARA'S PHONE WHEN I JOINED THE CROWD.
DO YOU KNOW WHO CALLED HER?
SHE SAID IT WAS A SCOOP FROM A PHOTOGRAPHER SHE HAD STAKING OUT A LOVE HOTEL.
WHAT DO YOU THINK, SIR?
THEY ALL HAVE THE SAME MOTIVE. MAYBE FURTHER QUESTIONING WILL SHED SOME LIGHT.
CHAK

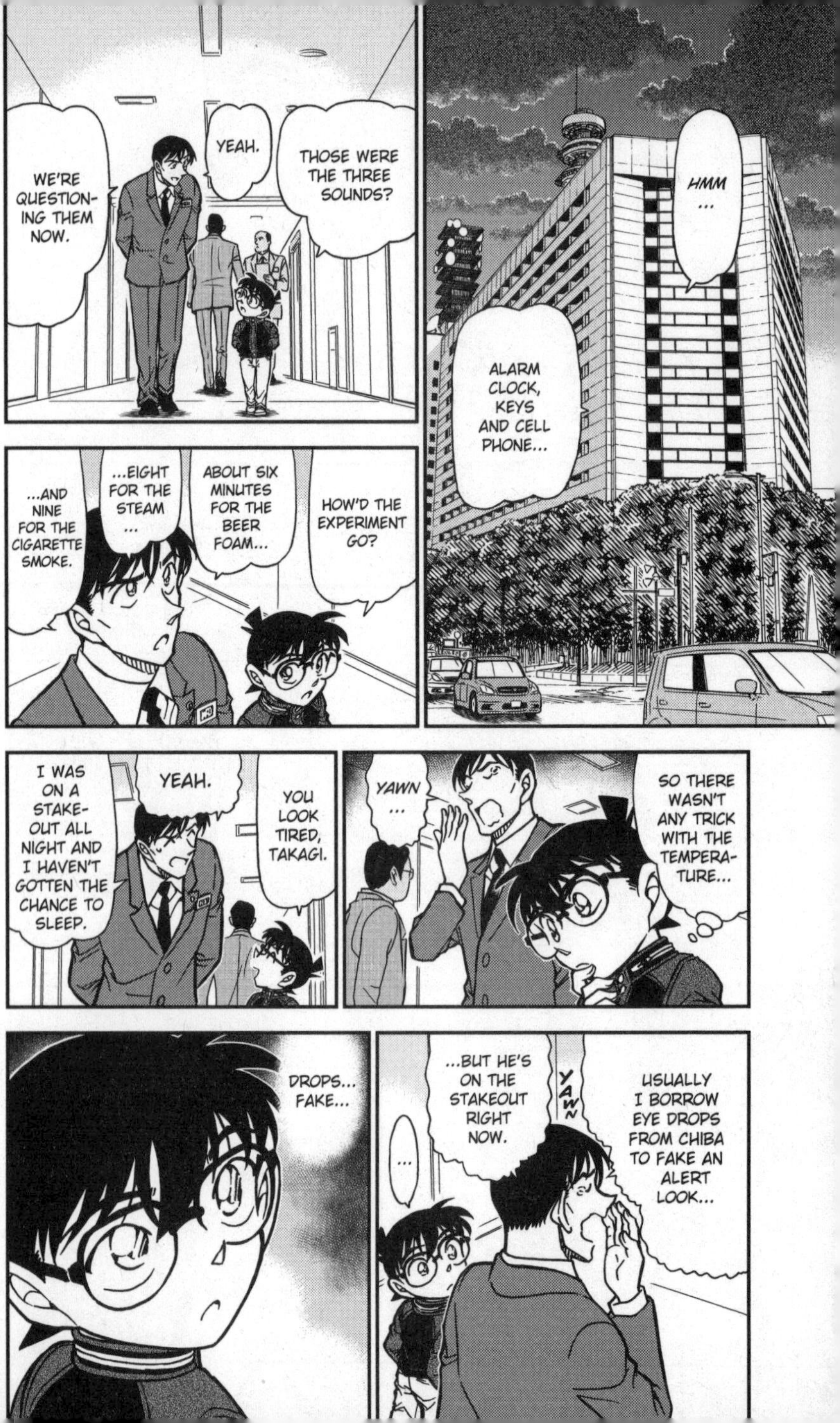
HMM...
ALARM CLOCK, KEYS AND CELL PHONE...
THOSE WERE THE THREE SOUNDS?
YEAH.
WE'RE QUESTIONING THEM NOW.
HOW'D THE EXPERIMENT GO?
ABOUT SIX MINUTES FOR THE BEER FOAM...
...EIGHT FOR THE STEAM...
...AND NINE FOR THE CIGARETTE SMOKE.
SO THERE WASN'T ANY TRICK WITH THE TEMPERATURE...
YAWN...
YOU LOOK TIRED, TAKAGI.
YEAH.
I WAS ON A STAKEOUT ALL NIGHT AND I HAVEN'T GOTTEN THE CHANCE TO SLEEP.
USUALLY I BORROW EYE DROPS FROM CHIBA TO FAKE AN ALERT LOOK...
YAWN
...BUT HE'S ON THE STAKEOUT RIGHT NOW.
...
DROPS... FAKE...

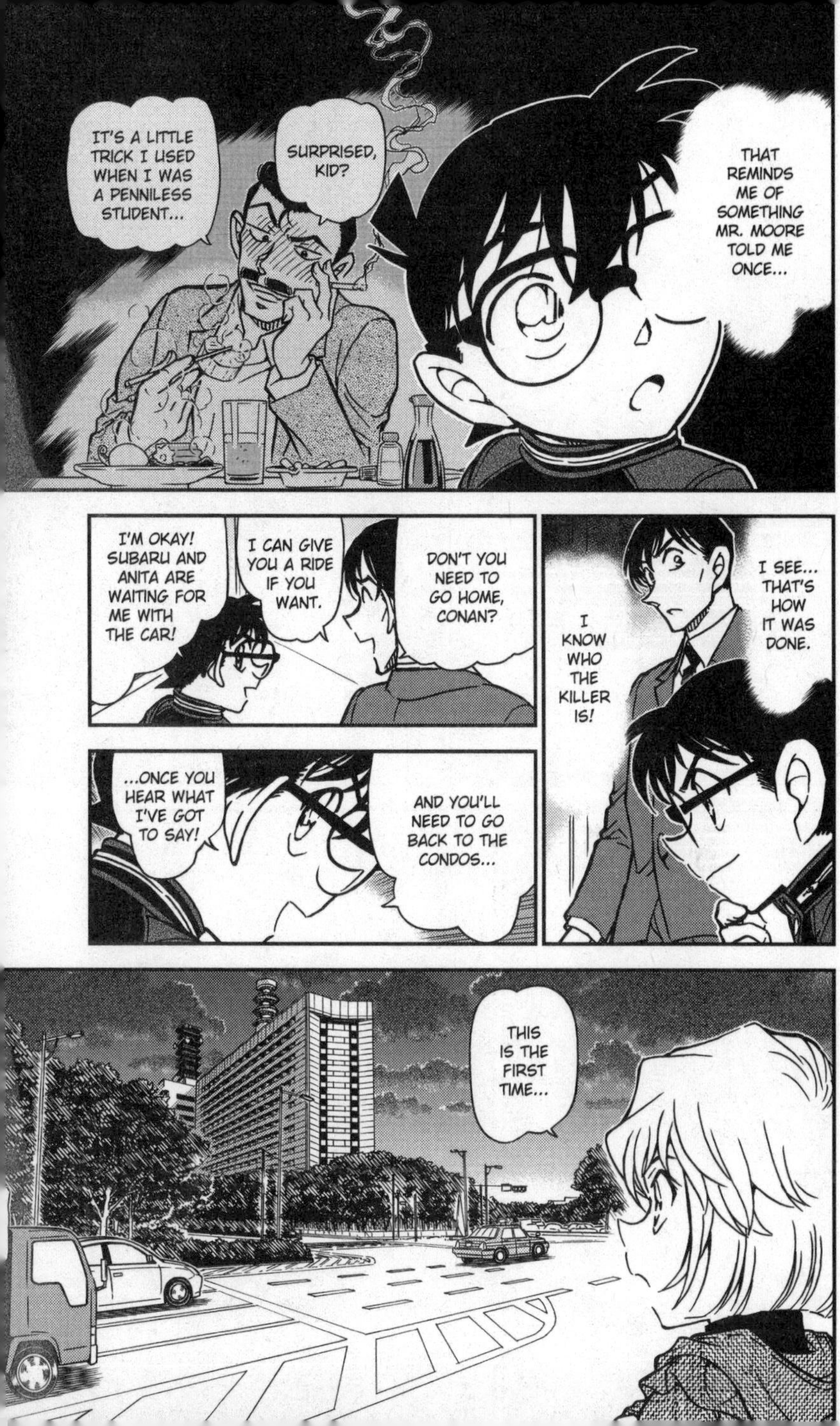
THAT REMINDS ME OF SOMETHING MR. MOORE TOLD ME ONCE...
SURPRISED, KID?
IT'S A LITTLE TRICK I USED WHEN I WAS A PENNILESS STUDENT...
I SEE... THAT'S HOW IT WAS DONE.
I KNOW WHO THE KILLER IS!
DON'T YOU NEED TO GO HOME, CONAN?
I CAN GIVE YOU A RIDE IF YOU WANT.
I'M OKAY! SUBARU AND ANITA ARE WAITING FOR ME WITH THE CAR!
AND YOU'LL NEED TO GO BACK TO THE CONDOS...
...ONCE YOU HEAR WHAT I'VE GOT TO SAY!
THIS IS THE FIRST TIME...

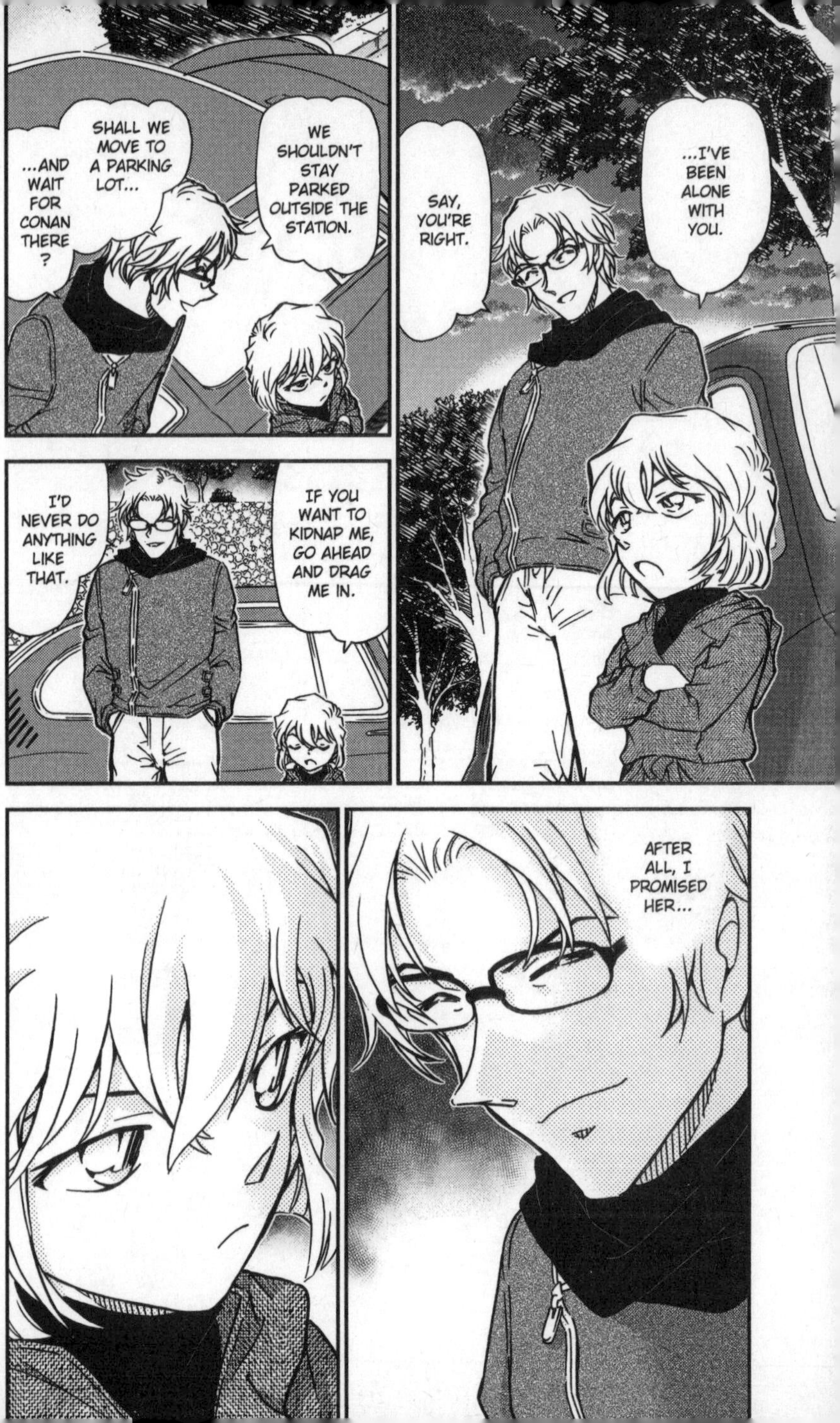
...I'VE BEEN ALONE WITH YOU.
SAY, YOU'RE RIGHT.
WE SHOULDN'T STAY PARKED OUTSIDE THE STATION.
SHALL WE MOVE TO A PARKING LOT...
...AND WAIT FOR CONAN THERE?
IF YOU WANT TO KIDNAP ME, GO AHEAD AND DRAG ME IN.
I'D NEVER DO ANYTHING LIKE THAT.
AFTER ALL, I PROMISED HER...

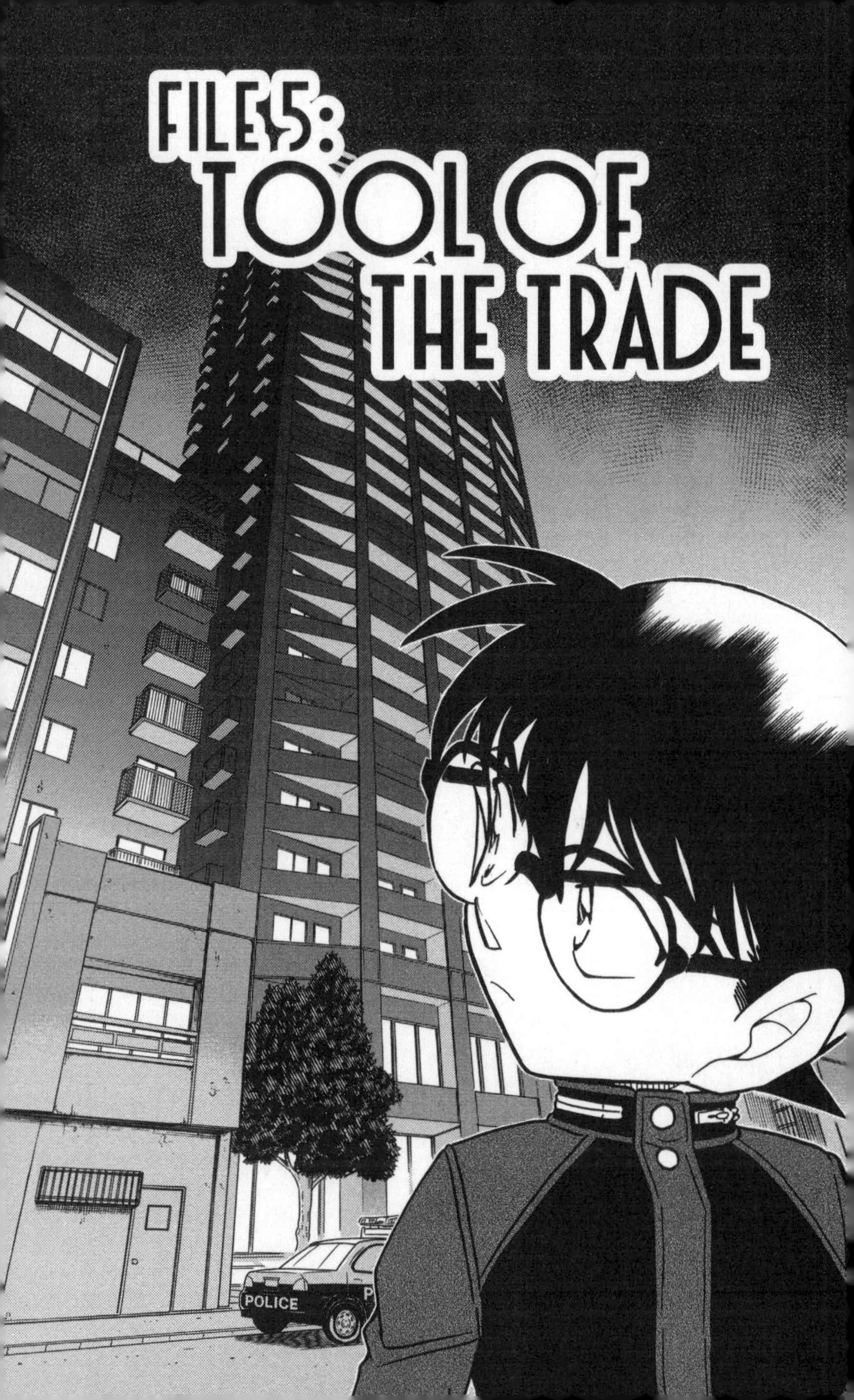
FILE 5:
TOOL OF THE TRADE
POLICE

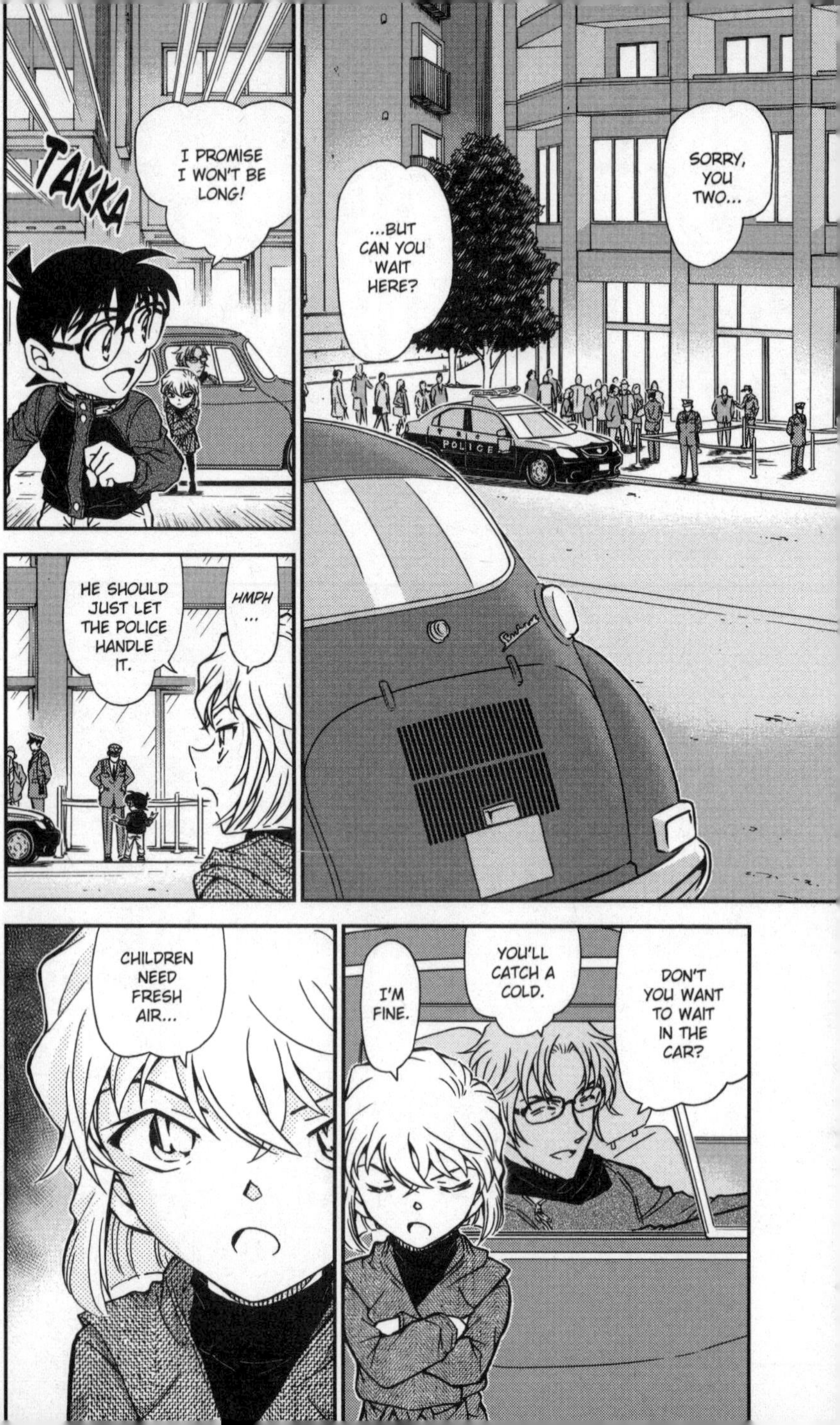
SORRY, YOU TWO...
...BUT CAN YOU WAIT HERE?
TAKKA
I PROMISE I WON'T BE LONG!
HMPH...
HE SHOULD JUST LET THE POLICE HANDLE IT.
DON'T YOU WANT TO WAIT IN THE CAR?
YOU'LL CATCH A COLD.
I'M FINE.
CHILDREN NEED FRESH AIR...

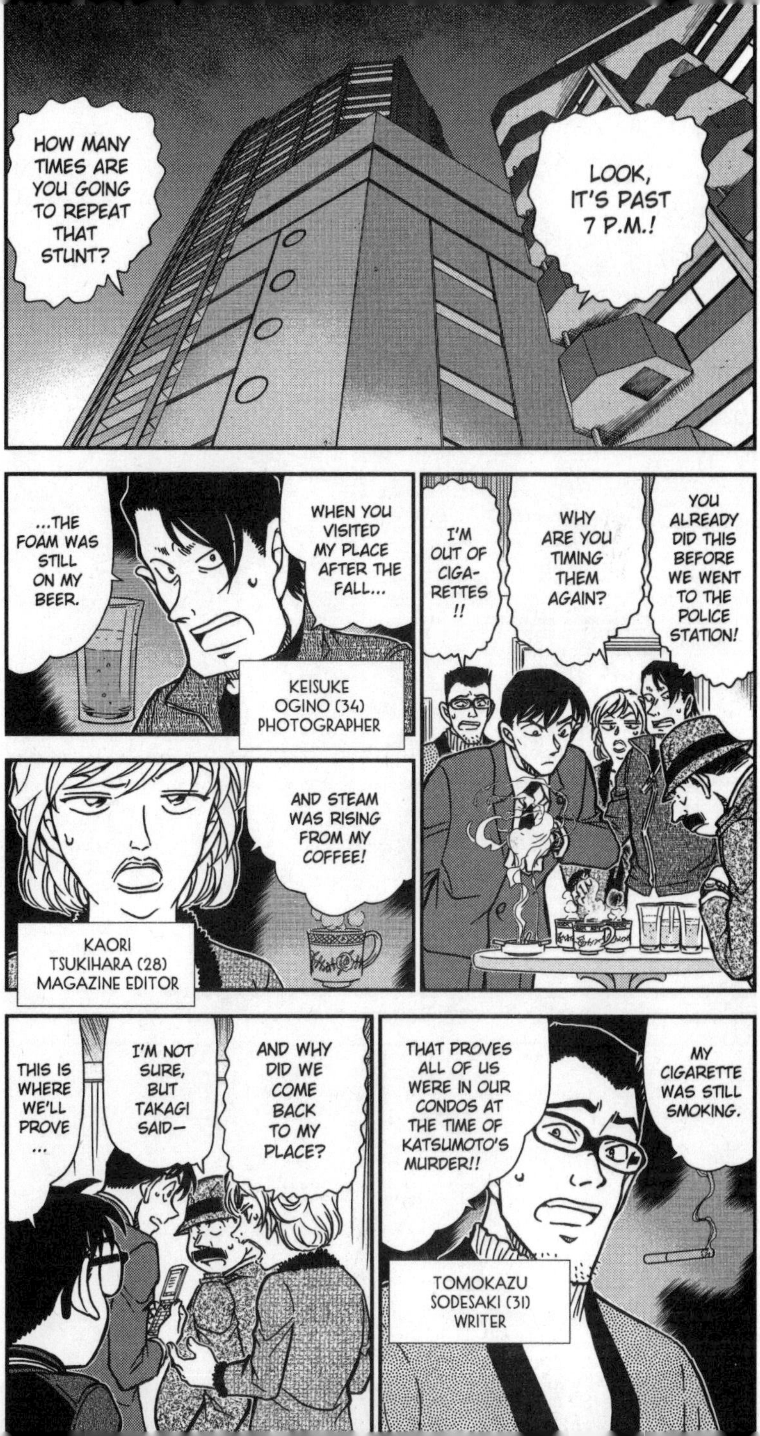
LOOK, IT'S PAST 7 P.M.!
HOW MANY TIMES ARE YOU GOING TO REPEAT THAT STUNT?
YOU ALREADY DID THIS BEFORE WE WENT TO THE POLICE STATION!
WHY ARE YOU TIMING THEM AGAIN?
I'M OUT OF CIGA- RETTES!!
WHEN YOU VISITED MY PLACE AFTER THE FALL...
...THE FOAM WAS STILL ON MY BEER.
KEISUKE OGINO (34) PHOTOGRAPHER
AND STEAM WAS RISING FROM MY COFFEE!
KAORI TSUKIHARA (28) MAGAZINE EDITOR
MY CIGARETTE WAS STILL SMOKING.
THAT PROVES ALL OF US WERE IN OUR CONDOS AT THE TIME OF KATSUMOTO'S MURDER!!
TOMOKAZU SODESAKI (31) WRITER
AND WHY DID WE COME BACK TO MY PLACE?
I'M NOT SURE, BUT TAKAGI SAID—
THIS IS WHERE WE'LL PROVE ...

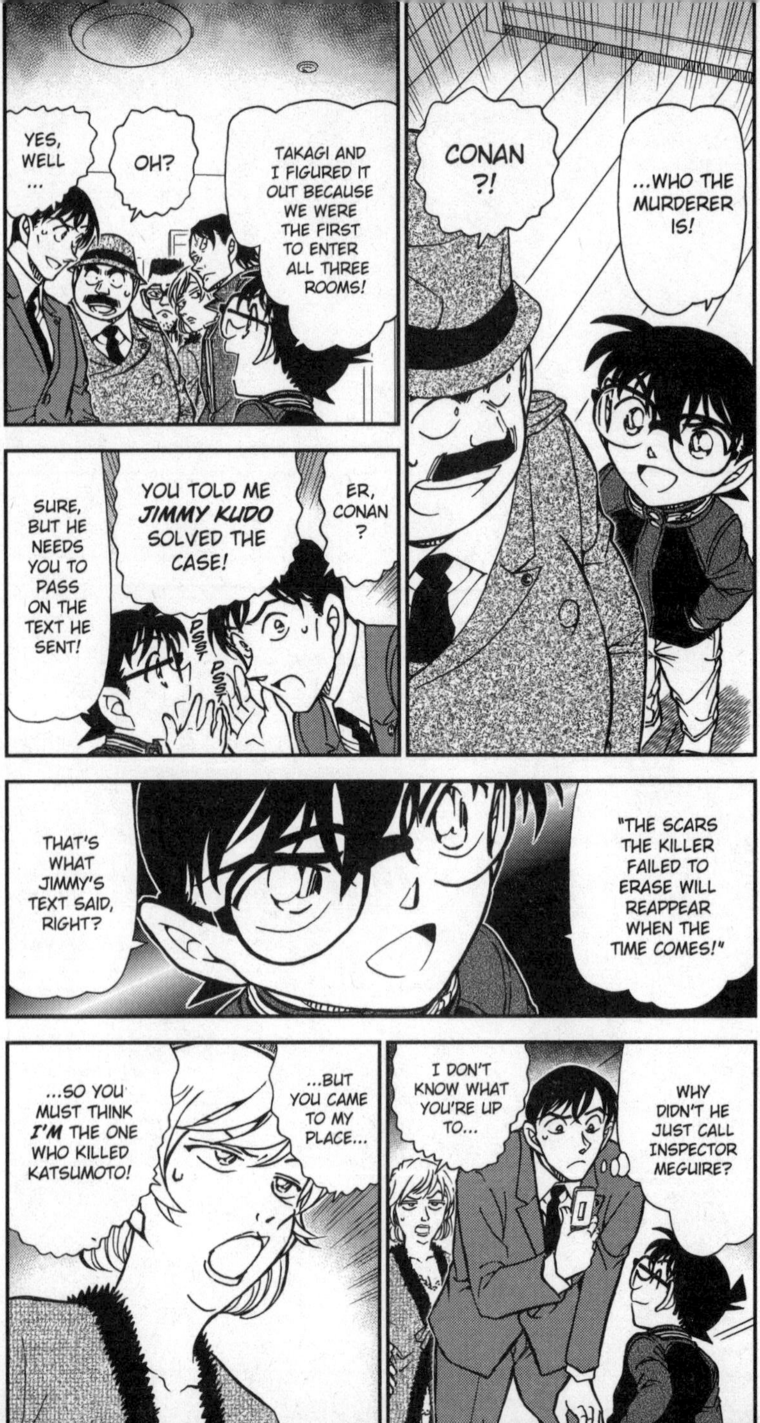
...WHO THE MURDERER IS!
CONAN ?!
TAKAGI AND I FIGURED IT OUT BECAUSE WE WERE THE FIRST TO ENTER ALL THREE ROOMS!
OH?
YES, WELL ...
ER, CONAN ?
YOU TOLD ME JIMMY KUDO SOLVED THE CASE!
PSST PSST
SURE, BUT HE NEEDS YOU TO PASS ON THE TEXT HE SENT!
"THE SCARS THE KILLER FAILED TO ERASE WILL REAPPEAR WHEN THE TIME COMES!"
THAT'S WHAT JIMMY'S TEXT SAID, RIGHT?
WHY DIDN'T HE JUST CALL INSPECTOR MEGUIRE?
I DON'T KNOW WHAT YOU'RE UP TO...
...BUT YOU CAME TO MY PLACE...
...SO YOU MUST THINK I'M THE ONE WHO KILLED KATSUMOTO!

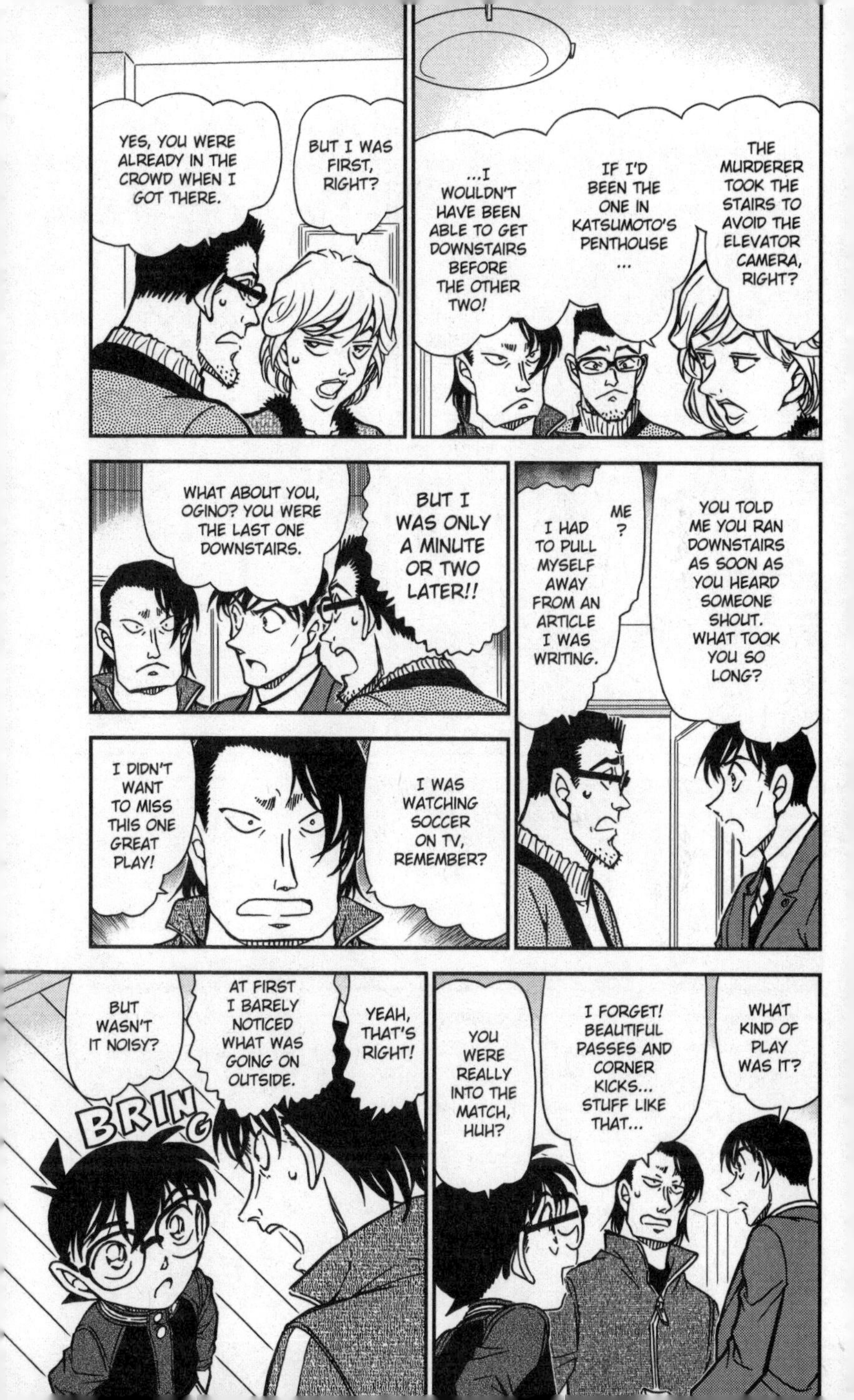
THE MURDERER TOOK THE STAIRS TO AVOID THE ELEVATOR CAMERA, RIGHT?
IF I'D BEEN THE ONE IN KATSUMOTO'S PENTHOUSE ...
...I WOULDN'T HAVE BEEN ABLE TO GET DOWNSTAIRS BEFORE THE OTHER TWO!
BUT I WAS FIRST, RIGHT?
YES, YOU WERE ALREADY IN THE CROWD WHEN I GOT THERE.
YOU TOLD ME YOU RAN DOWNSTAIRS AS SOON AS YOU HEARD SOMEONE SHOUT. WHAT TOOK YOU SO LONG?
ME?
I HAD TO PULL MYSELF AWAY FROM AN ARTICLE I WAS WRITING.
WHAT ABOUT YOU, OGINO? YOU WERE THE LAST ONE DOWNSTAIRS.
BUT I WAS ONLY A MINUTE OR TWO LATER!!
I WAS WATCHING SOCCER ON TV, REMEMBER?
I DIDN'T WANT TO MISS THIS ONE GREAT PLAY!
WHAT KIND OF PLAY WAS IT?
I FORGET! BEAUTIFUL PASSES AND CORNER KICKS... STUFF LIKE THAT...
YOU WERE REALLY INTO THE MATCH, HUH?
YEAH, THAT'S RIGHT!
AT FIRST I BARELY NOTICED WHAT WAS GOING ON OUTSIDE.
BUT WASN'T IT NOISY?
BRING

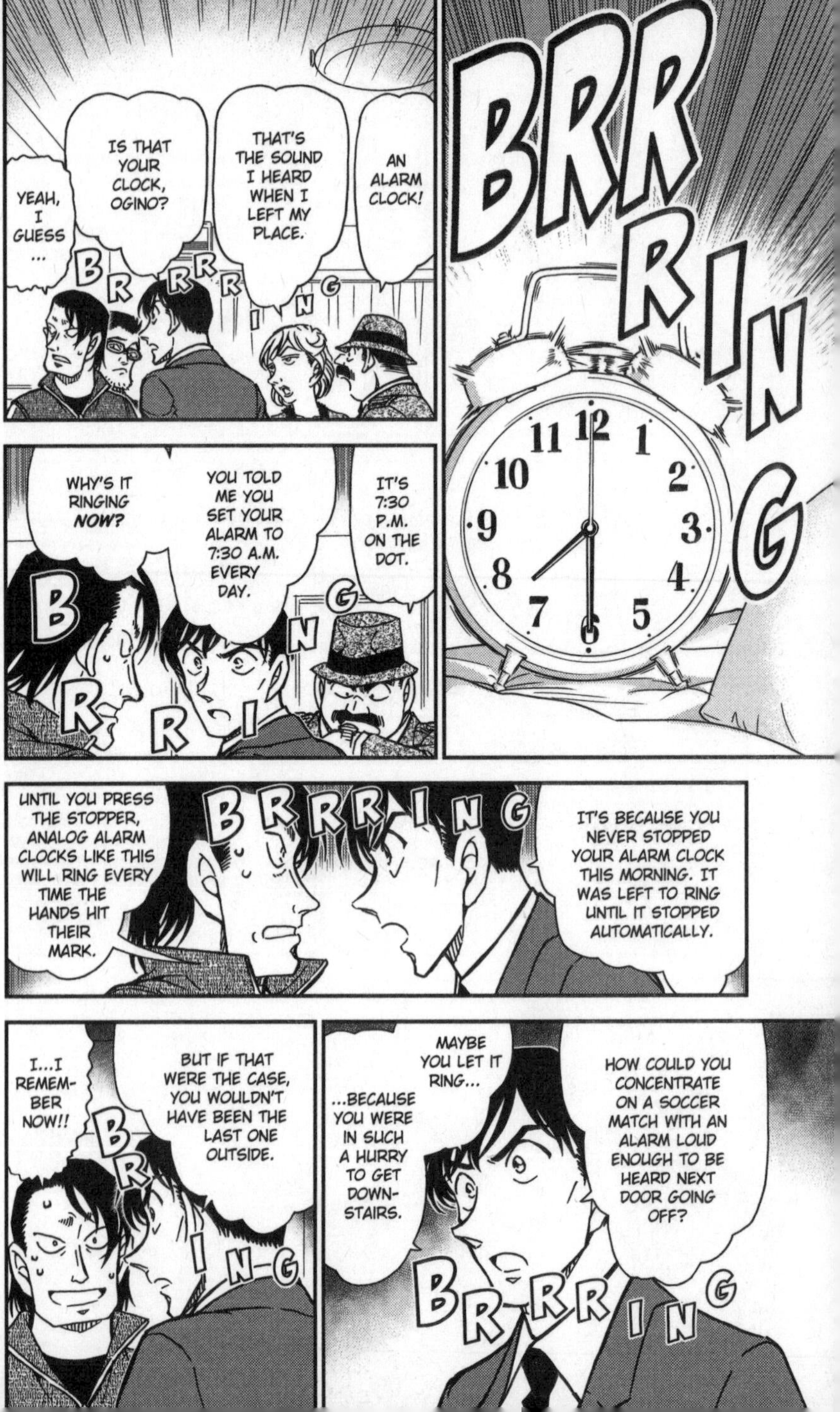
BRRRING
AN ALARM CLOCK!
THAT'S THE SOUND I HEARD WHEN I LEFT MY PLACE.
BRRRING
IS THAT YOUR CLOCK, OGINO?
YEAH, I GUESS ...
IT'S 7:30 P.M. ON THE DOT.
BRRRING
YOU TOLD ME YOU SET YOUR ALARM TO 7:30 A.M. EVERY DAY.
WHY'S IT RINGING *NOW?*
IT'S BECAUSE YOU NEVER STOPPED YOUR ALARM CLOCK THIS MORNING. IT WAS LEFT TO RING UNTIL IT STOPPED AUTOMATICALLY.
BRRRING
UNTIL YOU PRESS THE STOPPER, ANALOG ALARM CLOCKS LIKE THIS WILL RING EVERY TIME THE HANDS HIT THEIR MARK.
HOW COULD YOU CONCENTRATE ON A SOCCER MATCH WITH AN ALARM LOUD ENOUGH TO BE HEARD NEXT DOOR GOING OFF?
MAYBE YOU LET IT RING...
...BECAUSE YOU WERE IN SUCH A HURRY TO GET DOWN-STAIRS.
BRRRING
BUT IF THAT WERE THE CASE, YOU WOULDN'T HAVE BEEN THE LAST ONE OUTSIDE.
I...I REMEM-BER NOW!!
BRING

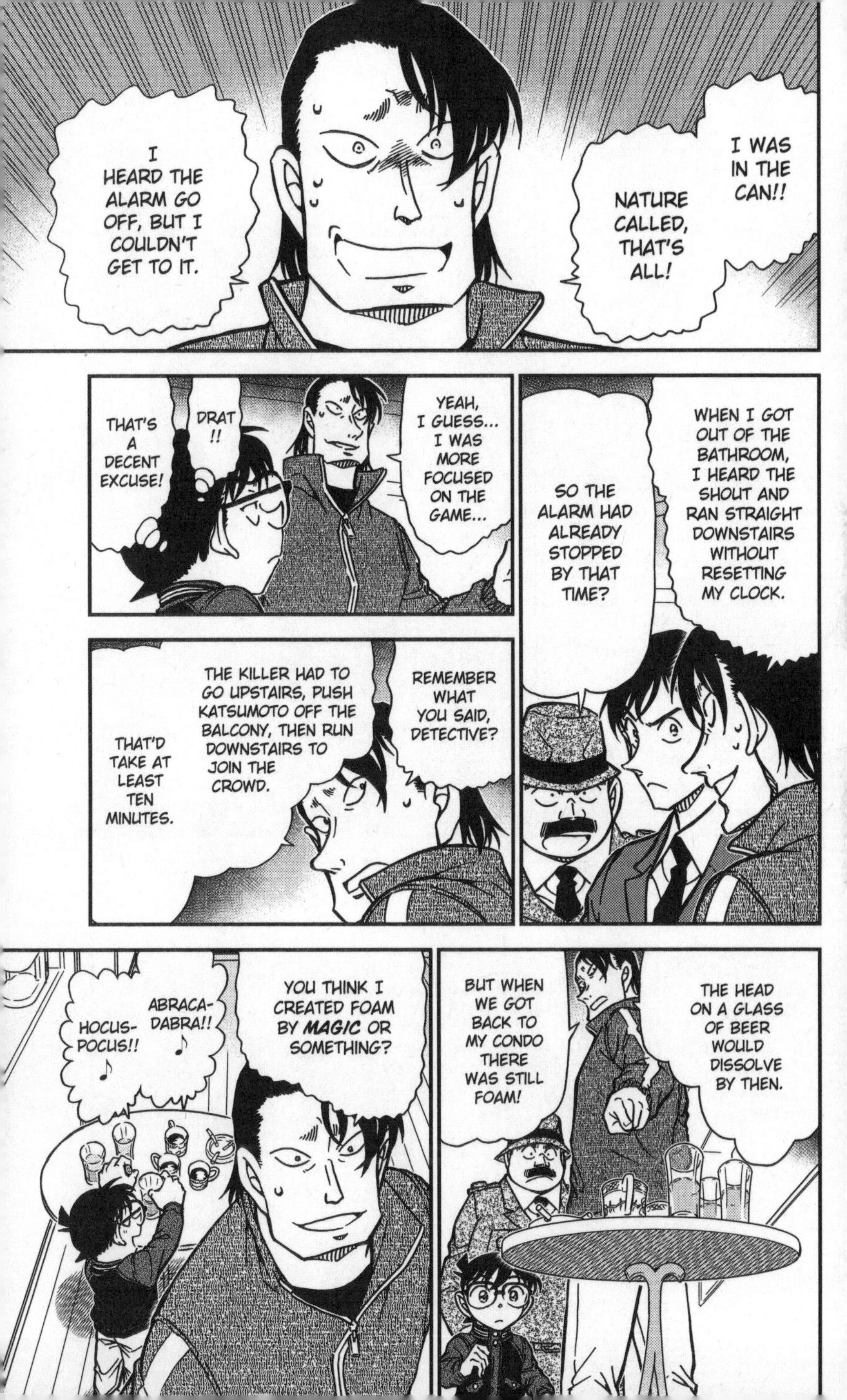
I WAS IN THE CAN!!
NATURE CALLED, THAT'S ALL!
I HEARD THE ALARM GO OFF, BUT I COULDN'T GET TO IT.
WHEN I GOT OUT OF THE BATHROOM, I HEARD THE SHOUT AND RAN STRAIGHT DOWNSTAIRS WITHOUT RESETTING MY CLOCK.
SO THE ALARM HAD ALREADY STOPPED BY THAT TIME?
YEAH, I GUESS... I WAS MORE FOCUSED ON THE GAME...
DRAT!!
THAT'S A DECENT EXCUSE!
REMEMBER WHAT YOU SAID, DETECTIVE?
THE KILLER HAD TO GO UPSTAIRS, PUSH KATSUMOTO OFF THE BALCONY, THEN RUN DOWNSTAIRS TO JOIN THE CROWD.
THAT'D TAKE AT LEAST TEN MINUTES.
THE HEAD ON A GLASS OF BEER WOULD DISSOLVE BY THEN.
BUT WHEN WE GOT BACK TO MY CONDO THERE WAS STILL FOAM!
YOU THINK I CREATED FOAM BY *MAGIC* OR SOMETHING?
ABRACA-DABRA!! ♪
HOCUS-POCUS!! ♪

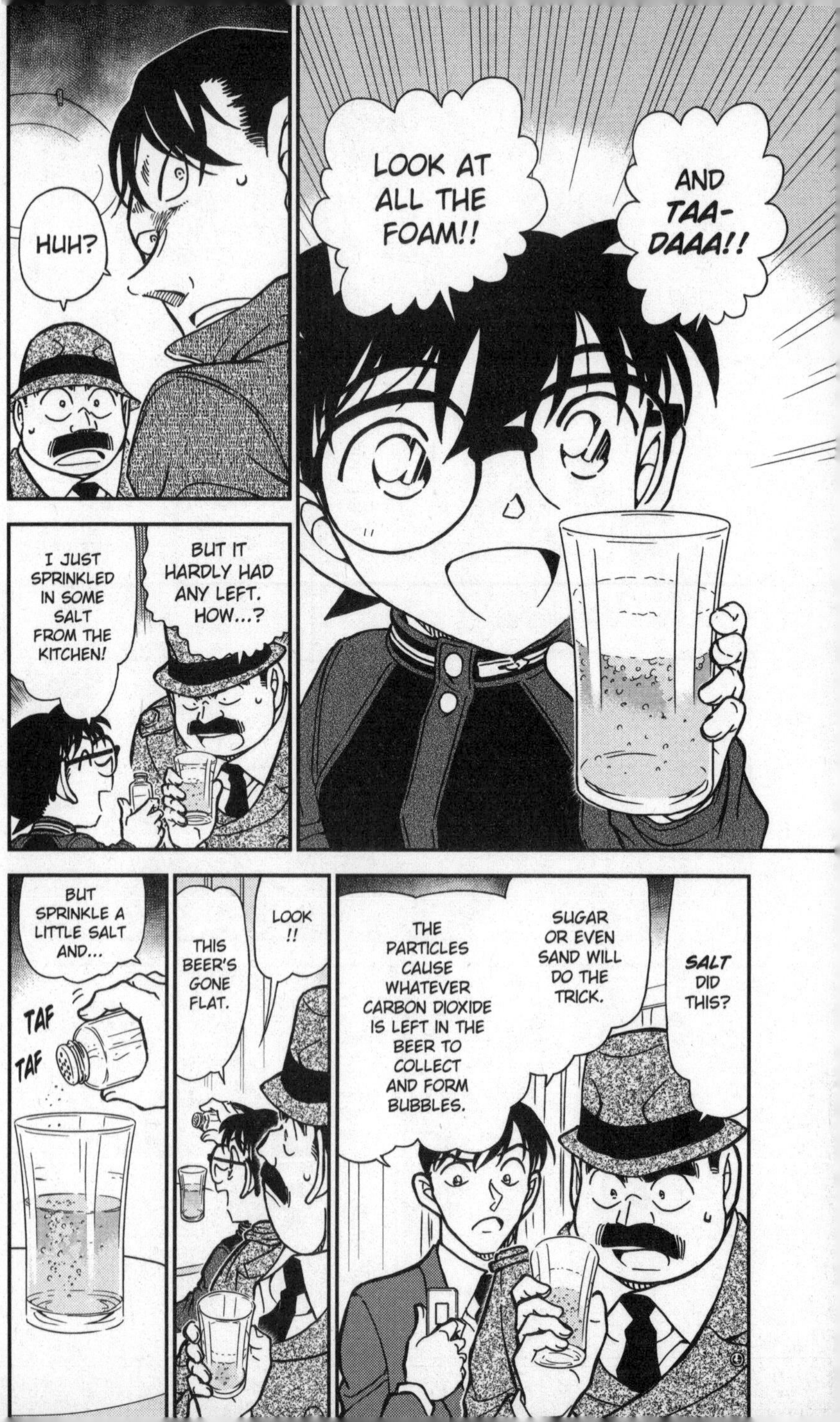
AND TAA-DAAA!!
LOOK AT ALL THE FOAM!!
HUH?
BUT IT HARDLY HAD ANY LEFT. HOW...?
I JUST SPRINKLED IN SOME SALT FROM THE KITCHEN!
SALT DID THIS?
SUGAR OR EVEN SAND WILL DO THE TRICK.
THE PARTICLES CAUSE WHATEVER CARBON DIOXIDE IS LEFT IN THE BEER TO COLLECT AND FORM BUBBLES.
LOOK!!
THIS BEER'S GONE FLAT.
BUT SPRINKLE A LITTLE SALT AND...
TAF
TAF

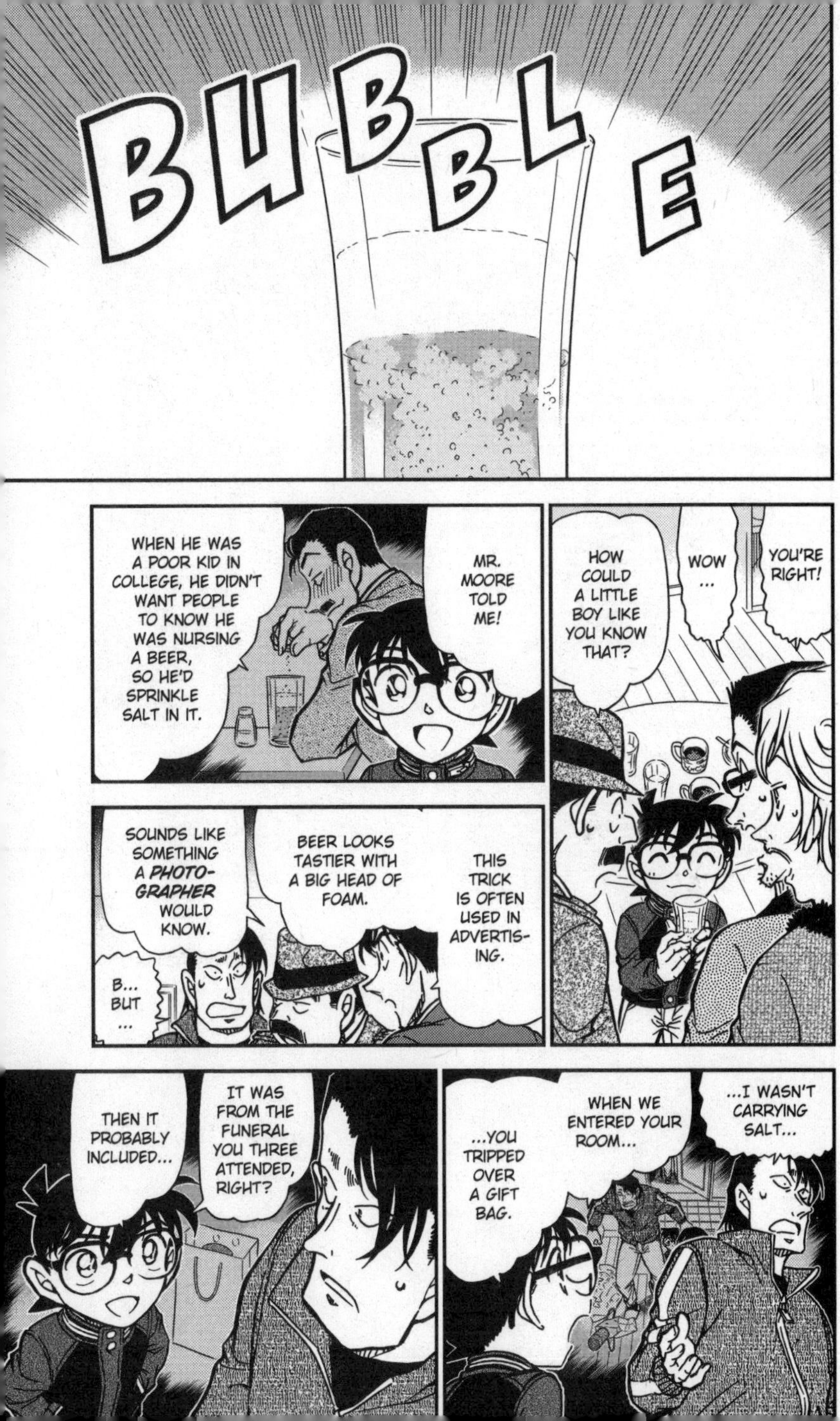
BUBBLE
YOU'RE RIGHT!
WOW...
HOW COULD A LITTLE BOY LIKE YOU KNOW THAT?
MR. MOORE TOLD ME!
WHEN HE WAS A POOR KID IN COLLEGE, HE DIDN'T WANT PEOPLE TO KNOW HE WAS NURSING A BEER, SO HE'D SPRINKLE SALT IN IT.
THIS TRICK IS OFTEN USED IN ADVERTISING.
BEER LOOKS TASTIER WITH A BIG HEAD OF FOAM.
SOUNDS LIKE SOMETHING A *PHOTOGRAPHER* WOULD KNOW.
B... BUT...
...I WASN'T CARRYING SALT...
WHEN WE ENTERED YOUR ROOM...
...YOU TRIPPED OVER A GIFT BAG.
IT WAS FROM THE FUNERAL YOU THREE ATTENDED, RIGHT?
THEN IT PROBABLY INCLUDED...

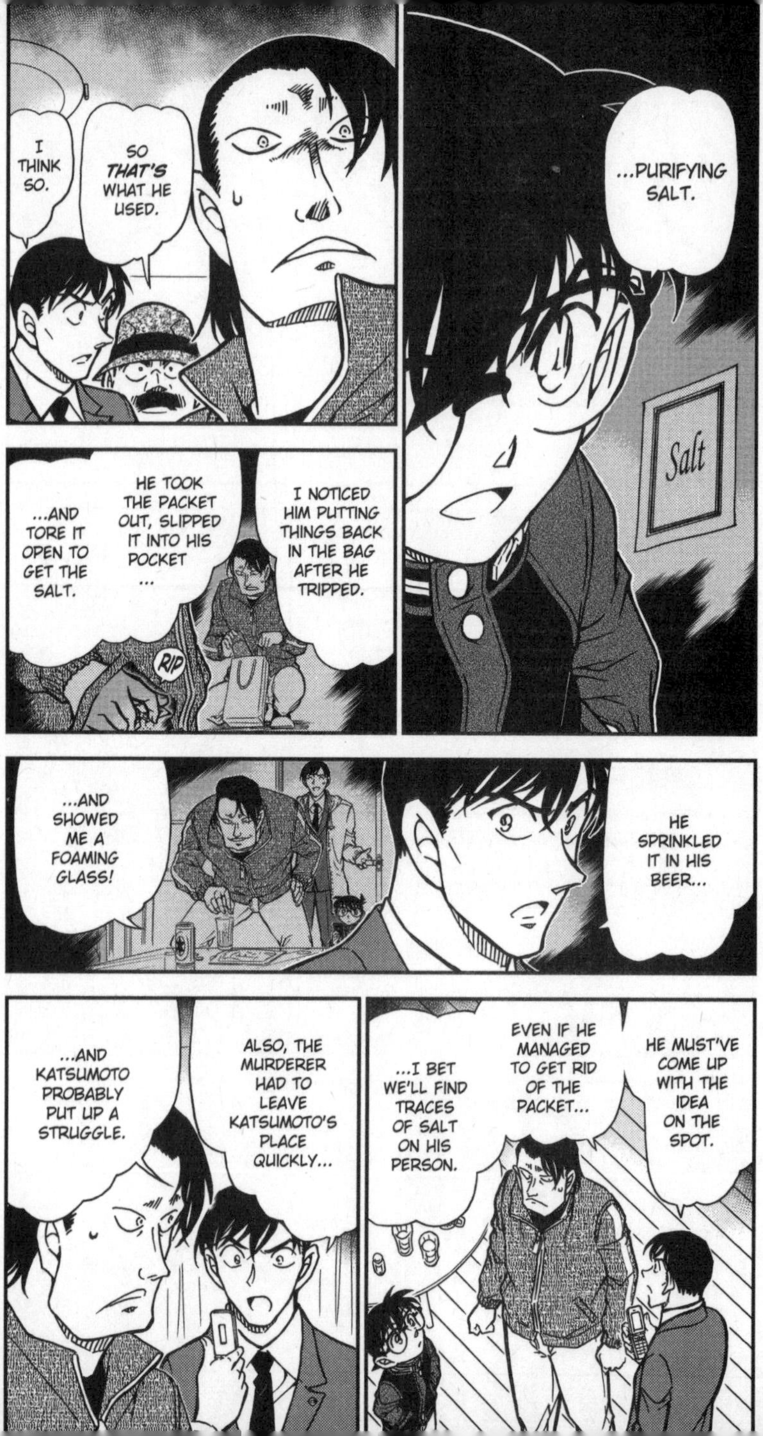
...PURIFYING SALT.
Salt
SO *THAT'S* WHAT HE USED.
I THINK SO.
I NOTICED HIM PUTTING THINGS BACK IN THE BAG AFTER HE TRIPPED.
HE TOOK THE PACKET OUT, SLIPPED IT INTO HIS POCKET...
...AND TORE IT OPEN TO GET THE SALT.
RIP
HE SPRINKLED IT IN HIS BEER...
...AND SHOWED ME A FOAMING GLASS!
HE MUST'VE COME UP WITH THE IDEA ON THE SPOT.
EVEN IF HE MANAGED TO GET RID OF THE PACKET...
...I BET WE'LL FIND TRACES OF SALT ON HIS PERSON.
ALSO, THE MURDERER HAD TO LEAVE KATSUMOTO'S PLACE QUICKLY...
...AND KATSUMOTO PROBABLY PUT UP A STRUGGLE.

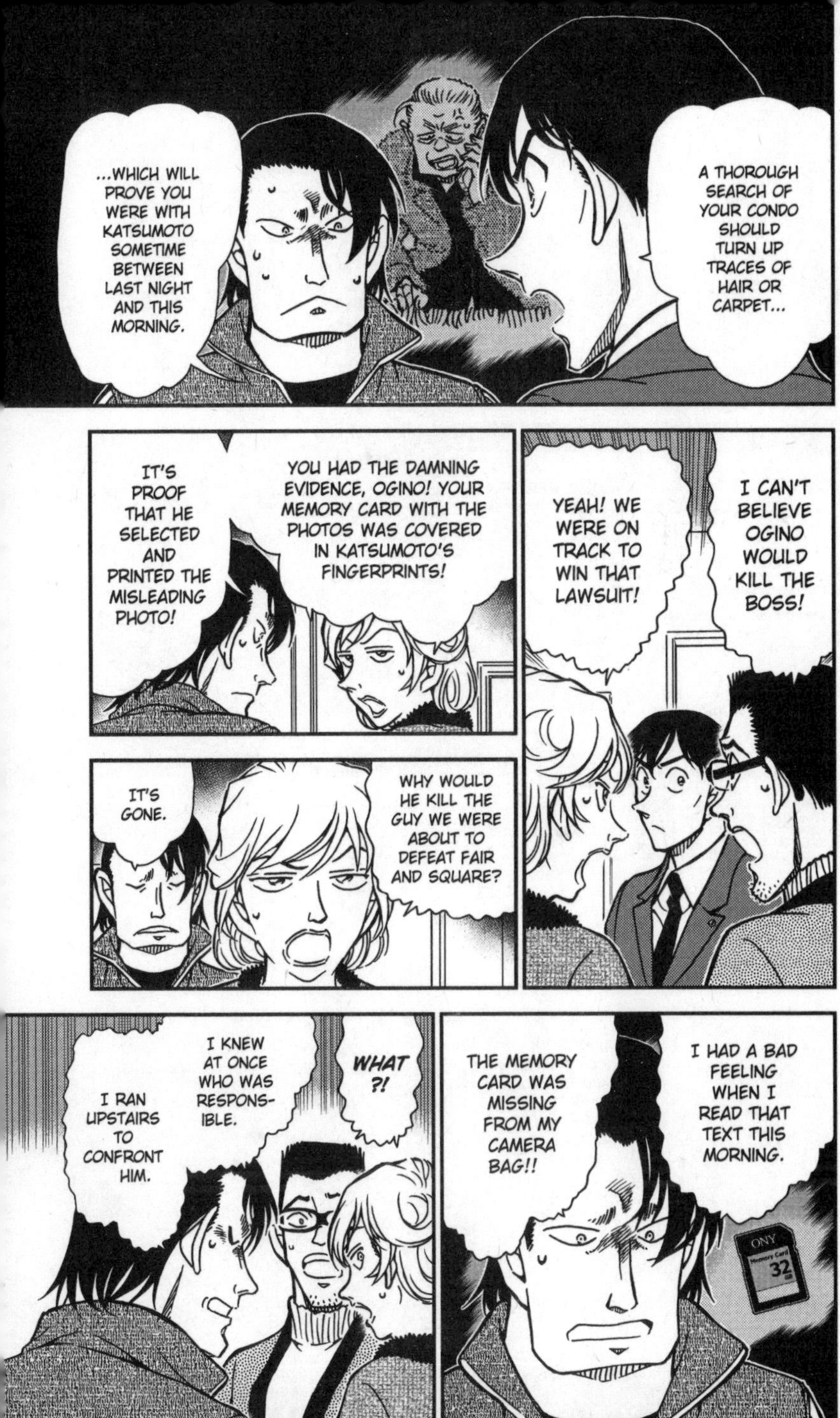
A THOROUGH SEARCH OF YOUR CONDO SHOULD TURN UP TRACES OF HAIR OR CARPET...
...WHICH WILL PROVE YOU WERE WITH KATSUMOTO SOMETIME BETWEEN LAST NIGHT AND THIS MORNING.
I CAN'T BELIEVE OGINO WOULD KILL THE BOSS!
YEAH! WE WERE ON TRACK TO WIN THAT LAWSUIT!
YOU HAD THE DAMNING EVIDENCE, OGINO! YOUR MEMORY CARD WITH THE PHOTOS WAS COVERED IN KATSUMOTO'S FINGERPRINTS!
IT'S PROOF THAT HE SELECTED AND PRINTED THE MISLEADING PHOTO!
WHY WOULD HE KILL THE GUY WE WERE ABOUT TO DEFEAT FAIR AND SQUARE?
IT'S GONE.
I HAD A BAD FEELING WHEN I READ THAT TEXT THIS MORNING.
THE MEMORY CARD WAS MISSING FROM MY CAMERA BAG!!
WHAT?!
I KNEW AT ONCE WHO WAS RESPONSIBLE.
I RAN UPSTAIRS TO CONFRONT HIM.

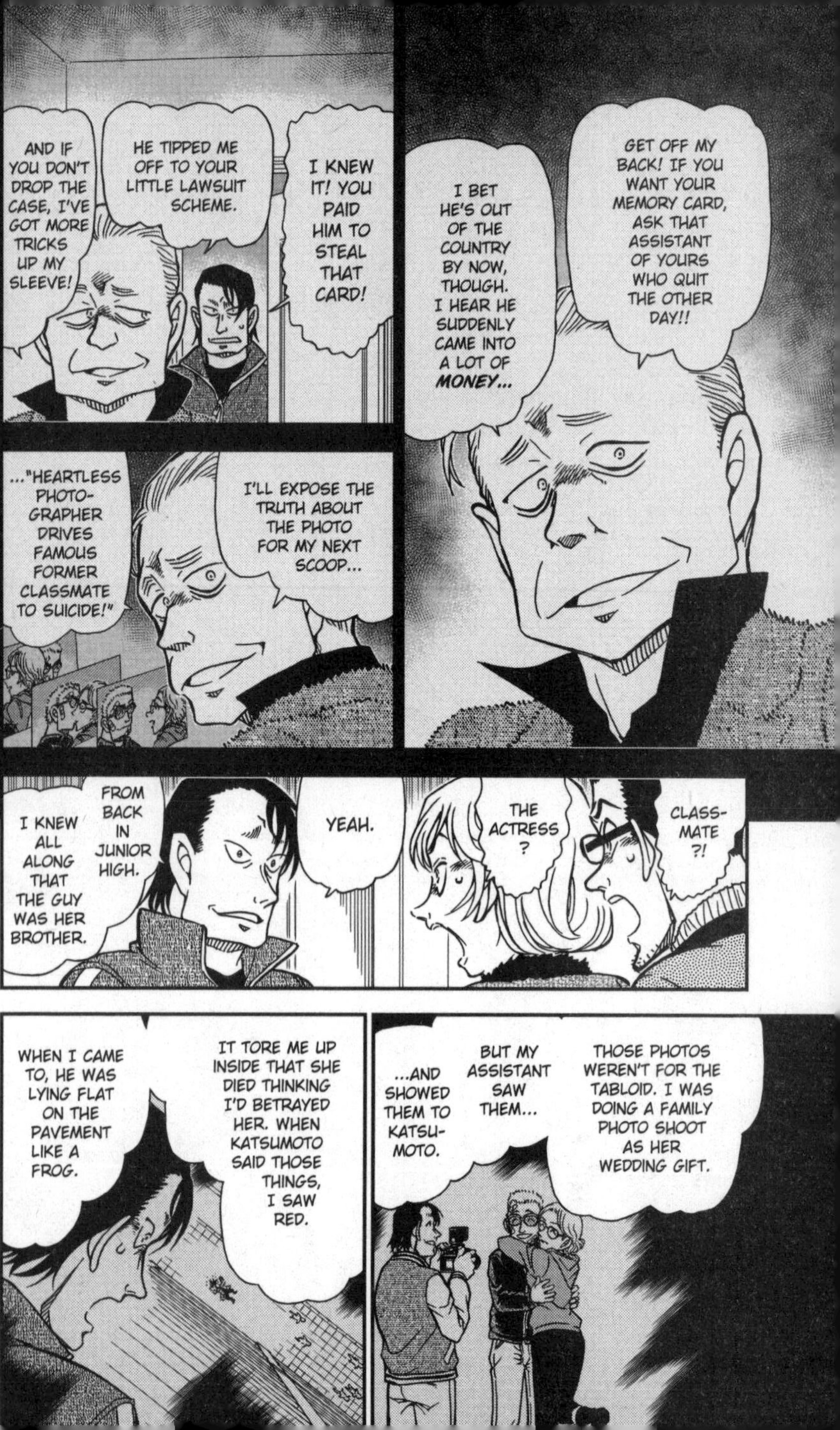
GET OFF MY BACK! IF YOU WANT YOUR MEMORY CARD, ASK THAT ASSISTANT OF YOURS WHO QUIT THE OTHER DAY!!
I BET HE'S OUT OF THE COUNTRY BY NOW, THOUGH. I HEAR HE SUDDENLY CAME INTO A LOT OF **MONEY...**
I KNEW IT! YOU PAID HIM TO STEAL THAT CARD!
HE TIPPED ME OFF TO YOUR LITTLE LAWSUIT SCHEME.
AND IF YOU DON'T DROP THE CASE, I'VE GOT MORE TRICKS UP MY SLEEVE!
I'LL EXPOSE THE TRUTH ABOUT THE PHOTO FOR MY NEXT SCOOP...
..."HEARTLESS PHOTOGRAPHER DRIVES FAMOUS FORMER CLASSMATE TO SUICIDE!"
CLASSMATE?!
THE ACTRESS?
YEAH.
FROM BACK IN JUNIOR HIGH.
I KNEW ALL ALONG THAT THE GUY WAS HER BROTHER.
THOSE PHOTOS WEREN'T FOR THE TABLOID. I WAS DOING A FAMILY PHOTO SHOOT AS HER WEDDING GIFT.
BUT MY ASSISTANT SAW THEM...
...AND SHOWED THEM TO KATSUMOTO.
IT TORE ME UP INSIDE THAT SHE DIED THINKING I'D BETRAYED HER. WHEN KATSUMOTO SAID THOSE THINGS, I SAW RED.
WHEN I CAME TO, HE WAS LYING FLAT ON THE PAVEMENT LIKE A FROG.

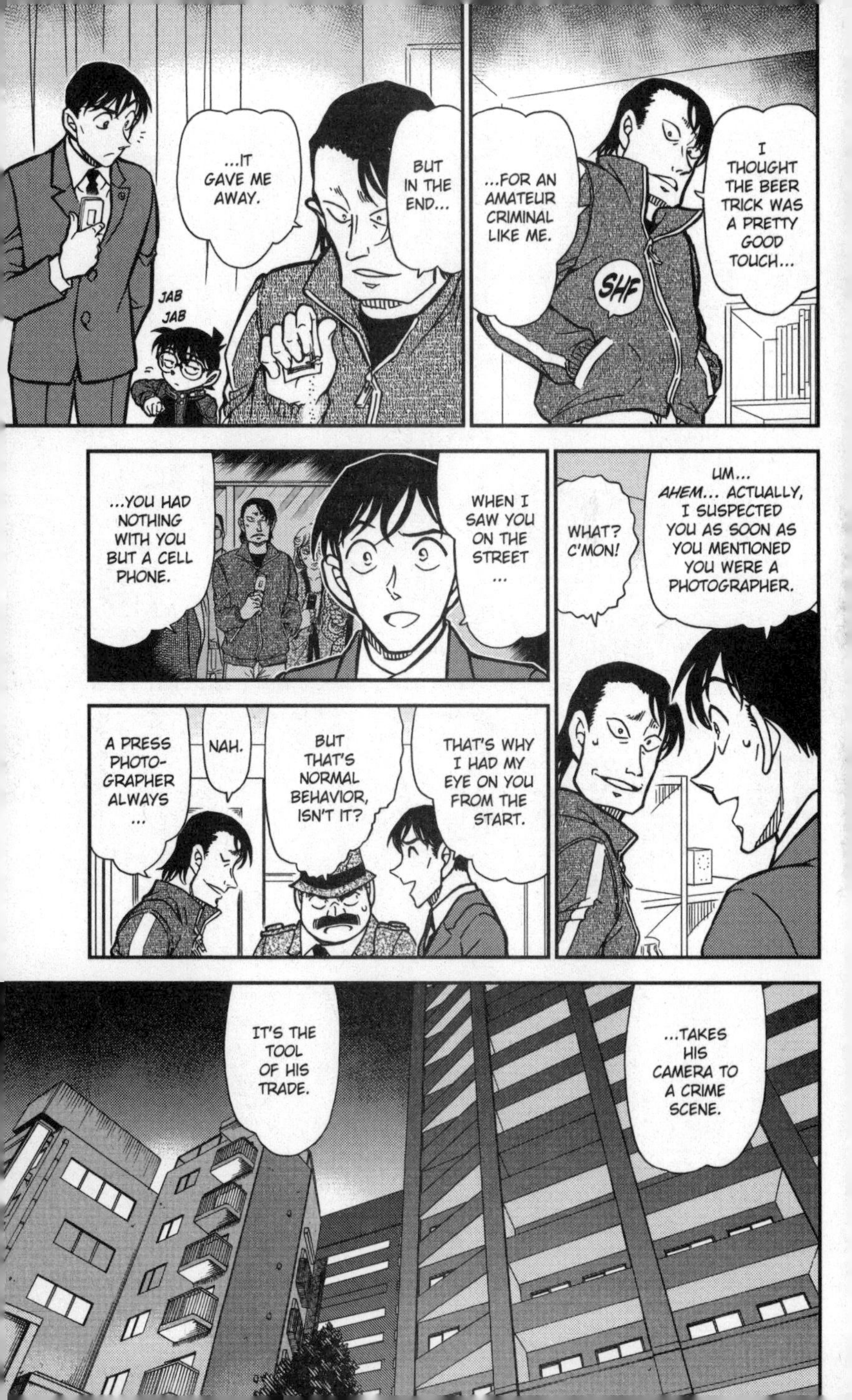
I THOUGHT THE BEER TRICK WAS A PRETTY GOOD TOUCH...
...FOR AN AMATEUR CRIMINAL LIKE ME.
SHF
BUT IN THE END...
...IT GAVE ME AWAY.
JAB JAB
UM... *AHEM*... ACTUALLY, I SUSPECTED YOU AS SOON AS YOU MENTIONED YOU WERE A PHOTOGRAPHER.
WHAT? C'MON!
WHEN I SAW YOU ON THE STREET...
...YOU HAD NOTHING WITH YOU BUT A CELL PHONE.
THAT'S WHY I HAD MY EYE ON YOU FROM THE START.
BUT THAT'S NORMAL BEHAVIOR, ISN'T IT?
NAH.
A PRESS PHOTOGRAPHER ALWAYS...
...TAKES HIS CAMERA TO A CRIME SCENE.
IT'S THE TOOL OF HIS TRADE.

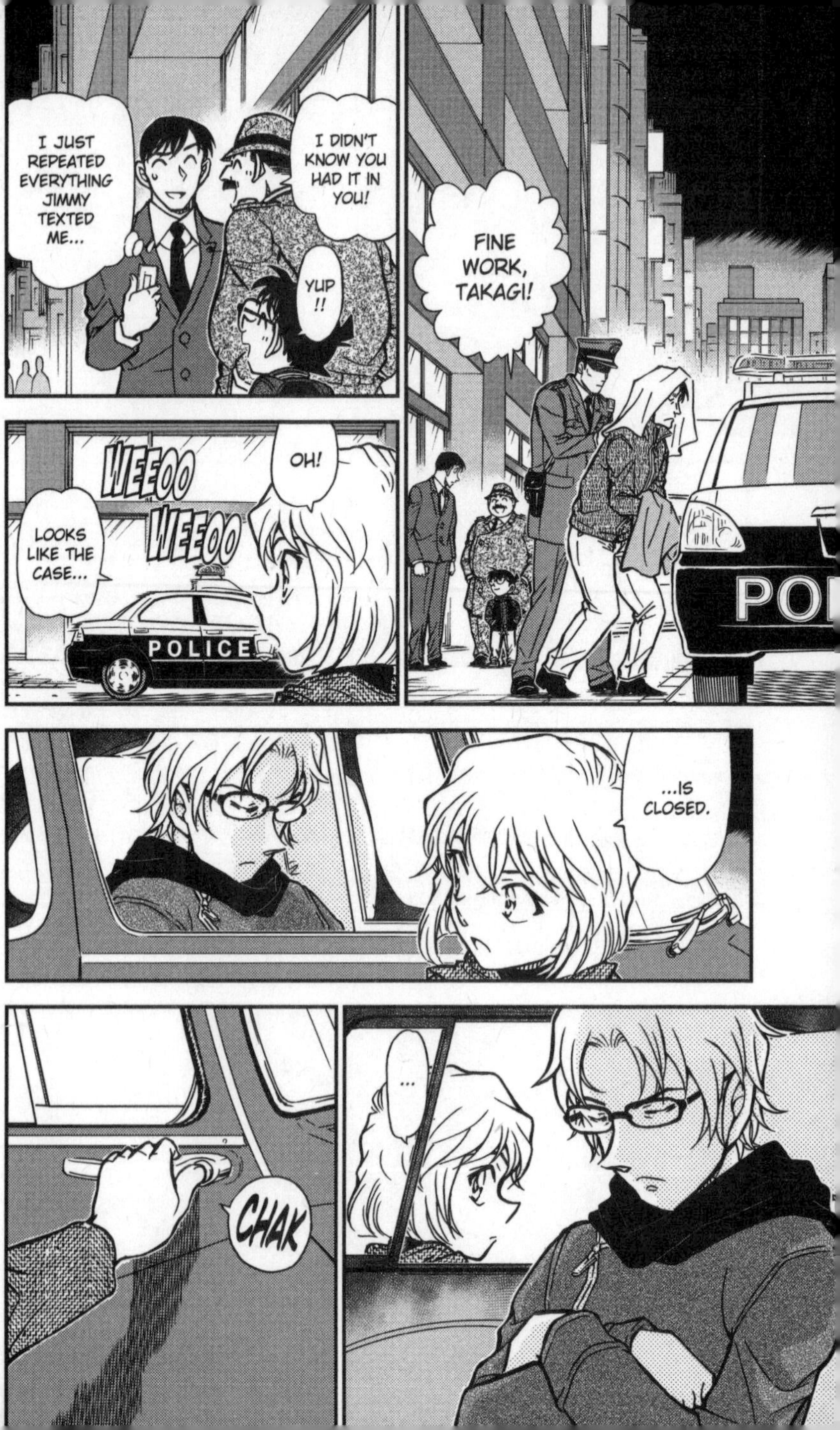
FINE WORK, TAKAGI!
I DIDN'T KNOW YOU HAD IT IN YOU!
YUP!!
I JUST REPEATED EVERYTHING JIMMY TEXTED ME...
OH!
WEEOO WEEOO
LOOKS LIKE THE CASE...
POLICE
...IS CLOSED.
...
CHAK

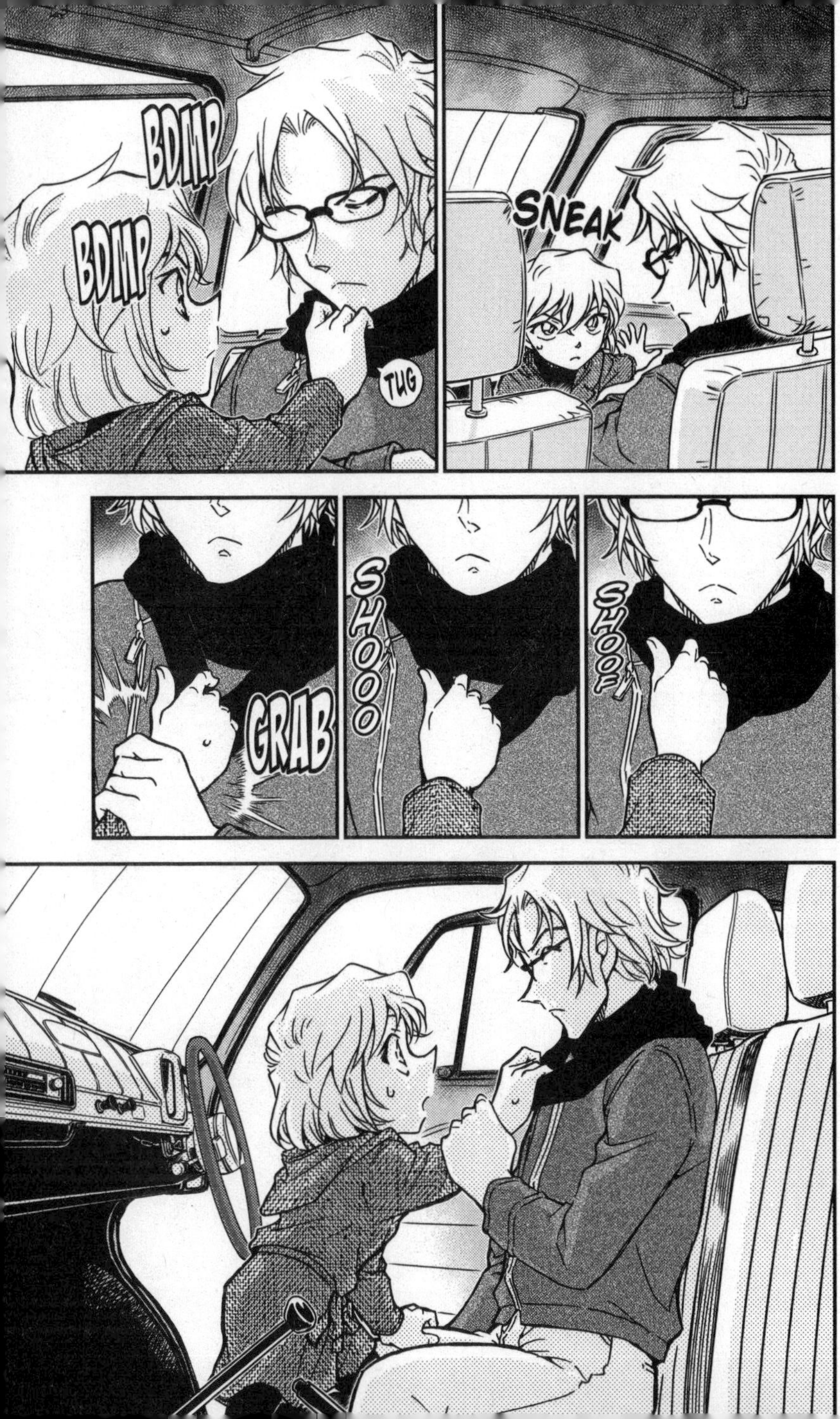
SNEAK
BDMP
BDMP
TUG
SHOOF
SHOOO
GRAB

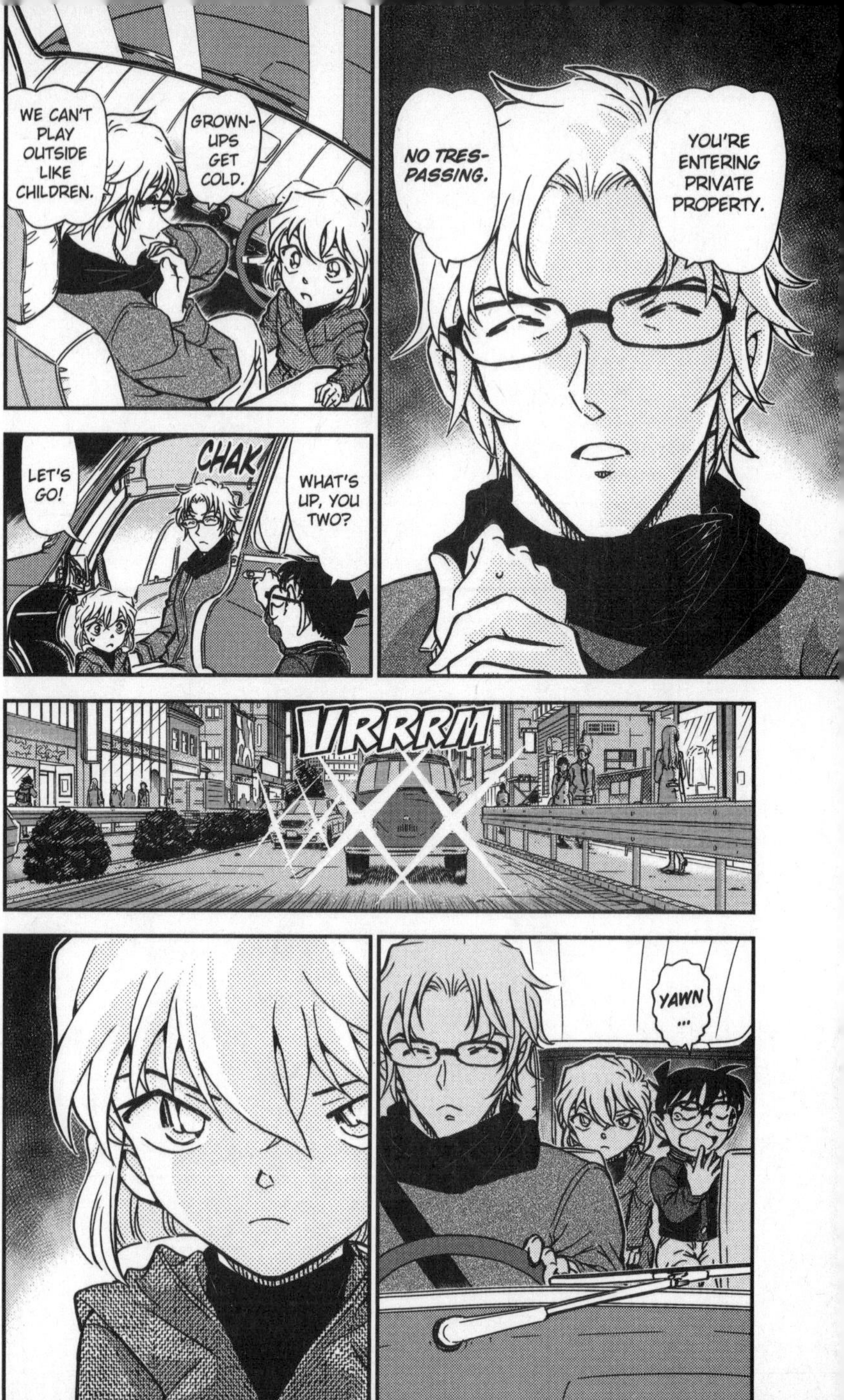
YOU'RE ENTERING PRIVATE PROPERTY.
NO TRES-PASSING.
GROWN-UPS GET COLD.
WE CAN'T PLAY OUTSIDE LIKE CHILDREN.
WHAT'S UP, YOU TWO?
CHAK
LET'S GO!
VRRRM
YAWN ...

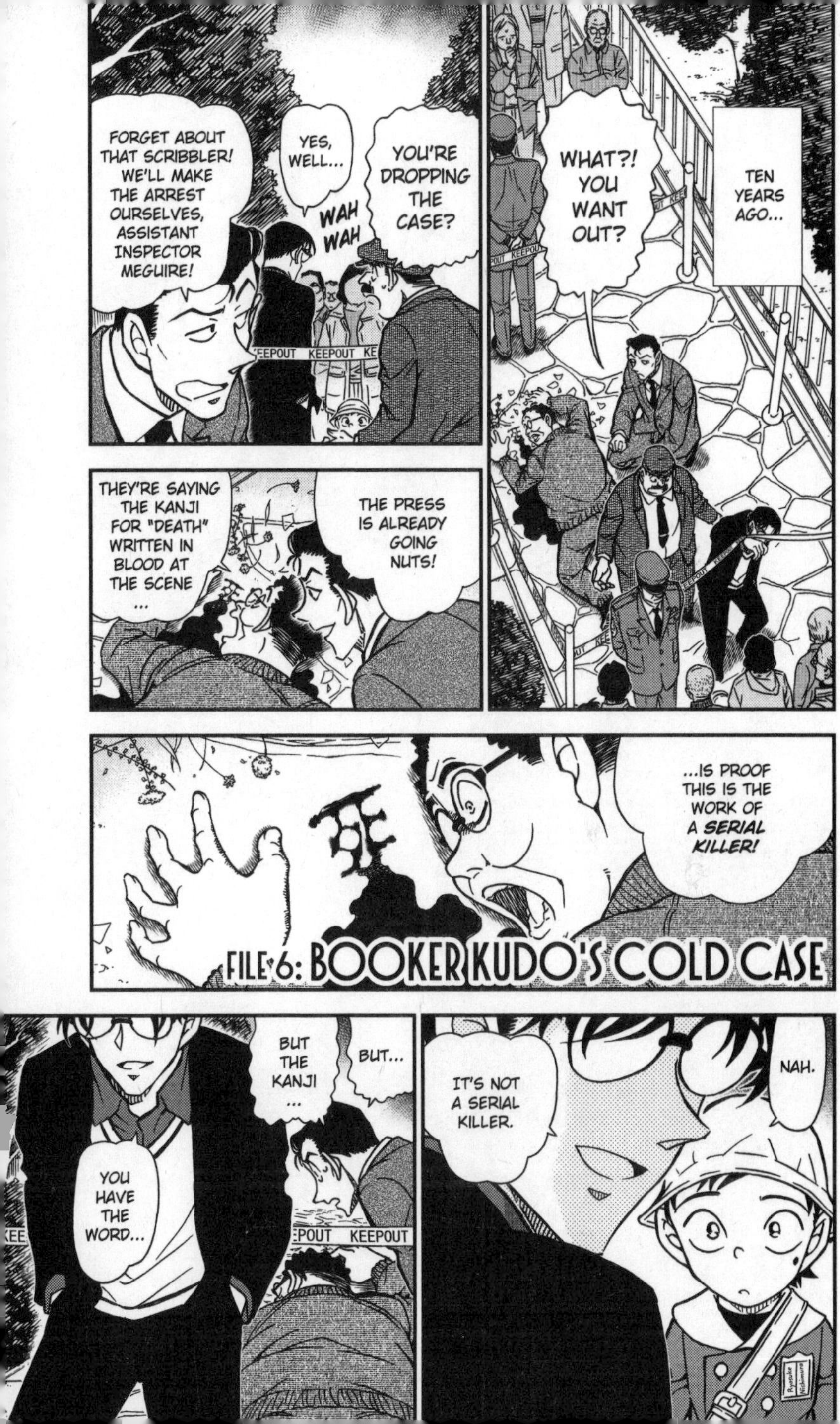
TEN YEARS AGO...
WHAT?! YOU WANT OUT?
YOU'RE DROPPING THE CASE?
YES, WELL...
WAH WAH
FORGET ABOUT THAT SCRIBBLER! WE'LL MAKE THE ARREST OURSELVES, ASSISTANT INSPECTOR MEGUIRE!
KEEPOUT KEEPOUT
THE PRESS IS ALREADY GOING NUTS!
THEY'RE SAYING THE KANJI FOR "DEATH" WRITTEN IN BLOOD AT THE SCENE ...
...IS PROOF THIS IS THE WORK OF A SERIAL KILLER!
FILE 6: BOOKER KUDO'S COLD CASE
NAH.
IT'S NOT A SERIAL KILLER.
BUT...
BUT THE KANJI ...
YOU HAVE THE WORD...

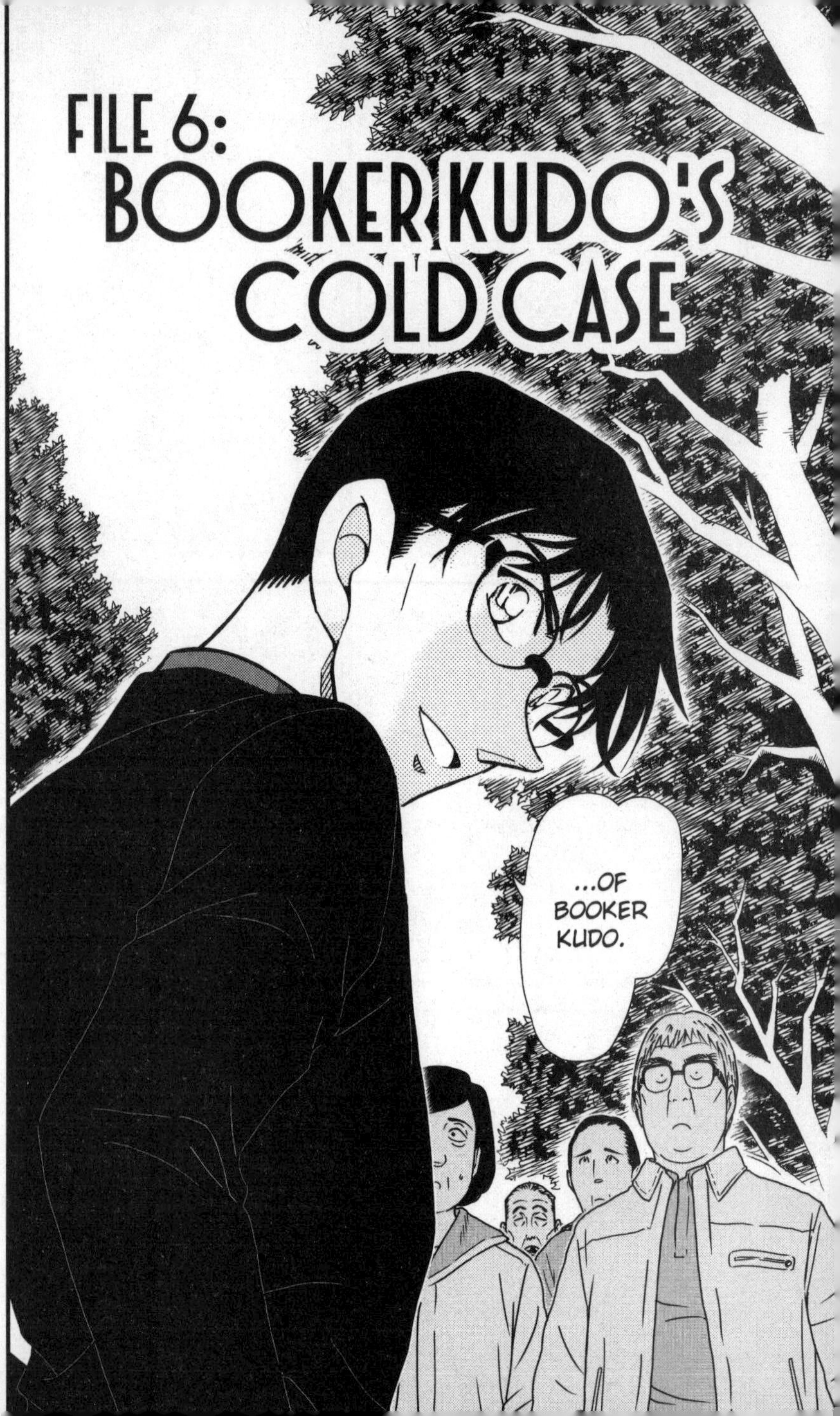
FILE 6:
BOOKER KUDO'S COLD CASE
...OF BOOKER KUDO.

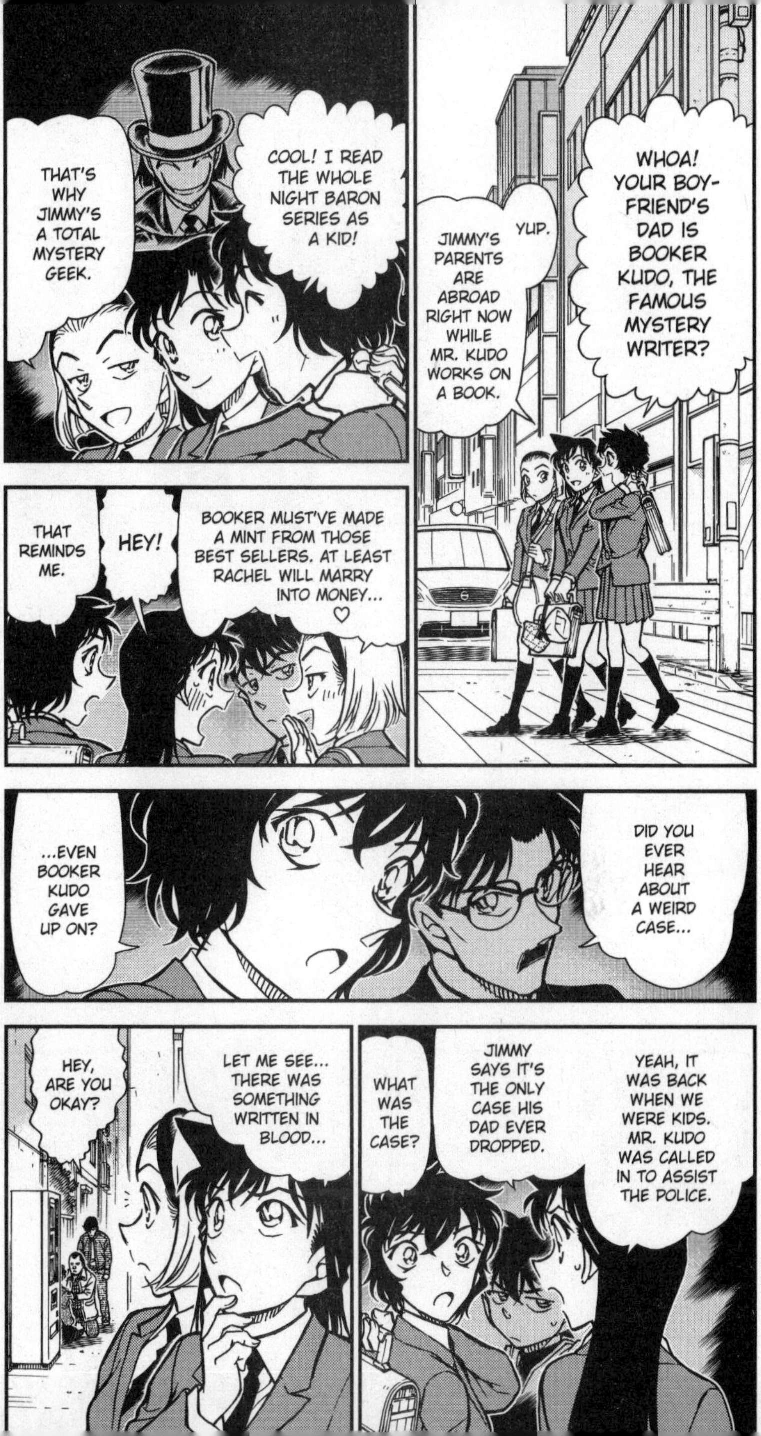
WHOA! YOUR BOY-FRIEND'S DAD IS BOOKER KUDO, THE FAMOUS MYSTERY WRITER?
YUP.
JIMMY'S PARENTS ARE ABROAD RIGHT NOW WHILE MR. KUDO WORKS ON A BOOK.
COOL! I READ THE WHOLE NIGHT BARON SERIES AS A KID!
THAT'S WHY JIMMY'S A TOTAL MYSTERY GEEK.
BOOKER MUST'VE MADE A MINT FROM THOSE BEST SELLERS. AT LEAST RACHEL WILL MARRY INTO MONEY... ♡
HEY!
THAT REMINDS ME.
DID YOU EVER HEAR ABOUT A WEIRD CASE...
...EVEN BOOKER KUDO GAVE UP ON?
YEAH, IT WAS BACK WHEN WE WERE KIDS. MR. KUDO WAS CALLED IN TO ASSIST THE POLICE.
JIMMY SAYS IT'S THE ONLY CASE HIS DAD EVER DROPPED.
WHAT WAS THE CASE?
LET ME SEE... THERE WAS SOMETHING WRITTEN IN BLOOD...
HEY, ARE YOU OKAY?

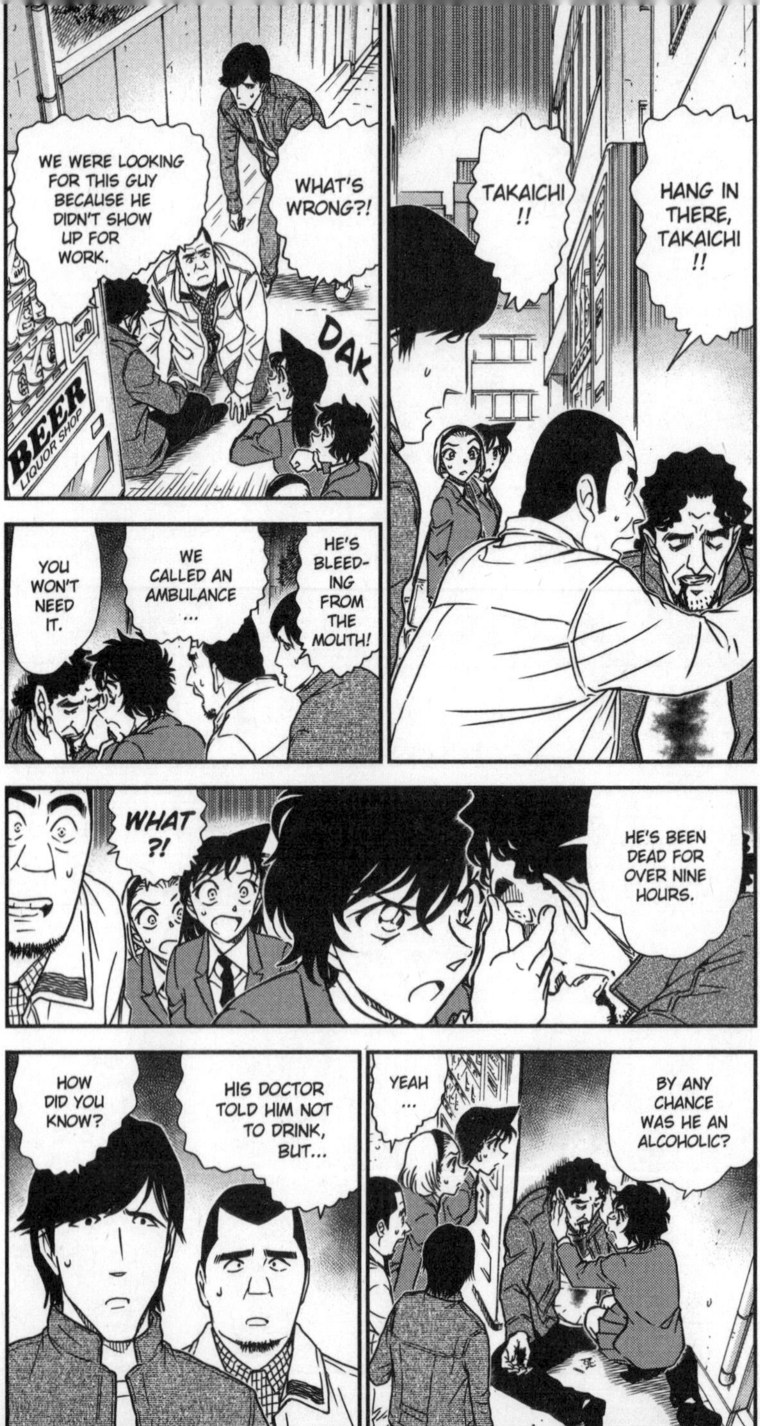
HANG IN THERE, TAKAICHI!!
TAKAICHI!!
WHAT'S WRONG?!
WE WERE LOOKING FOR THIS GUY BECAUSE HE DIDN'T SHOW UP FOR WORK.
DAK
HE'S BLEEDING FROM THE MOUTH!
WE CALLED AN AMBULANCE...
YOU WON'T NEED IT.
HE'S BEEN DEAD FOR OVER NINE HOURS.
WHAT?!
BY ANY CHANCE WAS HE AN ALCOHOLIC?
YEAH...
HIS DOCTOR TOLD HIM NOT TO DRINK, BUT...
HOW DID YOU KNOW?

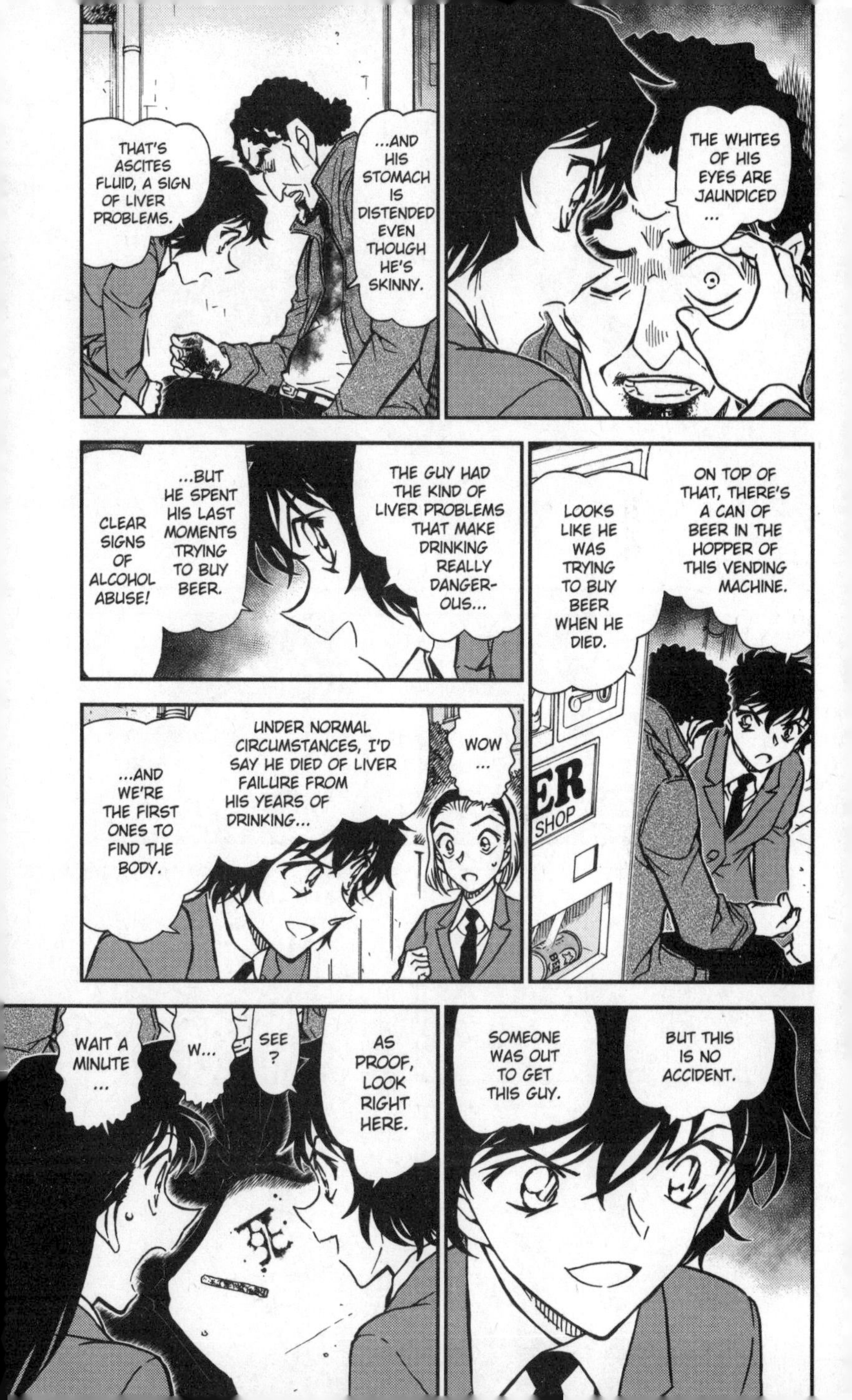
THE WHITES OF HIS EYES ARE JAUNDICED ...
...AND HIS STOMACH IS DISTENDED EVEN THOUGH HE'S SKINNY.
THAT'S ASCITES FLUID, A SIGN OF LIVER PROBLEMS.
ON TOP OF THAT, THERE'S A CAN OF BEER IN THE HOPPER OF THIS VENDING MACHINE.
LOOKS LIKE HE WAS TRYING TO BUY BEER WHEN HE DIED.
THE GUY HAD THE KIND OF LIVER PROBLEMS THAT MAKE DRINKING REALLY DANGER-OUS...
...BUT HE SPENT HIS LAST MOMENTS TRYING TO BUY BEER.
CLEAR SIGNS OF ALCOHOL ABUSE!
WOW ...
UNDER NORMAL CIRCUMSTANCES, I'D SAY HE DIED OF LIVER FAILURE FROM HIS YEARS OF DRINKING...
...AND WE'RE THE FIRST ONES TO FIND THE BODY.
BUT THIS IS NO ACCIDENT.
SOMEONE WAS OUT TO GET THIS GUY.
AS PROOF, LOOK RIGHT HERE.
SEE ?
W...
WAIT A MINUTE ...

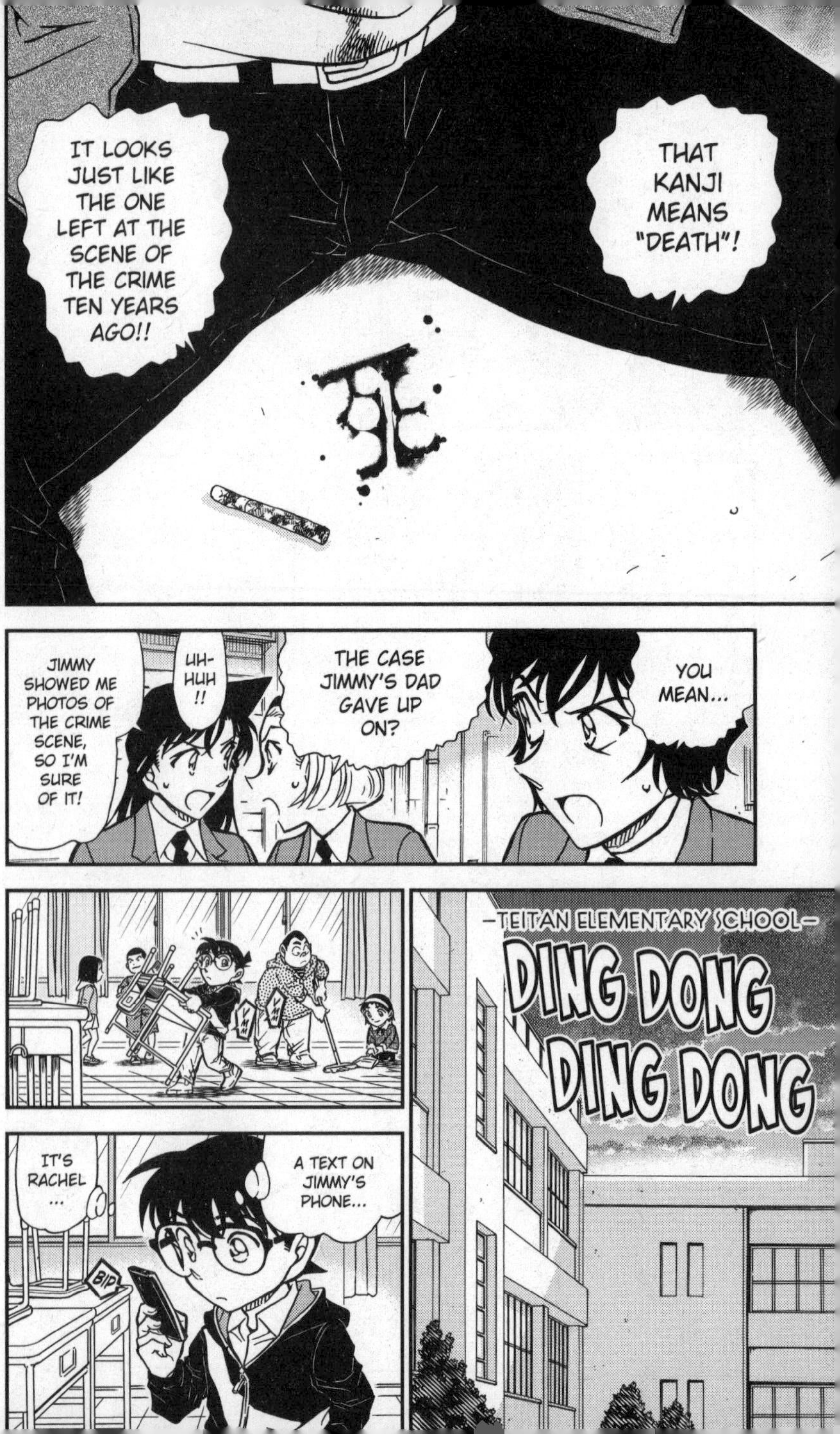
THAT KANJI MEANS "DEATH"!
IT LOOKS JUST LIKE THE ONE LEFT AT THE SCENE OF THE CRIME TEN YEARS AGO!!
YOU MEAN...
THE CASE JIMMY'S DAD GAVE UP ON?
UH-HUH!!
JIMMY SHOWED ME PHOTOS OF THE CRIME SCENE, SO I'M SURE OF IT!
—TEITAN ELEMENTARY SCHOOL—
DING DONG DING DONG
A TEXT ON JIMMY'S PHONE...
IT'S RACHEL...
BIP

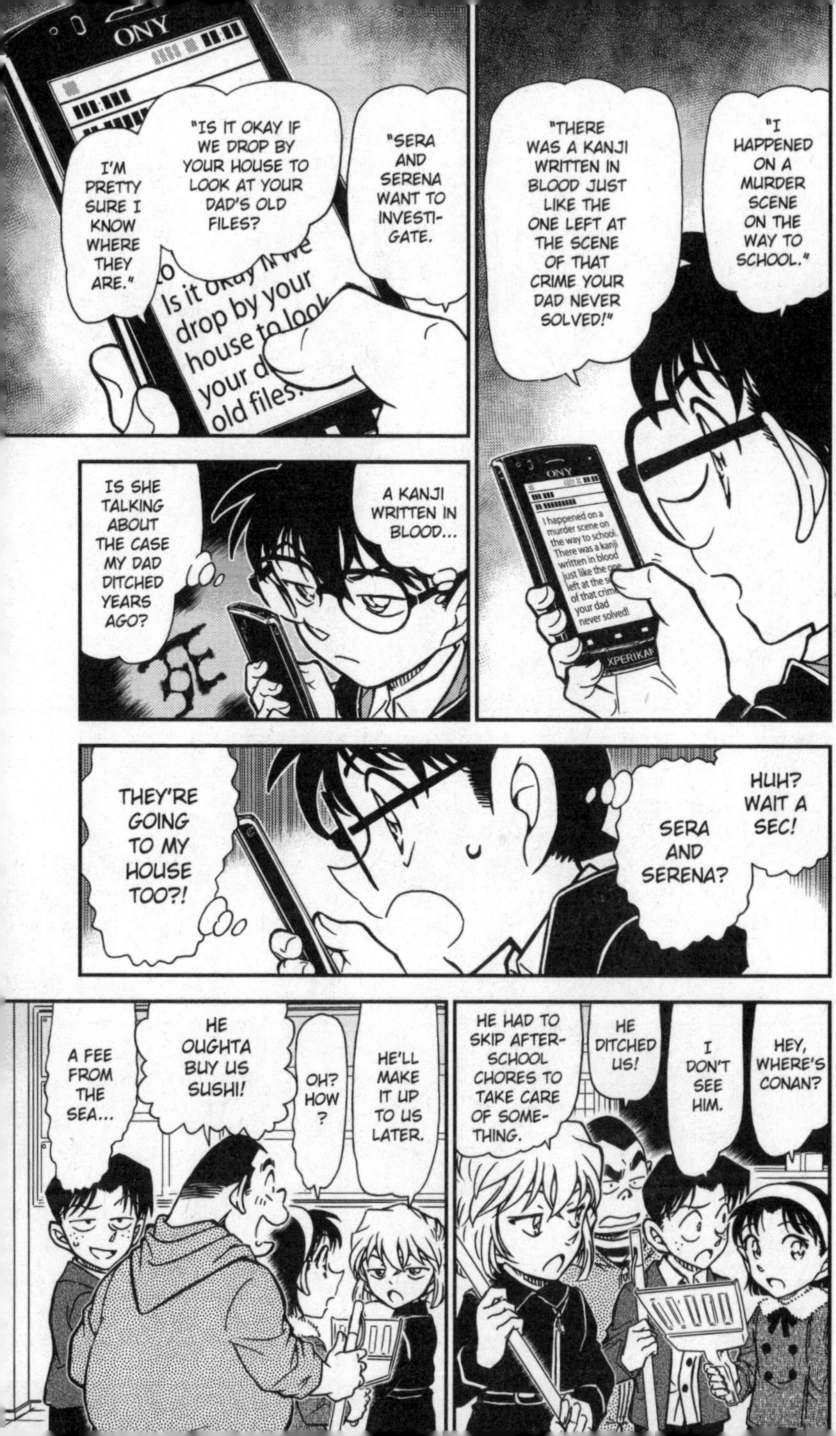

"I HAPPENED ON A MURDER SCENE ON THE WAY TO SCHOOL."
"THERE WAS A KANJI WRITTEN IN BLOOD JUST LIKE THE ONE LEFT AT THE SCENE OF THAT CRIME YOUR DAD NEVER SOLVED!"
ONY
I happened on a murder scene on the way to school. There was a kanji written in blood just like the one left at the s of that crim your dad never solved!
XPERIKAN
ONY
"SERA AND SERENA WANT TO INVESTI-GATE.
"IS IT OKAY IF WE DROP BY YOUR HOUSE TO LOOK AT YOUR DAD'S OLD FILES?
I'M PRETTY SURE I KNOW WHERE THEY ARE."
Is it okay if we
drop by your
house to look
old files?
A KANJI WRITTEN IN BLOOD...
IS SHE TALKING ABOUT THE CASE MY DAD DITCHED YEARS AGO?
HUH? WAIT A SEC!
SERA AND SERENA?
THEY'RE GOING TO MY HOUSE TOO?!
HEY, WHERE'S CONAN?
I DON'T SEE HIM.
HE DITCHED US!
HE HAD TO SKIP AFTER-SCHOOL CHORES TO TAKE CARE OF SOME-THING.
HE'LL MAKE IT UP TO US LATER.
OH? HOW?
HE OUGHTA BUY US SUSHI!
A FEE FROM THE SEA...

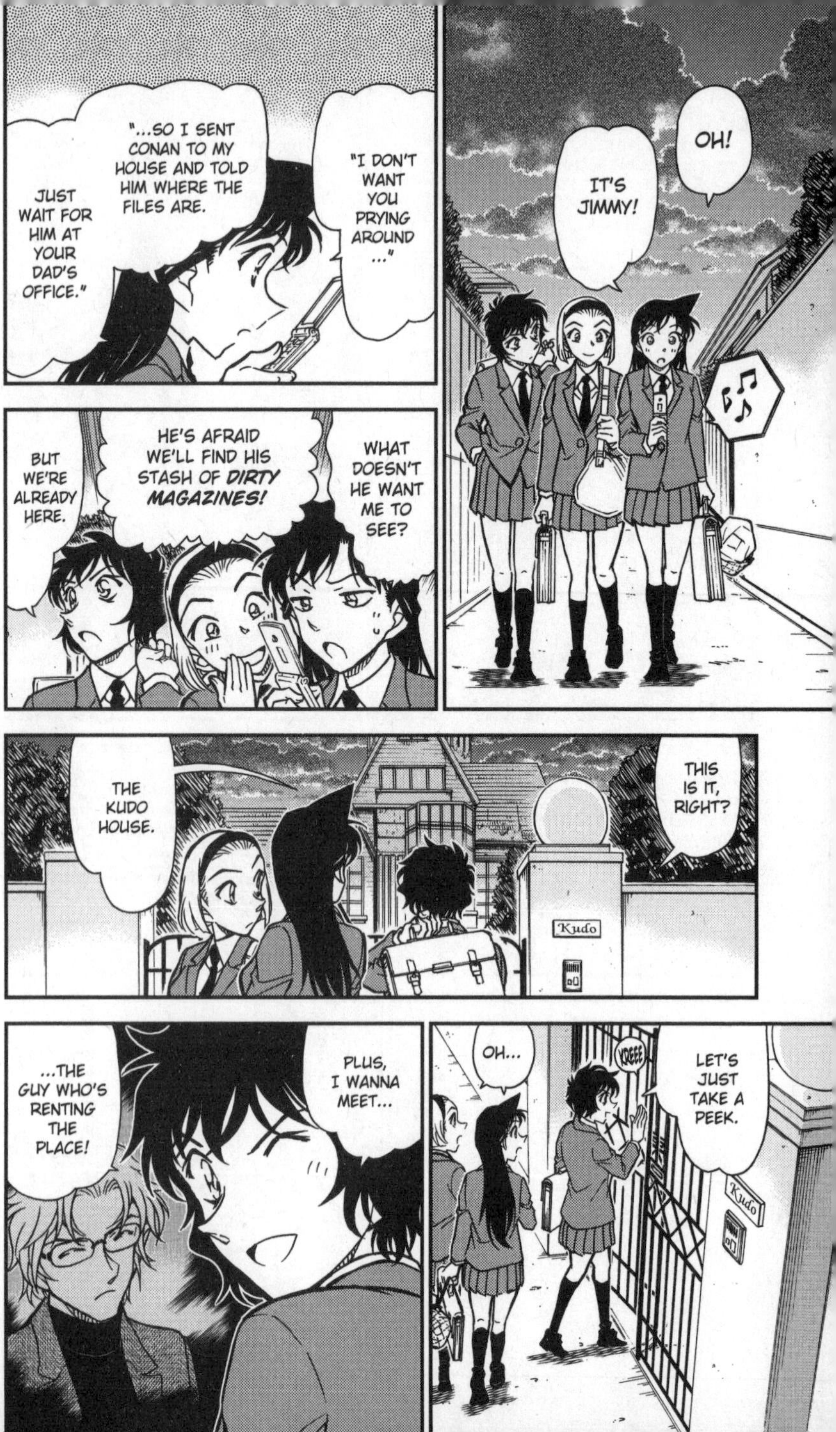
OH!
IT'S JIMMY!
"I DON'T WANT YOU PRYING AROUND ..."
"...SO I SENT CONAN TO MY HOUSE AND TOLD HIM WHERE THE FILES ARE.
JUST WAIT FOR HIM AT YOUR DAD'S OFFICE."
WHAT DOESN'T HE WANT ME TO SEE?
HE'S AFRAID WE'LL FIND HIS STASH OF DIRTY MAGAZINES!
BUT WE'RE ALREADY HERE.
THIS IS IT, RIGHT?
THE KUDO HOUSE.
Kudo
LET'S JUST TAKE A PEEK.
KREEE
OH...
Kudo
PLUS, I WANNA MEET...
...THE GUY WHO'S RENTING THE PLACE!

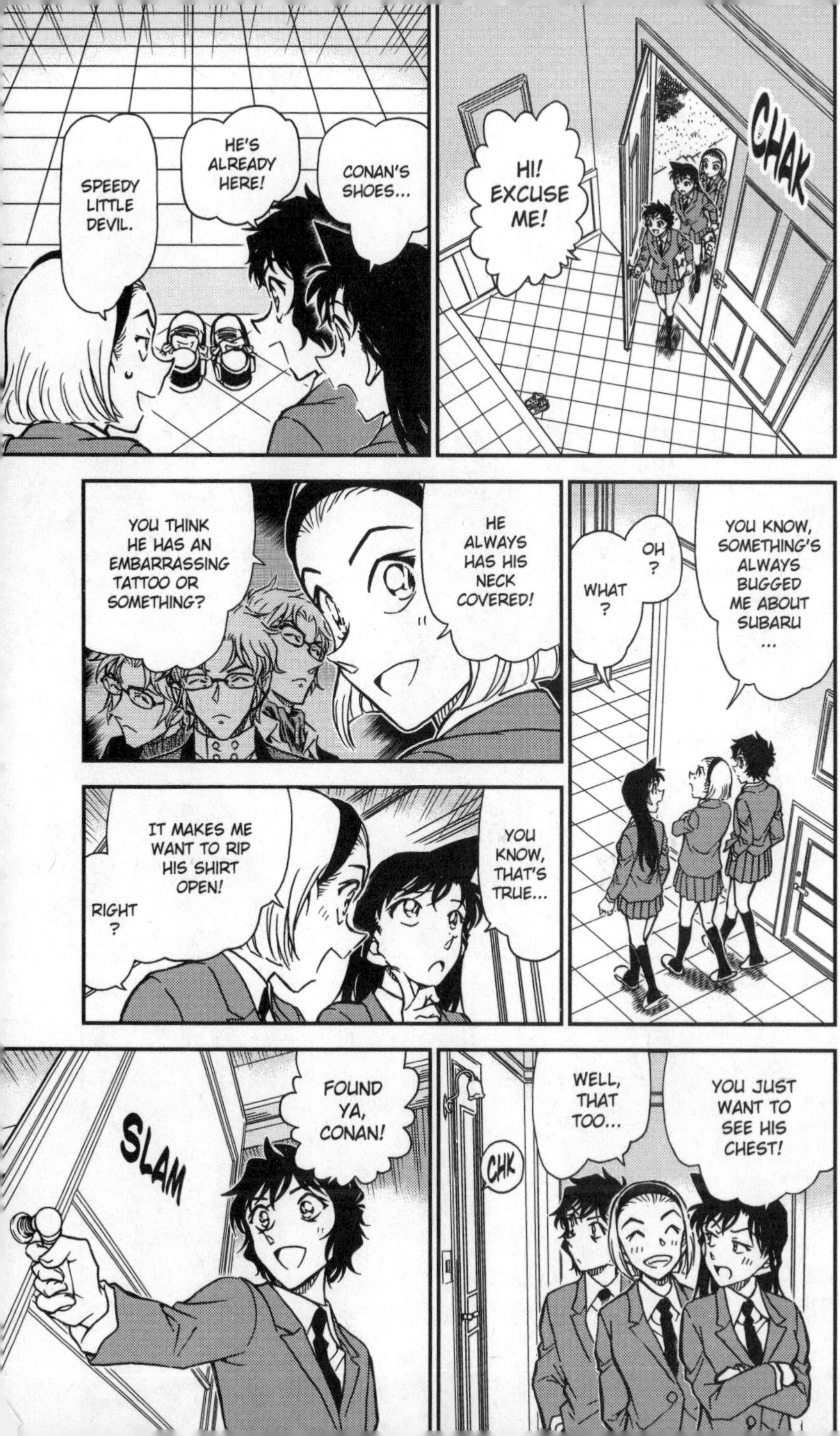
CHAK
HI! EXCUSE ME!
CONAN'S SHOES...
HE'S ALREADY HERE!
SPEEDY LITTLE DEVIL.
YOU KNOW, SOMETHING'S ALWAYS BUGGED ME ABOUT SUBARU...
OH?
WHAT?
HE ALWAYS HAS HIS NECK COVERED!
YOU THINK HE HAS AN EMBARRASSING TATTOO OR SOMETHING?
YOU KNOW, THAT'S TRUE...
IT MAKES ME WANT TO RIP HIS SHIRT OPEN!
RIGHT?
YOU JUST WANT TO SEE HIS CHEST!
WELL, THAT TOO...
CHK
FOUND YA, CONAN!
SLAM

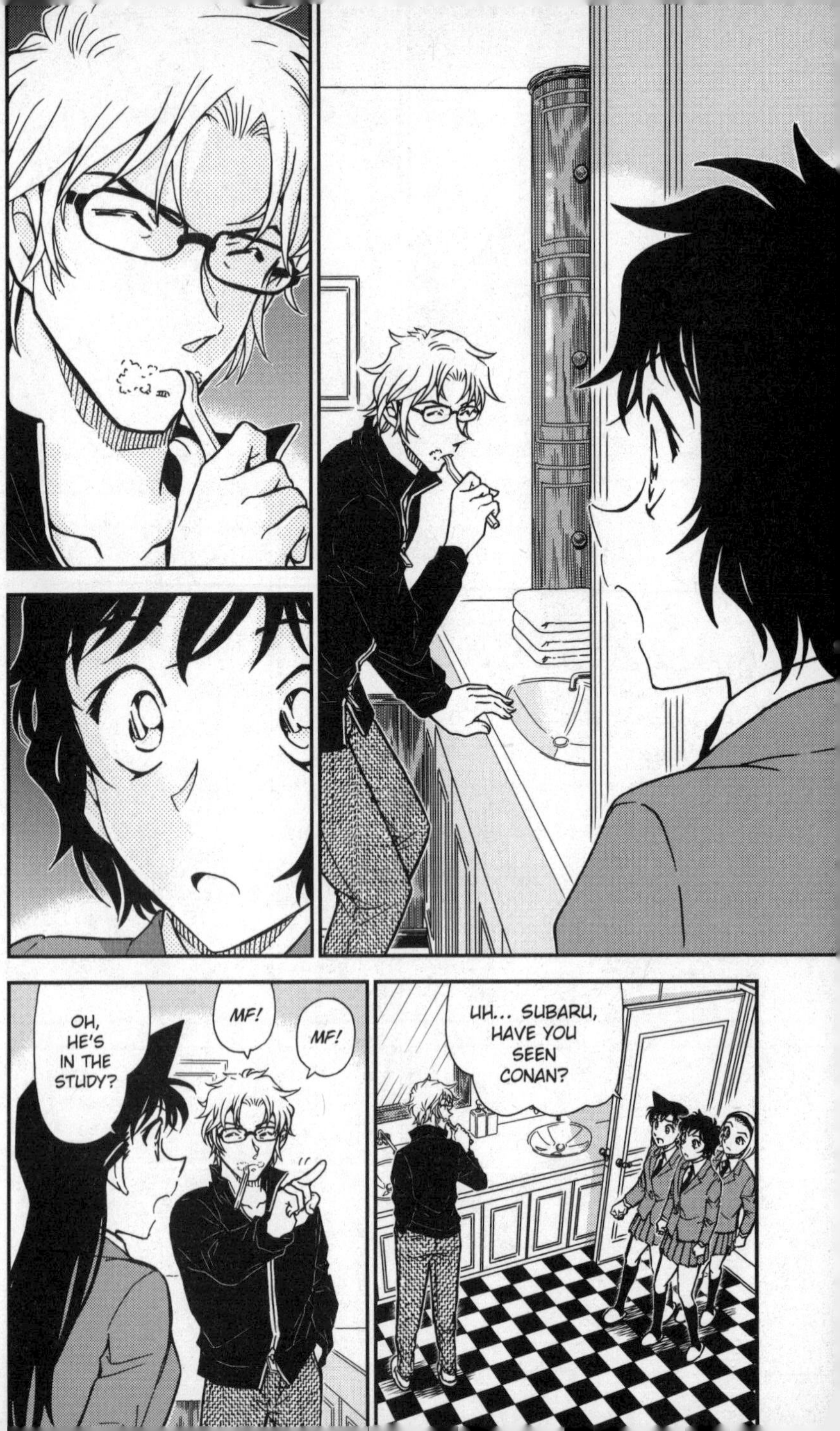
UH... SUBARU, HAVE YOU SEEN CONAN?
MF!
MF!
OH, HE'S IN THE STUDY?

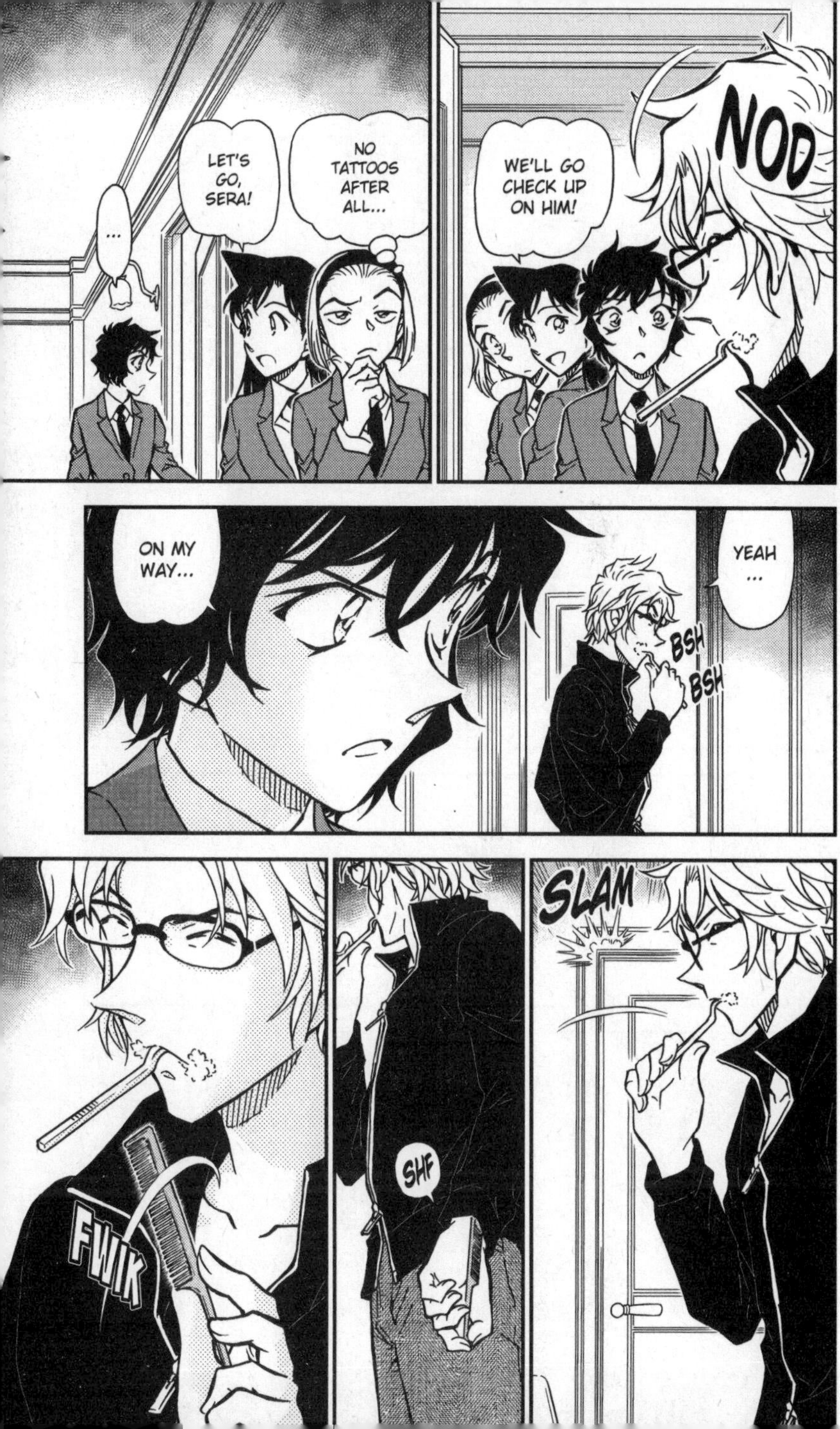
NOD
WE'LL GO CHECK UP ON HIM!
NO TATTOOS AFTER ALL...
LET'S GO, SERA!
...
YEAH ...
BSH
BSH
ON MY WAY...
SLAM
SHF
FWIK

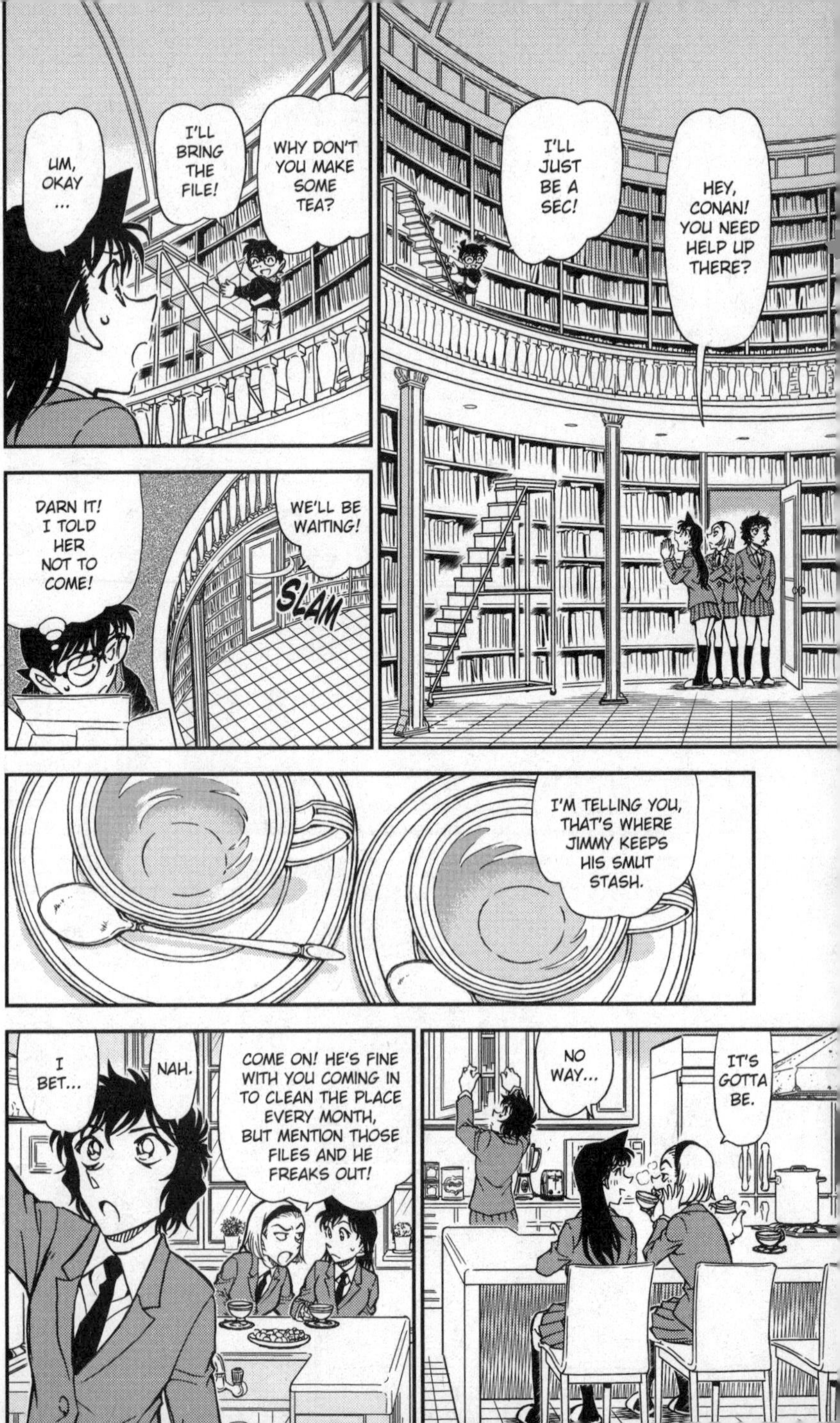
HEY, CONAN! YOU NEED HELP UP THERE?
I'LL JUST BE A SEC!
WHY DON'T YOU MAKE SOME TEA?
I'LL BRING THE FILE!
UM, OKAY ...
WE'LL BE WAITING!
SLAM
DARN IT! I TOLD HER NOT TO COME!
I'M TELLING YOU, THAT'S WHERE JIMMY KEEPS HIS SMUT STASH.
IT'S GOTTA BE.
NO WAY...
COME ON! HE'S FINE WITH YOU COMING IN TO CLEAN THE PLACE EVERY MONTH, BUT MENTION THOSE FILES AND HE FREAKS OUT!
NAH.
I BET...

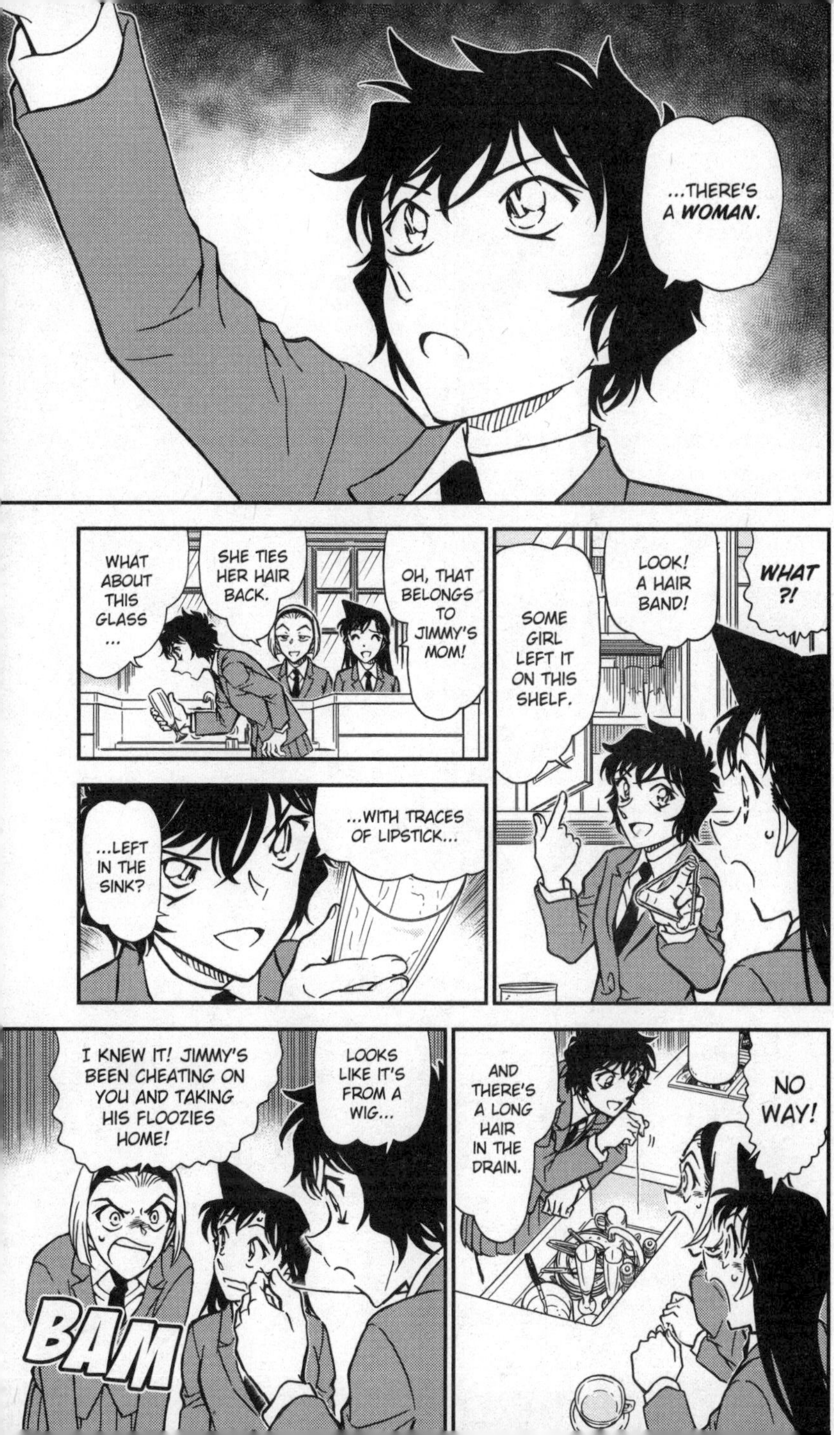
...THERE'S A *WOMAN*.
WHAT ?!
LOOK! A HAIR BAND!
SOME GIRL LEFT IT ON THIS SHELF.
OH, THAT BELONGS TO JIMMY'S MOM!
SHE TIES HER HAIR BACK.
WHAT ABOUT THIS GLASS ...
...WITH TRACES OF LIPSTICK...
...LEFT IN THE SINK?
NO WAY!
AND THERE'S A LONG HAIR IN THE DRAIN.
LOOKS LIKE IT'S FROM A WIG...
I KNEW IT! JIMMY'S BEEN CHEATING ON YOU AND TAKING HIS FLOOZIES HOME!
BAM

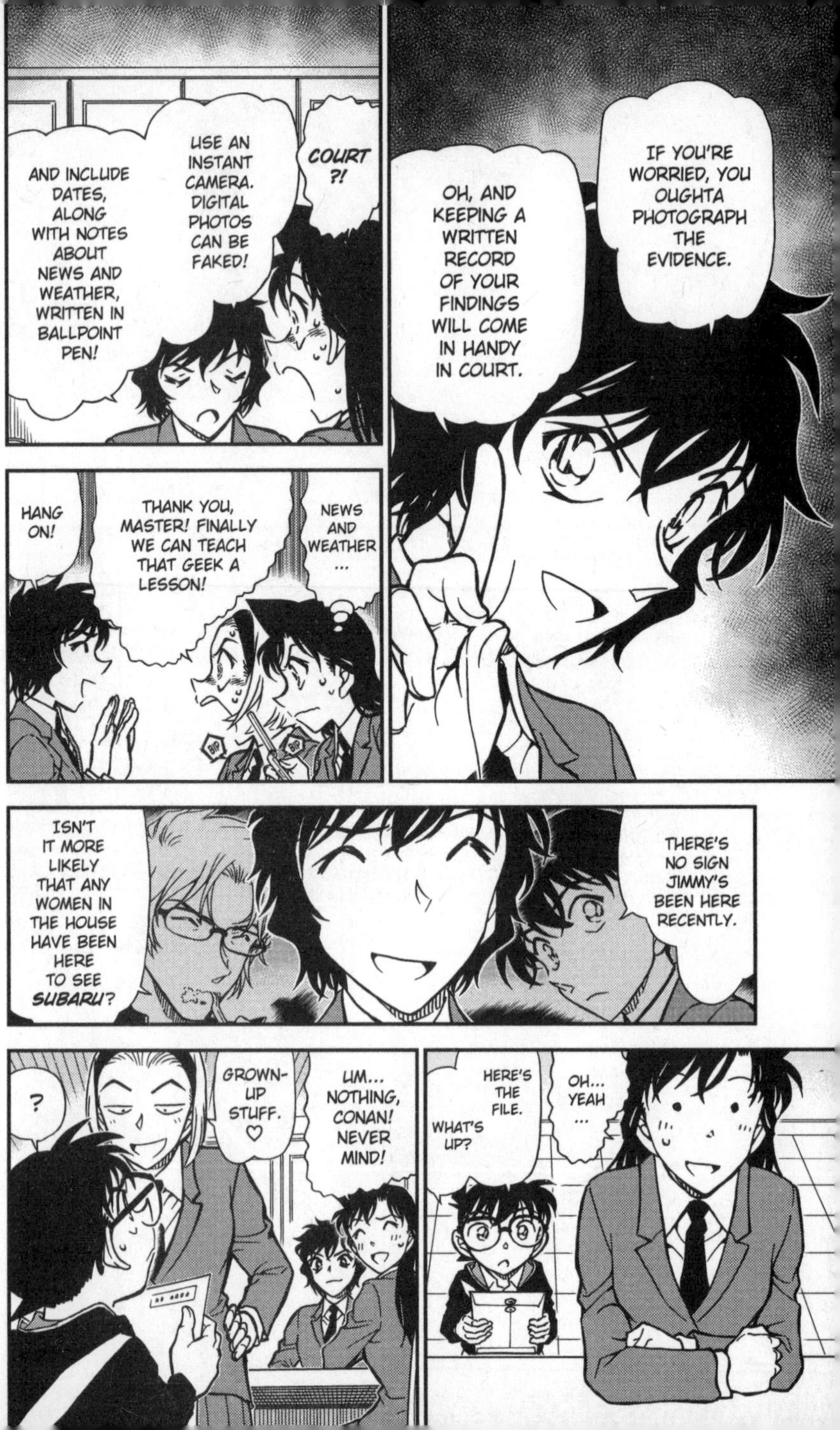
IF YOU'RE WORRIED, YOU OUGHTA PHOTOGRAPH THE EVIDENCE.
OH, AND KEEPING A WRITTEN RECORD OF YOUR FINDINGS WILL COME IN HANDY IN COURT.
COURT ?!
USE AN INSTANT CAMERA. DIGITAL PHOTOS CAN BE FAKED!
AND INCLUDE DATES, ALONG WITH NOTES ABOUT NEWS AND WEATHER, WRITTEN IN BALLPOINT PEN!
NEWS AND WEATHER ...
THANK YOU, MASTER! FINALLY WE CAN TEACH THAT GEEK A LESSON!
HANG ON!
BIP
BIP
THERE'S NO SIGN JIMMY'S BEEN HERE RECENTLY.
ISN'T IT MORE LIKELY THAT ANY WOMEN IN THE HOUSE HAVE BEEN HERE TO SEE SUBARU?
OH... YEAH ...
HERE'S THE FILE.
WHAT'S UP?
UM... NOTHING, CONAN! NEVER MIND!
GROWN-UP STUFF. ♡
?

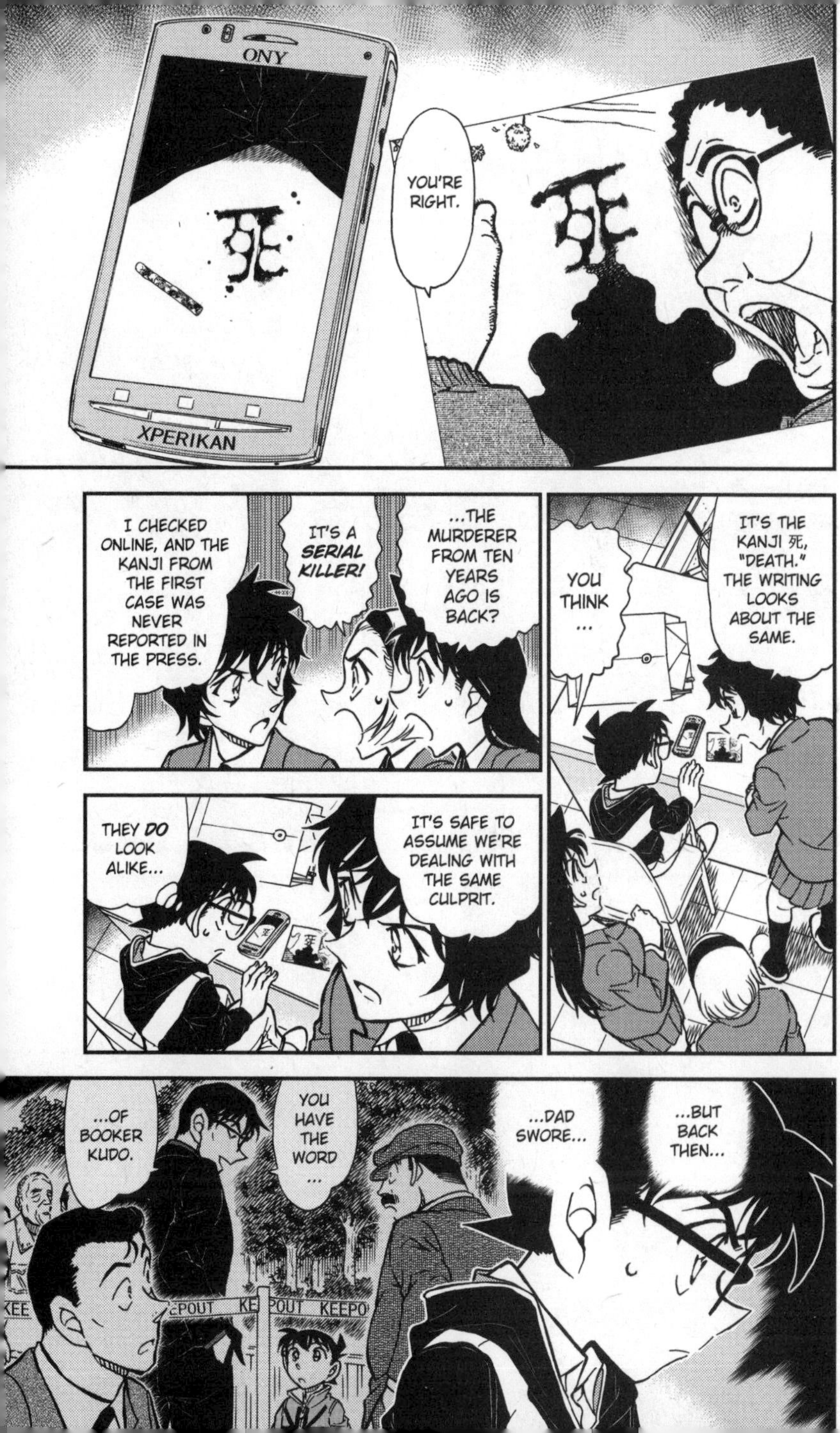
YOU'RE RIGHT.
ONY
XPERIKAN
IT'S THE KANJI 死, "DEATH." THE WRITING LOOKS ABOUT THE SAME.
YOU THINK ...
...THE MURDERER FROM TEN YEARS AGO IS BACK?
IT'S A *SERIAL KILLER!*
I CHECKED ONLINE, AND THE KANJI FROM THE FIRST CASE WAS NEVER REPORTED IN THE PRESS.
IT'S SAFE TO ASSUME WE'RE DEALING WITH THE SAME CULPRIT.
THEY *DO* LOOK ALIKE...
...BUT BACK THEN...
...DAD SWORE...
YOU HAVE THE WORD ...
...OF BOOKER KUDO.

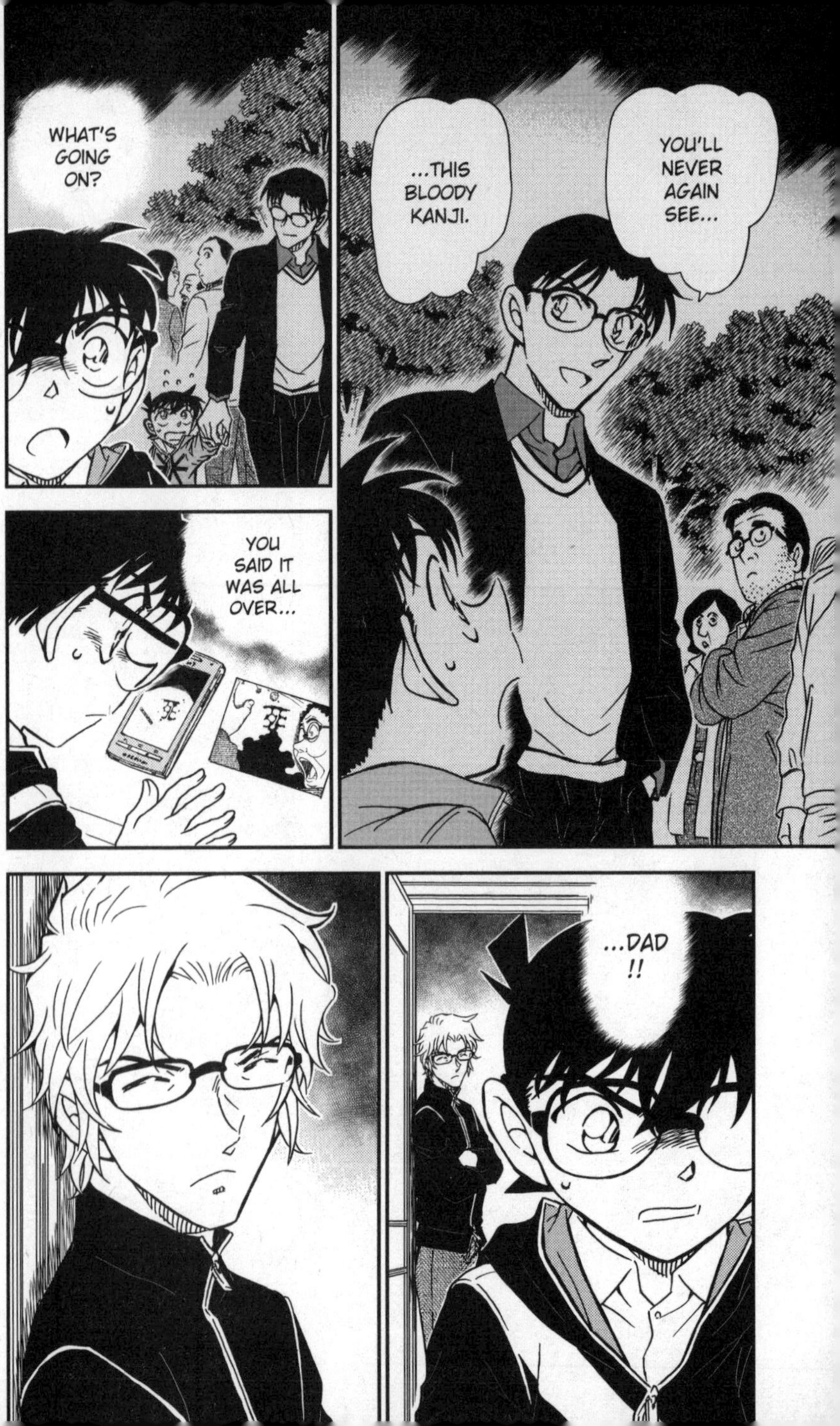
YOU'LL NEVER AGAIN SEE...
...THIS BLOODY KANJI.
WHAT'S GOING ON?
YOU SAID IT WAS ALL OVER...
...DAD !!

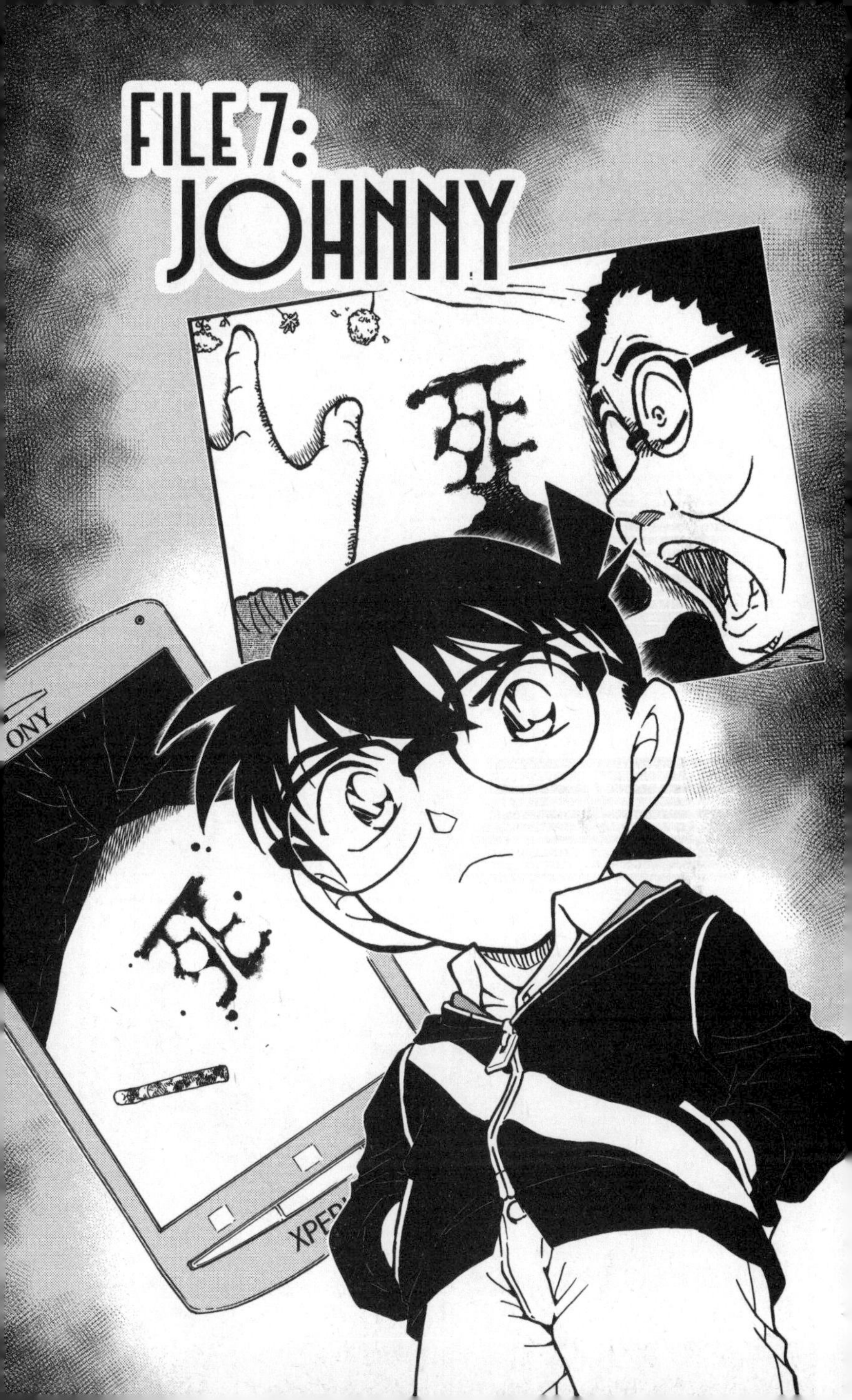
FILE 7:
JOHNNY

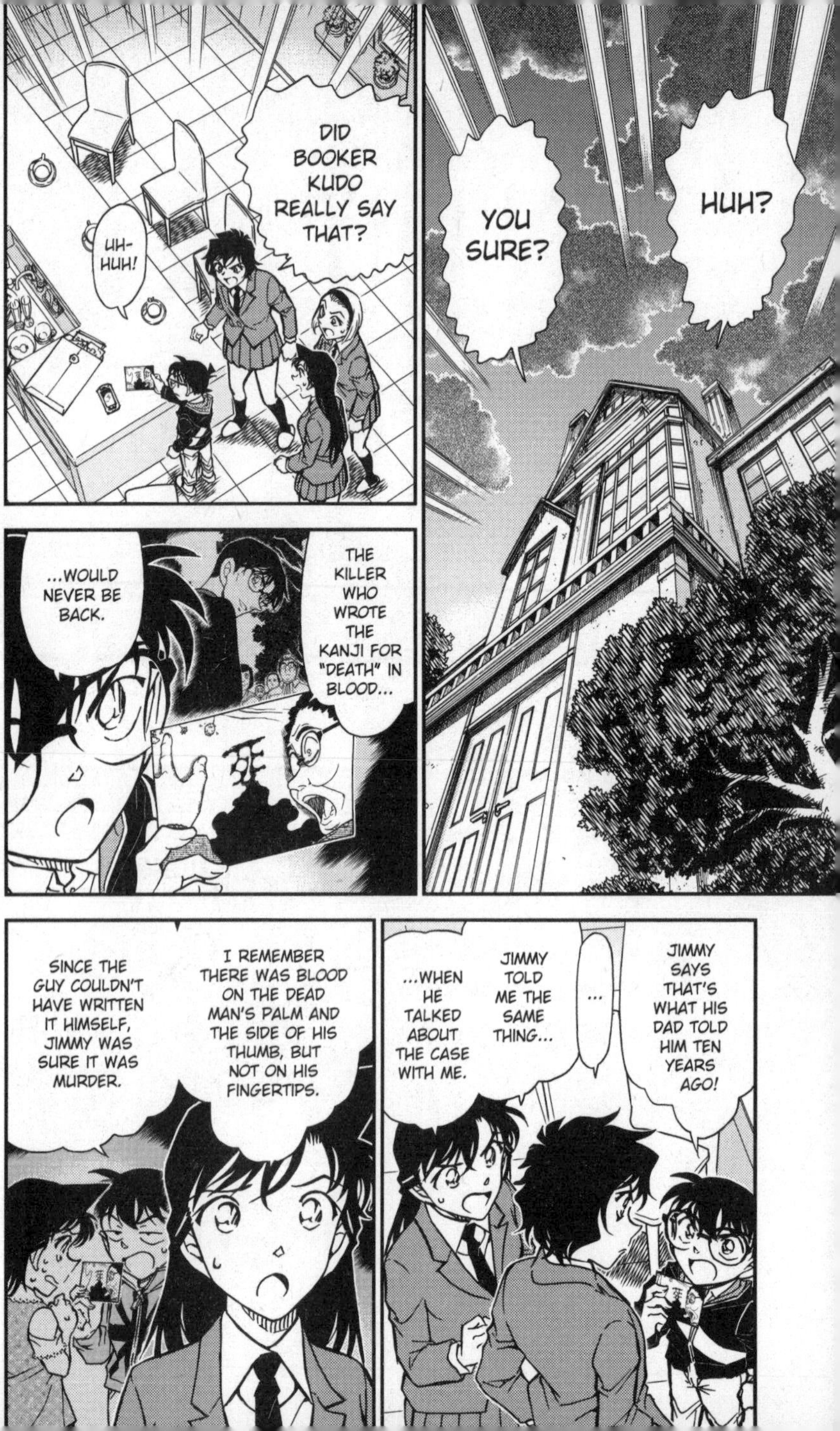
HUH?
YOU SURE?
DID BOOKER KUDO REALLY SAY THAT?
UH-HUH!
THE KILLER WHO WROTE THE KANJI FOR "DEATH" IN BLOOD...
...WOULD NEVER BE BACK.
JIMMY SAYS THAT'S WHAT HIS DAD TOLD HIM TEN YEARS AGO!
...
JIMMY TOLD ME THE SAME THING...
...WHEN HE TALKED ABOUT THE CASE WITH ME.
I REMEMBER THERE WAS BLOOD ON THE DEAD MAN'S PALM AND THE SIDE OF HIS THUMB, BUT NOT ON HIS FINGERTIPS.
SINCE THE GUY COULDN'T HAVE WRITTEN IT HIMSELF, JIMMY WAS SURE IT WAS MURDER.

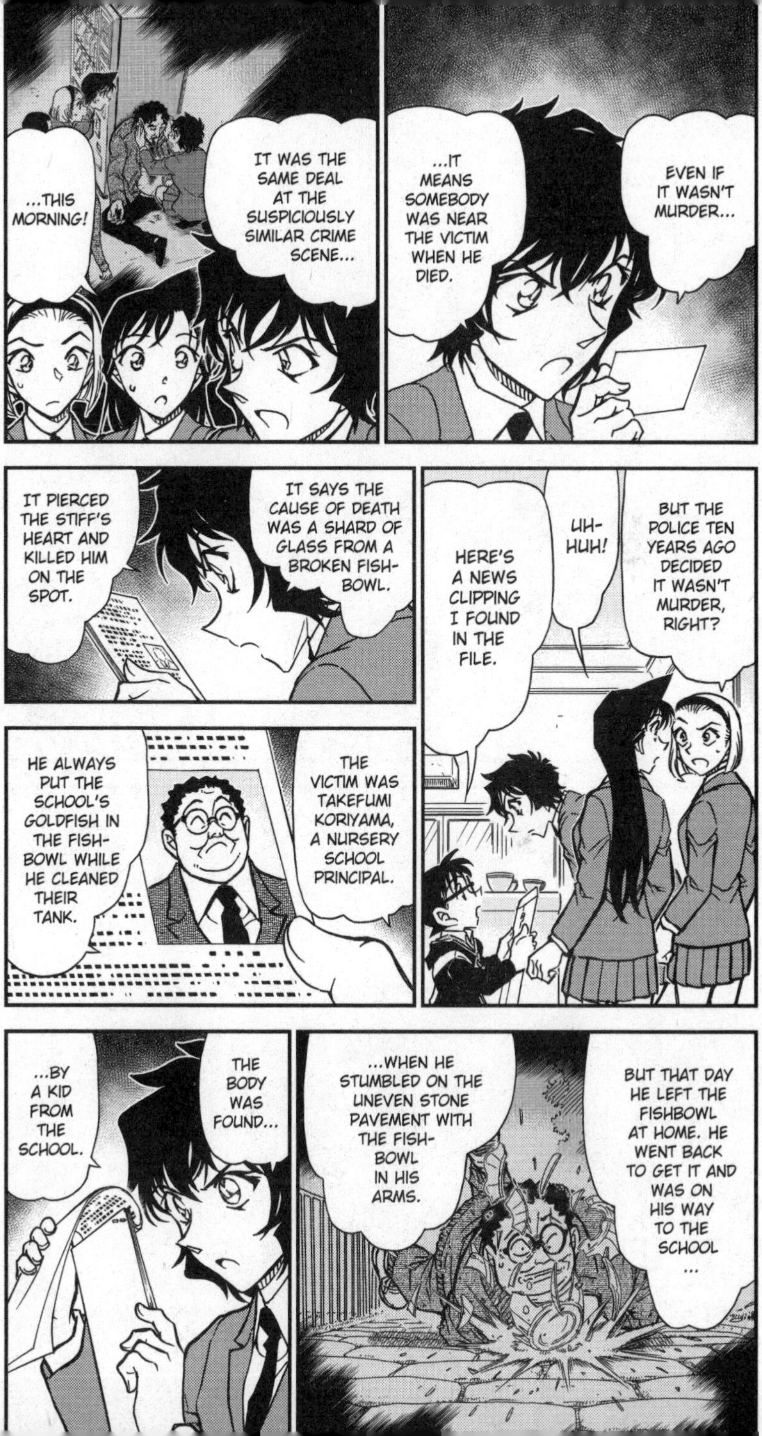
EVEN IF IT WASN'T MURDER...
...IT MEANS SOMEBODY WAS NEAR THE VICTIM WHEN HE DIED.
IT WAS THE SAME DEAL AT THE SUSPICIOUSLY SIMILAR CRIME SCENE...
...THIS MORNING!
BUT THE POLICE TEN YEARS AGO DECIDED IT WASN'T MURDER, RIGHT?
UH-HUH!
HERE'S A NEWS CLIPPING I FOUND IN THE FILE.
IT SAYS THE CAUSE OF DEATH WAS A SHARD OF GLASS FROM A BROKEN FISH-BOWL.
IT PIERCED THE STIFF'S HEART AND KILLED HIM ON THE SPOT.
THE VICTIM WAS TAKEFUMI KORIYAMA, A NURSERY SCHOOL PRINCIPAL.
HE ALWAYS PUT THE SCHOOL'S GOLDFISH IN THE FISH-BOWL WHILE HE CLEANED THEIR TANK.
BUT THAT DAY HE LEFT THE FISHBOWL AT HOME. HE WENT BACK TO GET IT AND WAS ON HIS WAY TO THE SCHOOL ...
...WHEN HE STUMBLED ON THE UNEVEN STONE PAVEMENT WITH THE FISH-BOWL IN HIS ARMS.
THE BODY WAS FOUND...
...BY A KID FROM THE SCHOOL.

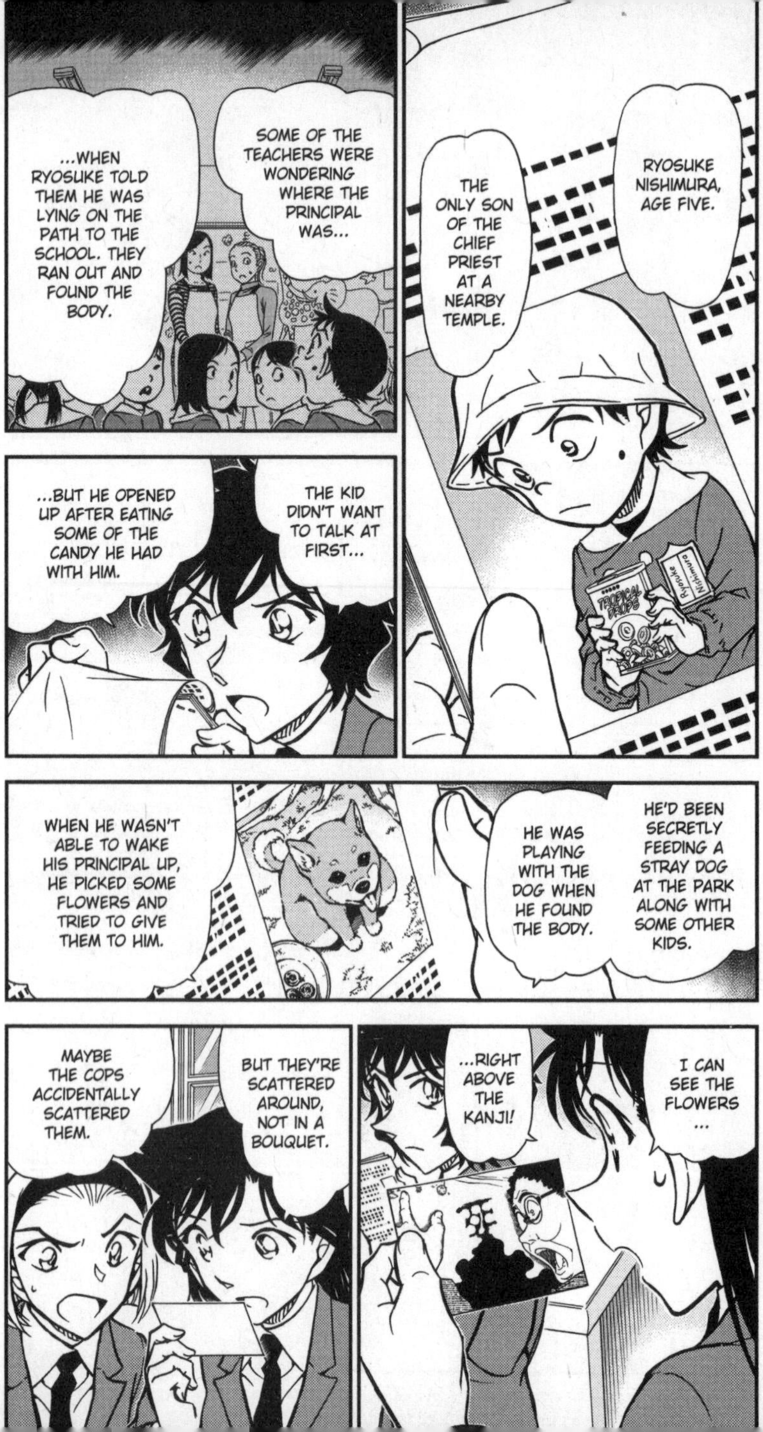
RYOSUKE NISHIMURA, AGE FIVE.
THE ONLY SON OF THE CHIEF PRIEST AT A NEARBY TEMPLE.
TROPICAL DROPS
Ryosuke Nishimura
SOME OF THE TEACHERS WERE WONDERING WHERE THE PRINCIPAL WAS...
...WHEN RYOSUKE TOLD THEM HE WAS LYING ON THE PATH TO THE SCHOOL. THEY RAN OUT AND FOUND THE BODY.
THE KID DIDN'T WANT TO TALK AT FIRST...
...BUT HE OPENED UP AFTER EATING SOME OF THE CANDY HE HAD WITH HIM.
HE'D BEEN SECRETLY FEEDING A STRAY DOG AT THE PARK ALONG WITH SOME OTHER KIDS.
HE WAS PLAYING WITH THE DOG WHEN HE FOUND THE BODY.
WHEN HE WASN'T ABLE TO WAKE HIS PRINCIPAL UP, HE PICKED SOME FLOWERS AND TRIED TO GIVE THEM TO HIM.
I CAN SEE THE FLOWERS ...
...RIGHT ABOVE THE KANJI!
BUT THEY'RE SCATTERED AROUND, NOT IN A BOUQUET.
MAYBE THE COPS ACCIDENTALLY SCATTERED THEM.

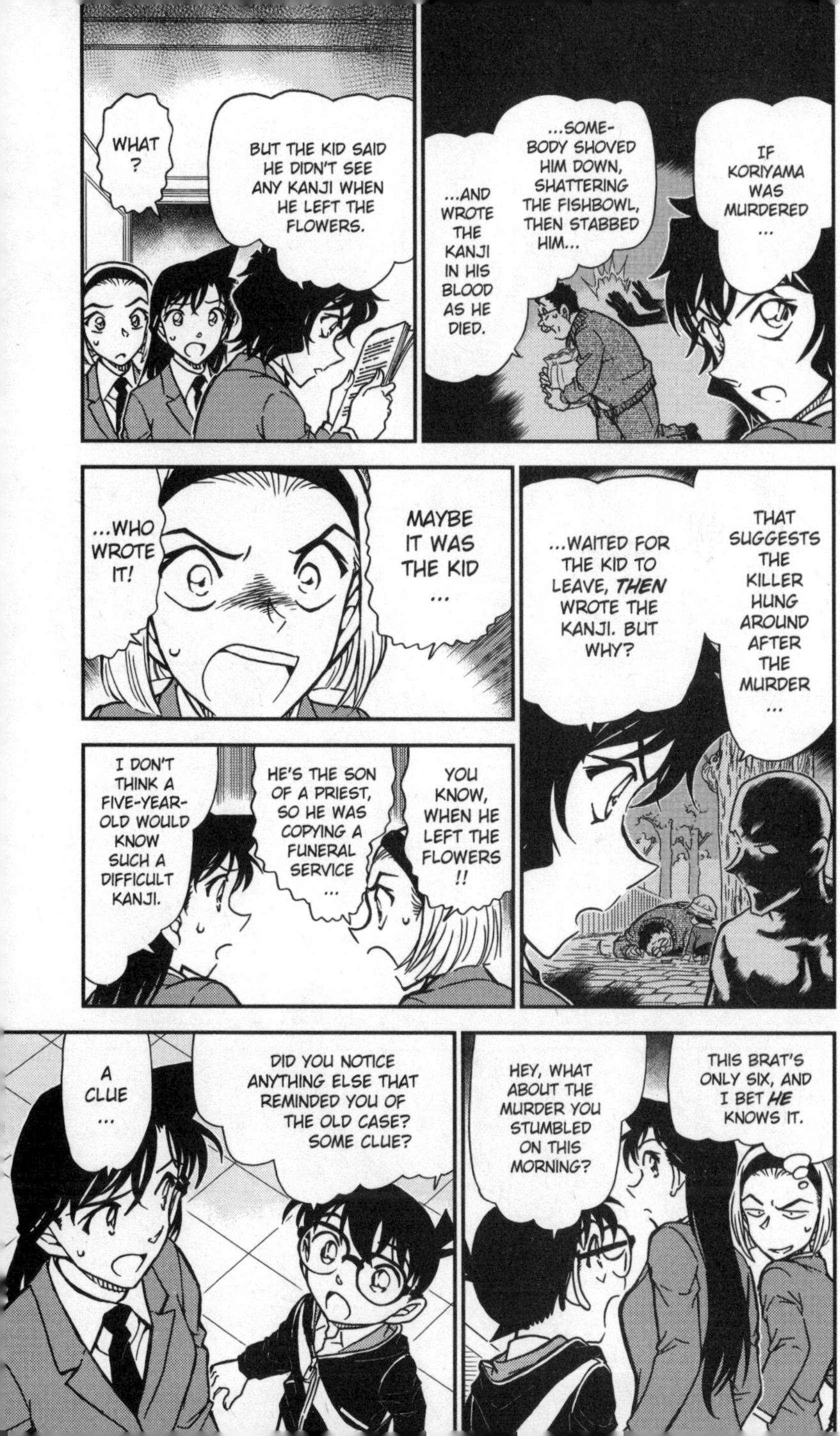
IF KORIYAMA WAS MURDERED ...
...SOMEBODY SHOVED HIM DOWN, SHATTERING THE FISHBOWL, THEN STABBED HIM...
...AND WROTE THE KANJI IN HIS BLOOD AS HE DIED.
BUT THE KID SAID HE DIDN'T SEE ANY KANJI WHEN HE LEFT THE FLOWERS.
WHAT?
THAT SUGGESTS THE KILLER HUNG AROUND AFTER THE MURDER ...
...WAITED FOR THE KID TO LEAVE, *THEN* WROTE THE KANJI. BUT WHY?
MAYBE IT WAS THE KID ...
...WHO WROTE IT!
YOU KNOW, WHEN HE LEFT THE FLOWERS!!
HE'S THE SON OF A PRIEST, SO HE WAS COPYING A FUNERAL SERVICE ...
I DON'T THINK A FIVE-YEAR-OLD WOULD KNOW SUCH A DIFFICULT KANJI.
THIS BRAT'S ONLY SIX, AND I BET *HE* KNOWS IT.
HEY, WHAT ABOUT THE MURDER YOU STUMBLED ON THIS MORNING?
DID YOU NOTICE ANYTHING ELSE THAT REMINDED YOU OF THE OLD CASE? SOME CLUE?
A CLUE ...

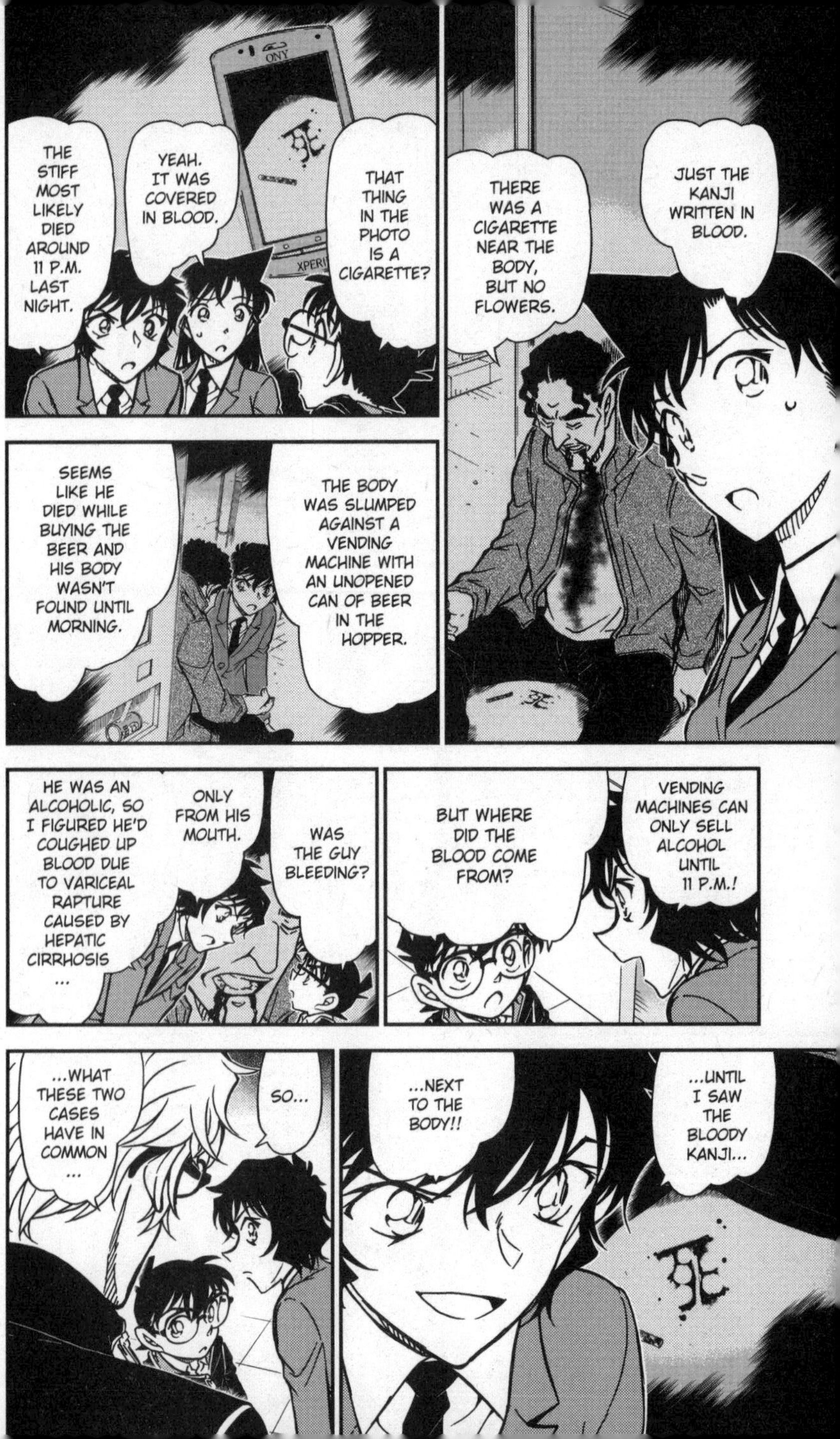
JUST THE KANJI WRITTEN IN BLOOD.
THERE WAS A CIGARETTE NEAR THE BODY, BUT NO FLOWERS.
THAT THING IN THE PHOTO IS A CIGARETTE?
YEAH. IT WAS COVERED IN BLOOD.
THE STIFF MOST LIKELY DIED AROUND 11 P.M. LAST NIGHT.
THE BODY WAS SLUMPED AGAINST A VENDING MACHINE WITH AN UNOPENED CAN OF BEER IN THE HOPPER.
SEEMS LIKE HE DIED WHILE BUYING THE BEER AND HIS BODY WASN'T FOUND UNTIL MORNING.
VENDING MACHINES CAN ONLY SELL ALCOHOL UNTIL 11 P.M.!
BUT WHERE DID THE BLOOD COME FROM?
WAS THE GUY BLEEDING?
ONLY FROM HIS MOUTH.
HE WAS AN ALCOHOLIC, SO I FIGURED HE'D COUGHED UP BLOOD DUE TO VARICEAL RAPTURE CAUSED BY HEPATIC CIRRHOSIS ...
...UNTIL I SAW THE BLOODY KANJI...
...NEXT TO THE BODY!!
SO...
...WHAT THESE TWO CASES HAVE IN COMMON ...

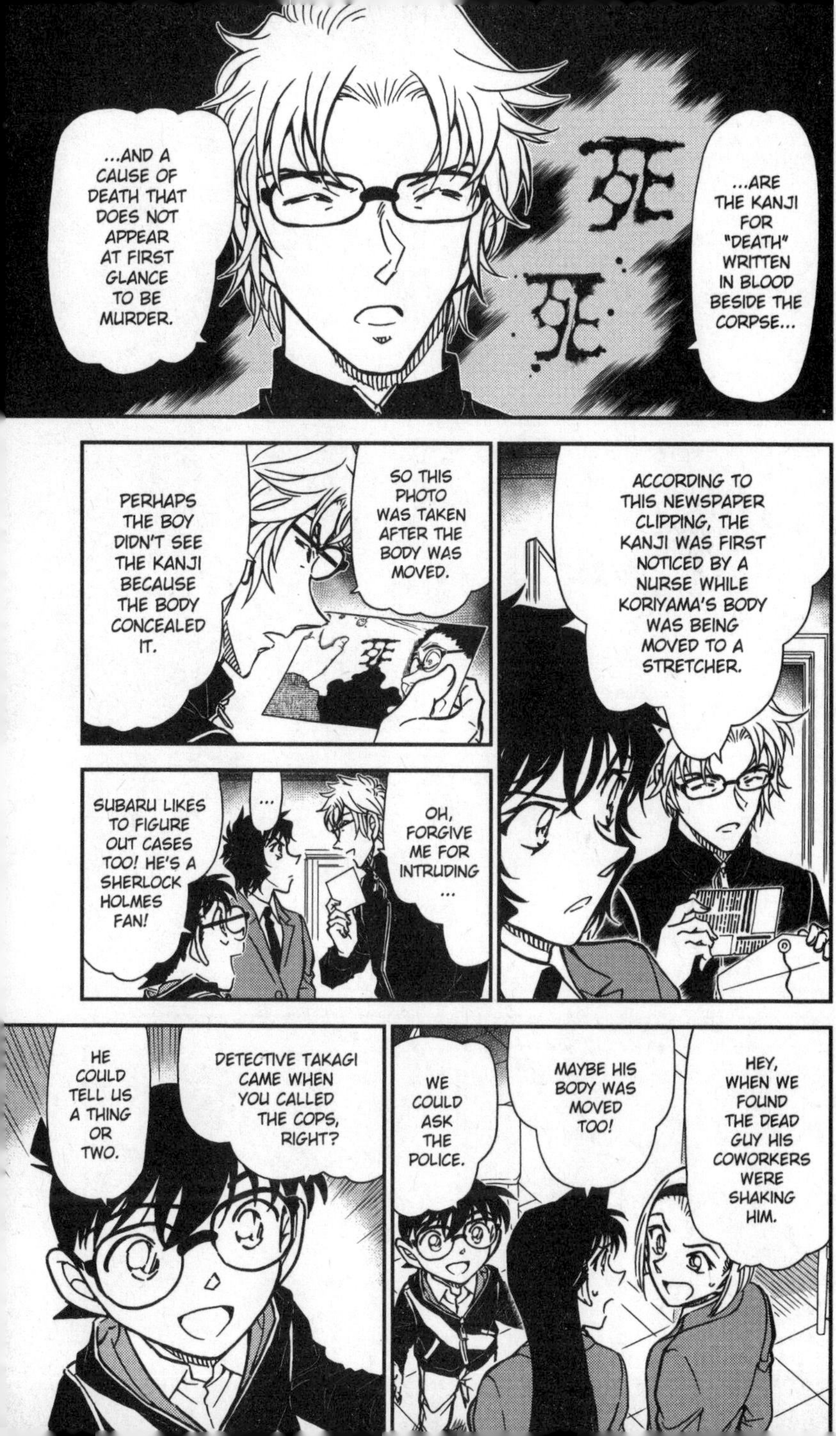
...ARE THE KANJI FOR "DEATH" WRITTEN IN BLOOD BESIDE THE CORPSE...
...AND A CAUSE OF DEATH THAT DOES NOT APPEAR AT FIRST GLANCE TO BE MURDER.
ACCORDING TO THIS NEWSPAPER CLIPPING, THE KANJI WAS FIRST NOTICED BY A NURSE WHILE KORIYAMA'S BODY WAS BEING MOVED TO A STRETCHER.
SO THIS PHOTO WAS TAKEN AFTER THE BODY WAS MOVED.
PERHAPS THE BOY DIDN'T SEE THE KANJI BECAUSE THE BODY CONCEALED IT.
OH, FORGIVE ME FOR INTRUDING ...
...
SUBARU LIKES TO FIGURE OUT CASES TOO! HE'S A SHERLOCK HOLMES FAN!
HEY, WHEN WE FOUND THE DEAD GUY HIS COWORKERS WERE SHAKING HIM.
MAYBE HIS BODY WAS MOVED TOO!
WE COULD ASK THE POLICE.
DETECTIVE TAKAGI CAME WHEN YOU CALLED THE COPS, RIGHT?
HE COULD TELL US A THING OR TWO.

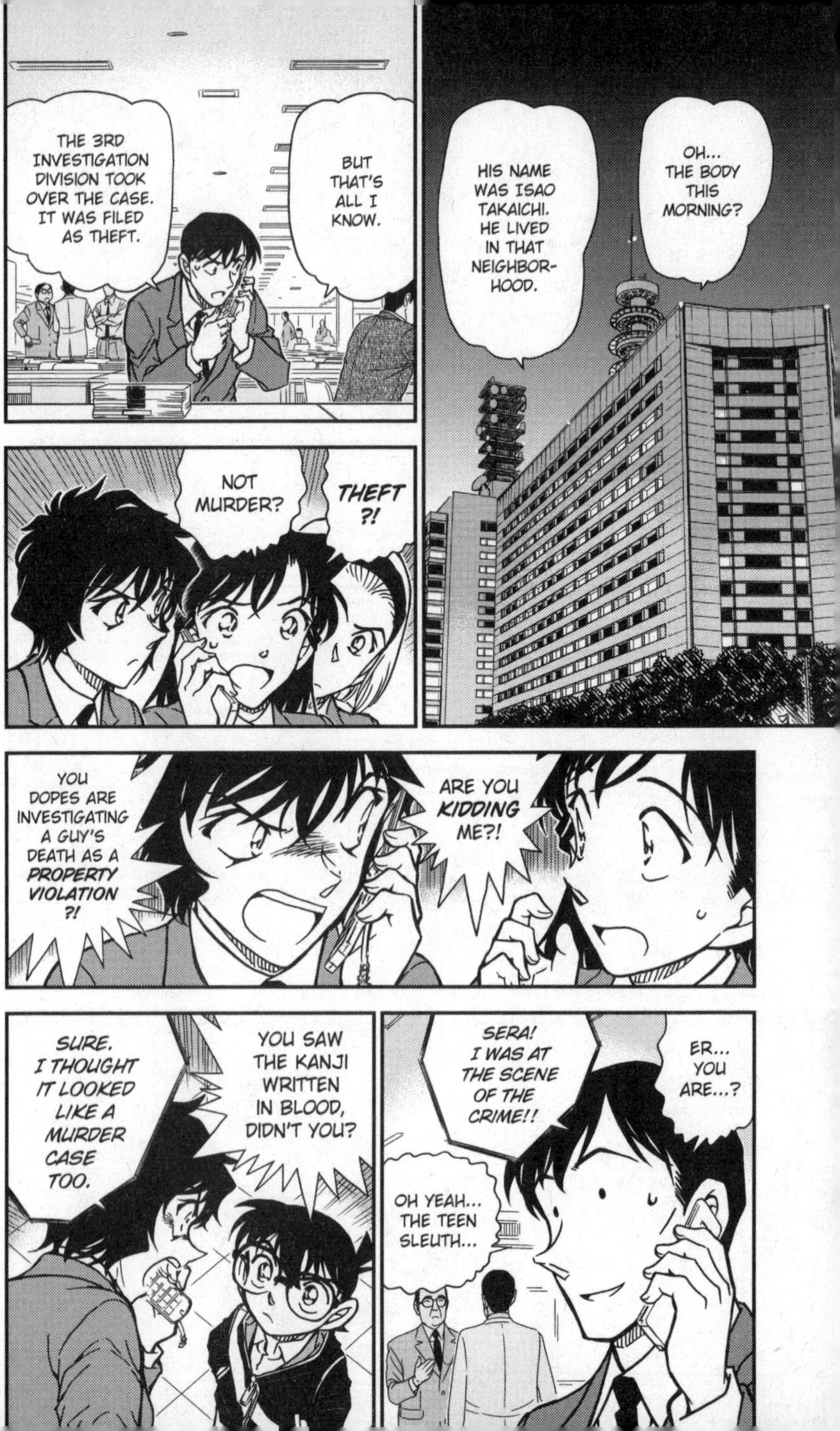
OH... THE BODY THIS MORNING?
HIS NAME WAS ISAO TAKAICHI. HE LIVED IN THAT NEIGHBORHOOD.
THE 3RD INVESTIGATION DIVISION TOOK OVER THE CASE. IT WAS FILED AS THEFT.
BUT THAT'S ALL I KNOW.
THEFT ?!
NOT MURDER?
ARE YOU KIDDING ME?!
YOU DOPES ARE INVESTIGATING A GUY'S DEATH AS A PROPERTY VIOLATION ?!
ER... YOU ARE...?
SERA! I WAS AT THE SCENE OF THE CRIME!!
OH YEAH... THE TEEN SLEUTH...
YOU SAW THE KANJI WRITTEN IN BLOOD, DIDN'T YOU?
SURE. I THOUGHT IT LOOKED LIKE A MURDER CASE TOO.

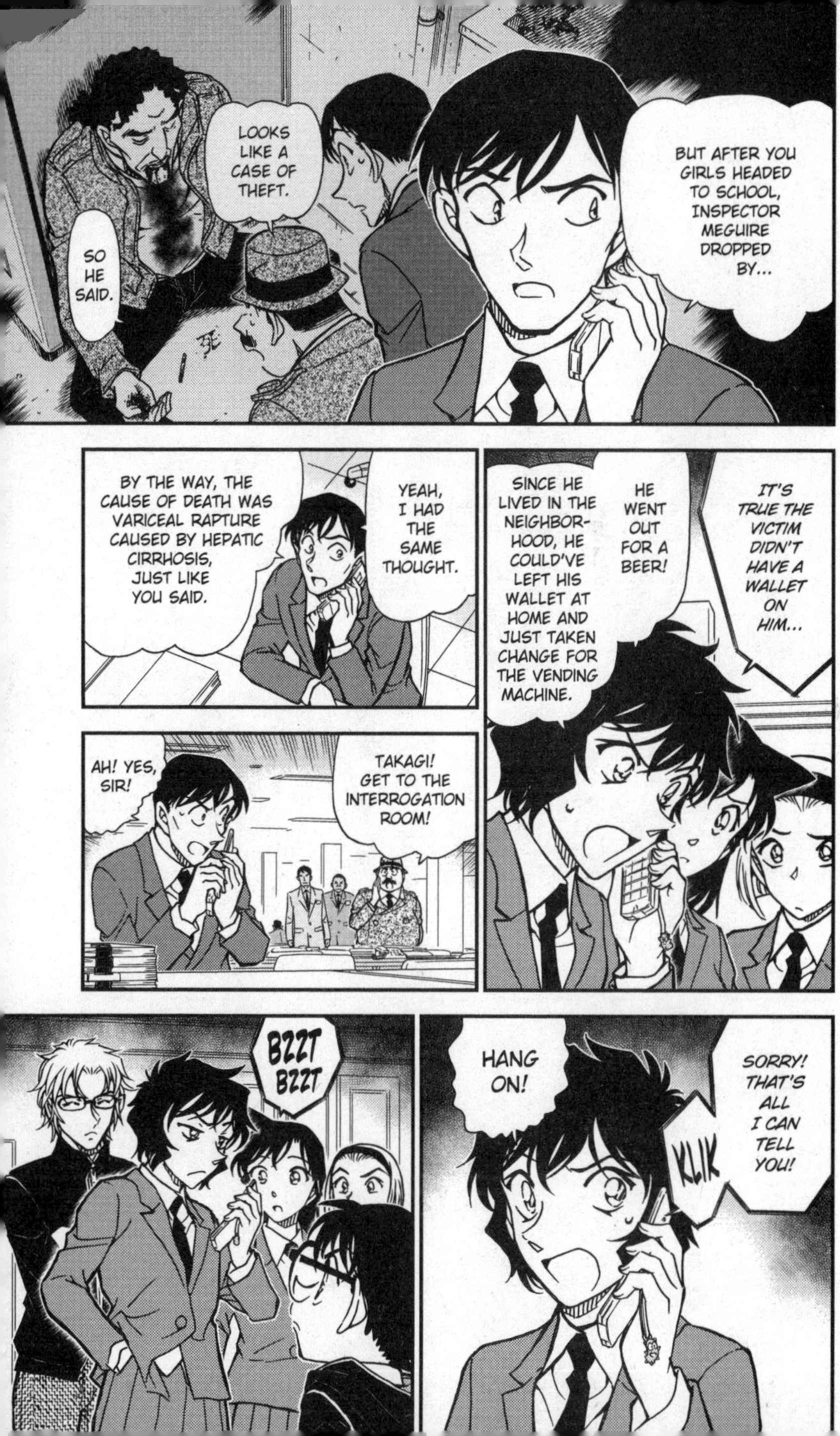
BUT AFTER YOU GIRLS HEADED TO SCHOOL, INSPECTOR MEGUIRE DROPPED BY...
LOOKS LIKE A CASE OF THEFT.
SO HE SAID.
IT'S TRUE THE VICTIM DIDN'T HAVE A WALLET ON HIM...
HE WENT OUT FOR A BEER!
SINCE HE LIVED IN THE NEIGHBOR-HOOD, HE COULD'VE LEFT HIS WALLET AT HOME AND JUST TAKEN CHANGE FOR THE VENDING MACHINE.
YEAH, I HAD THE SAME THOUGHT.
BY THE WAY, THE CAUSE OF DEATH WAS VARICEAL RAPTURE CAUSED BY HEPATIC CIRRHOSIS, JUST LIKE YOU SAID.
TAKAGI! GET TO THE INTERROGATION ROOM!
AH! YES, SIR!
SORRY! THAT'S ALL I CAN TELL YOU!
KLIK
HANG ON!
BZZT BZZT

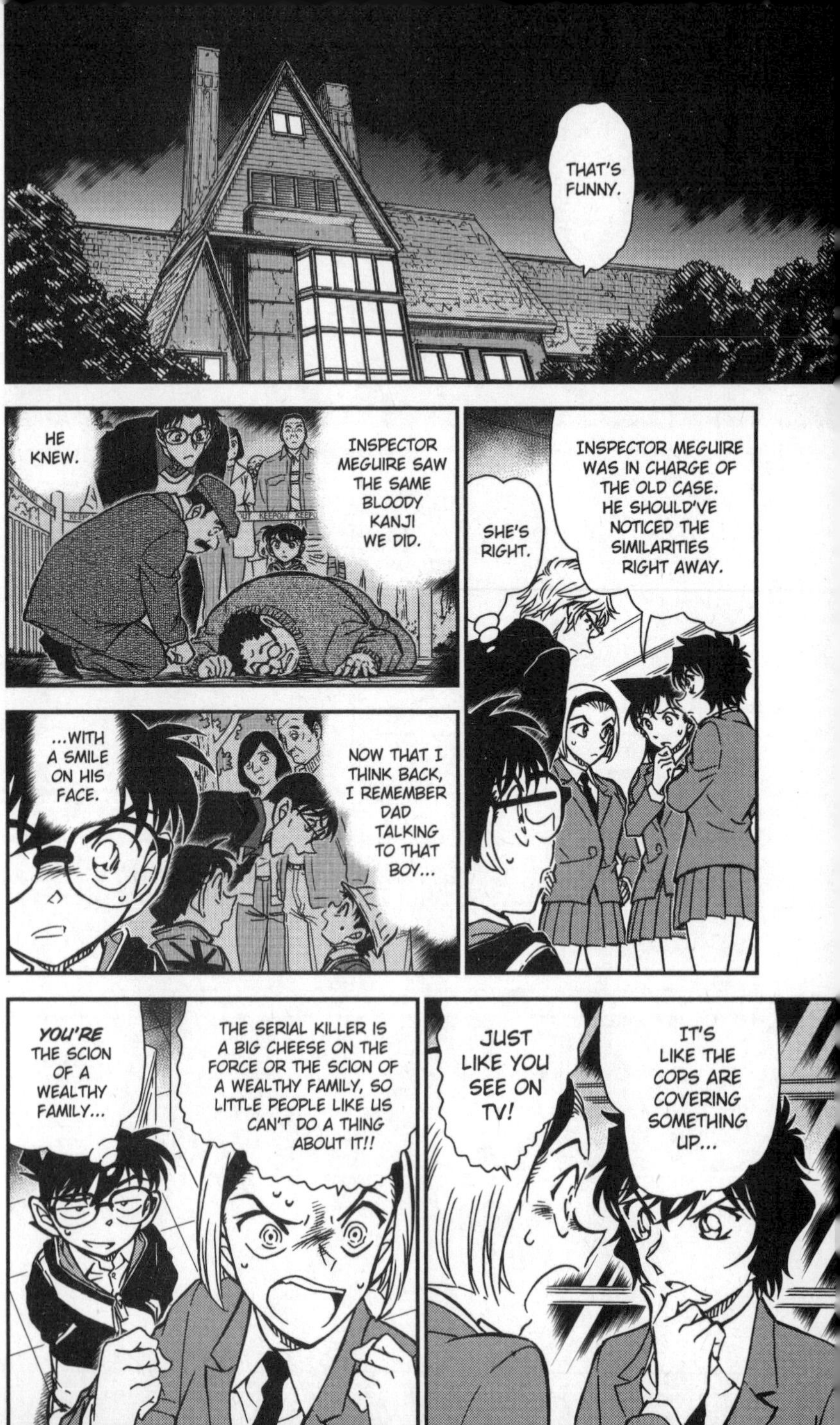
THAT'S FUNNY.
INSPECTOR MEGUIRE WAS IN CHARGE OF THE OLD CASE. HE SHOULD'VE NOTICED THE SIMILARITIES RIGHT AWAY.
SHE'S RIGHT.
INSPECTOR MEGUIRE SAW THE SAME BLOODY KANJI WE DID.
HE KNEW.
NOW THAT I THINK BACK, I REMEMBER DAD TALKING TO THAT BOY...
...WITH A SMILE ON HIS FACE.
IT'S LIKE THE COPS ARE COVERING SOMETHING UP...
JUST LIKE YOU SEE ON TV!
THE SERIAL KILLER IS A BIG CHEESE ON THE FORCE OR THE SCION OF A WEALTHY FAMILY, SO LITTLE PEOPLE LIKE US CAN'T DO A THING ABOUT IT!!
YOU'RE THE SCION OF A WEALTHY FAMILY...

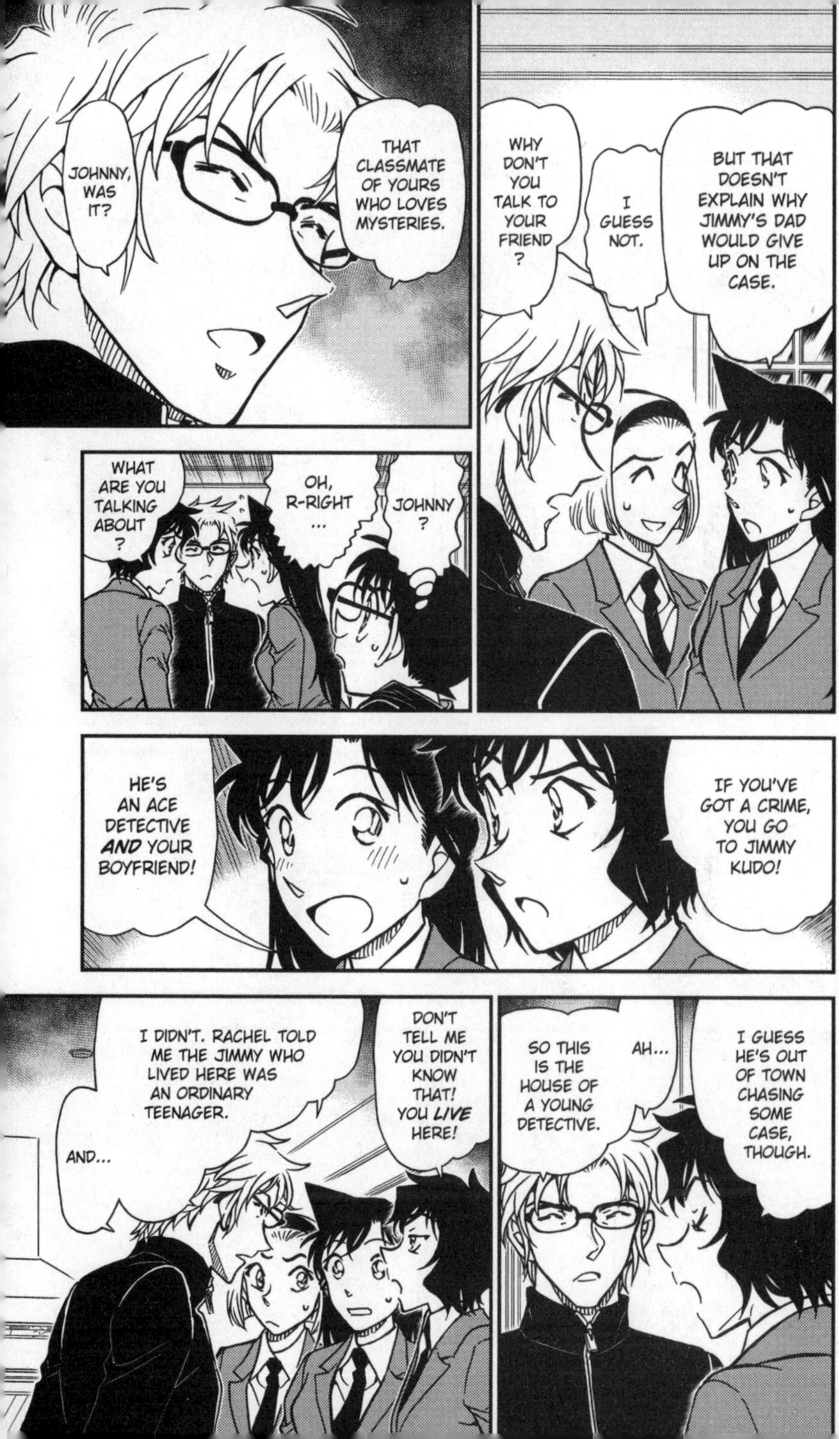
BUT THAT DOESN'T EXPLAIN WHY JIMMY'S DAD WOULD GIVE UP ON THE CASE.
I GUESS NOT.
WHY DON'T YOU TALK TO YOUR FRIEND?
THAT CLASSMATE OF YOURS WHO LOVES MYSTERIES.
JOHNNY, WAS IT?
JOHNNY?
OH, R-RIGHT...
WHAT ARE YOU TALKING ABOUT?
IF YOU'VE GOT A CRIME, YOU GO TO JIMMY KUDO!
HE'S AN ACE DETECTIVE ***AND*** YOUR BOYFRIEND!
I GUESS HE'S OUT OF TOWN CHASING SOME CASE, THOUGH.
AH...
SO THIS IS THE HOUSE OF A YOUNG DETECTIVE.
DON'T TELL ME YOU DIDN'T KNOW THAT! YOU ***LIVE*** HERE!
I DIDN'T. RACHEL TOLD ME THE JIMMY WHO LIVED HERE WAS AN ORDINARY TEENAGER.
AND...

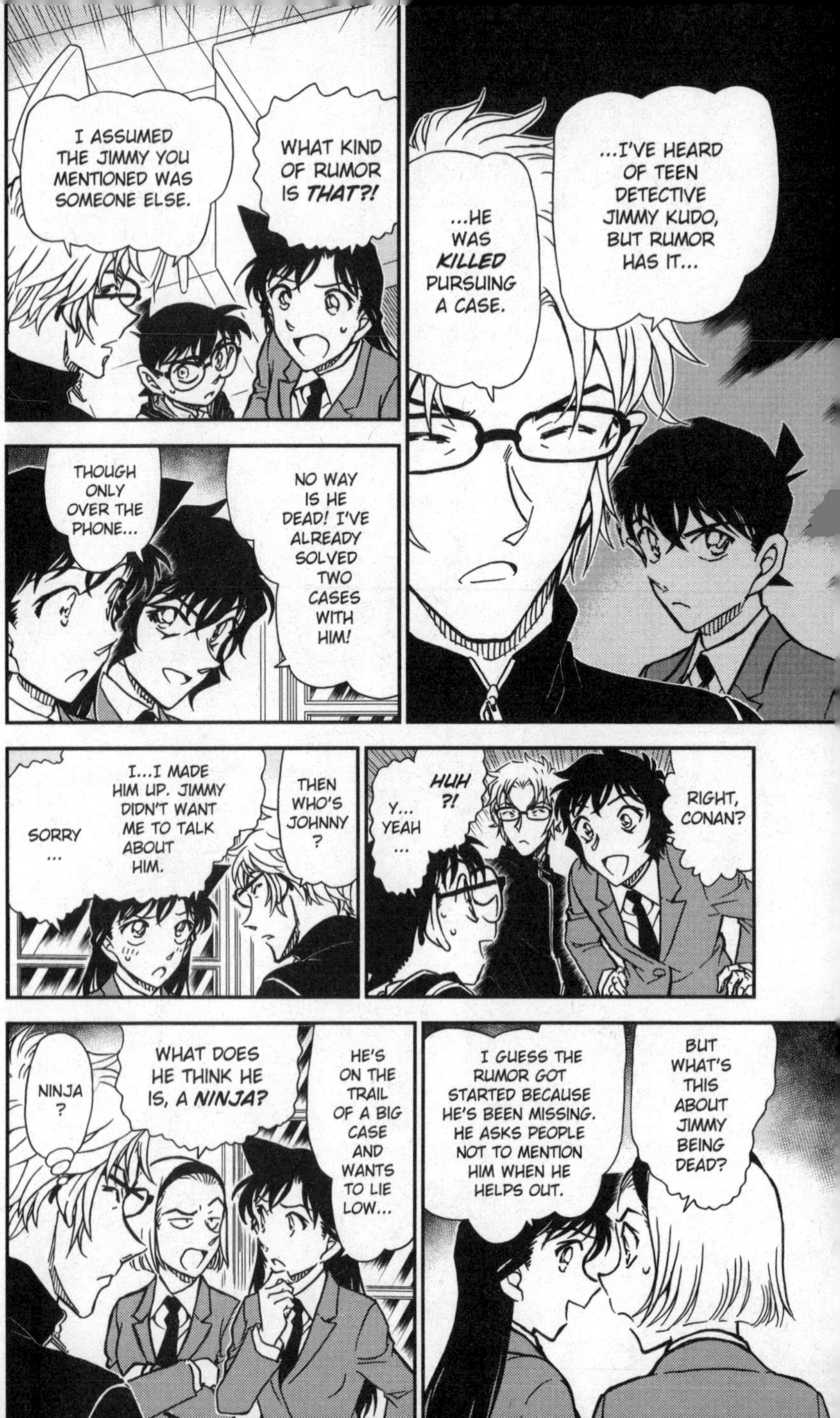
...I'VE HEARD OF TEEN DETECTIVE JIMMY KUDO, BUT RUMOR HAS IT...
...HE WAS ***KILLED*** PURSUING A CASE.
WHAT KIND OF RUMOR IS ***THAT?!***
I ASSUMED THE JIMMY YOU MENTIONED WAS SOMEONE ELSE.
NO WAY IS HE DEAD! I'VE ALREADY SOLVED TWO CASES WITH HIM!
THOUGH ONLY OVER THE PHONE...
RIGHT, CONAN?
HUH?!
Y... YEAH...
THEN WHO'S JOHNNY?
I...I MADE HIM UP. JIMMY DIDN'T WANT ME TO TALK ABOUT HIM.
SORRY...
BUT WHAT'S THIS ABOUT JIMMY BEING DEAD?
I GUESS THE RUMOR GOT STARTED BECAUSE HE'S BEEN MISSING. HE ASKS PEOPLE NOT TO MENTION HIM WHEN HE HELPS OUT.
HE'S ON THE TRAIL OF A BIG CASE AND WANTS TO LIE LOW...
WHAT DOES HE THINK HE IS, A ***NINJA?***
NINJA?

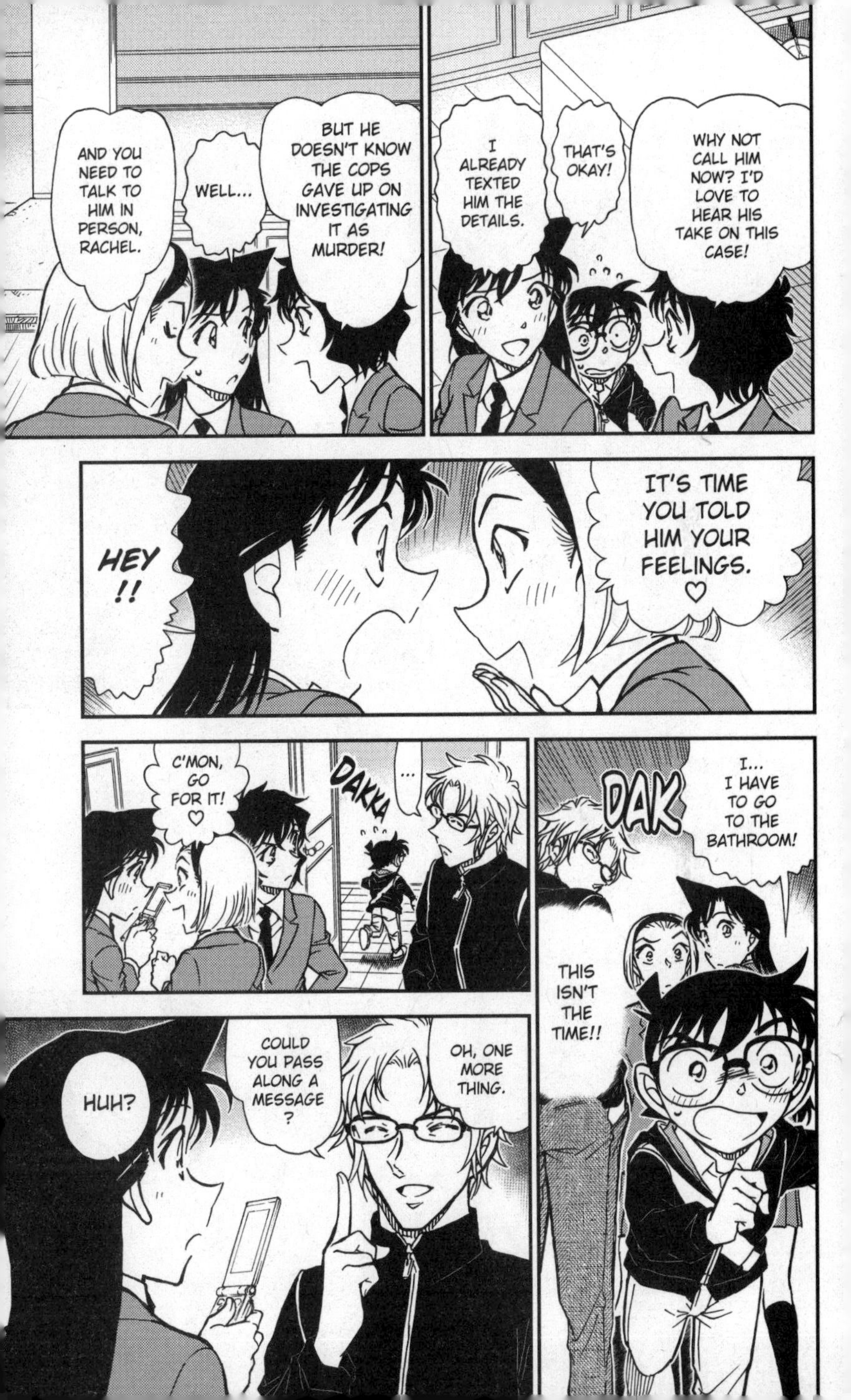
WHY NOT CALL HIM NOW? I'D LOVE TO HEAR HIS TAKE ON THIS CASE!
THAT'S OKAY!
I ALREADY TEXTED HIM THE DETAILS.
BUT HE DOESN'T KNOW THE COPS GAVE UP ON INVESTIGATING IT AS MURDER!
WELL...
AND YOU NEED TO TALK TO HIM IN PERSON, RACHEL.
IT'S TIME YOU TOLD HIM YOUR FEELINGS. ♡
HEY !!
I... I HAVE TO GO TO THE BATHROOM!
DAK
THIS ISN'T THE TIME!!
...
DAKKA
C'MON, GO FOR IT! ♡
OH, ONE MORE THING.
COULD YOU PASS ALONG A MESSAGE?
HUH?

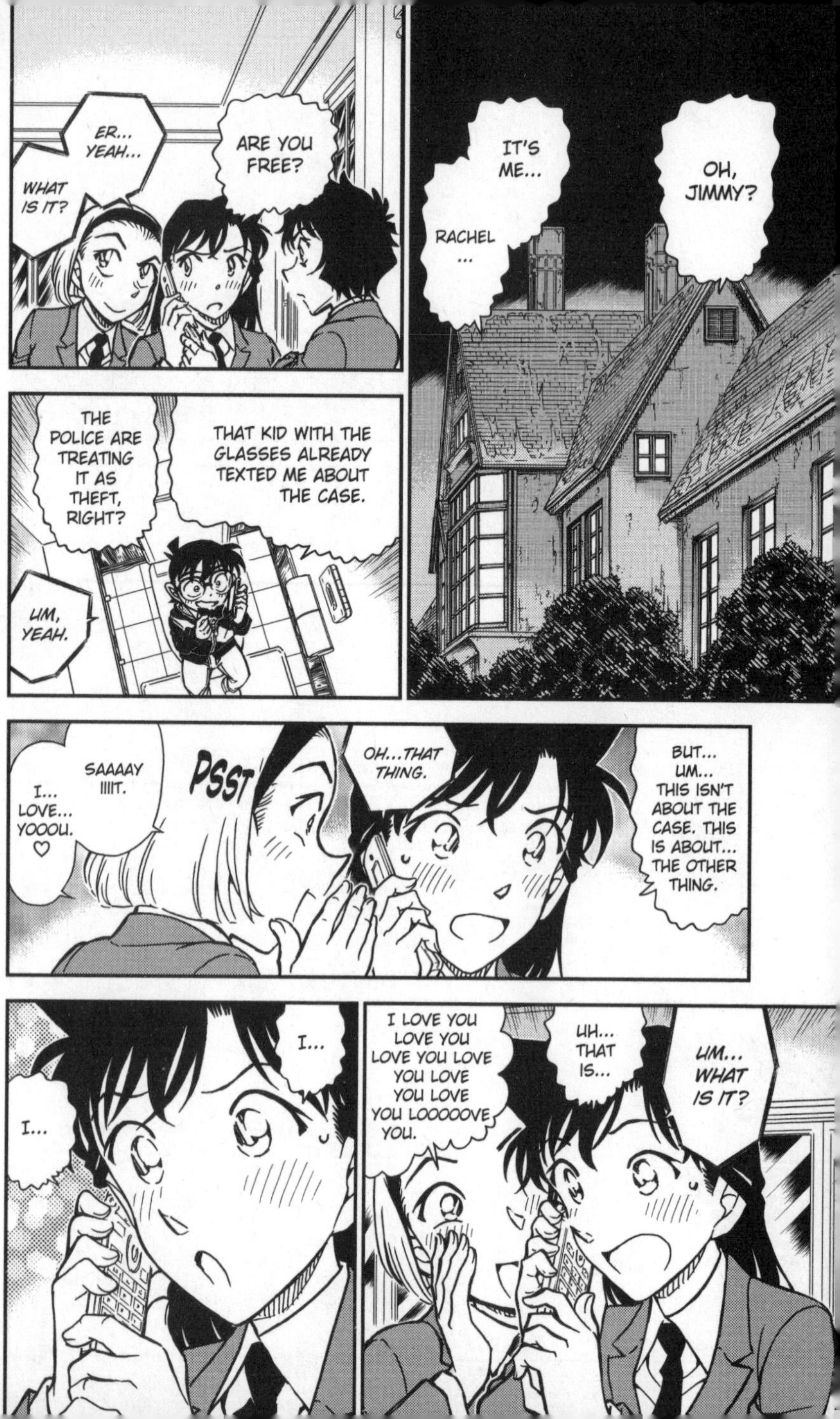
OH, JIMMY?
IT'S ME...
RACHEL ...
ARE YOU FREE?
ER... YEAH...
WHAT IS IT?
THAT KID WITH THE GLASSES ALREADY TEXTED ME ABOUT THE CASE.
THE POLICE ARE TREATING IT AS THEFT, RIGHT?
UM, YEAH.
BUT... UM... THIS ISN'T ABOUT THE CASE. THIS IS ABOUT... THE OTHER THING.
OH...THAT THING.
PSST
SAAAAY IIIIT.
I... LOVE... YOOOU. ♡
UM... WHAT IS IT?
UH... THAT IS...
I LOVE YOU LOVE YOU LOVE YOU LOVE YOU LOVE YOU LOVE YOU LOOOOOVE YOU.
I...
I...

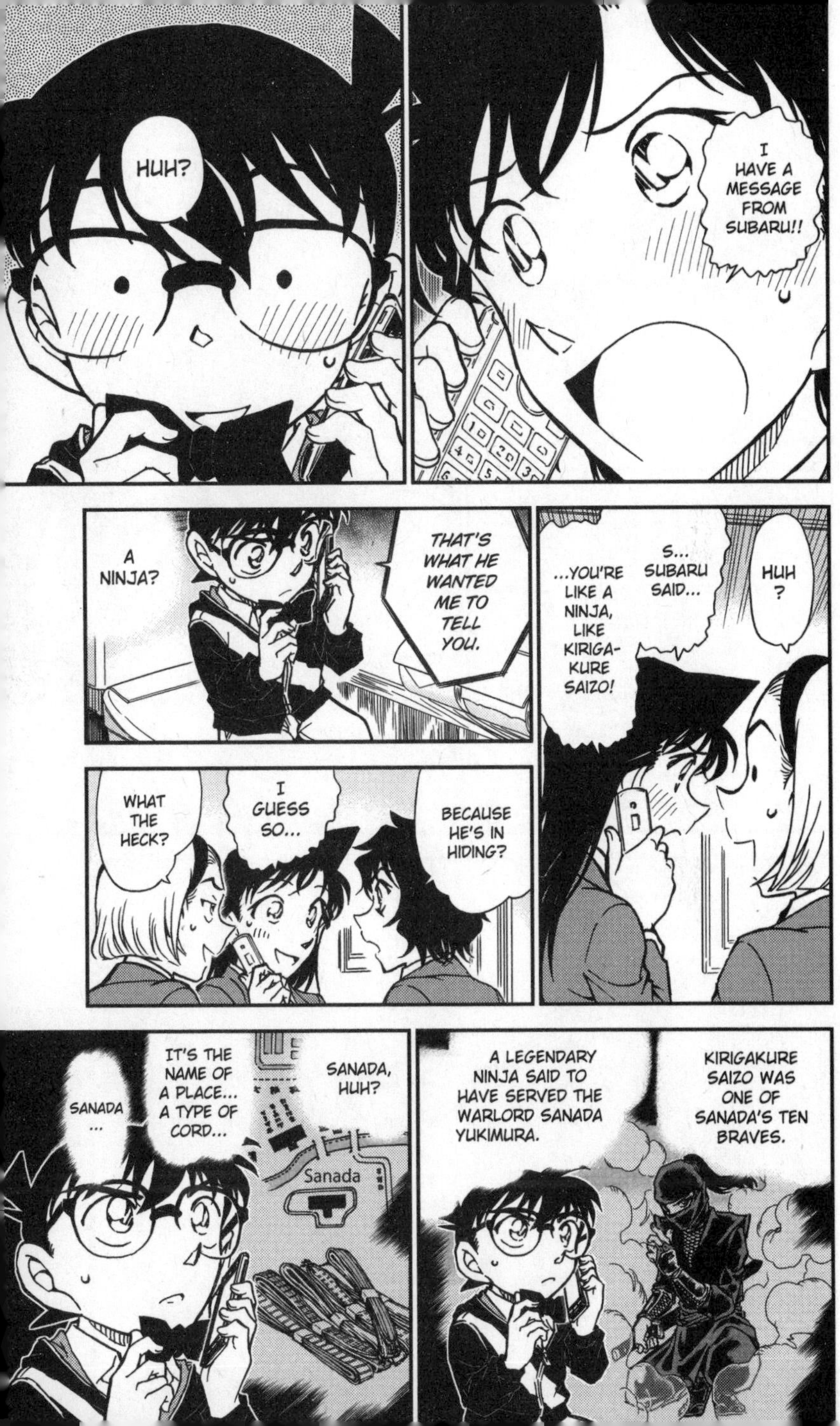
I HAVE A MESSAGE FROM SUBARU!!
HUH?
HUH?
S... SUBARU SAID...
...YOU'RE LIKE A NINJA, LIKE KIRIGAKURE SAIZO!
THAT'S WHAT HE WANTED ME TO TELL YOU.
A NINJA?
BECAUSE HE'S IN HIDING?
I GUESS SO...
WHAT THE HECK?
KIRIGAKURE SAIZO WAS ONE OF SANADA'S TEN BRAVES.
A LEGENDARY NINJA SAID TO HAVE SERVED THE WARLORD SANADA YUKIMURA.
SANADA, HUH?
Sanada
IT'S THE NAME OF A PLACE... A TYPE OF CORD...
SANADA ...

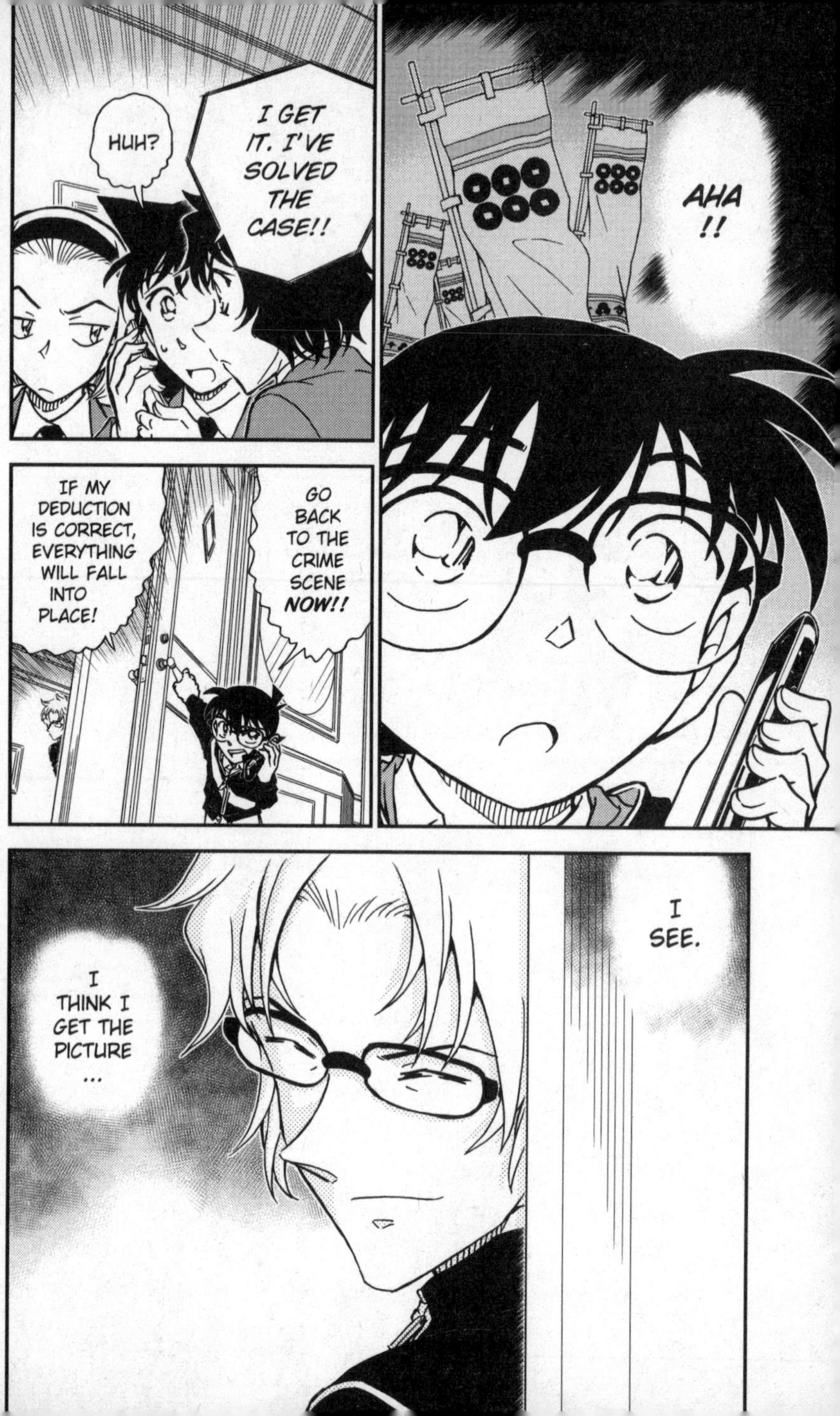
AHA !!
I GET IT. I'VE SOLVED THE CASE!!
HUH?
GO BACK TO THE CRIME SCENE NOW!!
IF MY DEDUCTION IS CORRECT, EVERYTHING WILL FALL INTO PLACE!
I SEE.
I THINK I GET THE PICTURE ...

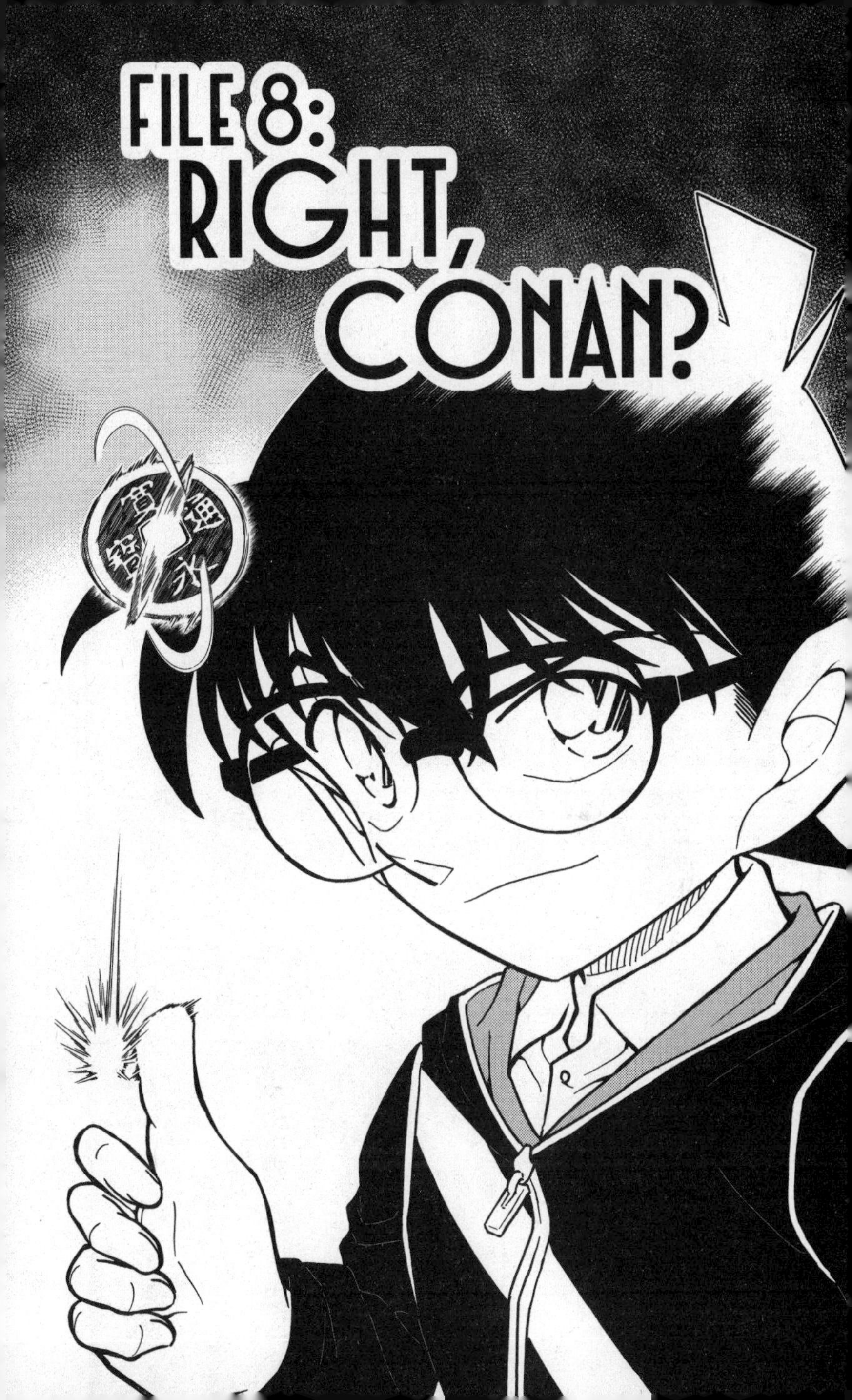
FILE 8:
RIGHT, CONAN?

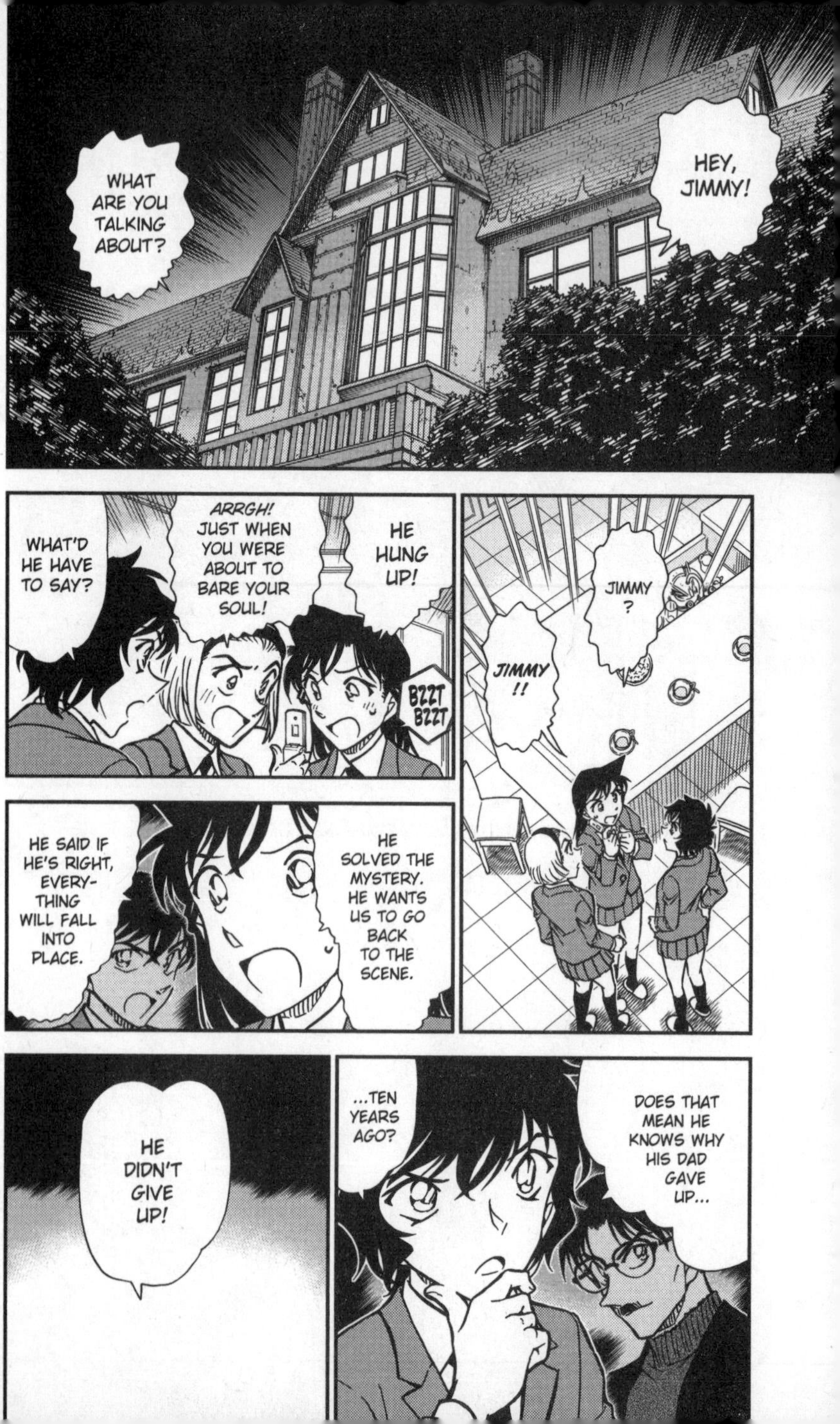
HEY, JIMMY!
WHAT ARE YOU TALKING ABOUT?
JIMMY ?
JIMMY !!
HE HUNG UP!
BZZT BZZT
ARRGH! JUST WHEN YOU WERE ABOUT TO BARE YOUR SOUL!
WHAT'D HE HAVE TO SAY?
HE SOLVED THE MYSTERY. HE WANTS US TO GO BACK TO THE SCENE.
HE SAID IF HE'S RIGHT, EVERY-THING WILL FALL INTO PLACE.
DOES THAT MEAN HE KNOWS WHY HIS DAD GAVE UP...
...TEN YEARS AGO?
HE DIDN'T GIVE UP!

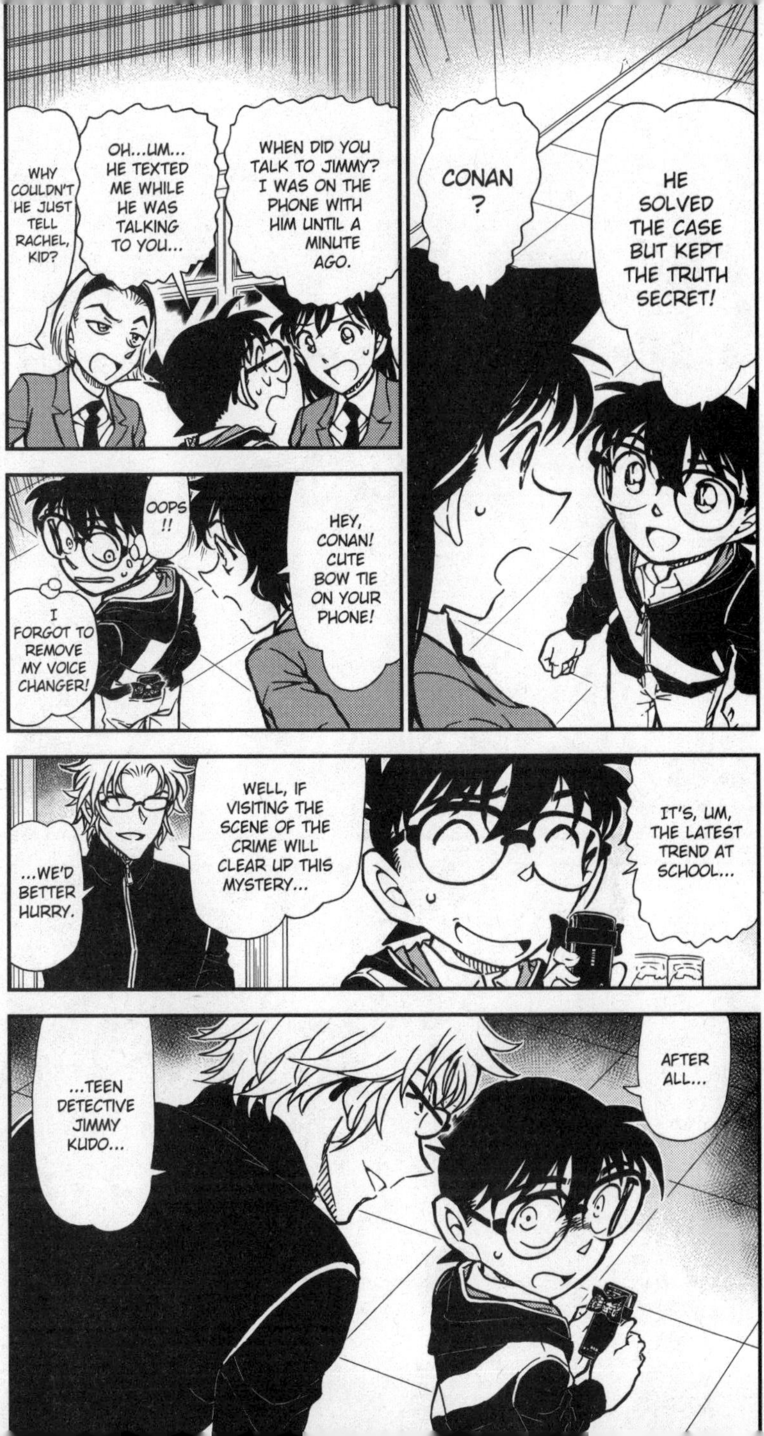
HE SOLVED THE CASE BUT KEPT THE TRUTH SECRET!
CONAN ?
WHEN DID YOU TALK TO JIMMY? I WAS ON THE PHONE WITH HIM UNTIL A MINUTE AGO.
OH...UM... HE TEXTED ME WHILE HE WAS TALKING TO YOU...
WHY COULDN'T HE JUST TELL RACHEL, KID?
HEY, CONAN! CUTE BOW TIE ON YOUR PHONE!
OOPS !!
I FORGOT TO REMOVE MY VOICE CHANGER!
IT'S, UM, THE LATEST TREND AT SCHOOL...
WELL, IF VISITING THE SCENE OF THE CRIME WILL CLEAR UP THIS MYSTERY...
...WE'D BETTER HURRY.
AFTER ALL...
...TEEN DETECTIVE JIMMY KUDO...

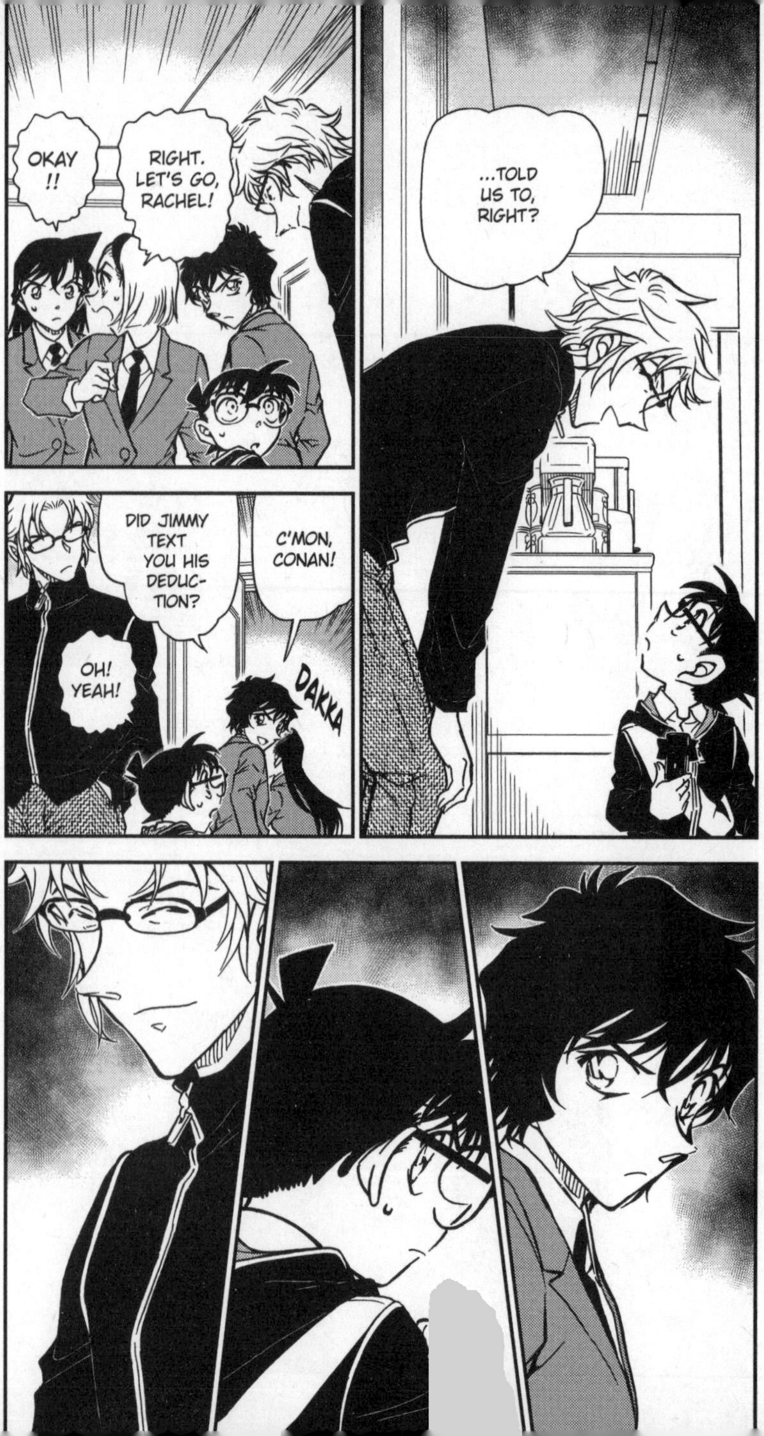
...TOLD US TO, RIGHT?
RIGHT. LET'S GO, RACHEL!
OKAY !!
C'MON, CONAN!
DID JIMMY TEXT YOU HIS DEDUC-TION?
DAKKA
OH! YEAH!

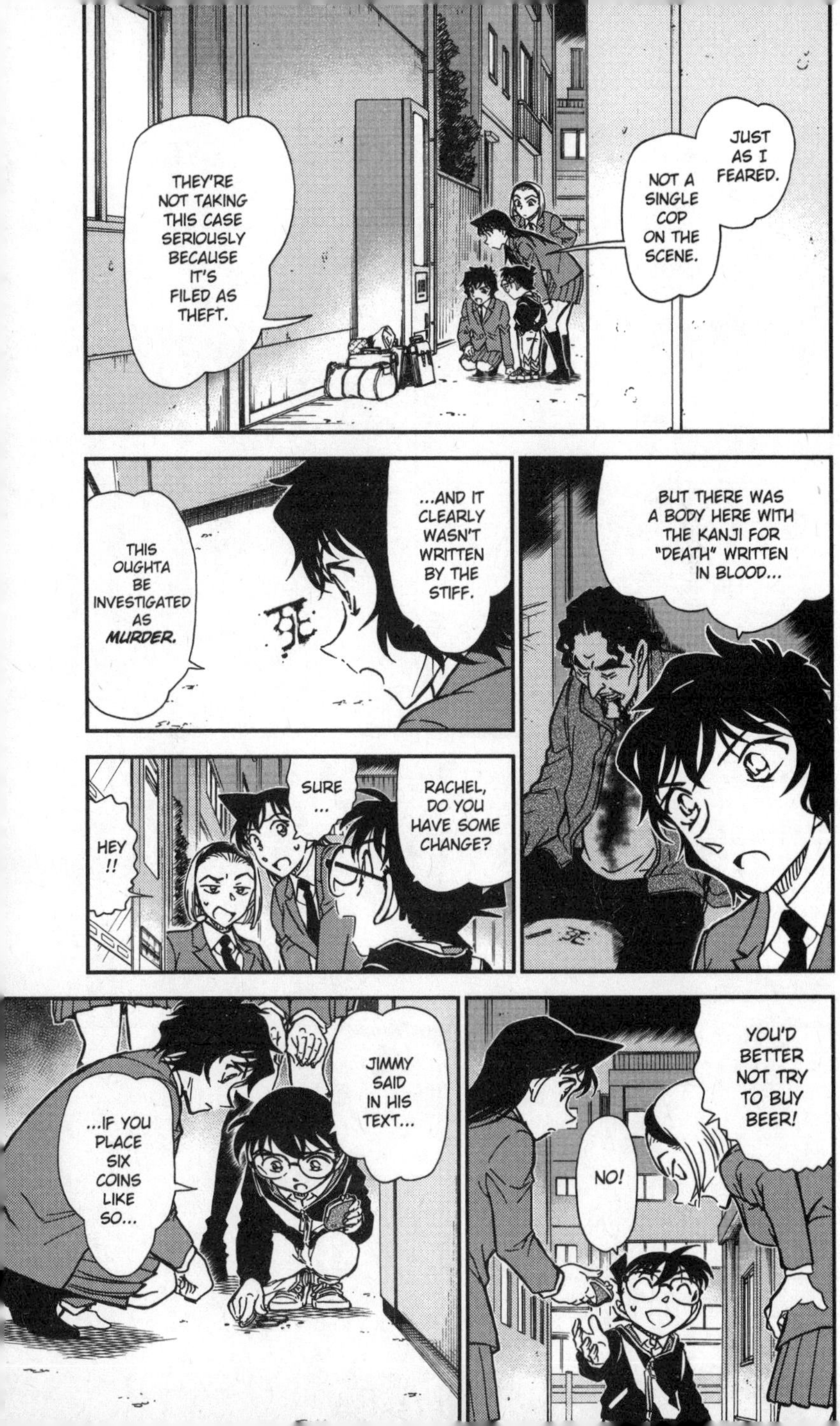
JUST AS I FEARED.
NOT A SINGLE COP ON THE SCENE.
THEY'RE NOT TAKING THIS CASE SERIOUSLY BECAUSE IT'S FILED AS THEFT.
BUT THERE WAS A BODY HERE WITH THE KANJI FOR "DEATH" WRITTEN IN BLOOD...
...AND IT CLEARLY WASN'T WRITTEN BY THE STIFF.
THIS OUGHTA BE INVESTIGATED AS MURDER.
RACHEL, DO YOU HAVE SOME CHANGE?
SURE ...
HEY !!
YOU'D BETTER NOT TRY TO BUY BEER!
NO!
JIMMY SAID IN HIS TEXT...
...IF YOU PLACE SIX COINS LIKE SO...

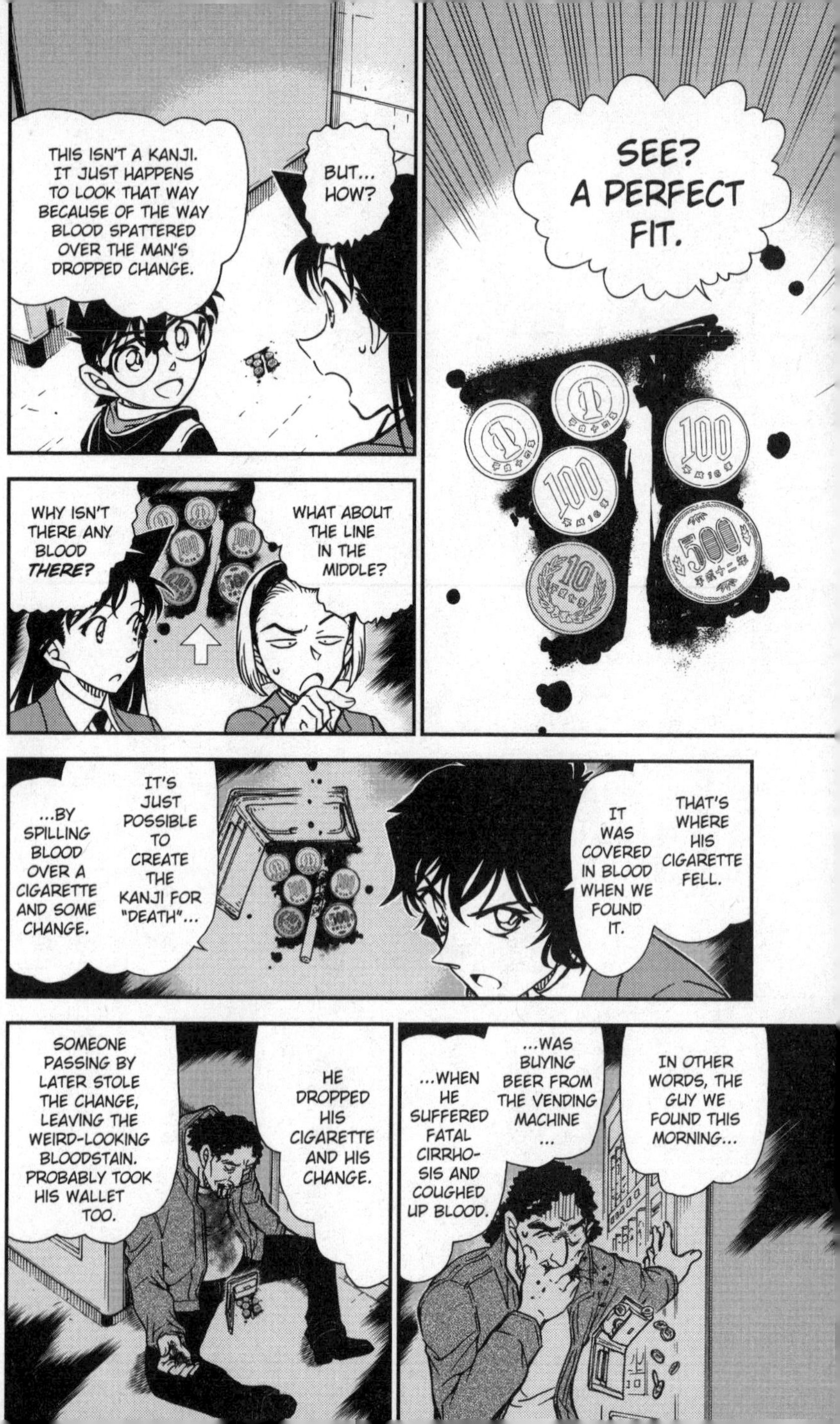
SEE? A PERFECT FIT.
BUT... HOW?
THIS ISN'T A KANJI. IT JUST HAPPENS TO LOOK THAT WAY BECAUSE OF THE WAY BLOOD SPATTERED OVER THE MAN'S DROPPED CHANGE.
WHAT ABOUT THE LINE IN THE MIDDLE?
WHY ISN'T THERE ANY BLOOD *THERE?*
THAT'S WHERE HIS CIGARETTE FELL.
IT WAS COVERED IN BLOOD WHEN WE FOUND IT.
IT'S JUST POSSIBLE TO CREATE THE KANJI FOR "DEATH"...
...BY SPILLING BLOOD OVER A CIGARETTE AND SOME CHANGE.
IN OTHER WORDS, THE GUY WE FOUND THIS MORNING...
...WAS BUYING BEER FROM THE VENDING MACHINE...
...WHEN HE SUFFERED FATAL CIRRHO-SIS AND COUGHED UP BLOOD.
HE DROPPED HIS CIGARETTE AND HIS CHANGE.
SOMEONE PASSING BY LATER STOLE THE CHANGE, LEAVING THE WEIRD-LOOKING BLOODSTAIN. PROBABLY TOOK HIS WALLET TOO.

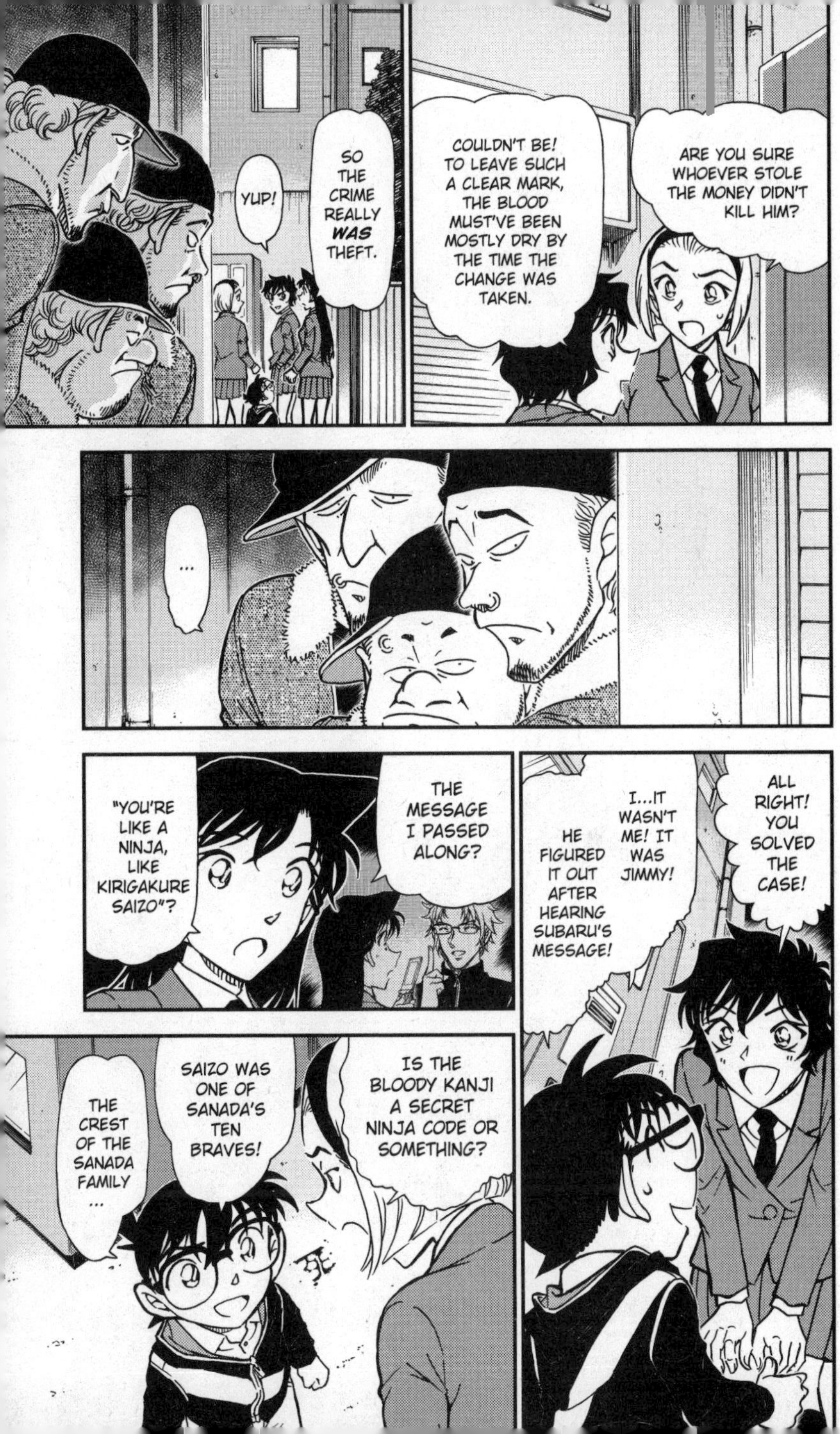

ARE YOU SURE WHOEVER STOLE THE MONEY DIDN'T KILL HIM?
COULDN'T BE! TO LEAVE SUCH A CLEAR MARK, THE BLOOD MUST'VE BEEN MOSTLY DRY BY THE TIME THE CHANGE WAS TAKEN.
SO THE CRIME REALLY WAS THEFT.
YUP!
...
ALL RIGHT! YOU SOLVED THE CASE!
I...IT WASN'T ME! IT WAS JIMMY!
HE FIGURED IT OUT AFTER HEARING SUBARU'S MESSAGE!
THE MESSAGE I PASSED ALONG?
"YOU'RE LIKE A NINJA, LIKE KIRIGAKURE SAIZO"?
IS THE BLOODY KANJI A SECRET NINJA CODE OR SOMETHING?
SAIZO WAS ONE OF SANADA'S TEN BRAVES!
THE CREST OF THE SANADA FAMILY ...

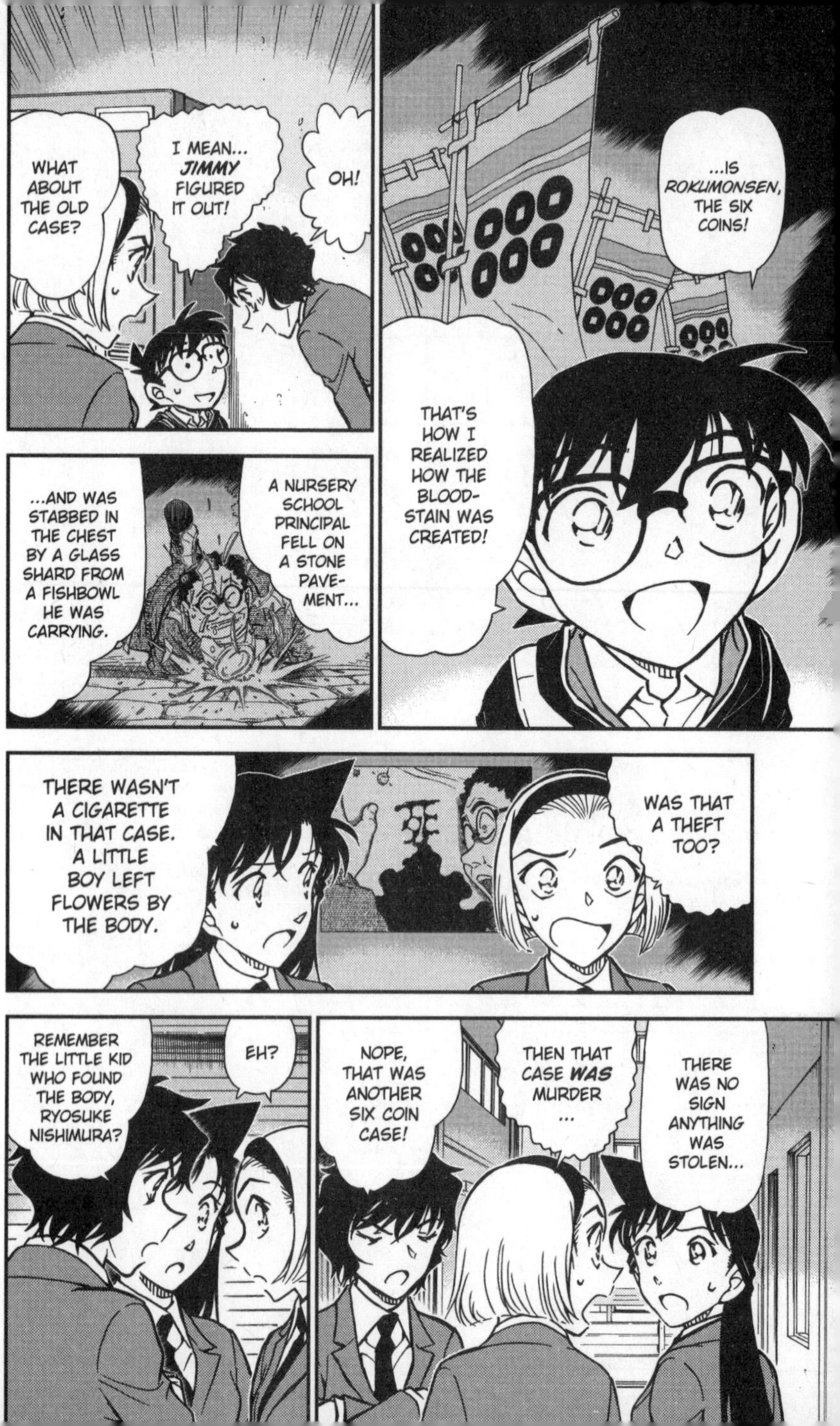
...IS ROKUMONSEN, THE SIX COINS!
THAT'S HOW I REALIZED HOW THE BLOOD-STAIN WAS CREATED!
OH!
I MEAN... JIMMY FIGURED IT OUT!
WHAT ABOUT THE OLD CASE?
A NURSERY SCHOOL PRINCIPAL FELL ON A STONE PAVE-MENT...
...AND WAS STABBED IN THE CHEST BY A GLASS SHARD FROM A FISHBOWL HE WAS CARRYING.
WAS THAT A THEFT TOO?
THERE WASN'T A CIGARETTE IN THAT CASE. A LITTLE BOY LEFT FLOWERS BY THE BODY.
THERE WAS NO SIGN ANYTHING WAS STOLEN...
THEN THAT CASE WAS MURDER ...
NOPE, THAT WAS ANOTHER SIX COIN CASE!
EH?
REMEMBER THE LITTLE KID WHO FOUND THE BODY, RYOSUKE NISHIMURA?

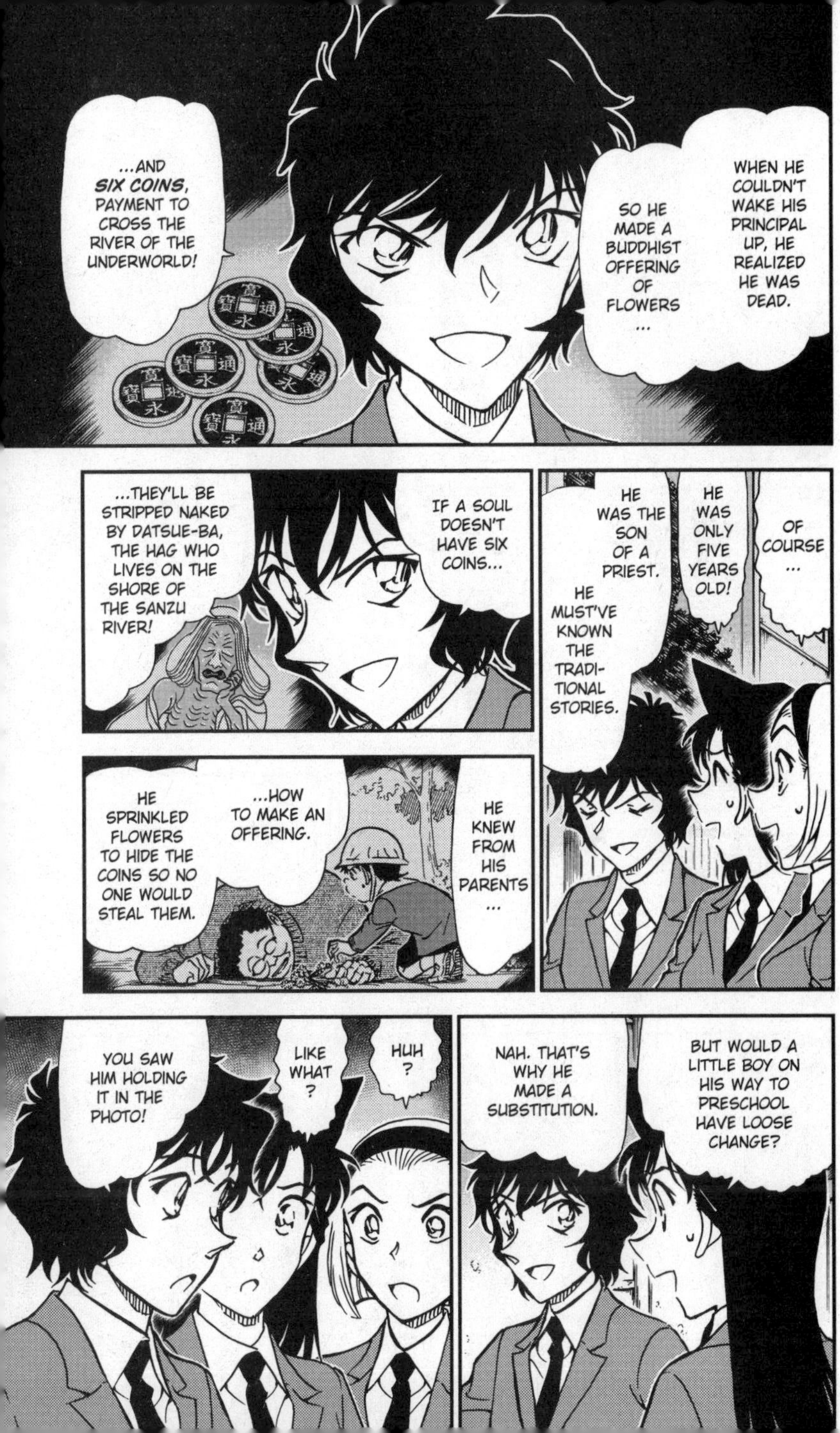
WHEN HE COULDN'T WAKE HIS PRINCIPAL UP, HE REALIZED HE WAS DEAD.
SO HE MADE A BUDDHIST OFFERING OF FLOWERS ...
...AND **SIX COINS**, PAYMENT TO CROSS THE RIVER OF THE UNDERWORLD!
OF COURSE ...
HE WAS ONLY FIVE YEARS OLD!
HE WAS THE SON OF A PRIEST.
HE MUST'VE KNOWN THE TRADI-TIONAL STORIES.
IF A SOUL DOESN'T HAVE SIX COINS...
...THEY'LL BE STRIPPED NAKED BY DATSUE-BA, THE HAG WHO LIVES ON THE SHORE OF THE SANZU RIVER!
HE KNEW FROM HIS PARENTS ...
...HOW TO MAKE AN OFFERING.
HE SPRINKLED FLOWERS TO HIDE THE COINS SO NO ONE WOULD STEAL THEM.
BUT WOULD A LITTLE BOY ON HIS WAY TO PRESCHOOL HAVE LOOSE CHANGE?
NAH. THAT'S WHY HE MADE A SUBSTITUTION.
HUH ?
LIKE WHAT ?
YOU SAW HIM HOLDING IT IN THE PHOTO!

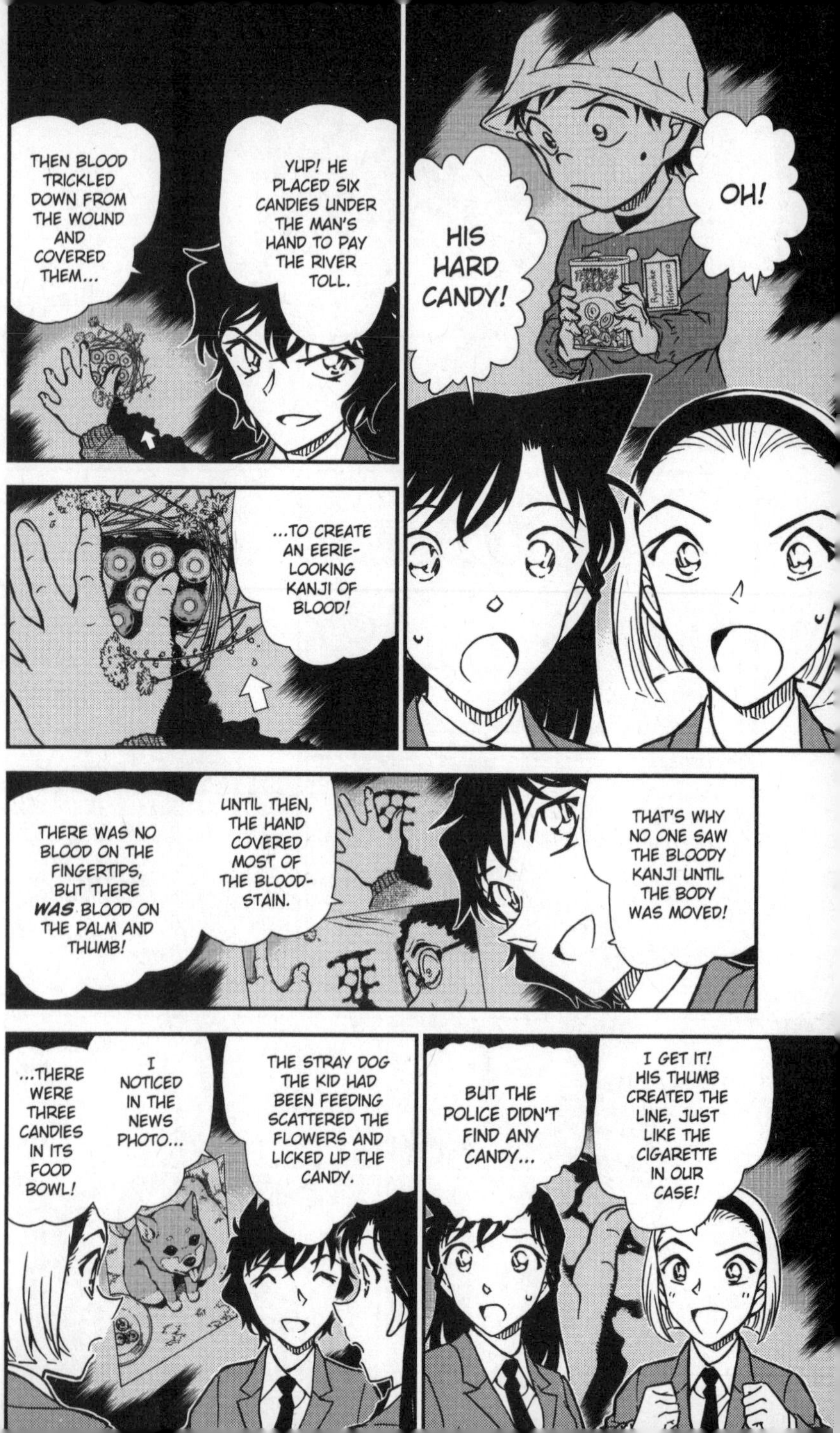
OH!
HIS HARD CANDY!
YUP! HE PLACED SIX CANDIES UNDER THE MAN'S HAND TO PAY THE RIVER TOLL.
THEN BLOOD TRICKLED DOWN FROM THE WOUND AND COVERED THEM...
...TO CREATE AN EERIE-LOOKING KANJI OF BLOOD!
THAT'S WHY NO ONE SAW THE BLOODY KANJI UNTIL THE BODY WAS MOVED!
UNTIL THEN, THE HAND COVERED MOST OF THE BLOOD-STAIN.
THERE WAS NO BLOOD ON THE FINGERTIPS, BUT THERE ***WAS*** BLOOD ON THE PALM AND THUMB!
I GET IT! HIS THUMB CREATED THE LINE, JUST LIKE THE CIGARETTE IN OUR CASE!
BUT THE POLICE DIDN'T FIND ANY CANDY...
THE STRAY DOG THE KID HAD BEEN FEEDING SCATTERED THE FLOWERS AND LICKED UP THE CANDY.
I NOTICED IN THE NEWS PHOTO...
...THERE WERE THREE CANDIES IN ITS FOOD BOWL!

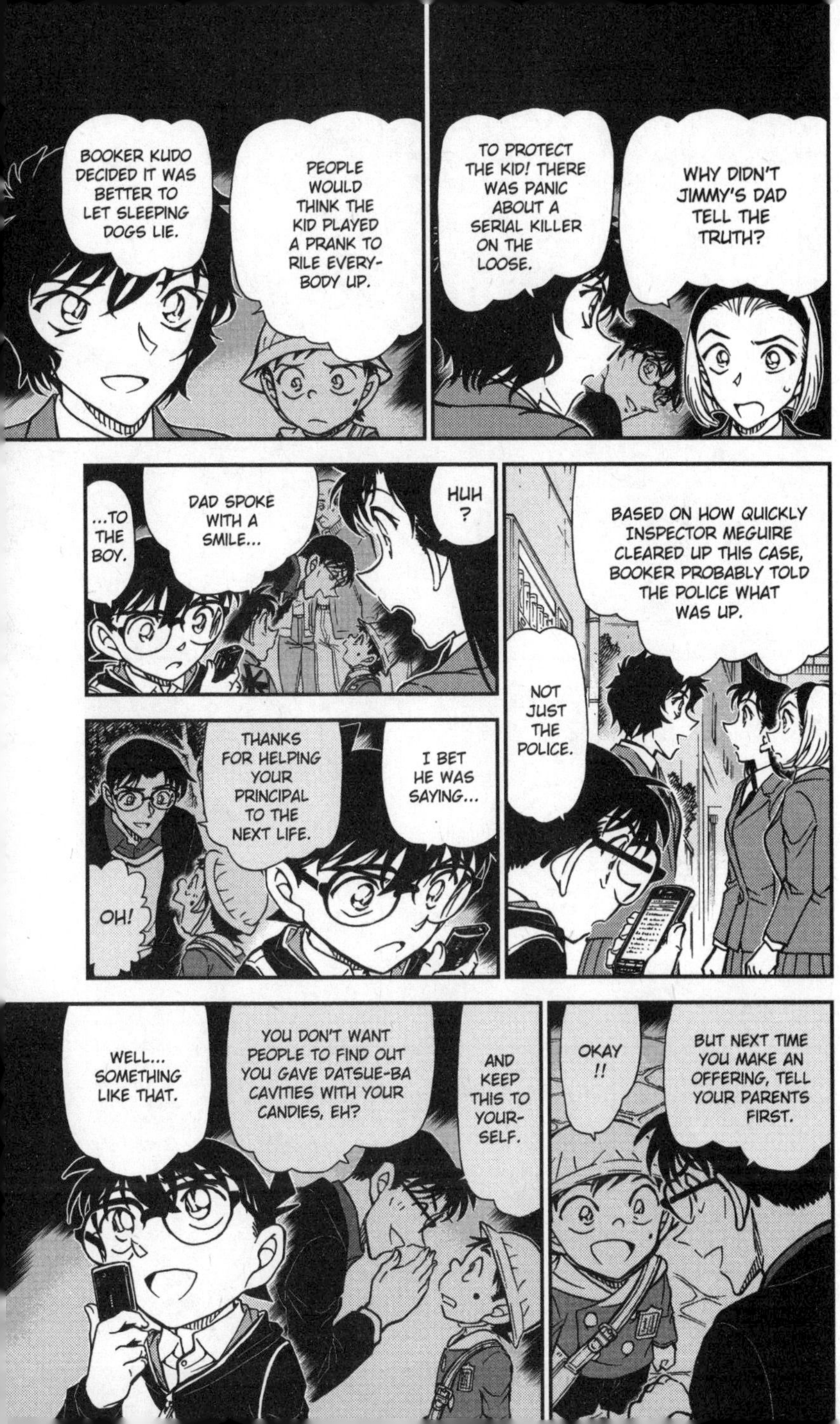
WHY DIDN'T JIMMY'S DAD TELL THE TRUTH?
TO PROTECT THE KID! THERE WAS PANIC ABOUT A SERIAL KILLER ON THE LOOSE.
PEOPLE WOULD THINK THE KID PLAYED A PRANK TO RILE EVERY-BODY UP.
BOOKER KUDO DECIDED IT WAS BETTER TO LET SLEEPING DOGS LIE.
BASED ON HOW QUICKLY INSPECTOR MEGUIRE CLEARED UP THIS CASE, BOOKER PROBABLY TOLD THE POLICE WHAT WAS UP.
NOT JUST THE POLICE.
HUH ?
DAD SPOKE WITH A SMILE...
...TO THE BOY.
I BET HE WAS SAYING...
THANKS FOR HELPING YOUR PRINCIPAL TO THE NEXT LIFE.
OH!
BUT NEXT TIME YOU MAKE AN OFFERING, TELL YOUR PARENTS FIRST.
OKAY !!
AND KEEP THIS TO YOUR-SELF.
YOU DON'T WANT PEOPLE TO FIND OUT YOU GAVE DATSUE-BA CAVITIES WITH YOUR CANDIES, EH?
WELL... SOMETHING LIKE THAT.

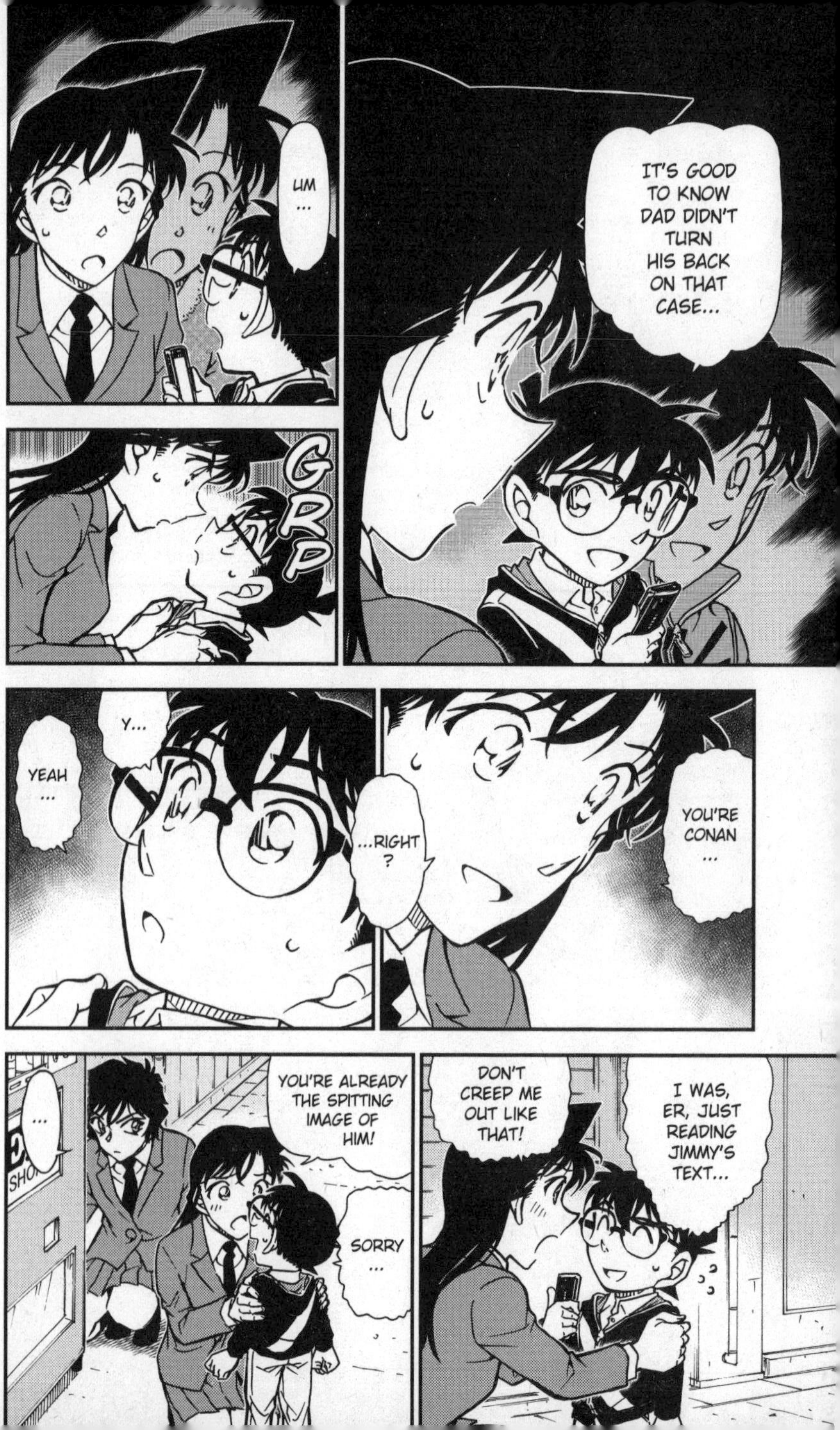
IT'S GOOD TO KNOW DAD DIDN'T TURN HIS BACK ON THAT CASE...
UM ...
GRP
YOU'RE CONAN ...
...RIGHT ?
Y...
YEAH ...
I WAS, ER, JUST READING JIMMY'S TEXT...
DON'T CREEP ME OUT LIKE THAT!
YOU'RE ALREADY THE SPITTING IMAGE OF HIM!
SORRY ...
...

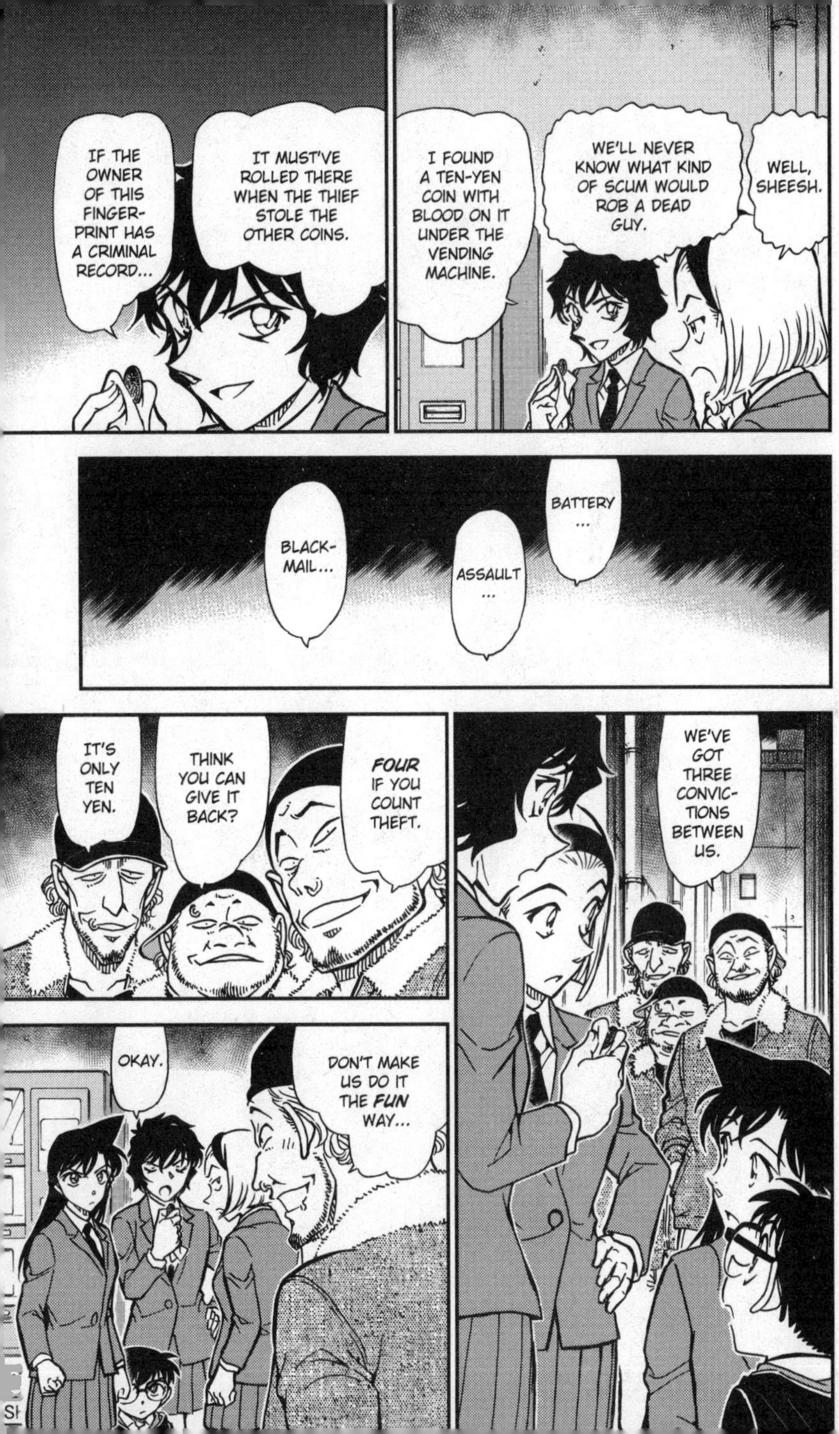
WELL, SHEESH.
WE'LL NEVER KNOW WHAT KIND OF SCUM WOULD ROB A DEAD GUY.
I FOUND A TEN-YEN COIN WITH BLOOD ON IT UNDER THE VENDING MACHINE.
IT MUST'VE ROLLED THERE WHEN THE THIEF STOLE THE OTHER COINS.
IF THE OWNER OF THIS FINGER-PRINT HAS A CRIMINAL RECORD...
BATTERY...
ASSAULT...
BLACK-MAIL...
WE'VE GOT THREE CONVIC-TIONS BETWEEN US.
FOUR IF YOU COUNT THEFT.
THINK YOU CAN GIVE IT BACK?
IT'S ONLY TEN YEN.
DON'T MAKE US DO IT THE **FUN** WAY...
OKAY.

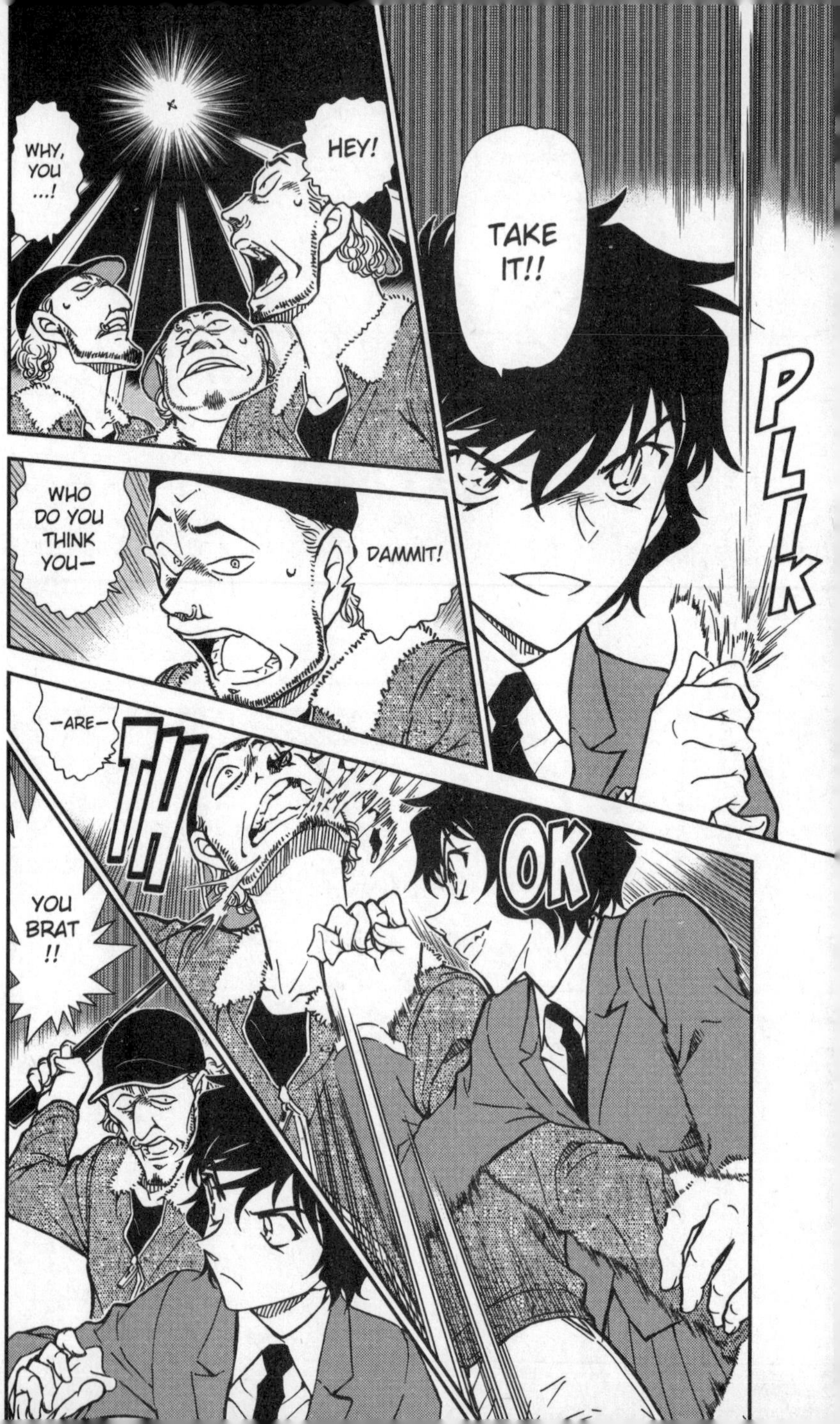
TAKE IT!!
PLIK
HEY!
WHY, YOU ...!
DAMMIT!
WHO DO YOU THINK YOU—
—ARE—
THOK
YOU BRAT !!

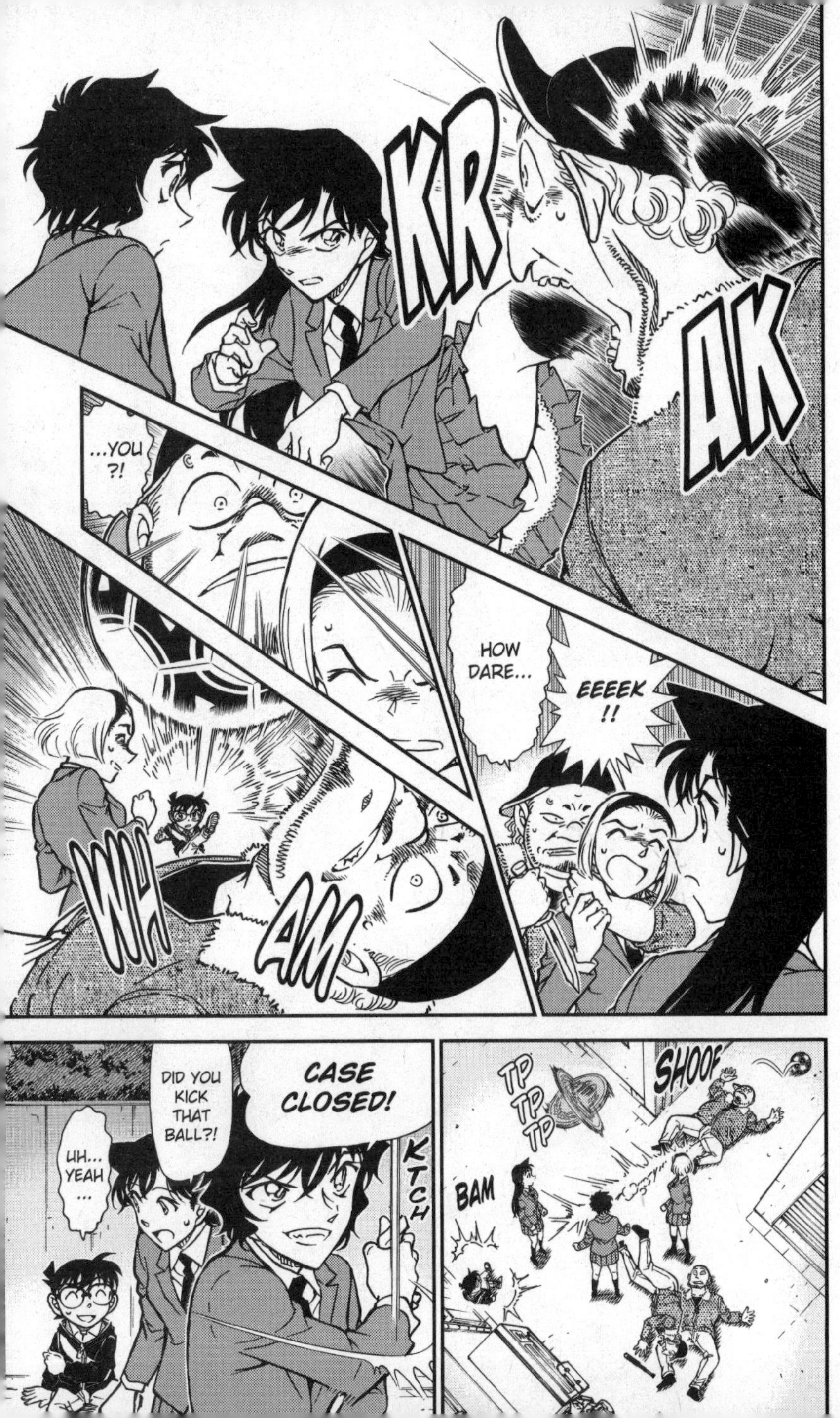
KRAK
HOW DARE...
EEEEK!!
...YOU ?!
WHAM
SHOOF
TP TP TP
BAM
CASE CLOSED!
KTCH
DID YOU KICK THAT BALL?!
UH... YEAH ...

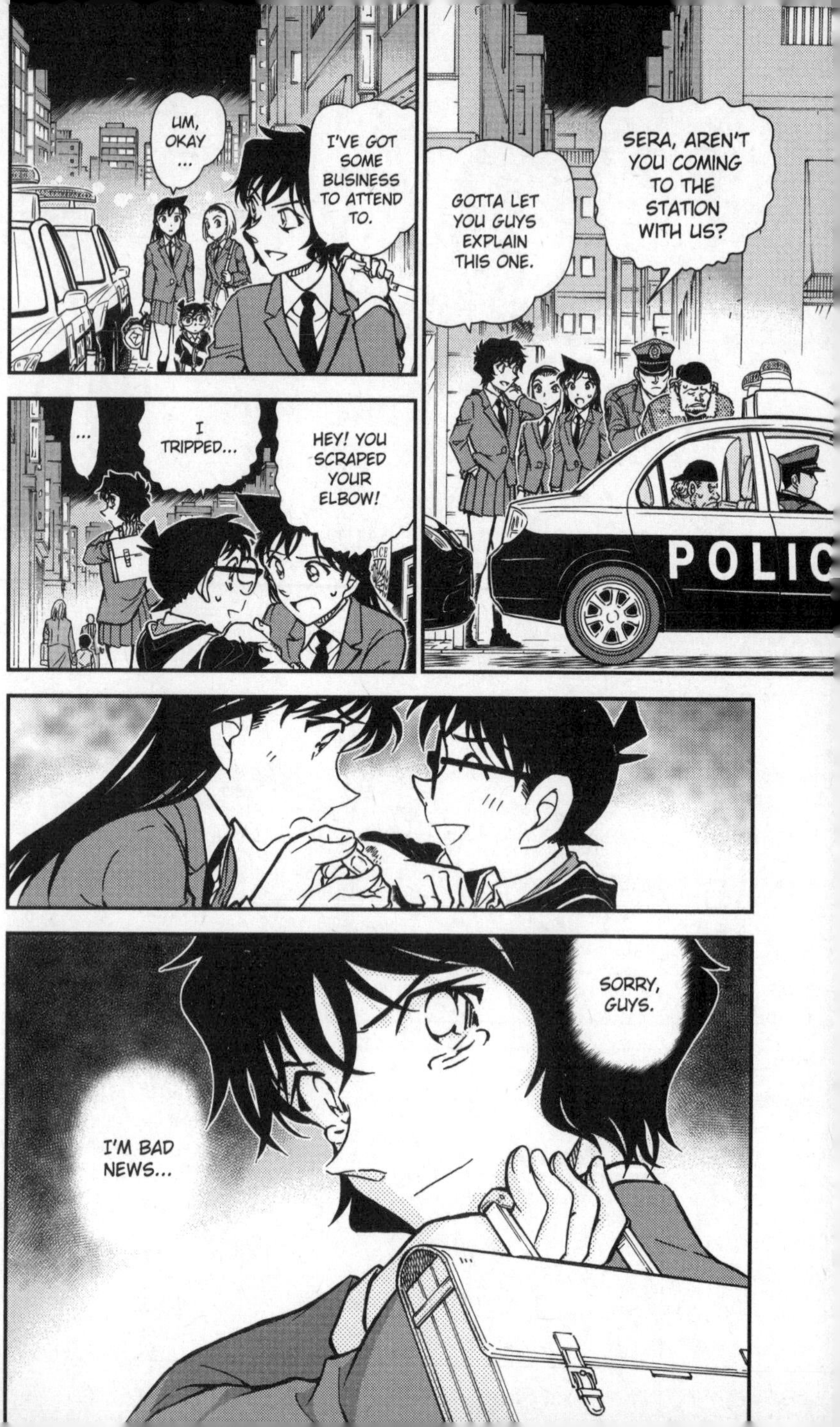
SERA, AREN'T YOU COMING TO THE STATION WITH US?
GOTTA LET YOU GUYS EXPLAIN THIS ONE.
POLIC
I'VE GOT SOME BUSINESS TO ATTEND TO.
UM, OKAY ...
HEY! YOU SCRAPED YOUR ELBOW!
I TRIPPED...
...
SORRY, GUYS.
I'M BAD NEWS...

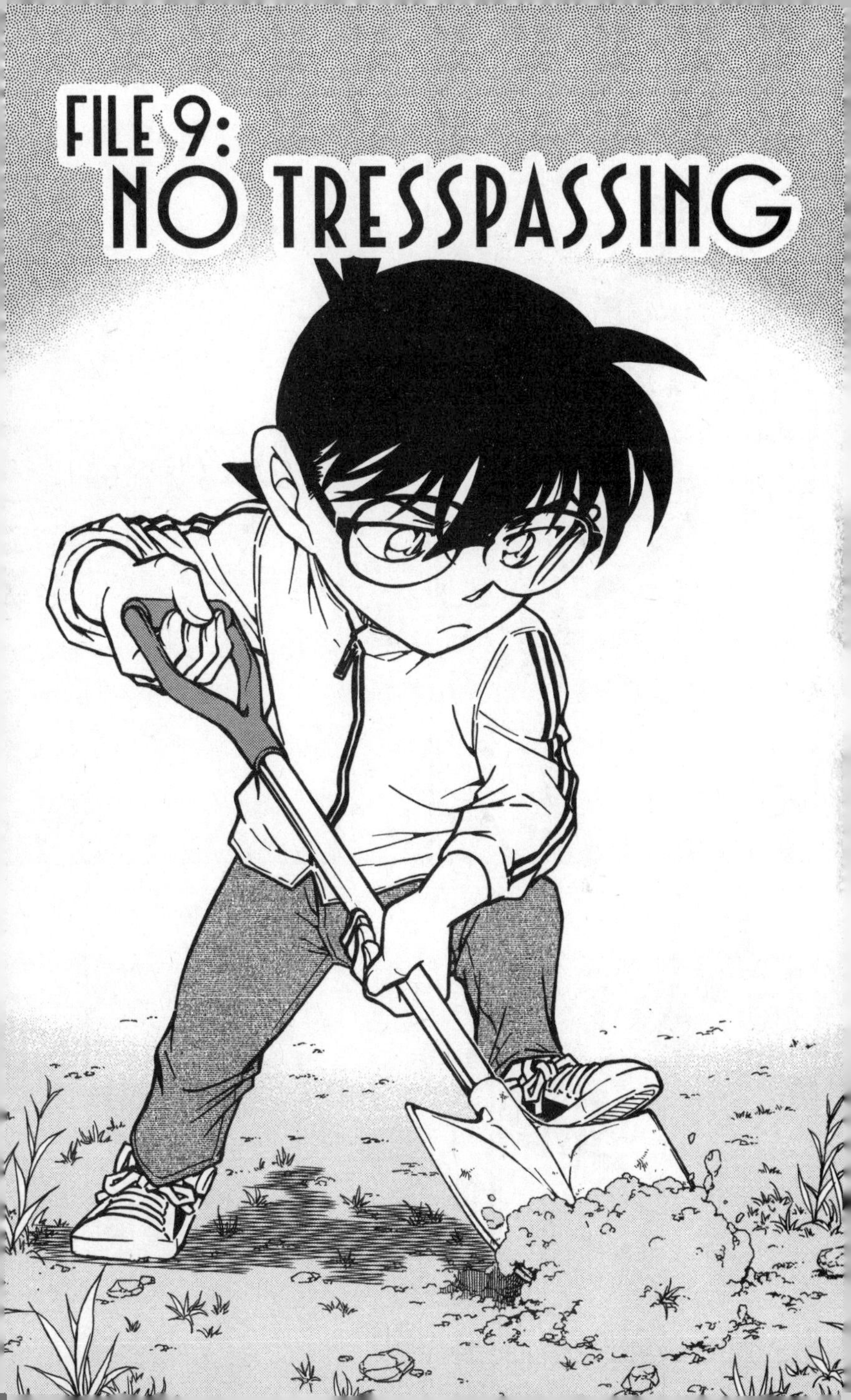
FILE 9:
NO TRESSPASSING

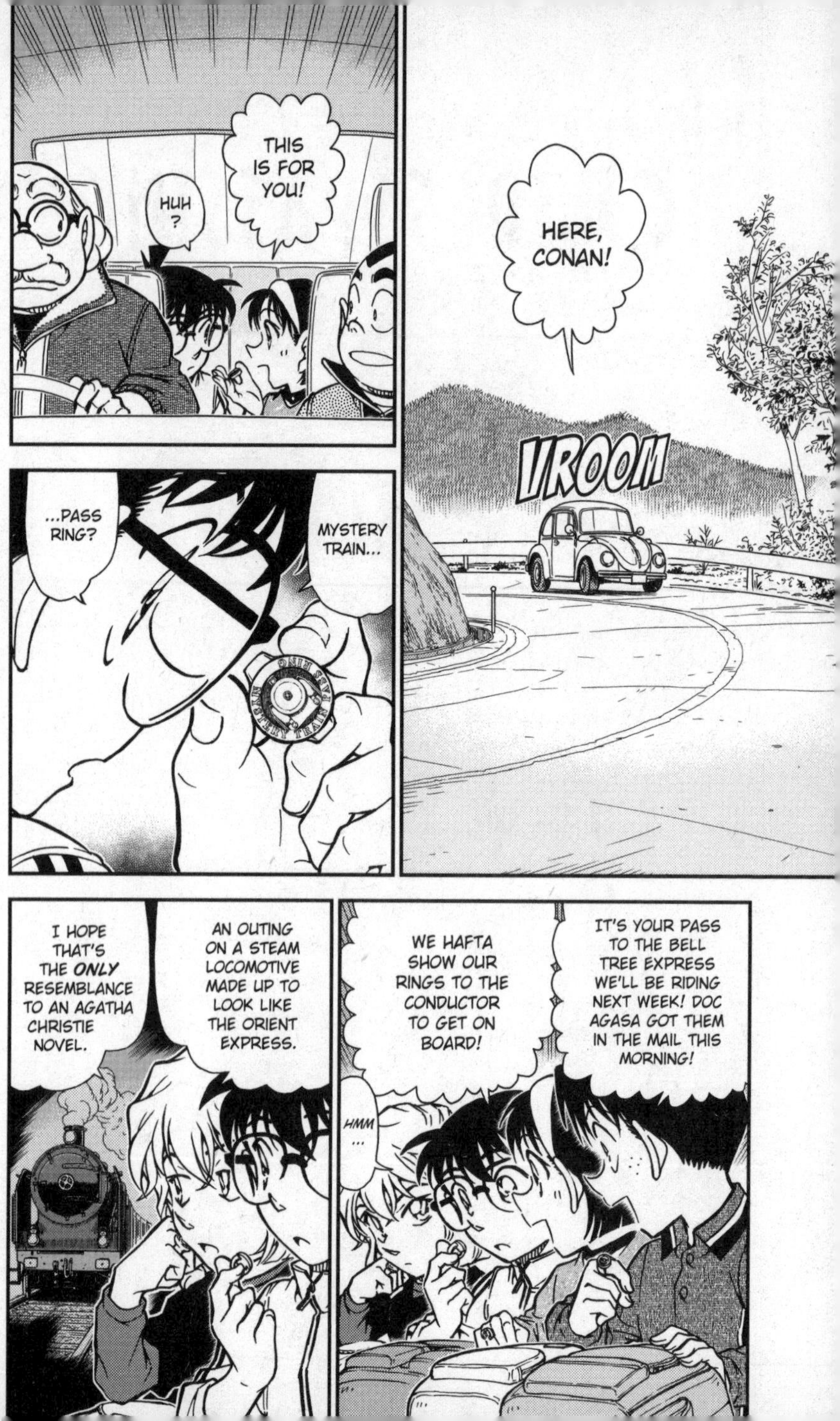
HERE, CONAN!
VROOM
THIS IS FOR YOU!
HUH?
MYSTERY TRAIN...
...PASS RING?
IT'S YOUR PASS TO THE BELL TREE EXPRESS WE'LL BE RIDING NEXT WEEK! DOC AGASA GOT THEM IN THE MAIL THIS MORNING!
WE HAFTA SHOW OUR RINGS TO THE CONDUCTOR TO GET ON BOARD!
HMM...
AN OUTING ON A STEAM LOCOMOTIVE MADE UP TO LOOK LIKE THE ORIENT EXPRESS.
I HOPE THAT'S THE *ONLY* RESEMBLANCE TO AN AGATHA CHRISTIE NOVEL.

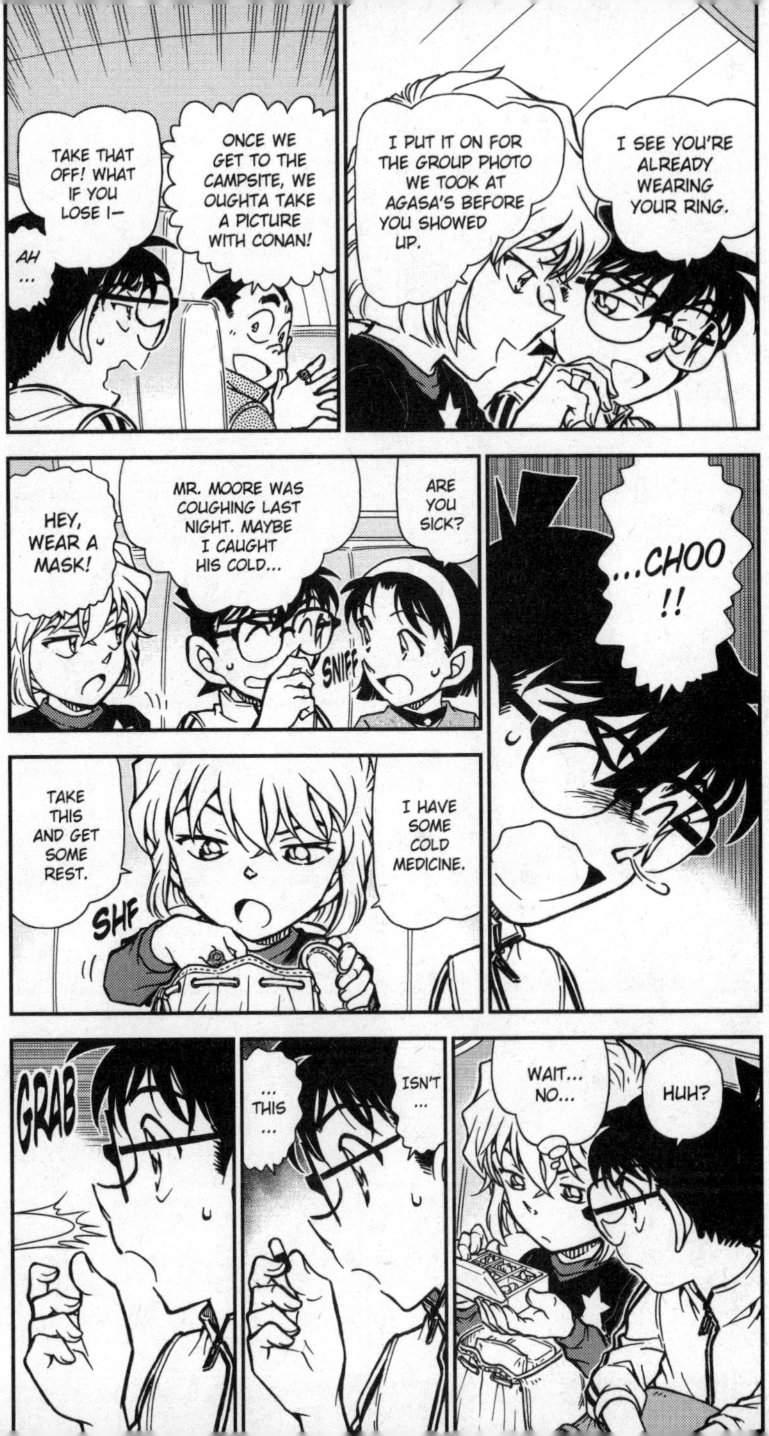
I SEE YOU'RE ALREADY WEARING YOUR RING.
I PUT IT ON FOR THE GROUP PHOTO WE TOOK AT AGASA'S BEFORE YOU SHOWED UP.
ONCE WE GET TO THE CAMPSITE, WE OUGHTA TAKE A PICTURE WITH CONAN!
TAKE THAT OFF! WHAT IF YOU LOSE I—
AH ...
...CHOO !!
ARE YOU SICK?
MR. MOORE WAS COUGHING LAST NIGHT. MAYBE I CAUGHT HIS COLD...
SNIFF
HEY, WEAR A MASK!
I HAVE SOME COLD MEDICINE.
TAKE THIS AND GET SOME REST.
SHF
HUH?
WAIT... NO...
ISN'T ...
... THIS ...
GRAB

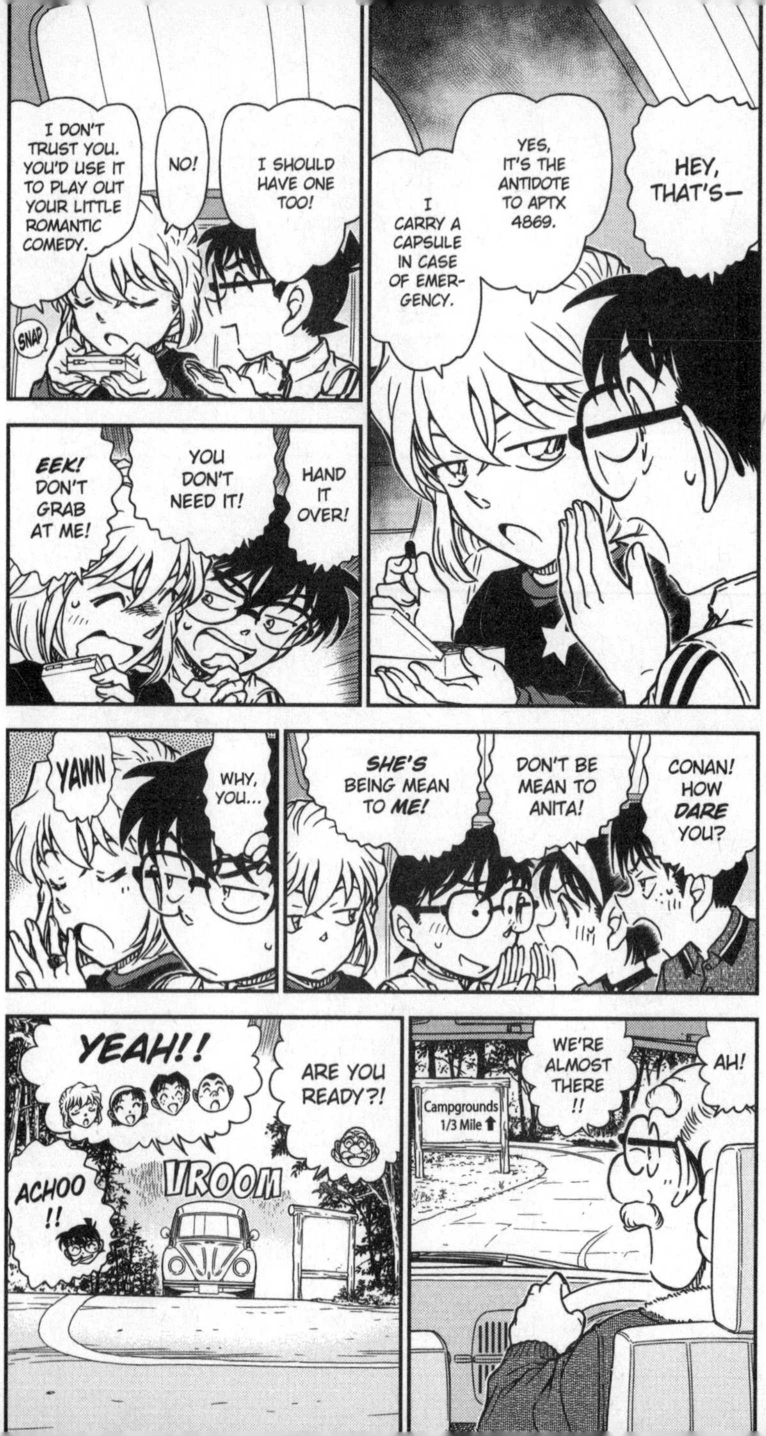
HEY, THAT'S—
YES, IT'S THE ANTIDOTE TO APTX 4869.
I CARRY A CAPSULE IN CASE OF EMERGENCY.
I SHOULD HAVE ONE TOO!
NO!
I DON'T TRUST YOU. YOU'D USE IT TO PLAY OUT YOUR LITTLE ROMANTIC COMEDY.
SNAP
HAND IT OVER!
YOU DON'T NEED IT!
EEK! DON'T GRAB AT ME!
CONAN! HOW DARE YOU?
DON'T BE MEAN TO ANITA!
SHE'S BEING MEAN TO ME!
WHY, YOU...
YAWN
AH!
WE'RE ALMOST THERE !!
Campgrounds
1/3 Mile
ARE YOU READY?!
YEAH!!
VROOM
ACHOO !!

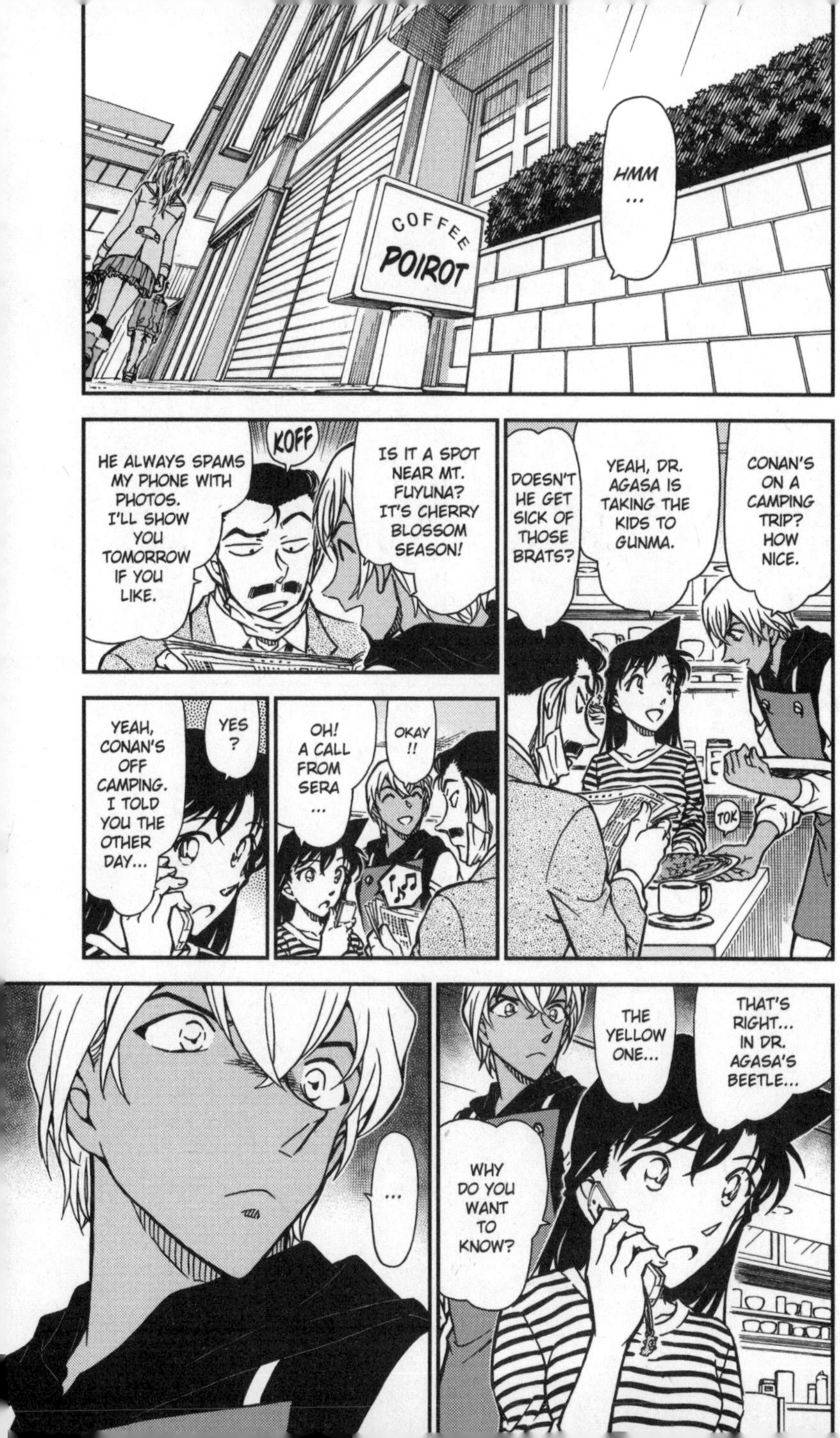
COFFEE
POIROT
HMM ...
CONAN'S ON A CAMPING TRIP? HOW NICE.
YEAH, DR. AGASA IS TAKING THE KIDS TO GUNMA.
DOESN'T HE GET SICK OF THOSE BRATS?
TOK
IS IT A SPOT NEAR MT. FUYUNA? IT'S CHERRY BLOSSOM SEASON!
KOFF
HE ALWAYS SPAMS MY PHONE WITH PHOTOS. I'LL SHOW YOU TOMORROW IF YOU LIKE.
OKAY !!
OH! A CALL FROM SERA ...
YES ?
YEAH, CONAN'S OFF CAMPING. I TOLD YOU THE OTHER DAY...
THAT'S RIGHT... IN DR. AGASA'S BEETLE...
THE YELLOW ONE...
WHY DO YOU WANT TO KNOW?
...

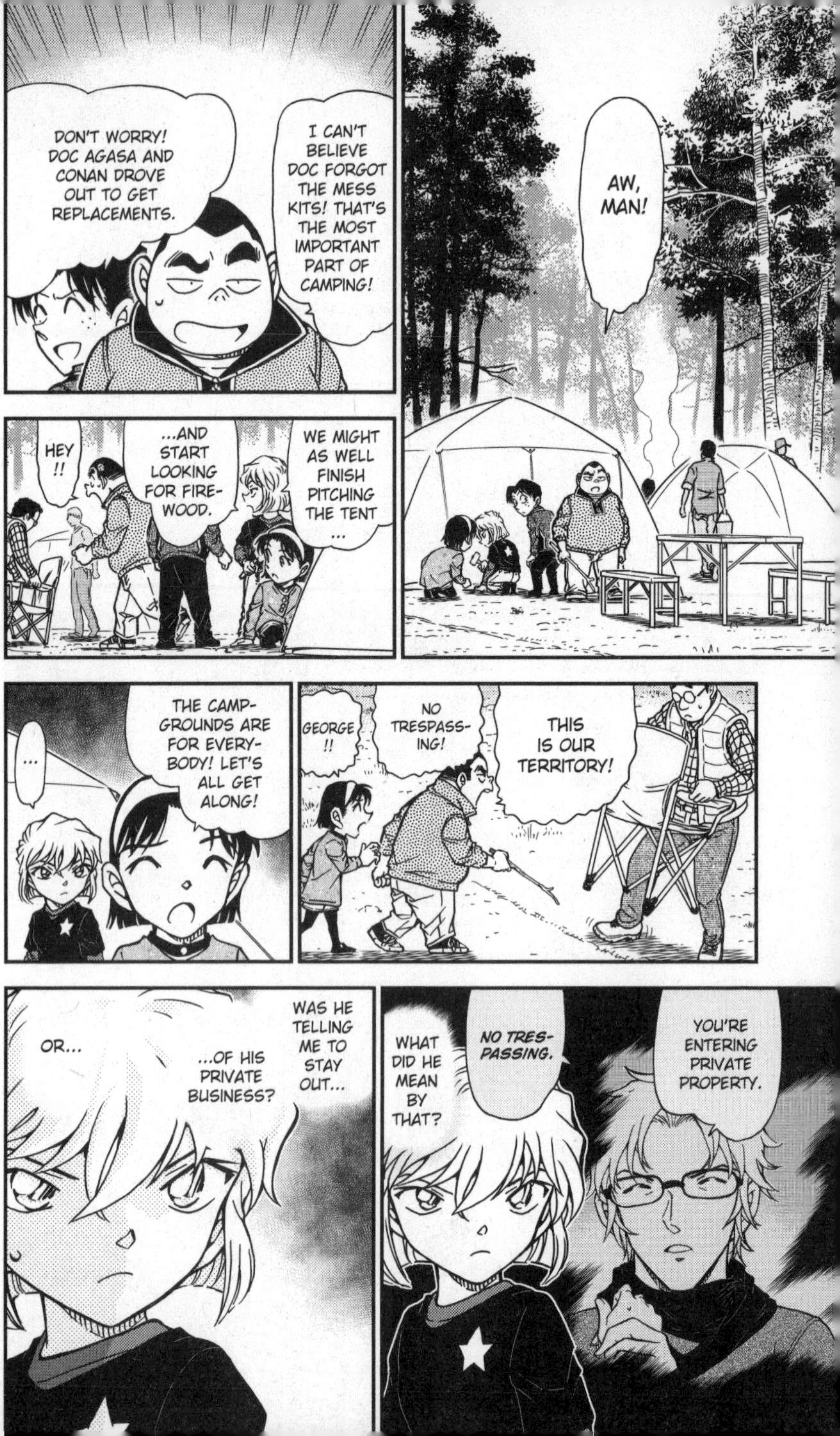
AW, MAN!
I CAN'T BELIEVE DOC FORGOT THE MESS KITS! THAT'S THE MOST IMPORTANT PART OF CAMPING!
DON'T WORRY! DOC AGASA AND CONAN DROVE OUT TO GET REPLACEMENTS.
WE MIGHT AS WELL FINISH PITCHING THE TENT ...
...AND START LOOKING FOR FIRE-WOOD.
HEY !!
THIS IS OUR TERRITORY!
NO TRESPASS-ING!
GEORGE !!
THE CAMP-GROUNDS ARE FOR EVERY-BODY! LET'S ALL GET ALONG!
...
YOU'RE ENTERING PRIVATE PROPERTY.
NO TRES-PASSING.
WHAT DID HE MEAN BY THAT?
WAS HE TELLING ME TO STAY OUT...
...OF HIS PRIVATE BUSINESS?
OR...

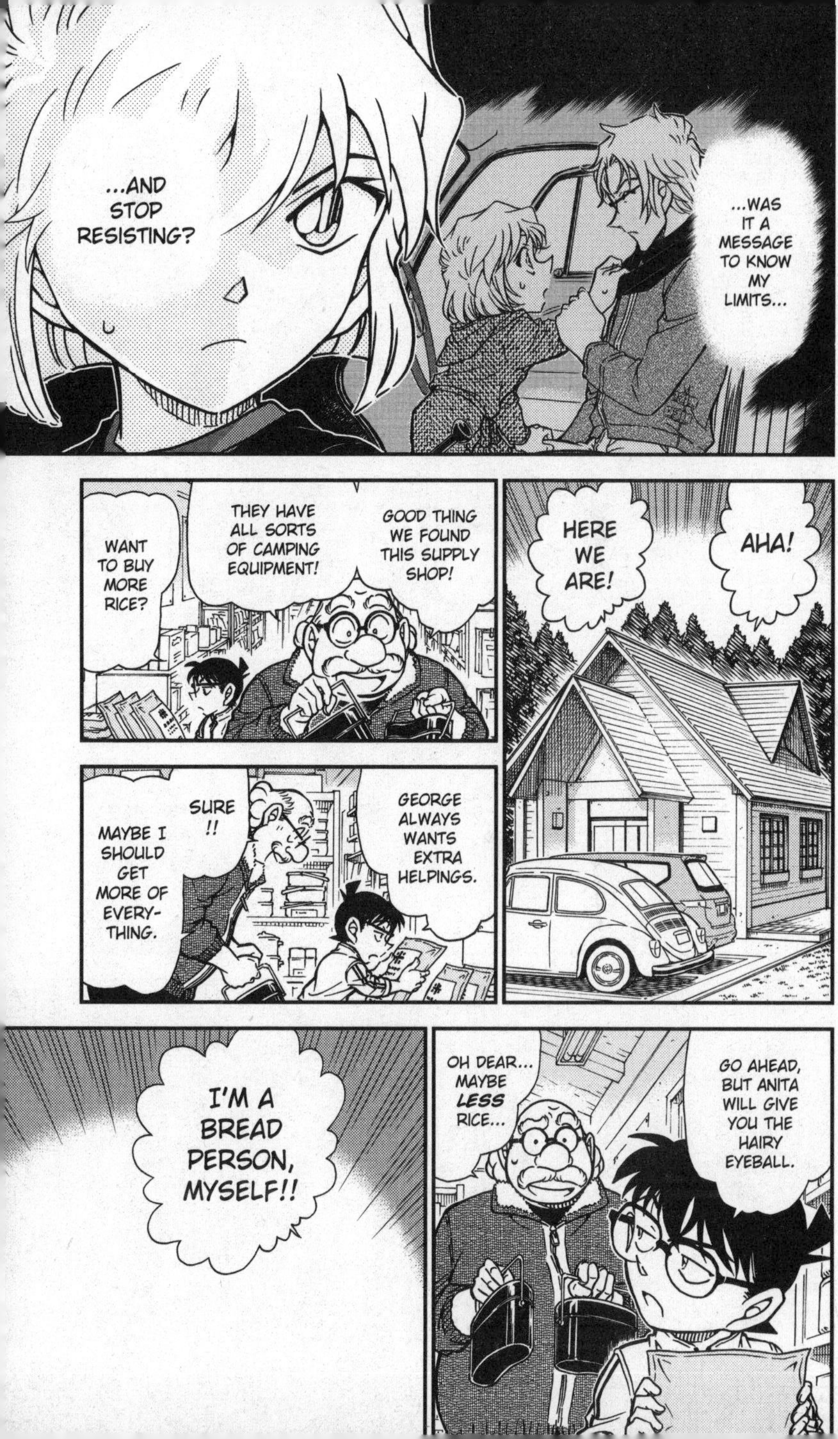
...WAS IT A MESSAGE TO KNOW MY LIMITS...
...AND STOP RESISTING?
AHA!
HERE WE ARE!
GOOD THING WE FOUND THIS SUPPLY SHOP!
THEY HAVE ALL SORTS OF CAMPING EQUIPMENT!
WANT TO BUY MORE RICE?
GEORGE ALWAYS WANTS EXTRA HELPINGS.
SURE!!
MAYBE I SHOULD GET MORE OF EVERYTHING.
GO AHEAD, BUT ANITA WILL GIVE YOU THE HAIRY EYEBALL.
OH DEAR... MAYBE LESS RICE...
I'M A BREAD PERSON, MYSELF!!

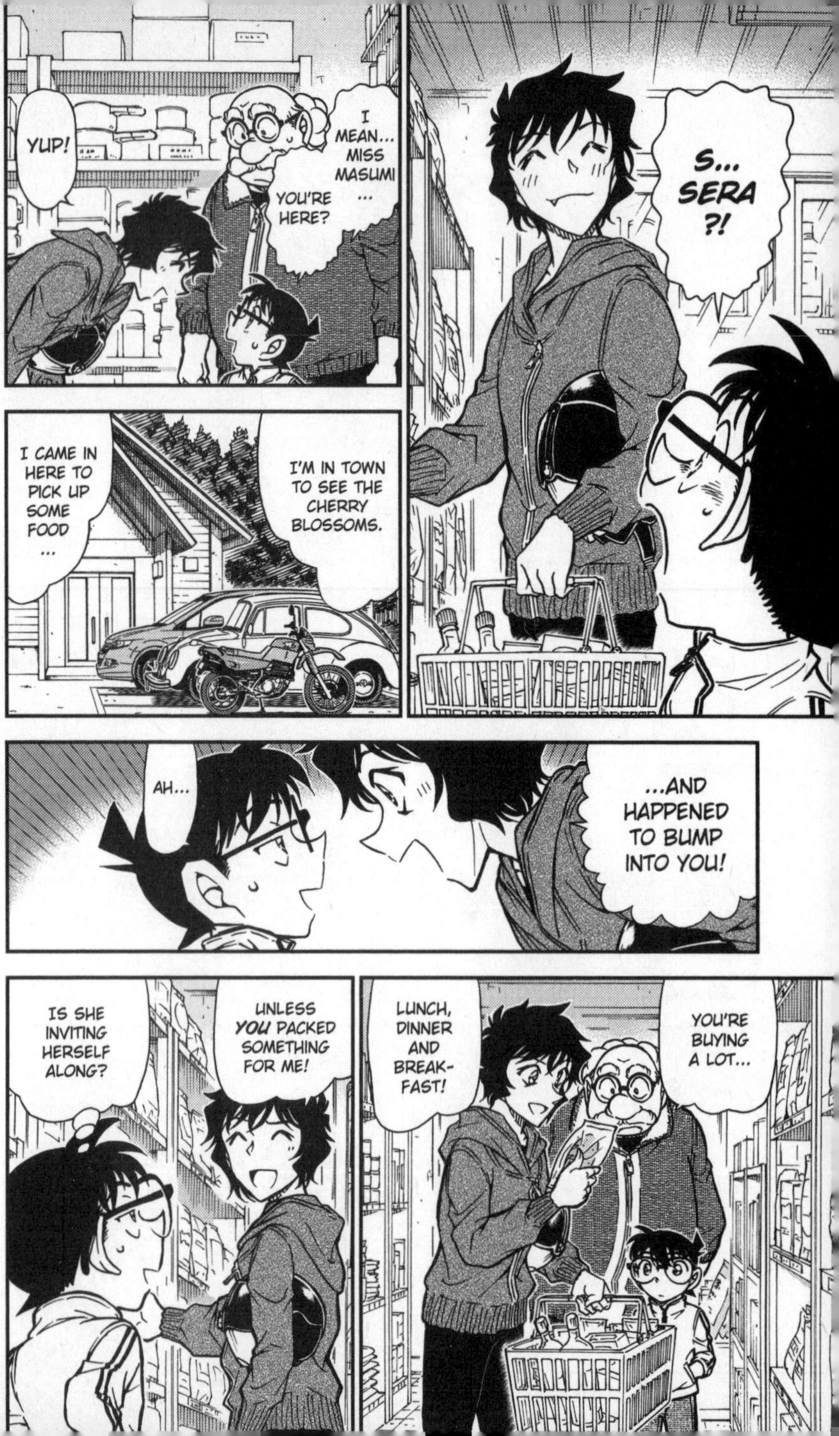
S... SERA?!
I MEAN... MISS MASUMI... YOU'RE HERE?
YUP!
I'M IN TOWN TO SEE THE CHERRY BLOSSOMS.
I CAME IN HERE TO PICK UP SOME FOOD...
...AND HAPPENED TO BUMP INTO YOU!
AH...
YOU'RE BUYING A LOT...
LUNCH, DINNER AND BREAKFAST!
UNLESS YOU PACKED SOMETHING FOR ME!
IS SHE INVITING HERSELF ALONG?

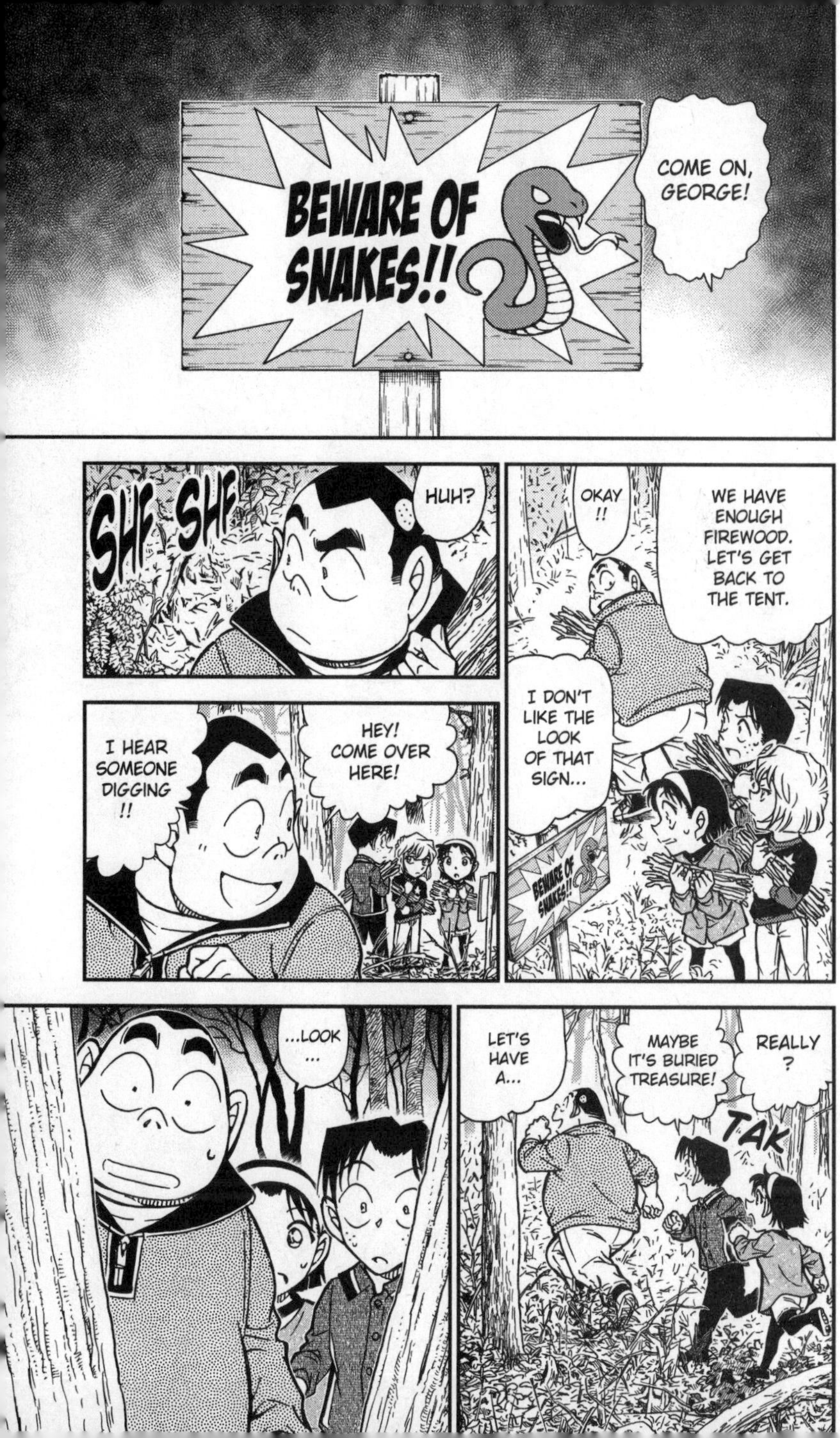
COME ON, GEORGE!
BEWARE OF SNAKES!!
WE HAVE ENOUGH FIREWOOD. LET'S GET BACK TO THE TENT.
OKAY!!
I DON'T LIKE THE LOOK OF THAT SIGN...
BEWARE OF SNAKES!!
HUH?
SHF SHF
HEY! COME OVER HERE!
I HEAR SOMEONE DIGGING!!
REALLY?
MAYBE IT'S BURIED TREASURE!
LET'S HAVE A...
TAK
...LOOK...

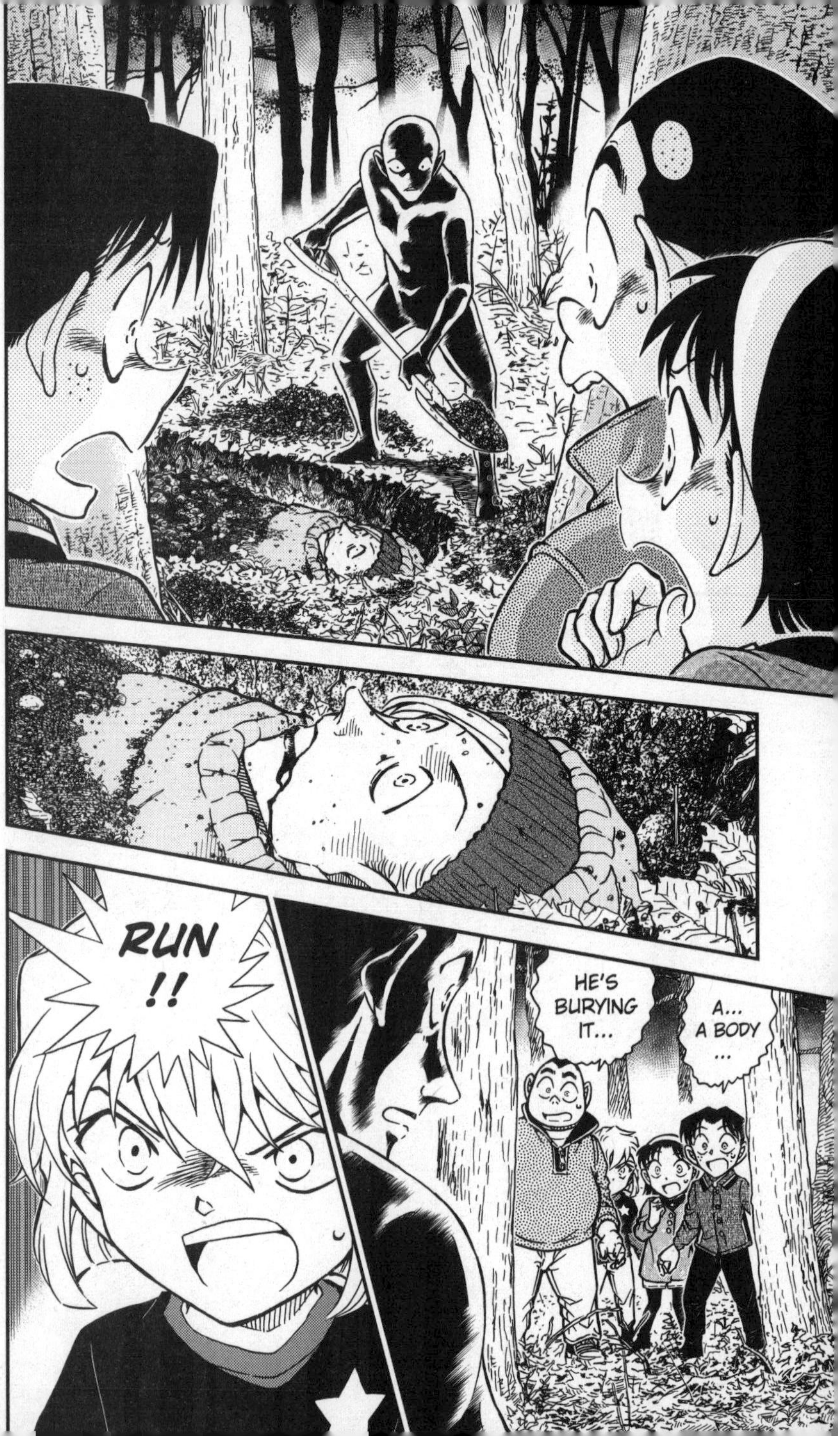
A... A BODY ...
HE'S BURYING IT...
RUN !!

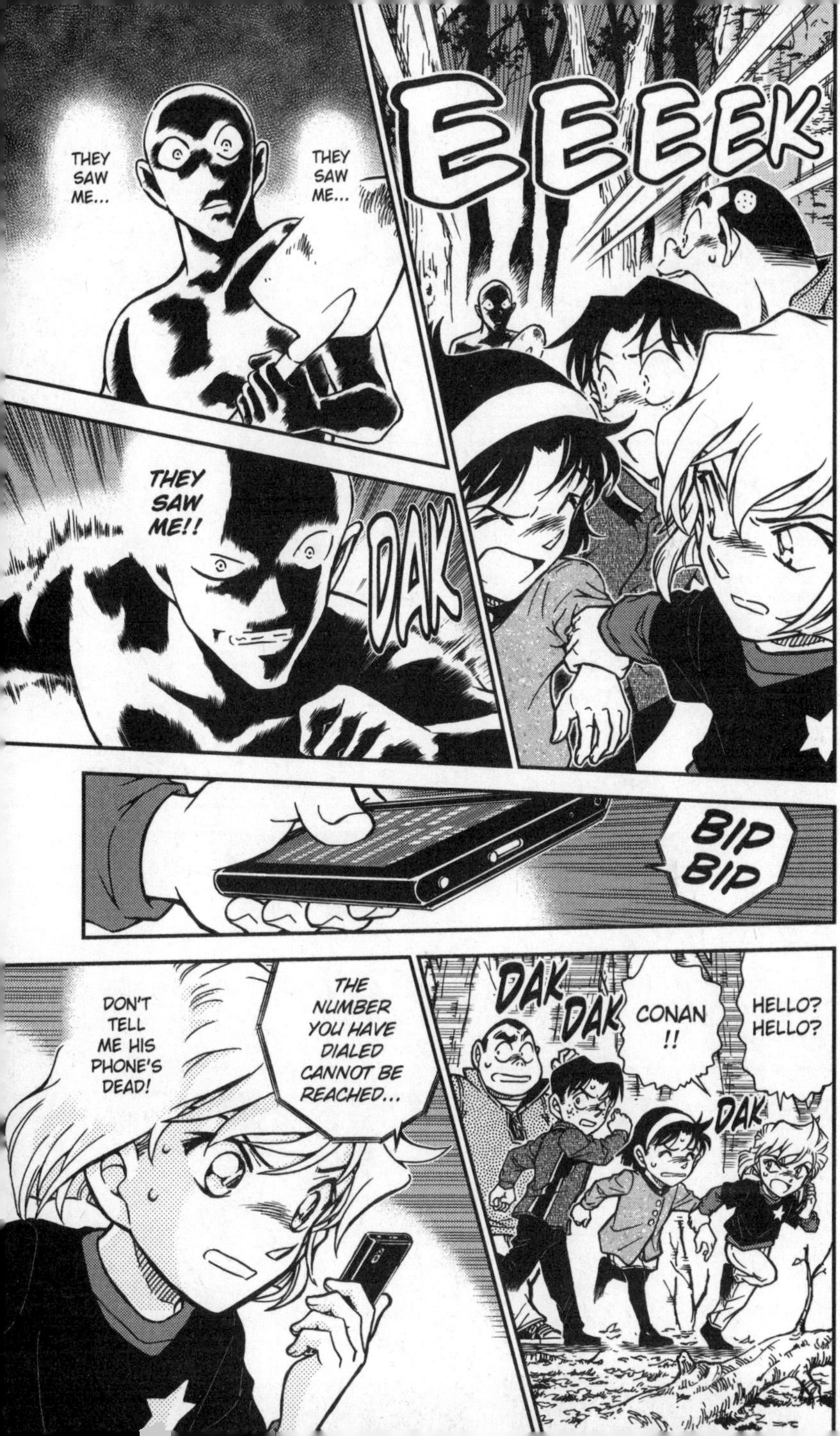
EEEEK
THEY SAW ME...
THEY SAW ME...
THEY SAW ME!!
DAK
BIP BIP
HELLO? HELLO?
CONAN !!
DAK DAK
DAK
THE NUMBER YOU HAVE DIALED CANNOT BE REACHED...
DON'T TELL ME HIS PHONE'S DEAD!

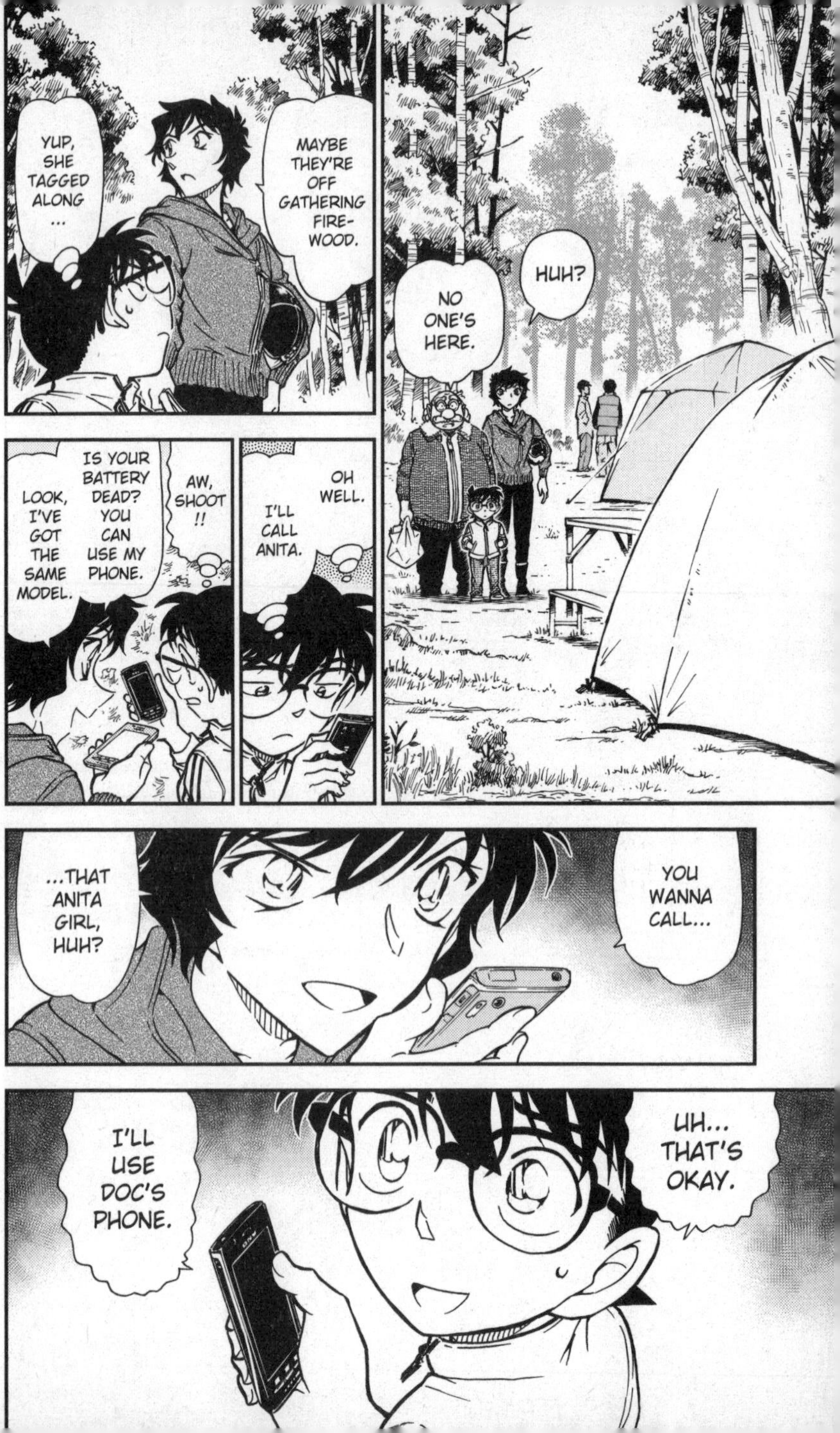
HUH?
NO ONE'S HERE.
MAYBE THEY'RE OFF GATHERING FIRE-WOOD.
YUP, SHE TAGGED ALONG ...
OH WELL. I'LL CALL ANITA.
AW, SHOOT !!
IS YOUR BATTERY DEAD? YOU CAN USE MY PHONE.
LOOK, I'VE GOT THE SAME MODEL.
YOU WANNA CALL...
...THAT ANITA GIRL, HUH?
UH... THAT'S OKAY.
I'LL USE DOC'S PHONE.

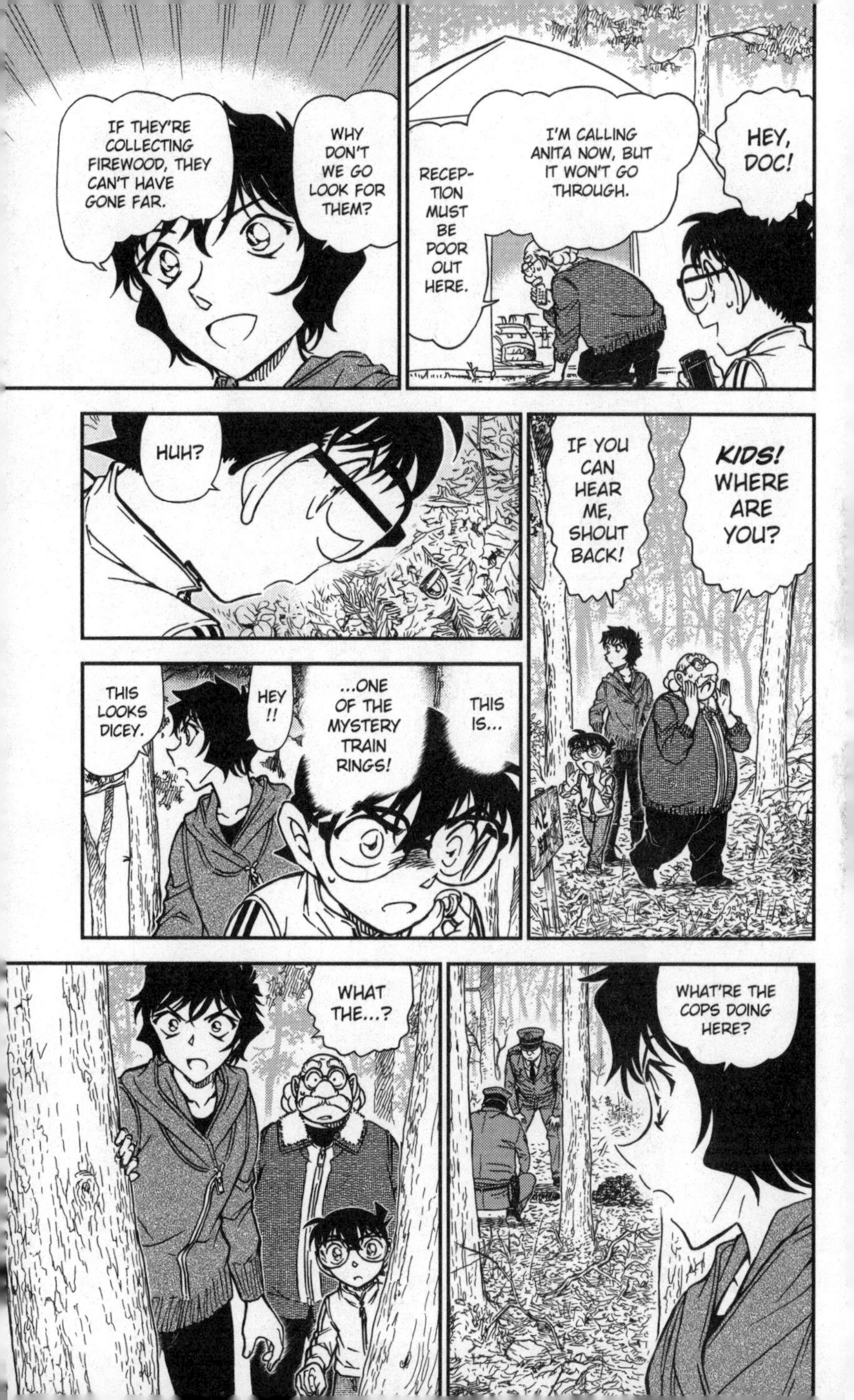
HEY, DOC!
I'M CALLING ANITA NOW, BUT IT WON'T GO THROUGH.
RECEPTION MUST BE POOR OUT HERE.
WHY DON'T WE GO LOOK FOR THEM?
IF THEY'RE COLLECTING FIREWOOD, THEY CAN'T HAVE GONE FAR.
KIDS! WHERE ARE YOU?
IF YOU CAN HEAR ME, SHOUT BACK!
HUH?
THIS IS...
...ONE OF THE MYSTERY TRAIN RINGS!
HEY!!
THIS LOOKS DICEY.
WHAT'RE THE COPS DOING HERE?
WHAT THE...?

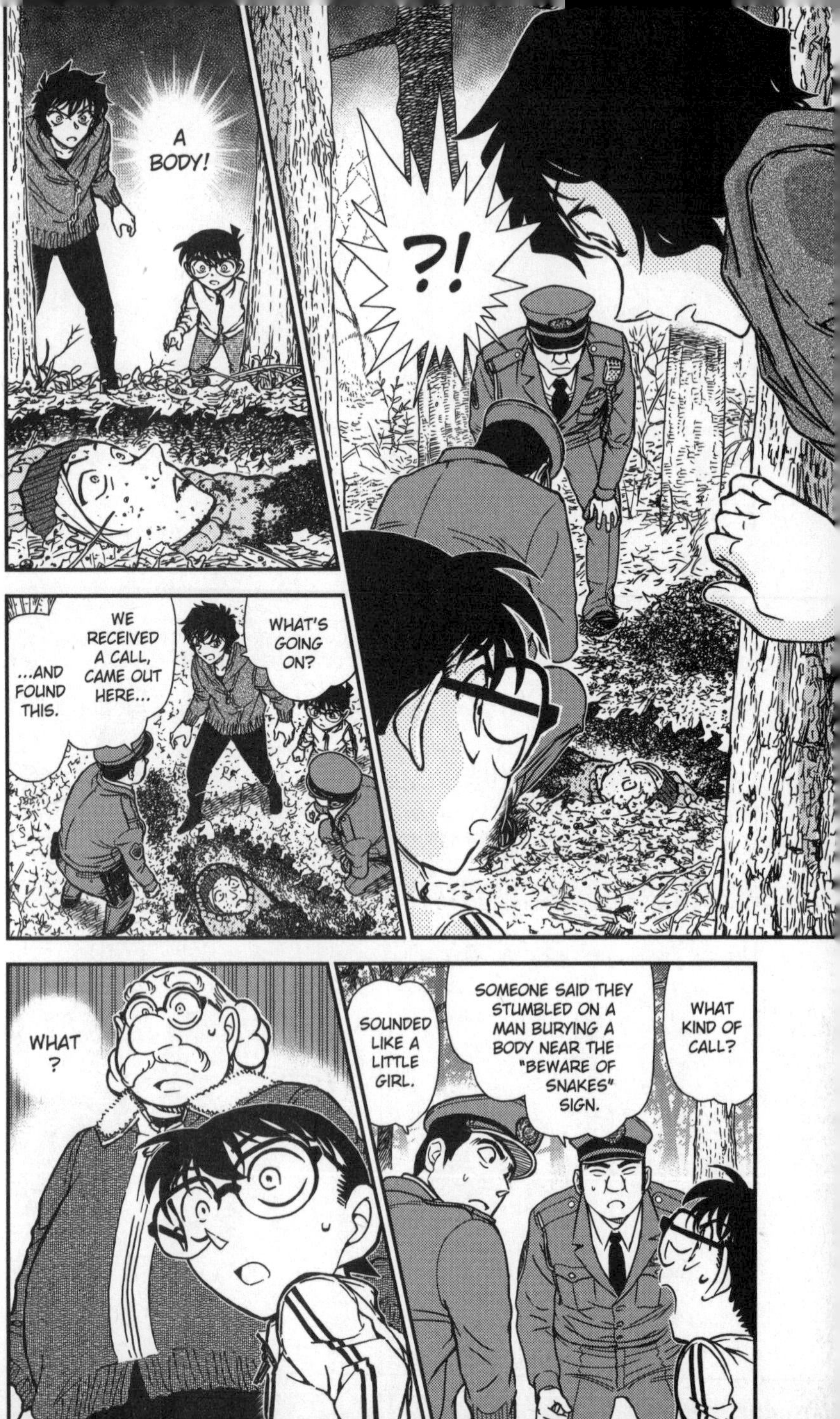
?!
A BODY!
WHAT'S GOING ON?
WE RECEIVED A CALL, CAME OUT HERE...
...AND FOUND THIS.
WHAT KIND OF CALL?
SOMEONE SAID THEY STUMBLED ON A MAN BURYING A BODY NEAR THE "BEWARE OF SNAKES" SIGN.
SOUNDED LIKE A LITTLE GIRL.
WHAT?

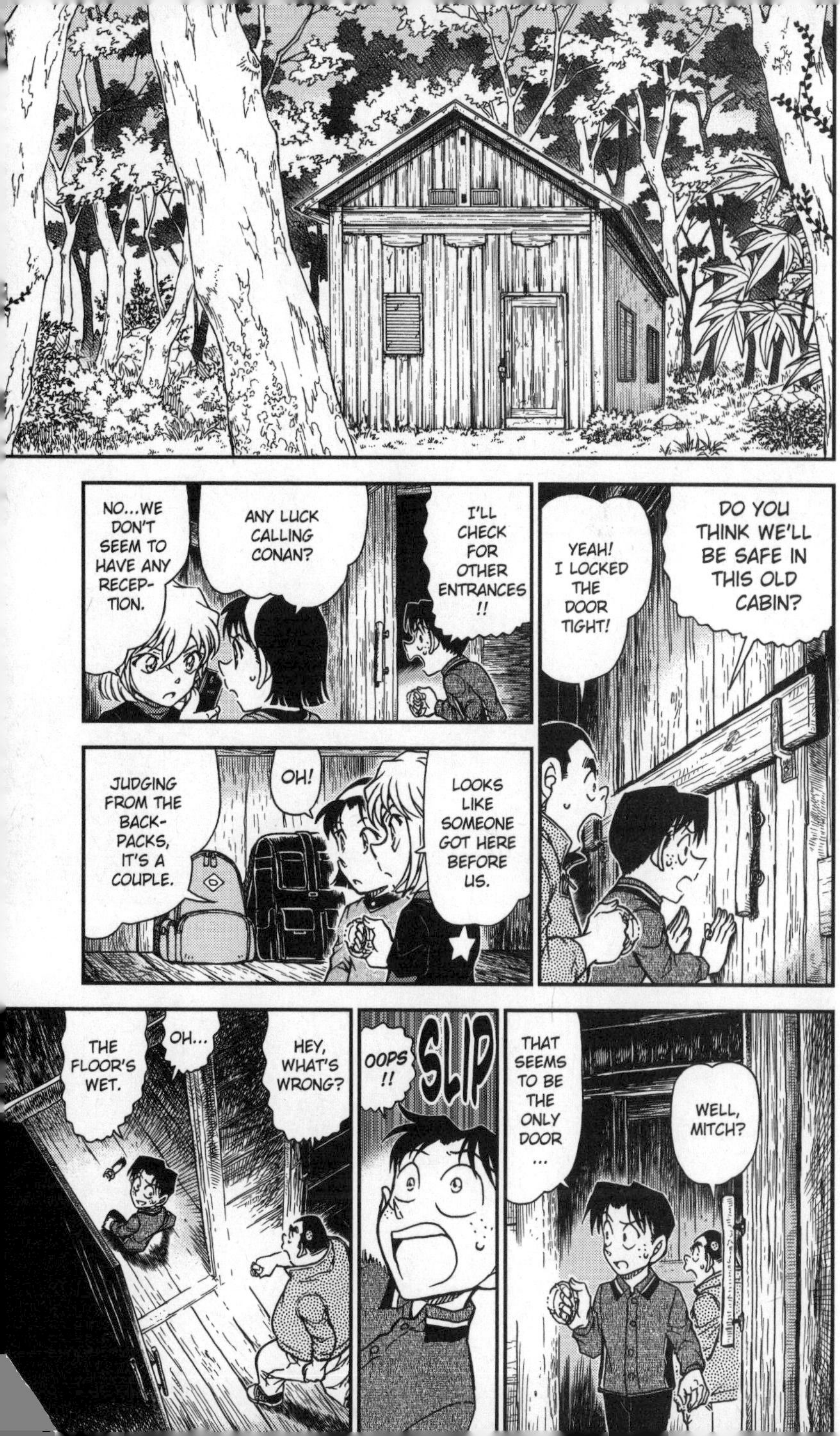
DO YOU THINK WE'LL BE SAFE IN THIS OLD CABIN?
YEAH! I LOCKED THE DOOR TIGHT!
I'LL CHECK FOR OTHER ENTRANCES !!
ANY LUCK CALLING CONAN?
NO...WE DON'T SEEM TO HAVE ANY RECEP-TION.
LOOKS LIKE SOMEONE GOT HERE BEFORE US.
OH!
JUDGING FROM THE BACK-PACKS, IT'S A COUPLE.
WELL, MITCH?
THAT SEEMS TO BE THE ONLY DOOR ...
SLIP
OOPS !!
HEY, WHAT'S WRONG?
OH...
THE FLOOR'S WET.

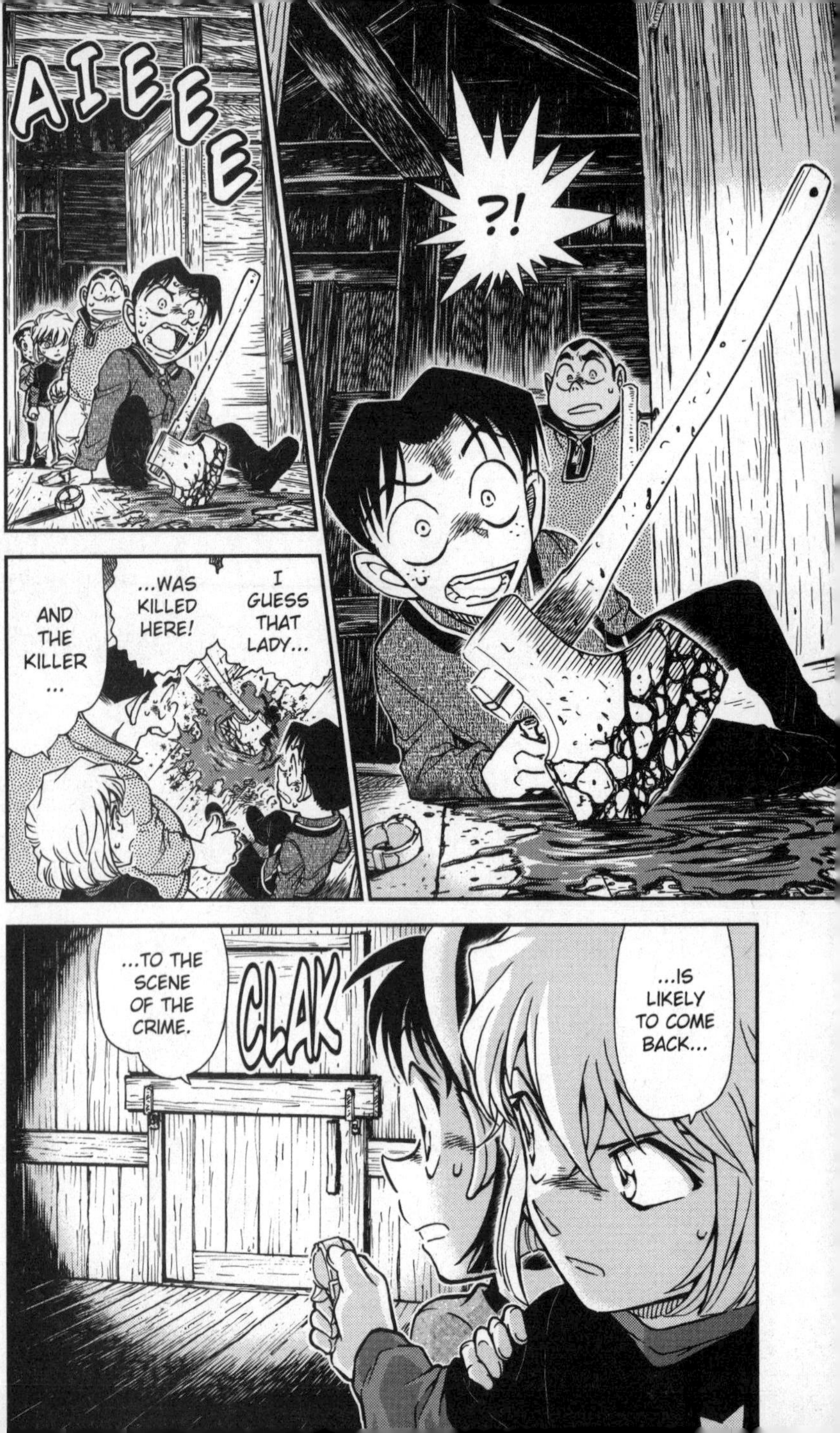

?!
AIEEE
I GUESS THAT LADY...
...WAS KILLED HERE!
AND THE KILLER ...
...IS LIKELY TO COME BACK...
CLAK
...TO THE SCENE OF THE CRIME.

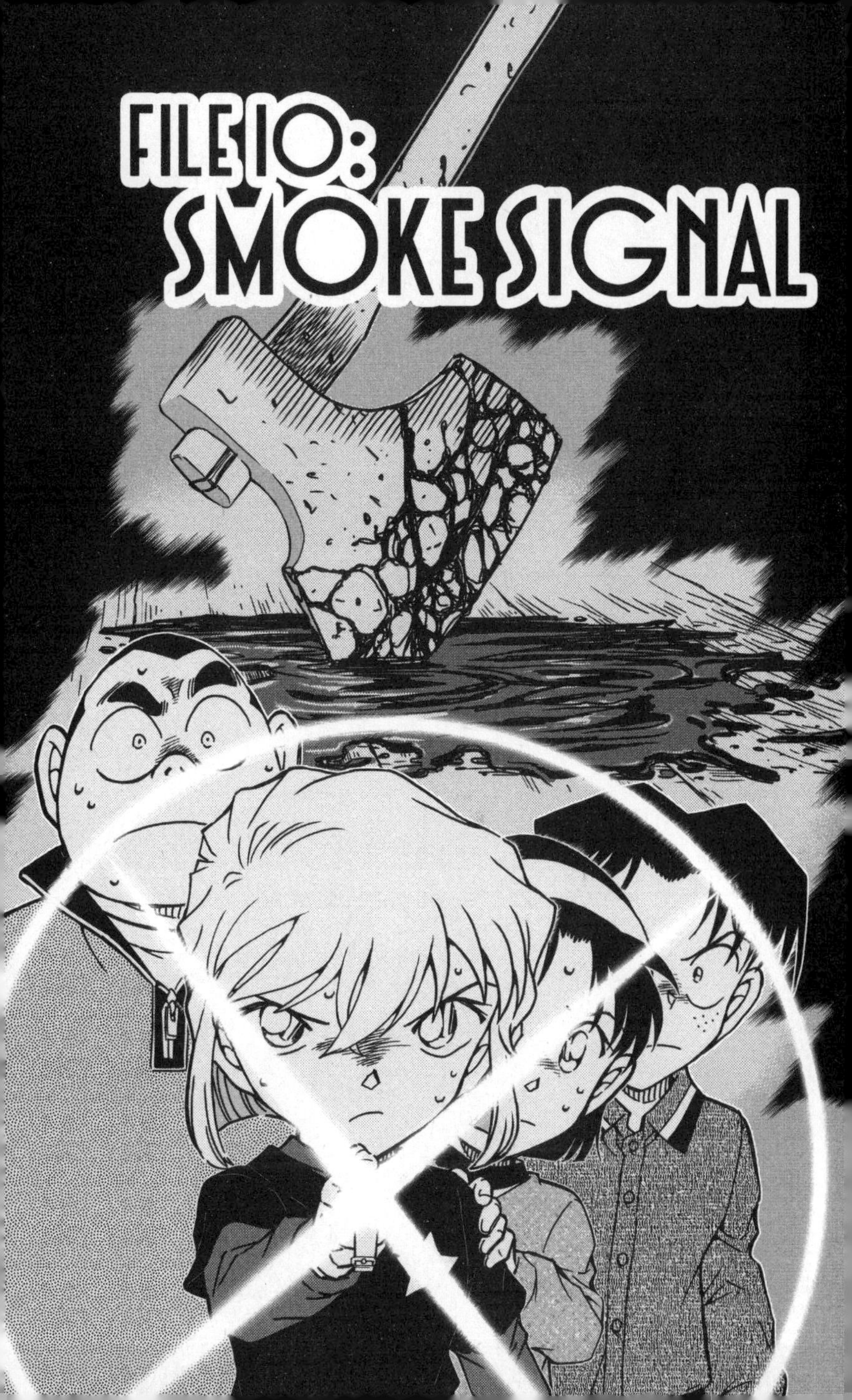
FILE 10:
SMOKE SIGNAL

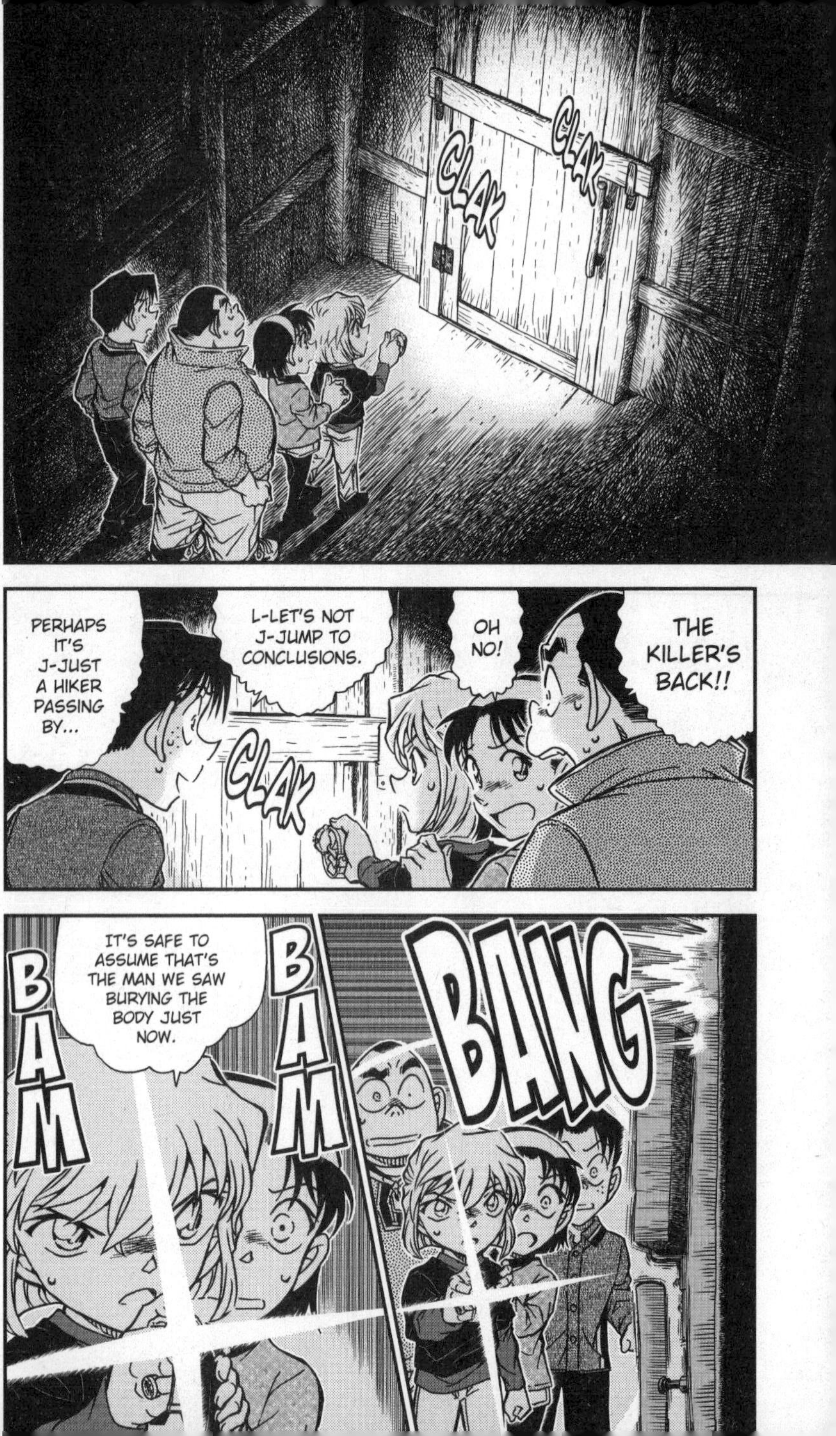
CLAK
CLAK
THE KILLER'S BACK!!
OH NO!
L-LET'S NOT J-JUMP TO CONCLUSIONS.
CLAK
PERHAPS IT'S J-JUST A HIKER PASSING BY...
BANG
BAM
IT'S SAFE TO ASSUME THAT'S THE MAN WE SAW BURYING THE BODY JUST NOW.
BAM

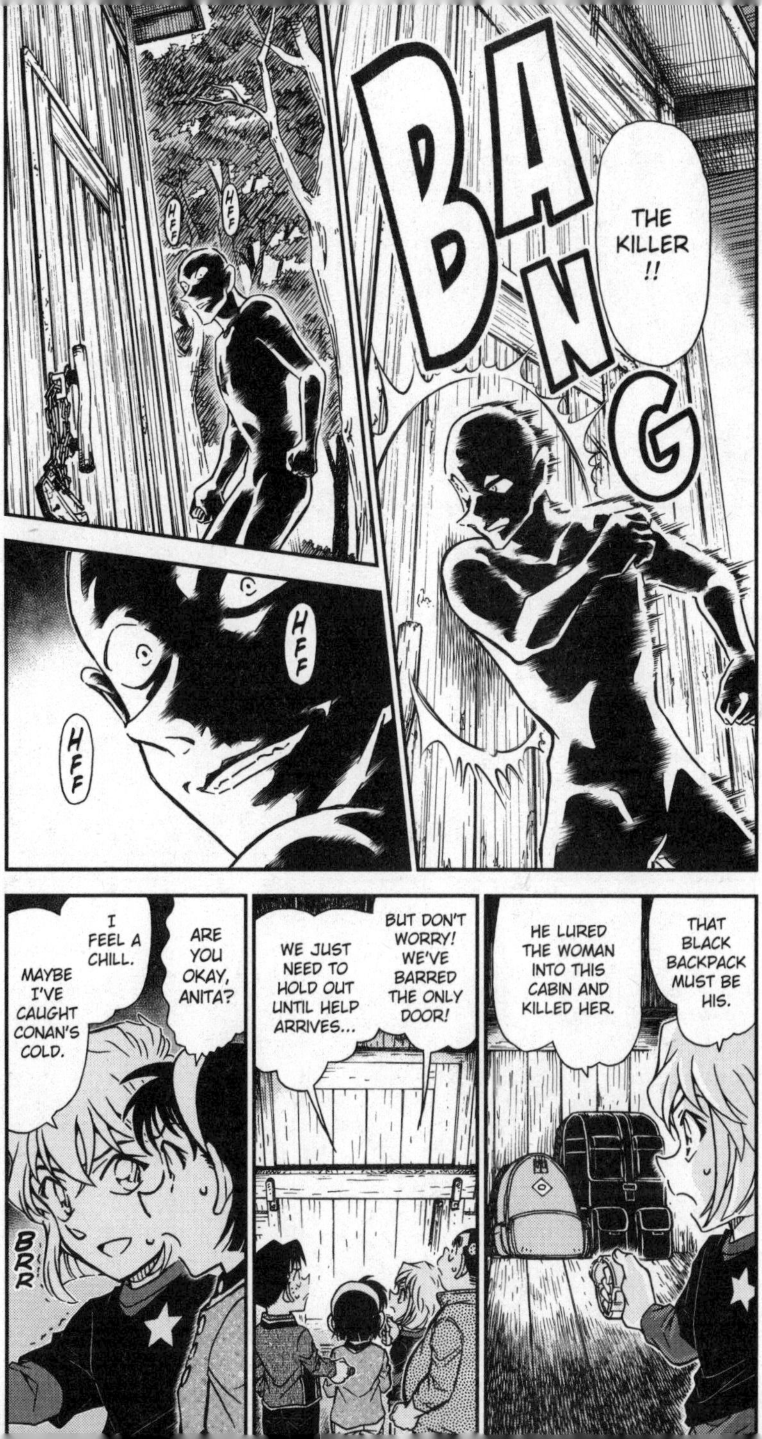
BANG
THE KILLER!!
HFF
HFF
HFF
HFF
THAT BLACK BACKPACK MUST BE HIS.
HE LURED THE WOMAN INTO THIS CABIN AND KILLED HER.
BUT DON'T WORRY! WE'VE BARRED THE ONLY DOOR!
WE JUST NEED TO HOLD OUT UNTIL HELP ARRIVES...
ARE YOU OKAY, ANITA?
I FEEL A CHILL.
MAYBE I'VE CAUGHT CONAN'S COLD.
BRR

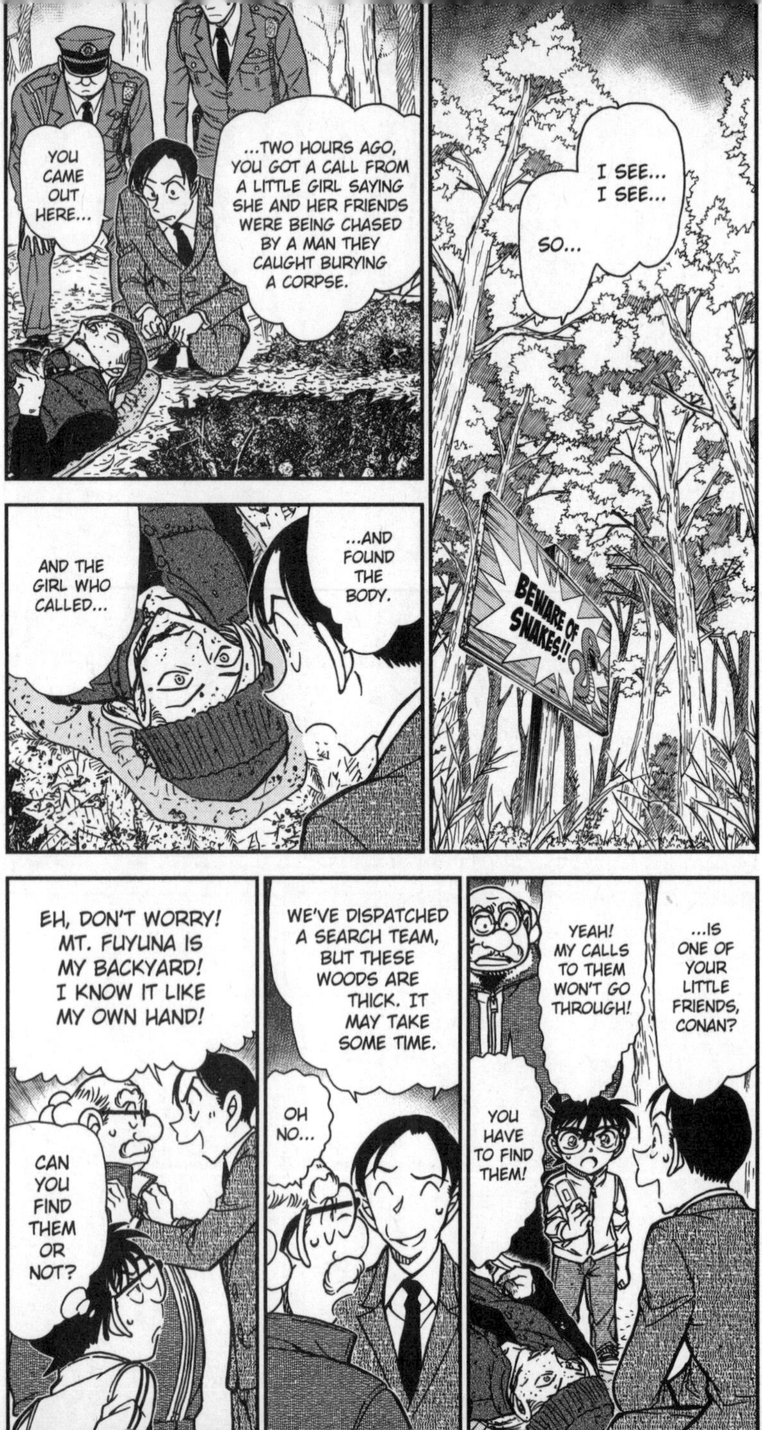
I SEE... I SEE...
SO...
BEWARE OF SNAKES!!
...TWO HOURS AGO, YOU GOT A CALL FROM A LITTLE GIRL SAYING SHE AND HER FRIENDS WERE BEING CHASED BY A MAN THEY CAUGHT BURYING A CORPSE.
YOU CAME OUT HERE...
...AND FOUND THE BODY.
AND THE GIRL WHO CALLED...
...IS ONE OF YOUR LITTLE FRIENDS, CONAN?
YEAH! MY CALLS TO THEM WON'T GO THROUGH!
YOU HAVE TO FIND THEM!
WE'VE DISPATCHED A SEARCH TEAM, BUT THESE WOODS ARE THICK. IT MAY TAKE SOME TIME.
OH NO...
EH, DON'T WORRY! MT. FUYUNA IS MY BACKYARD! I KNOW IT LIKE MY OWN HAND!
CAN YOU FIND THEM OR NOT?

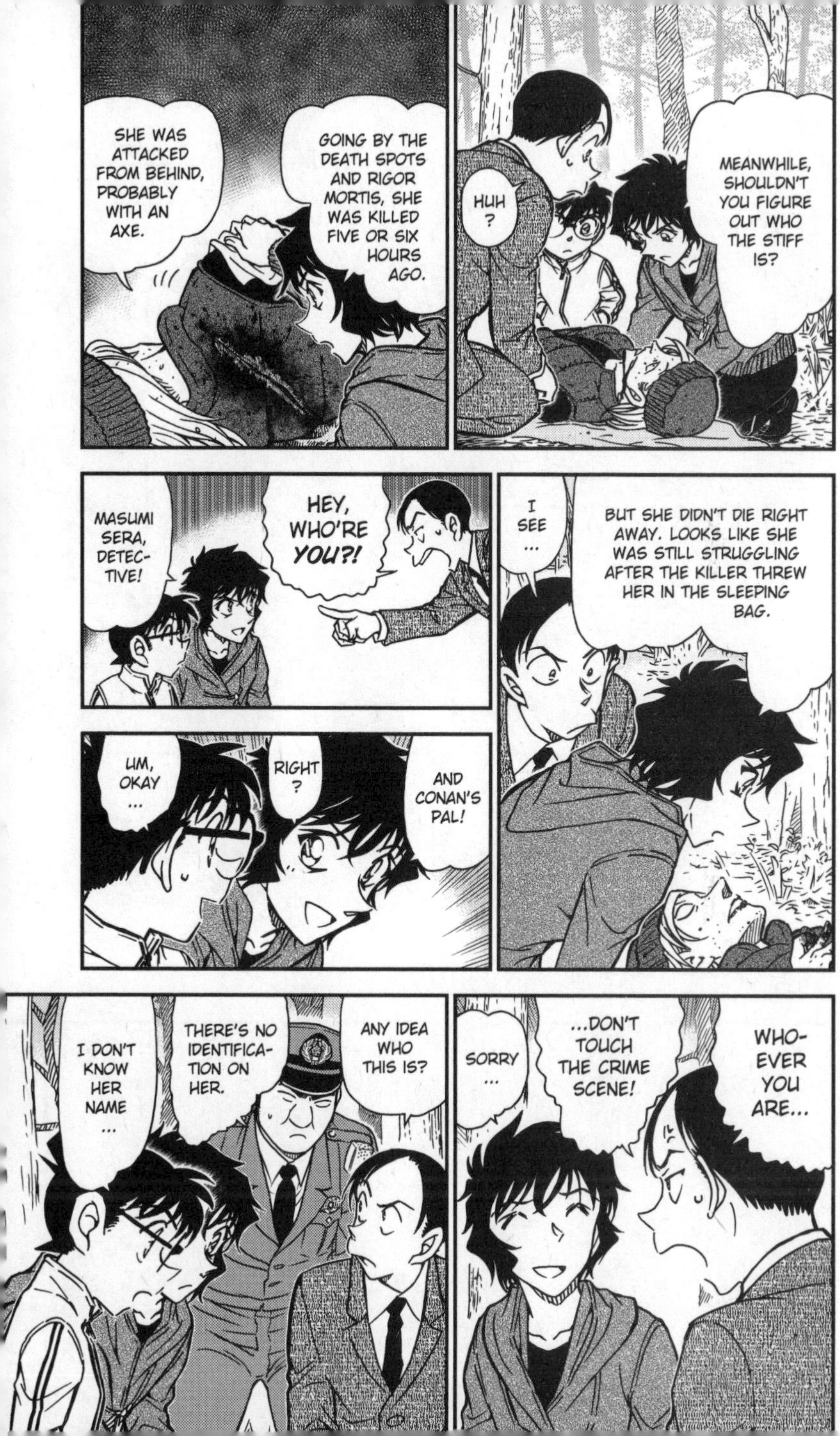
MEANWHILE, SHOULDN'T YOU FIGURE OUT WHO THE STIFF IS?
HUH?
GOING BY THE DEATH SPOTS AND RIGOR MORTIS, SHE WAS KILLED FIVE OR SIX HOURS AGO.
SHE WAS ATTACKED FROM BEHIND, PROBABLY WITH AN AXE.
BUT SHE DIDN'T DIE RIGHT AWAY. LOOKS LIKE SHE WAS STILL STRUGGLING AFTER THE KILLER THREW HER IN THE SLEEPING BAG.
I SEE...
HEY, WHO'RE *YOU?!*
MASUMI SERA, DETECTIVE!
AND CONAN'S PAL!
RIGHT?
UM, OKAY...
WHOEVER YOU ARE...
...DON'T TOUCH THE CRIME SCENE!
SORRY...
ANY IDEA WHO THIS IS?
THERE'S NO IDENTIFICATION ON HER.
I DON'T KNOW HER NAME...

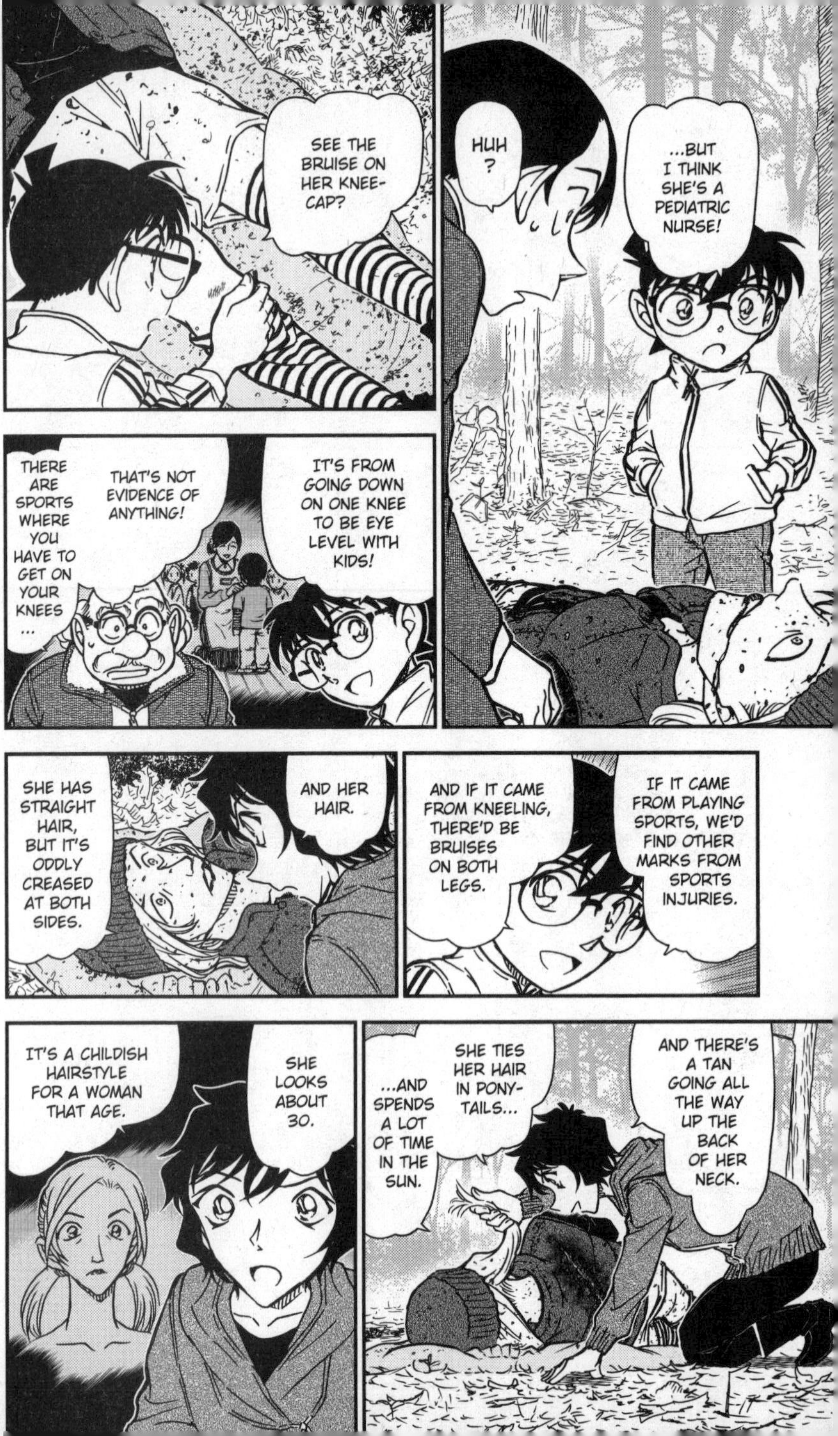
...BUT I THINK SHE'S A PEDIATRIC NURSE!
HUH?
SEE THE BRUISE ON HER KNEE-CAP?
IT'S FROM GOING DOWN ON ONE KNEE TO BE EYE LEVEL WITH KIDS!
THAT'S NOT EVIDENCE OF ANYTHING!
THERE ARE SPORTS WHERE YOU HAVE TO GET ON YOUR KNEES...
IF IT CAME FROM PLAYING SPORTS, WE'D FIND OTHER MARKS FROM SPORTS INJURIES.
AND IF IT CAME FROM KNEELING, THERE'D BE BRUISES ON BOTH LEGS.
AND HER HAIR.
SHE HAS STRAIGHT HAIR, BUT IT'S ODDLY CREASED AT BOTH SIDES.
AND THERE'S A TAN GOING ALL THE WAY UP THE BACK OF HER NECK.
SHE TIES HER HAIR IN PONY-TAILS...
...AND SPENDS A LOT OF TIME IN THE SUN.
SHE LOOKS ABOUT 30.
IT'S A CHILDISH HAIRSTYLE FOR A WOMAN THAT AGE.

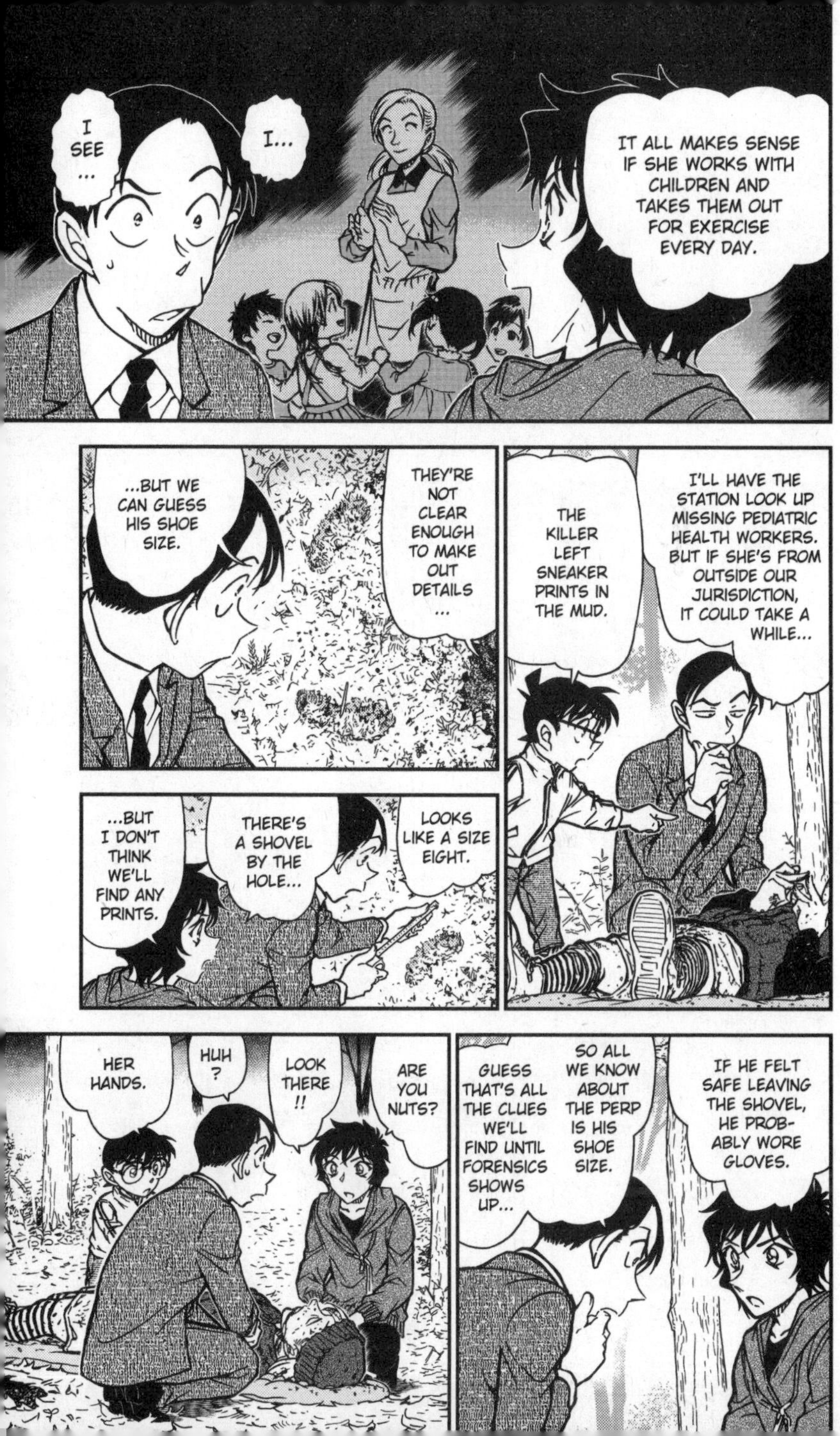
IT ALL MAKES SENSE IF SHE WORKS WITH CHILDREN AND TAKES THEM OUT FOR EXERCISE EVERY DAY.
I...
I SEE ...
I'LL HAVE THE STATION LOOK UP MISSING PEDIATRIC HEALTH WORKERS. BUT IF SHE'S FROM OUTSIDE OUR JURISDICTION, IT COULD TAKE A WHILE...
THE KILLER LEFT SNEAKER PRINTS IN THE MUD.
THEY'RE NOT CLEAR ENOUGH TO MAKE OUT DETAILS ...
...BUT WE CAN GUESS HIS SHOE SIZE.
LOOKS LIKE A SIZE EIGHT.
THERE'S A SHOVEL BY THE HOLE...
...BUT I DON'T THINK WE'LL FIND ANY PRINTS.
IF HE FELT SAFE LEAVING THE SHOVEL, HE PROB-ABLY WORE GLOVES.
SO ALL WE KNOW ABOUT THE PERP IS HIS SHOE SIZE.
GUESS THAT'S ALL THE CLUES WE'LL FIND UNTIL FORENSICS SHOWS UP...
ARE YOU NUTS?
LOOK THERE !!
HUH ?
HER HANDS.

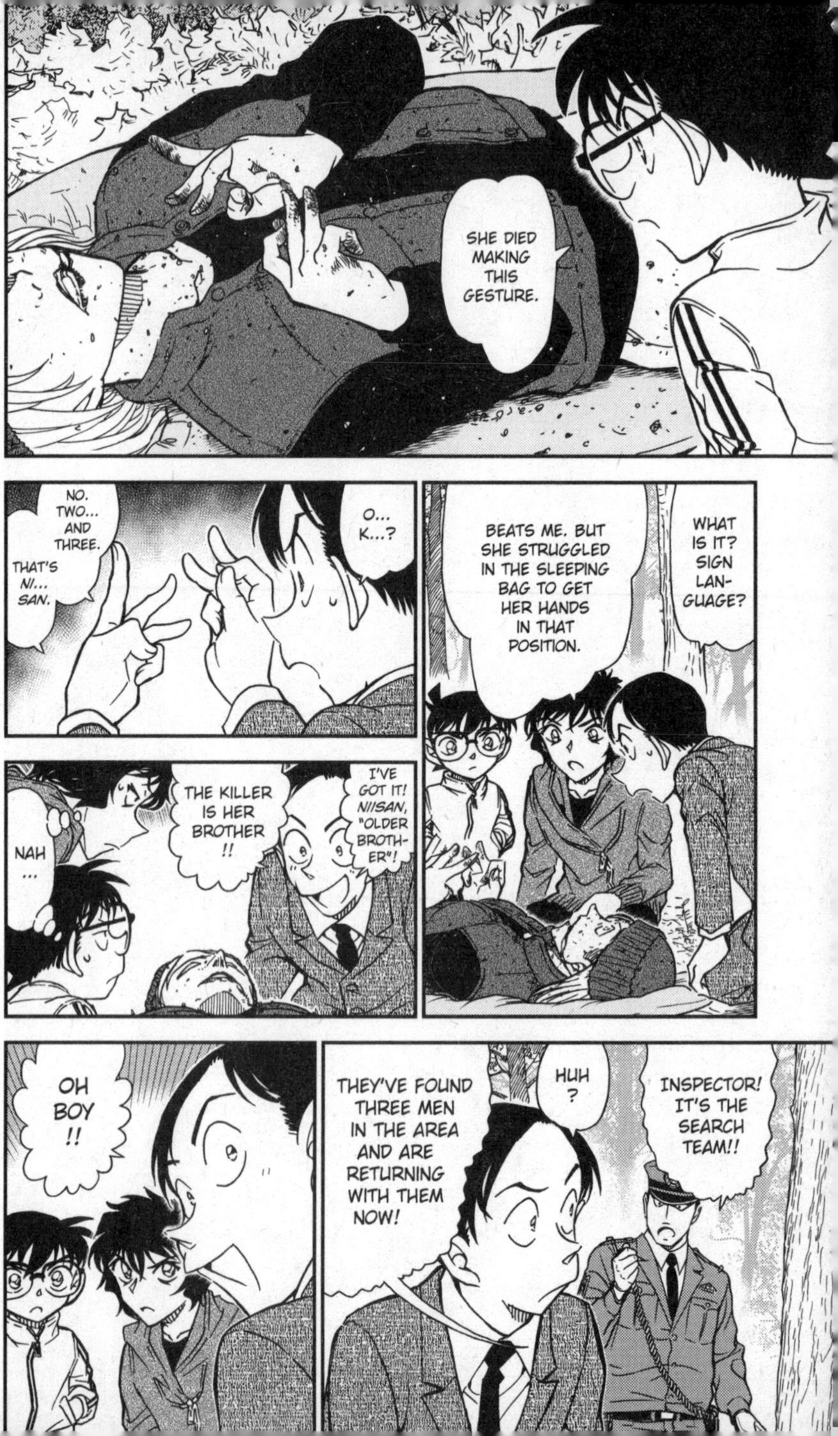
SHE DIED MAKING THIS GESTURE.
WHAT IS IT? SIGN LAN-GUAGE?
BEATS ME. BUT SHE STRUGGLED IN THE SLEEPING BAG TO GET HER HANDS IN THAT POSITION.
O... K...?
NO. TWO... AND THREE.
THAT'S NI... SAN.
I'VE GOT IT! NIISAN, "OLDER BROTH-ER"!
THE KILLER IS HER BROTHER!!
NAH...
INSPECTOR! IT'S THE SEARCH TEAM!!
HUH?
THEY'VE FOUND THREE MEN IN THE AREA AND ARE RETURNING WITH THEM NOW!
OH BOY!!

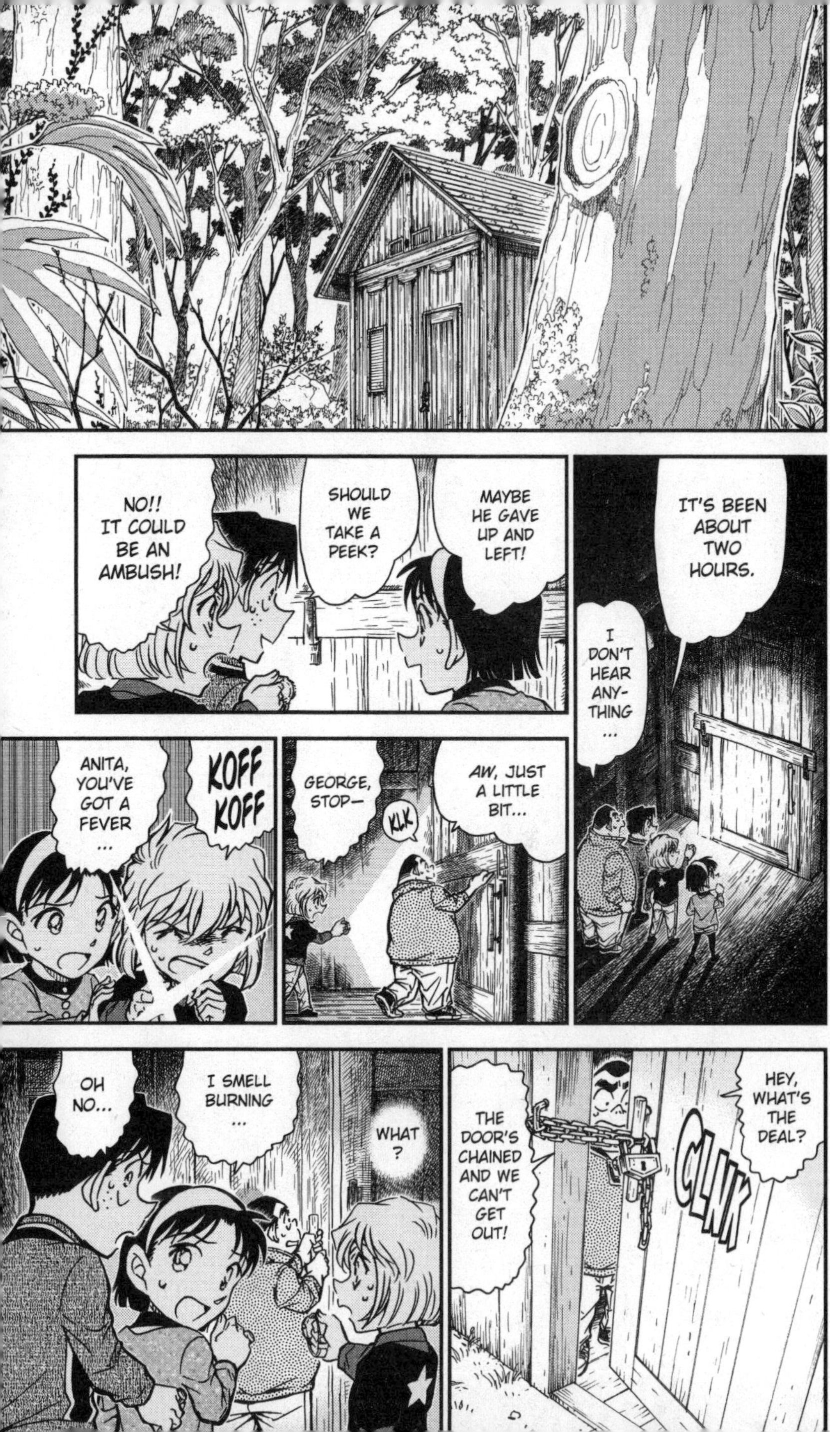
IT'S BEEN ABOUT TWO HOURS.
I DON'T HEAR ANY-THING...
MAYBE HE GAVE UP AND LEFT!
SHOULD WE TAKE A PEEK?
NO!! IT COULD BE AN AMBUSH!
AW, JUST A LITTLE BIT...
GEORGE, STOP—
KLK
KOFF KOFF
ANITA, YOU'VE GOT A FEVER...
HEY, WHAT'S THE DEAL?
CLNK
THE DOOR'S CHAINED AND WE CAN'T GET OUT!
WHAT?
I SMELL BURNING...
OH NO...

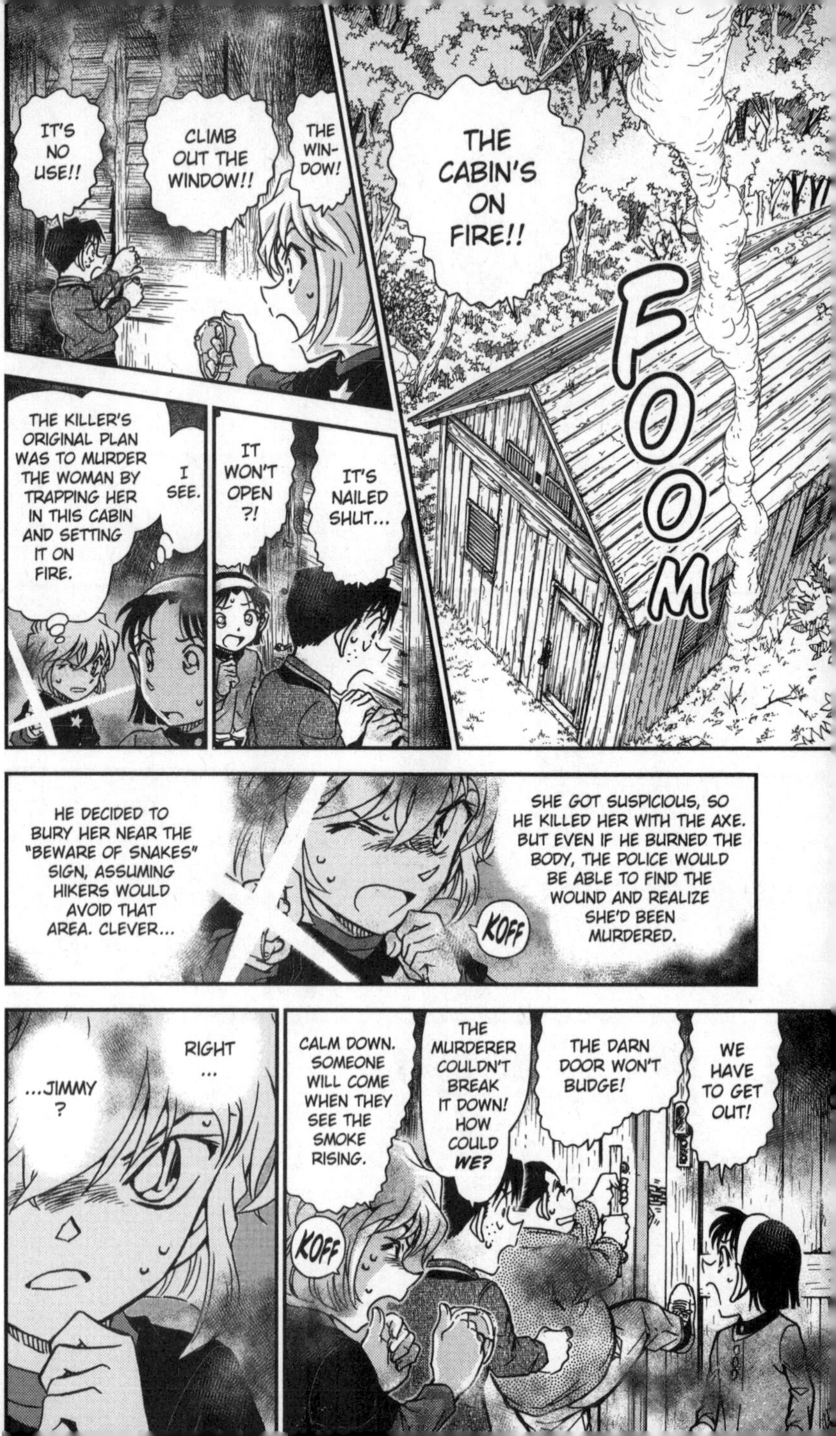
THE CABIN'S ON FIRE!!
FOOM
THE WIN-DOW!
CLIMB OUT THE WINDOW!!
IT'S NO USE!!
IT'S NAILED SHUT...
IT WON'T OPEN ?!
I SEE.
THE KILLER'S ORIGINAL PLAN WAS TO MURDER THE WOMAN BY TRAPPING HER IN THIS CABIN AND SETTING IT ON FIRE.
SHE GOT SUSPICIOUS, SO HE KILLED HER WITH THE AXE. BUT EVEN IF HE BURNED THE BODY, THE POLICE WOULD BE ABLE TO FIND THE WOUND AND REALIZE SHE'D BEEN MURDERED.
KOFF
HE DECIDED TO BURY HER NEAR THE "BEWARE OF SNAKES" SIGN, ASSUMING HIKERS WOULD AVOID THAT AREA. CLEVER...
WE HAVE TO GET OUT!
THE DARN DOOR WON'T BUDGE!
THE MURDERER COULDN'T BREAK IT DOWN! HOW COULD WE?
CALM DOWN. SOMEONE WILL COME WHEN THEY SEE THE SMOKE RISING.
KOFF
RIGHT ...
...JIMMY ?

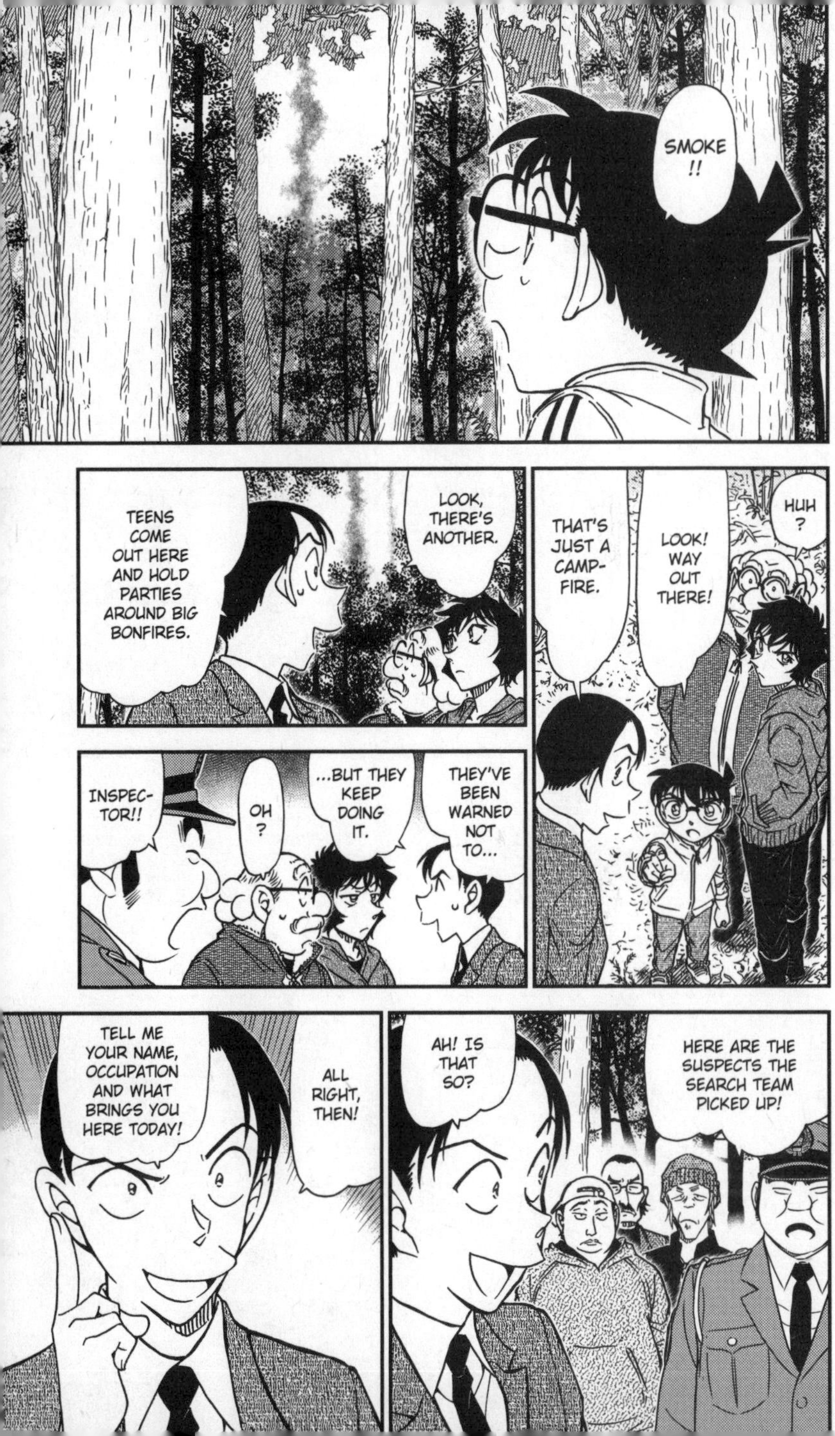
SMOKE !!
HUH ?
LOOK! WAY OUT THERE!
THAT'S JUST A CAMP-FIRE.
LOOK, THERE'S ANOTHER.
TEENS COME OUT HERE AND HOLD PARTIES AROUND BIG BONFIRES.
THEY'VE BEEN WARNED NOT TO...
...BUT THEY KEEP DOING IT.
OH ?
INSPECTOR!!
HERE ARE THE SUSPECTS THE SEARCH TEAM PICKED UP!
AH! IS THAT SO?
ALL RIGHT, THEN!
TELL ME YOUR NAME, OCCUPATION AND WHAT BRINGS YOU HERE TODAY!

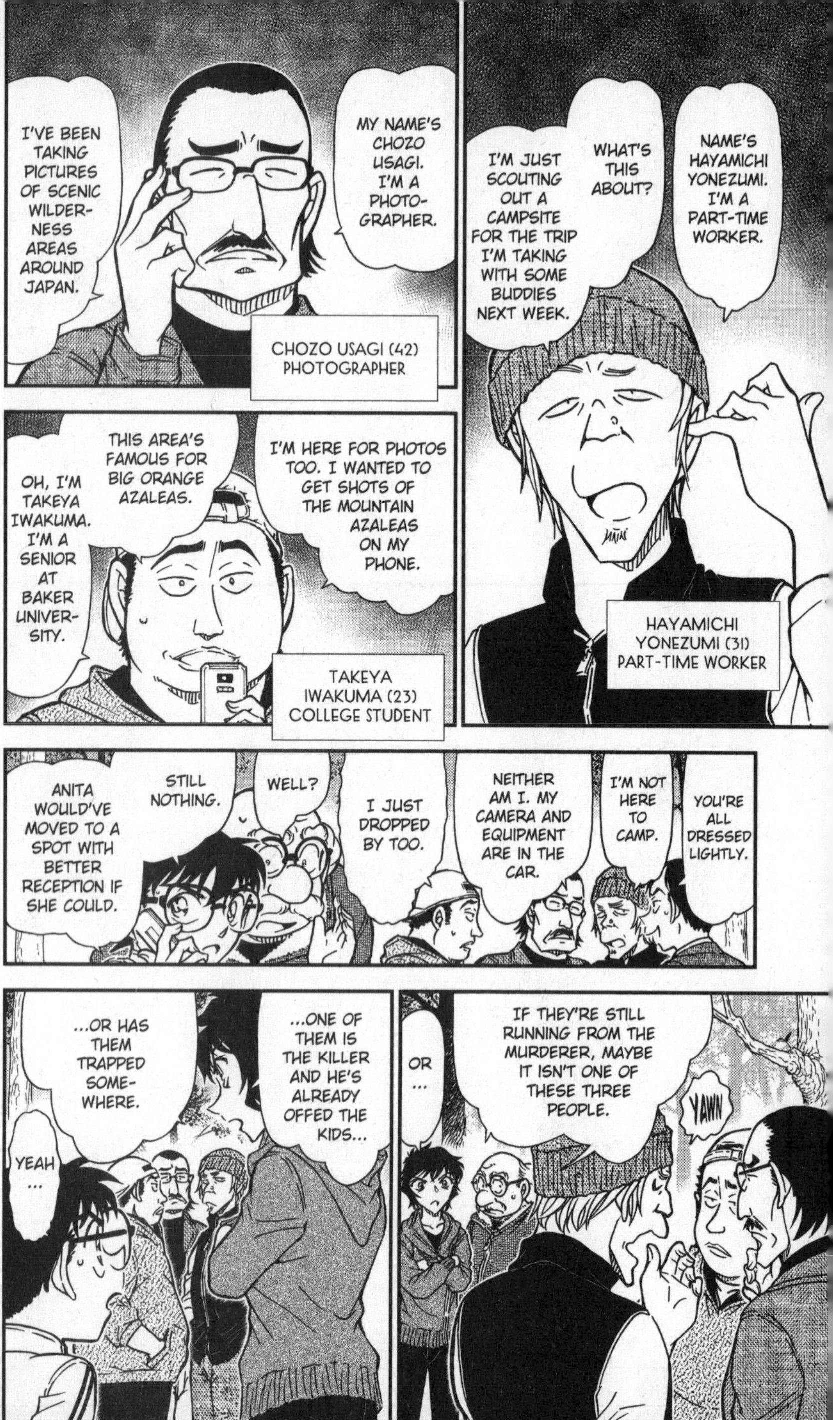
NAME'S HAYAMICHI YONEZUMI. I'M A PART-TIME WORKER.
WHAT'S THIS ABOUT?
I'M JUST SCOUTING OUT A CAMPSITE FOR THE TRIP I'M TAKING WITH SOME BUDDIES NEXT WEEK.
HAYAMICHI YONEZUMI (31) PART-TIME WORKER
MY NAME'S CHOZO USAGI. I'M A PHOTO-GRAPHER.
I'VE BEEN TAKING PICTURES OF SCENIC WILDER-NESS AREAS AROUND JAPAN.
CHOZO USAGI (42) PHOTOGRAPHER
I'M HERE FOR PHOTOS TOO. I WANTED TO GET SHOTS OF THE MOUNTAIN AZALEAS ON MY PHONE.
THIS AREA'S FAMOUS FOR BIG ORANGE AZALEAS.
OH, I'M TAKEYA IWAKUMA. I'M A SENIOR AT BAKER UNIVER-SITY.
TAKEYA IWAKUMA (23) COLLEGE STUDENT
YOU'RE ALL DRESSED LIGHTLY.
I'M NOT HERE TO CAMP.
NEITHER AM I. MY CAMERA AND EQUIPMENT ARE IN THE CAR.
I JUST DROPPED BY TOO.
WELL?
STILL NOTHING.
ANITA WOULD'VE MOVED TO A SPOT WITH BETTER RECEPTION IF SHE COULD.
IF THEY'RE STILL RUNNING FROM THE MURDERER, MAYBE IT ISN'T ONE OF THESE THREE PEOPLE.
YAWN
OR ...
...ONE OF THEM IS THE KILLER AND HE'S ALREADY OFFED THE KIDS...
...OR HAS THEM TRAPPED SOME-WHERE.
YEAH ...

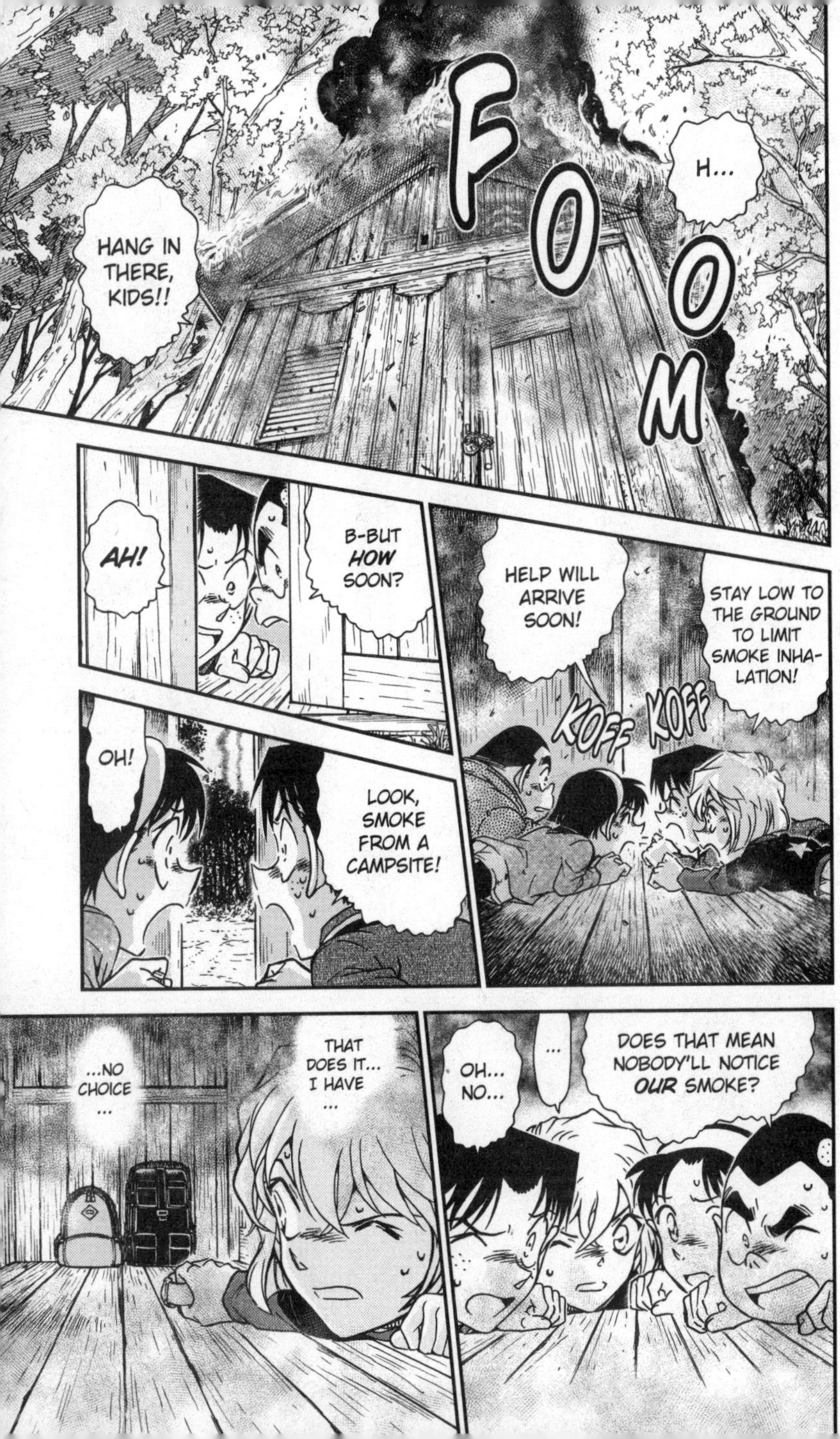
H...
FOOM
HANG IN THERE, KIDS!!
STAY LOW TO THE GROUND TO LIMIT SMOKE INHALATION!
HELP WILL ARRIVE SOON!
KOFF KOFF
B-BUT *HOW* SOON?
AH!
OH!
LOOK, SMOKE FROM A CAMPSITE!
DOES THAT MEAN NOBODY'LL NOTICE *OUR* SMOKE?
...
OH... NO...
THAT DOES IT... I HAVE ...
...NO CHOICE ...

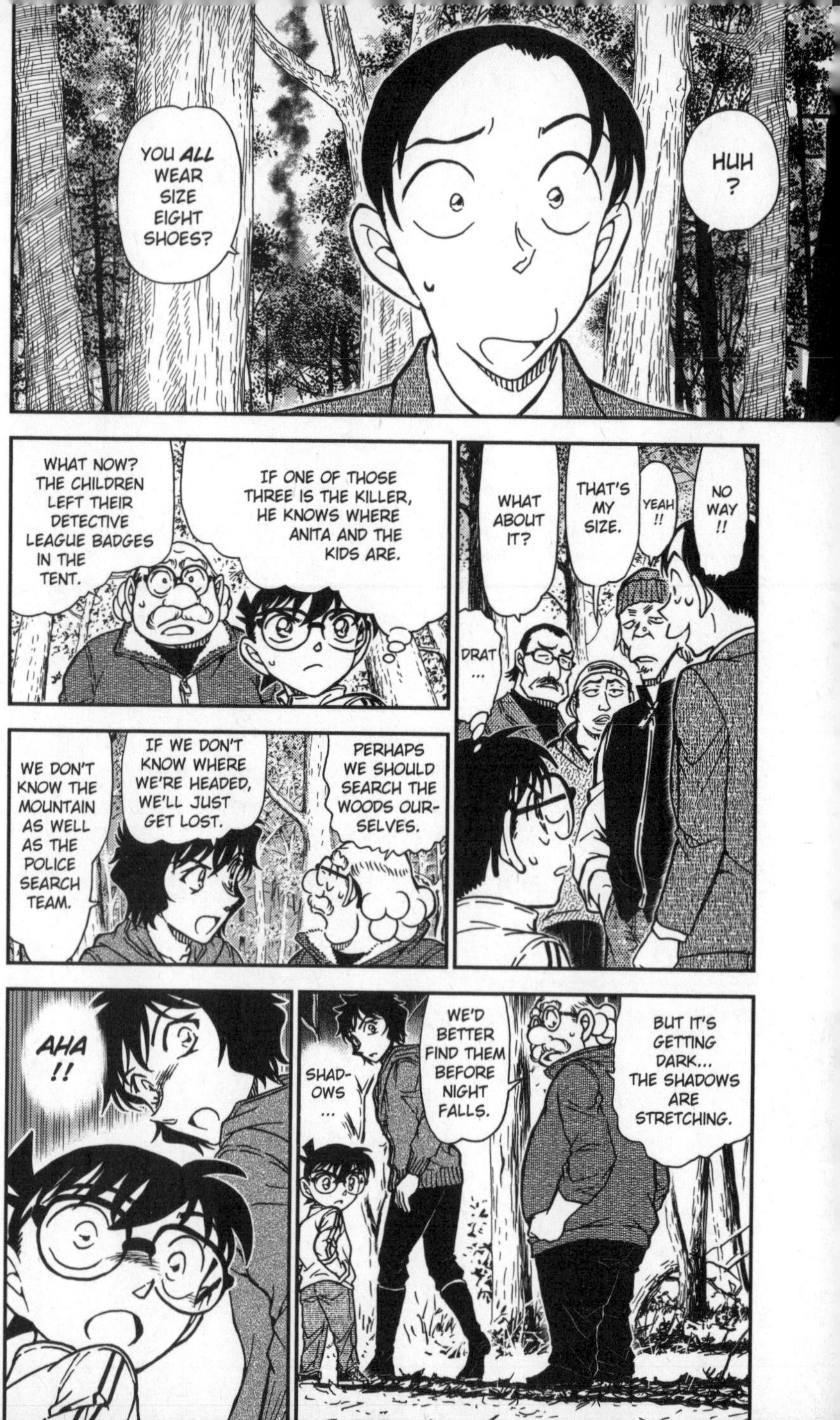
HUH ?
YOU ALL WEAR SIZE EIGHT SHOES?
NO WAY !!
YEAH !!
THAT'S MY SIZE.
WHAT ABOUT IT?
DRAT ...
IF ONE OF THOSE THREE IS THE KILLER, HE KNOWS WHERE ANITA AND THE KIDS ARE.
WHAT NOW? THE CHILDREN LEFT THEIR DETECTIVE LEAGUE BADGES IN THE TENT.
PERHAPS WE SHOULD SEARCH THE WOODS OUR-SELVES.
IF WE DON'T KNOW WHERE WE'RE HEADED, WE'LL JUST GET LOST.
WE DON'T KNOW THE MOUNTAIN AS WELL AS THE POLICE SEARCH TEAM.
BUT IT'S GETTING DARK... THE SHADOWS ARE STRETCHING.
WE'D BETTER FIND THEM BEFORE NIGHT FALLS.
SHAD-OWS ...
AHA !!

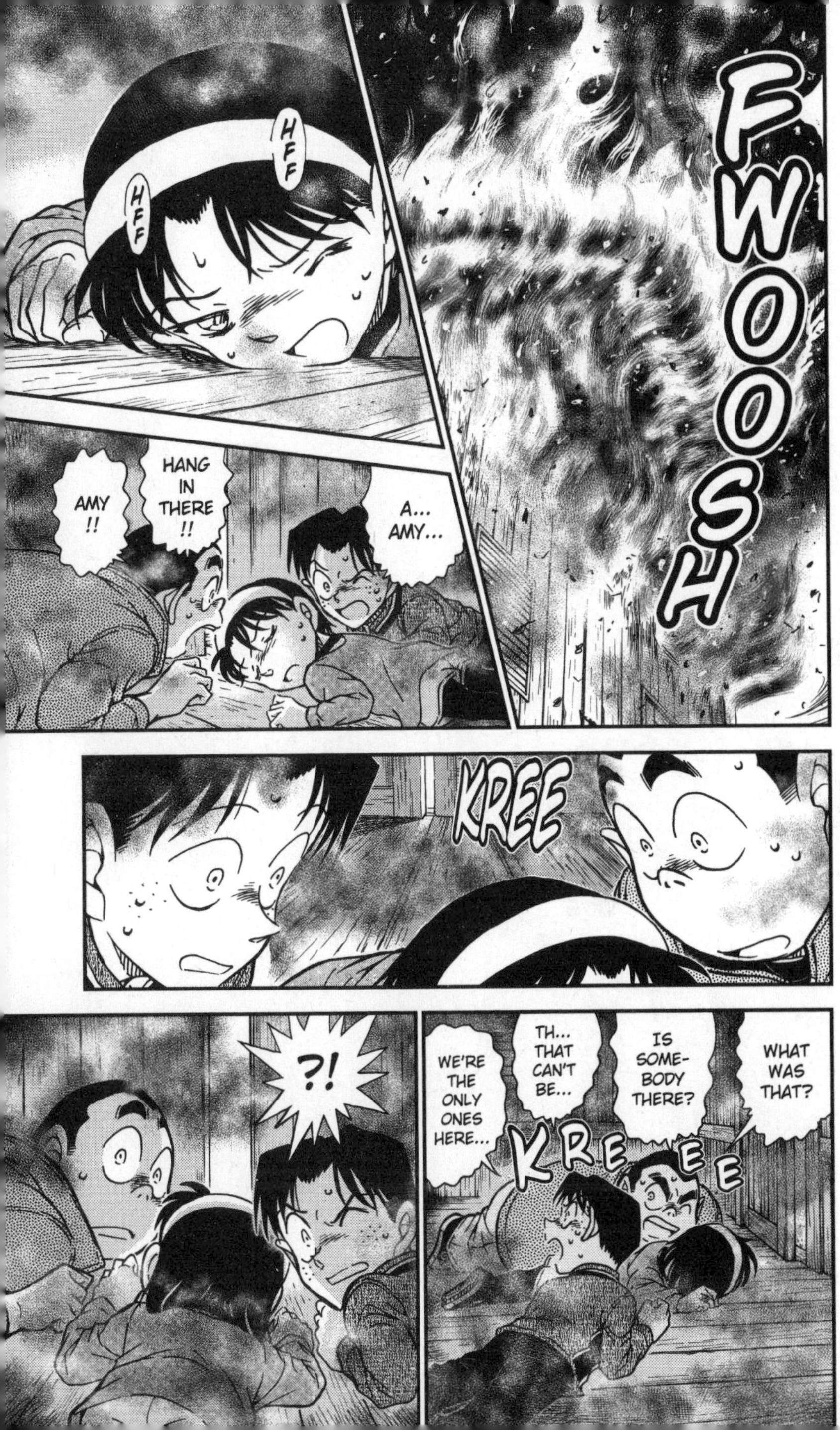
FWOOSH
HFF
HFF
A... AMY...
HANG IN THERE!!
AMY!!
KREE
WHAT WAS THAT?
IS SOME-BODY THERE?
TH... THAT CAN'T BE...
WE'RE THE ONLY ONES HERE...
KREEEE
?!

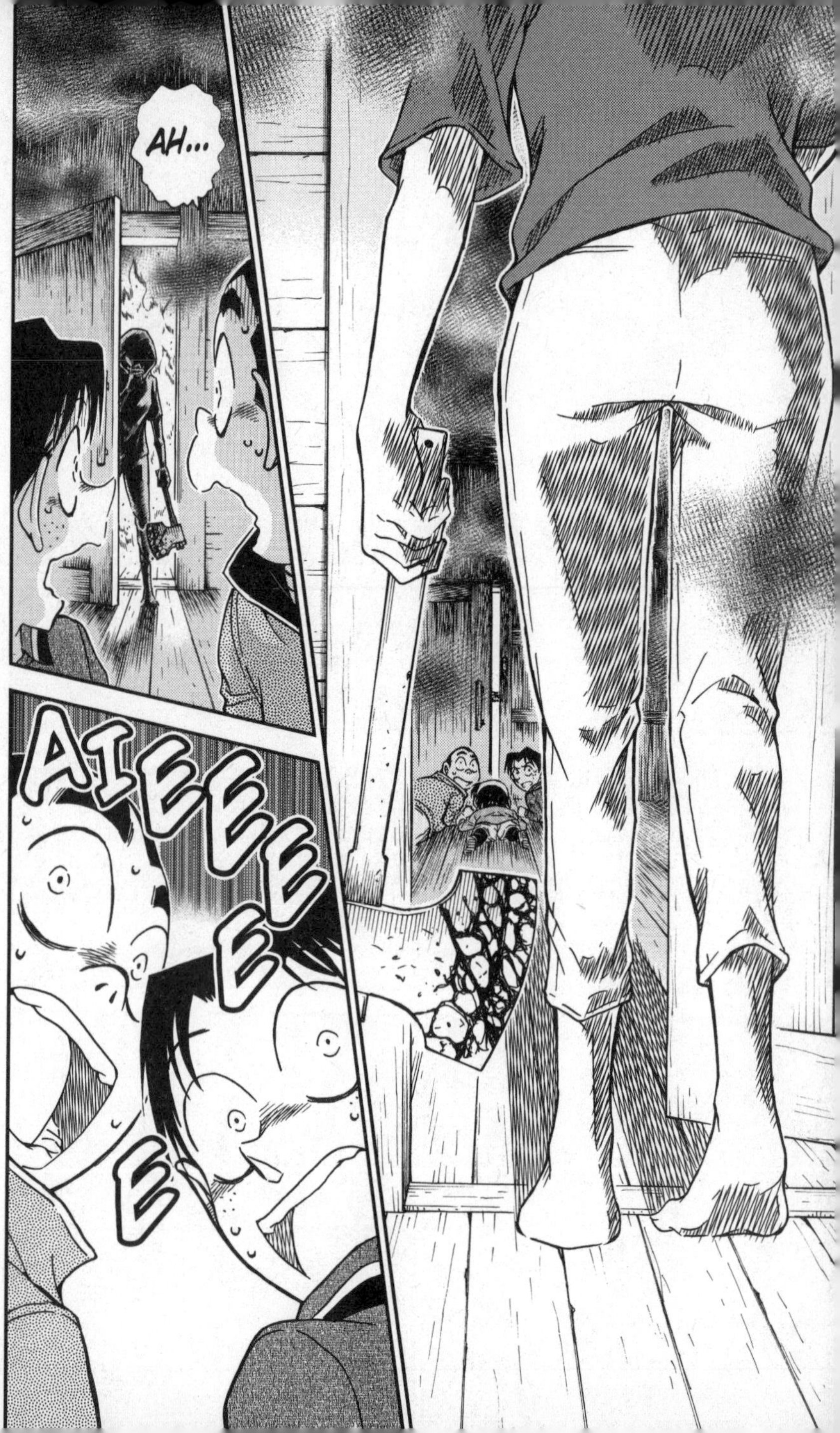
AH...
AIEEEEE

FILE 11: THE LONELY FIGURE IN THE LIGHT

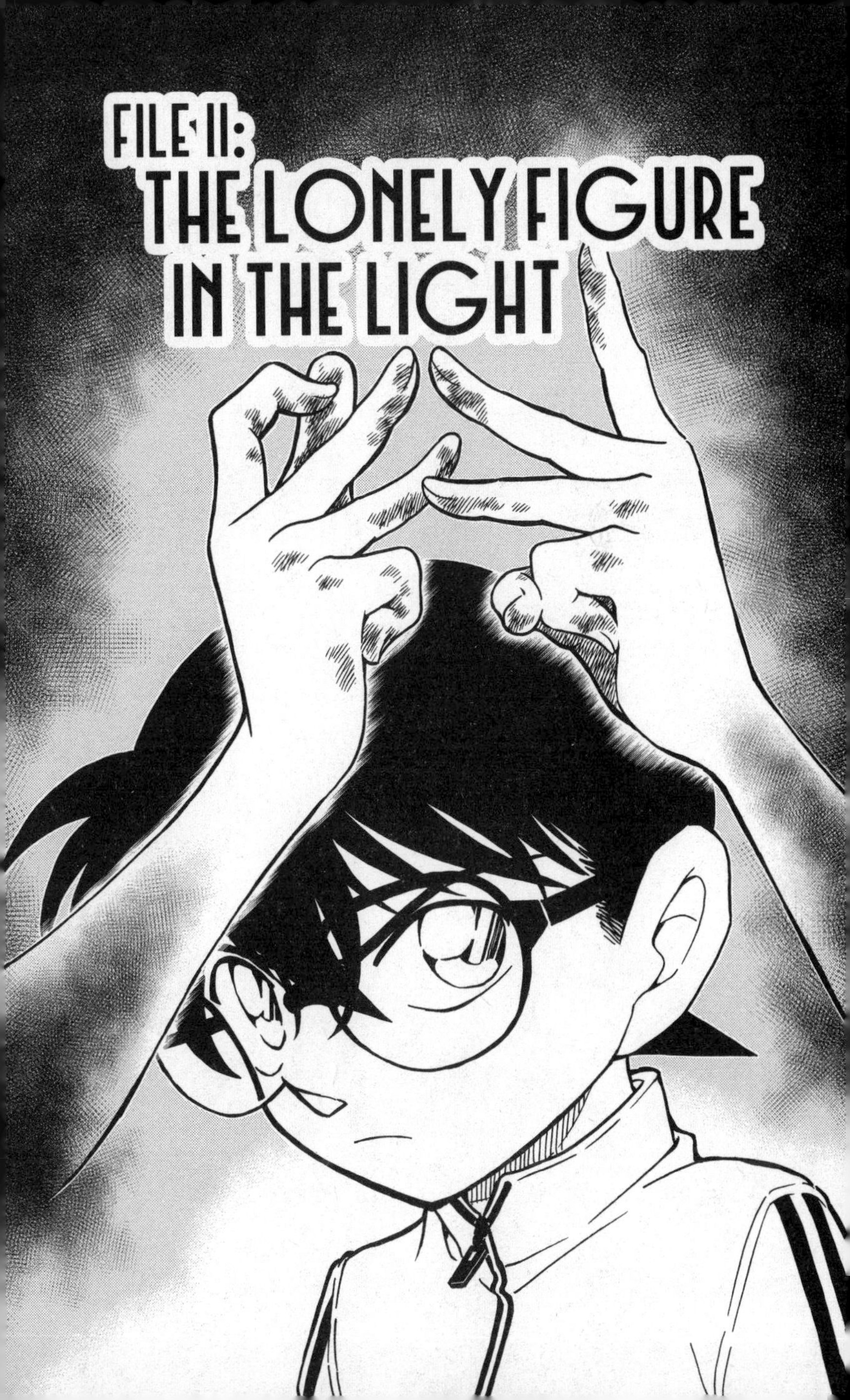

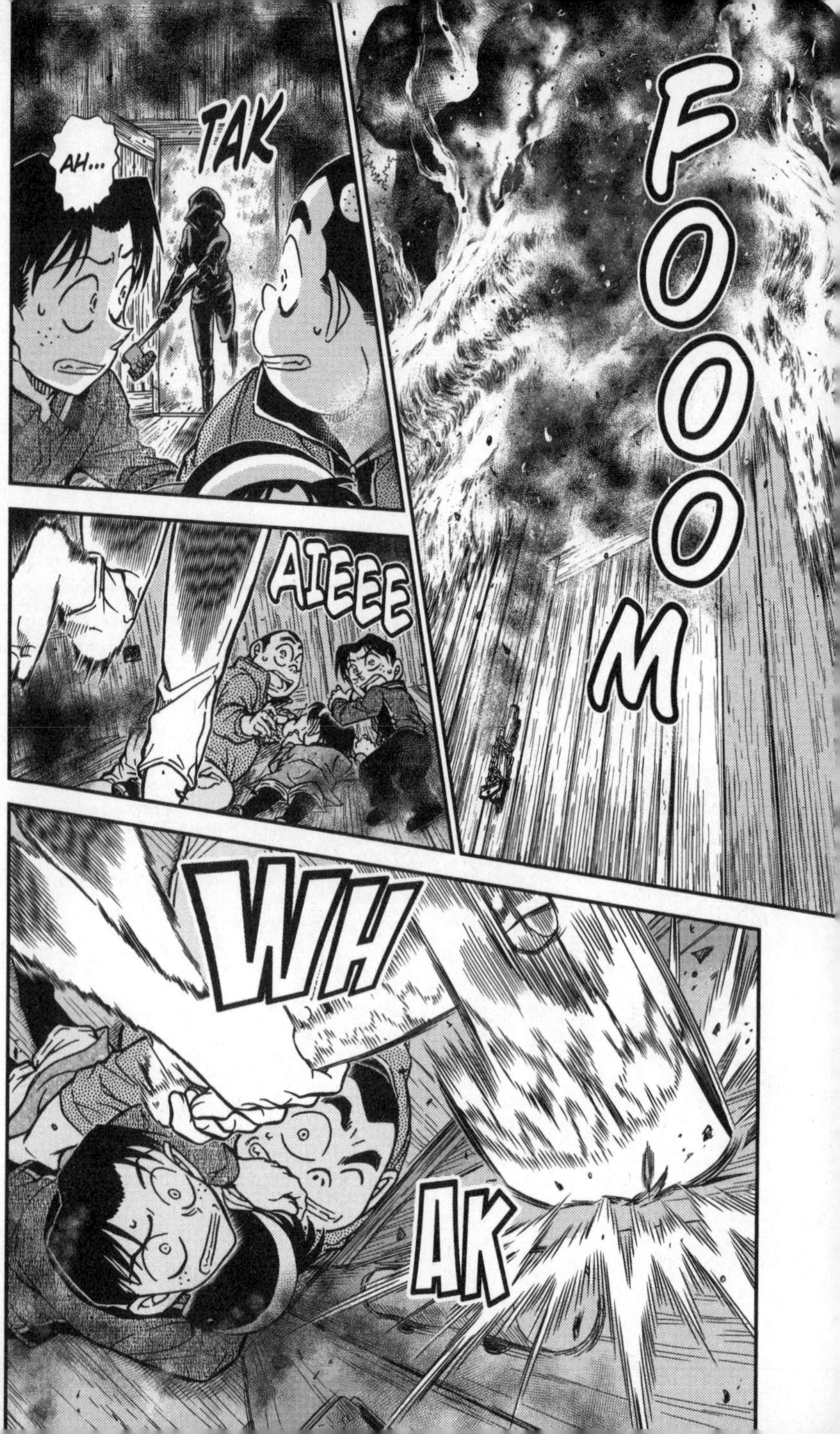
FOOOOM
TAK
AH...
AIEEE
WH
AK

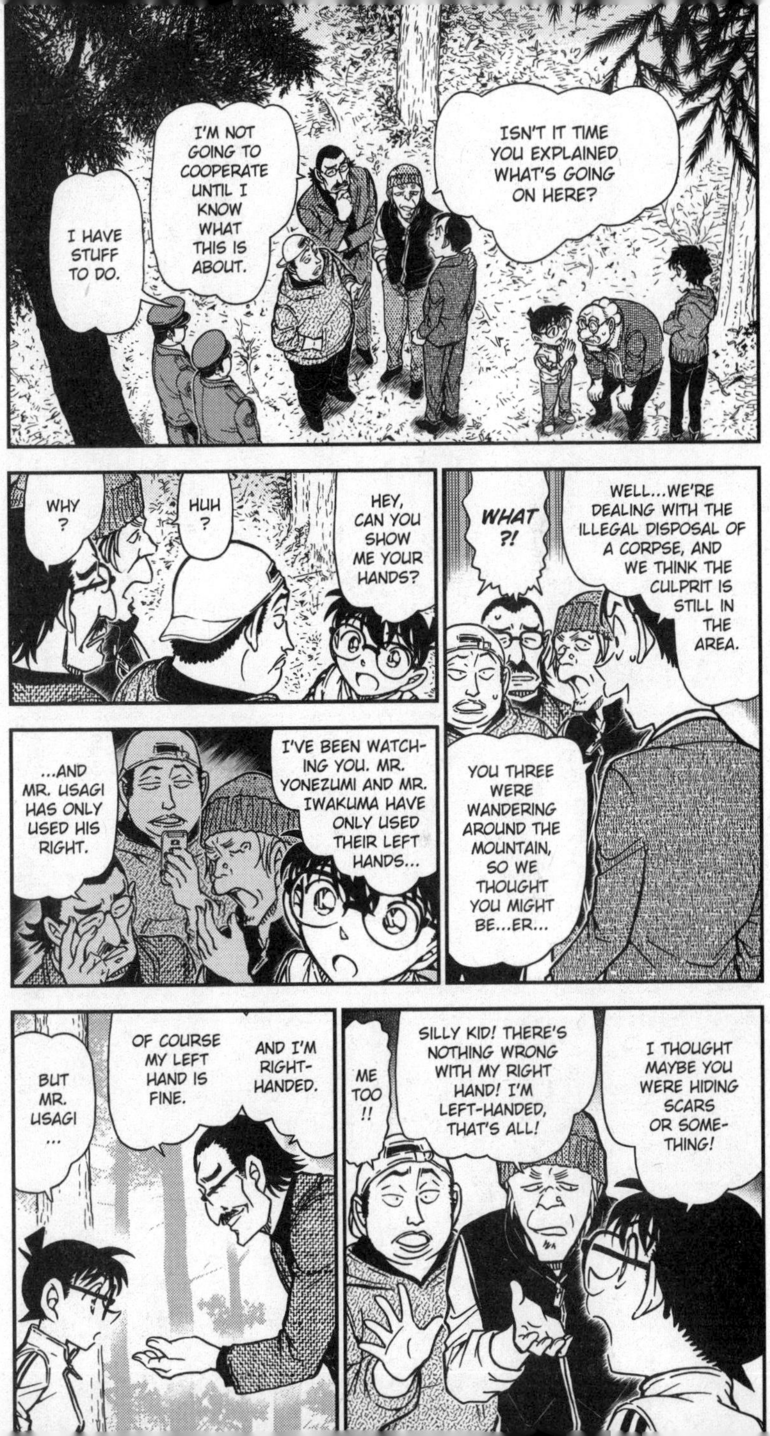
ISN'T IT TIME YOU EXPLAINED WHAT'S GOING ON HERE?
I'M NOT GOING TO COOPERATE UNTIL I KNOW WHAT THIS IS ABOUT.
I HAVE STUFF TO DO.
WELL...WE'RE DEALING WITH THE ILLEGAL DISPOSAL OF A CORPSE, AND WE THINK THE CULPRIT IS STILL IN THE AREA.
WHAT?!
YOU THREE WERE WANDERING AROUND THE MOUNTAIN, SO WE THOUGHT YOU MIGHT BE...ER...
HEY, CAN YOU SHOW ME YOUR HANDS?
HUH?
WHY?
I'VE BEEN WATCHING YOU. MR. YONEZUMI AND MR. IWAKUMA HAVE ONLY USED THEIR LEFT HANDS...
...AND MR. USAGI HAS ONLY USED HIS RIGHT.
I THOUGHT MAYBE YOU WERE HIDING SCARS OR SOMETHING!
SILLY KID! THERE'S NOTHING WRONG WITH MY RIGHT HAND! I'M LEFT-HANDED, THAT'S ALL!
ME TOO!!
AND I'M RIGHT-HANDED.
OF COURSE MY LEFT HAND IS FINE.
BUT MR. USAGI...

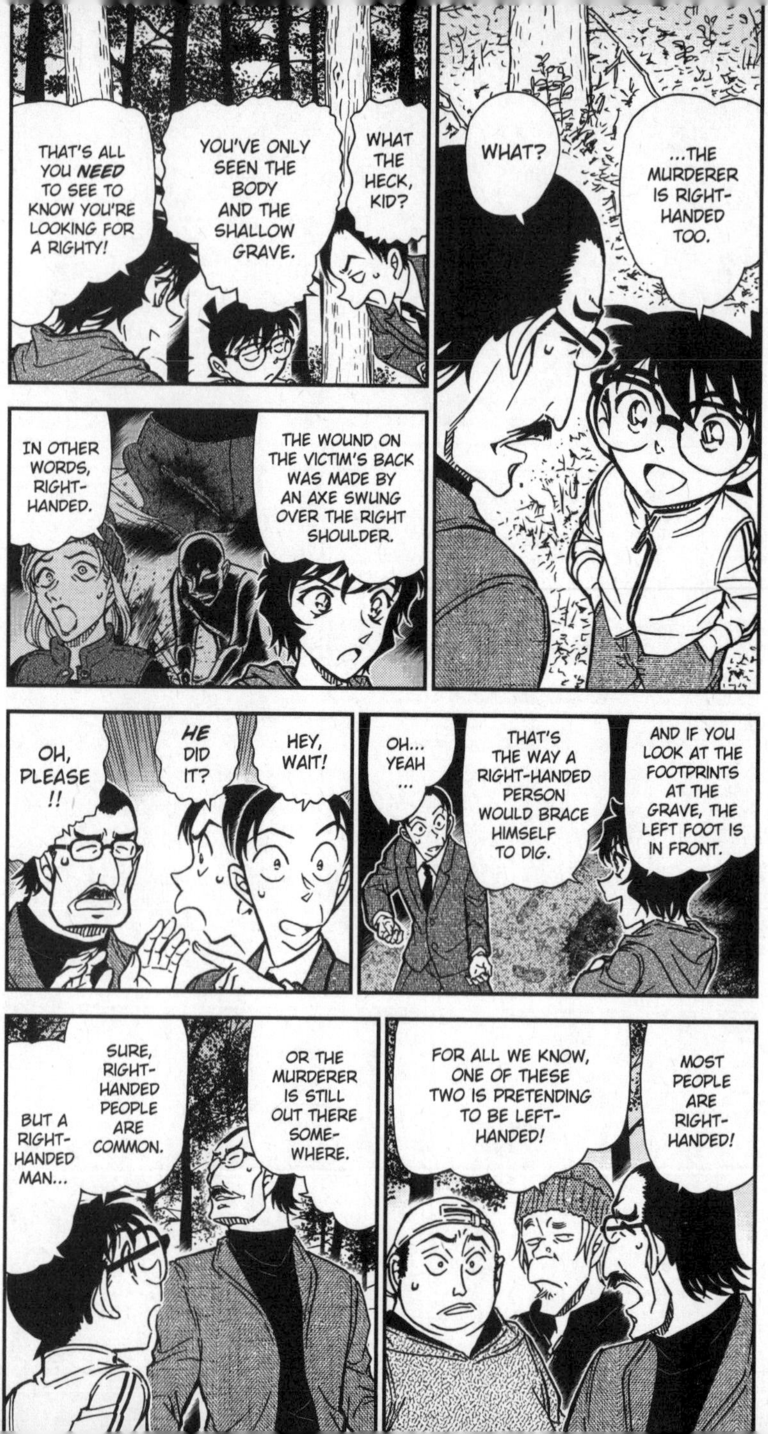
...THE MURDERER IS RIGHT-HANDED TOO.
WHAT?
WHAT THE HECK, KID?
YOU'VE ONLY SEEN THE BODY AND THE SHALLOW GRAVE.
THAT'S ALL YOU NEED TO SEE TO KNOW YOU'RE LOOKING FOR A RIGHTY!
THE WOUND ON THE VICTIM'S BACK WAS MADE BY AN AXE SWUNG OVER THE RIGHT SHOULDER.
IN OTHER WORDS, RIGHT-HANDED.
AND IF YOU LOOK AT THE FOOTPRINTS AT THE GRAVE, THE LEFT FOOT IS IN FRONT.
THAT'S THE WAY A RIGHT-HANDED PERSON WOULD BRACE HIMSELF TO DIG.
OH... YEAH ...
HEY, WAIT!
HE DID IT?
OH, PLEASE !!
MOST PEOPLE ARE RIGHT-HANDED!
FOR ALL WE KNOW, ONE OF THESE TWO IS PRETENDING TO BE LEFT-HANDED!
OR THE MURDERER IS STILL OUT THERE SOMEWHERE.
SURE, RIGHT-HANDED PEOPLE ARE COMMON.
BUT A RIGHT-HANDED MAN...

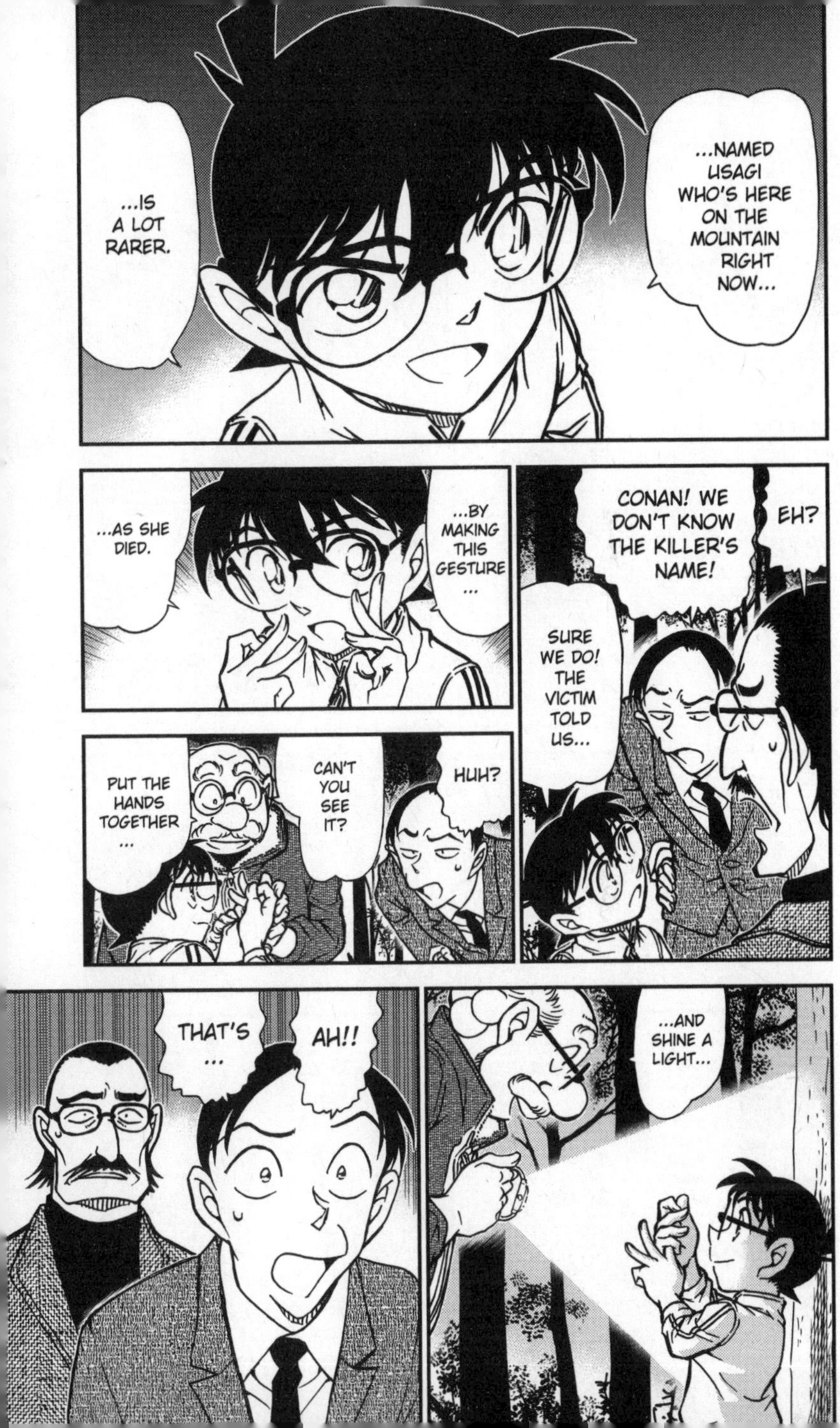
...NAMED USAGI WHO'S HERE ON THE MOUNTAIN RIGHT NOW...
...IS A LOT RARER.
EH?
CONAN! WE DON'T KNOW THE KILLER'S NAME!
SURE WE DO! THE VICTIM TOLD US...
...BY MAKING THIS GESTURE ...
...AS SHE DIED.
HUH?
CAN'T YOU SEE IT?
PUT THE HANDS TOGETHER ...
...AND SHINE A LIGHT...
AH!!
THAT'S ...

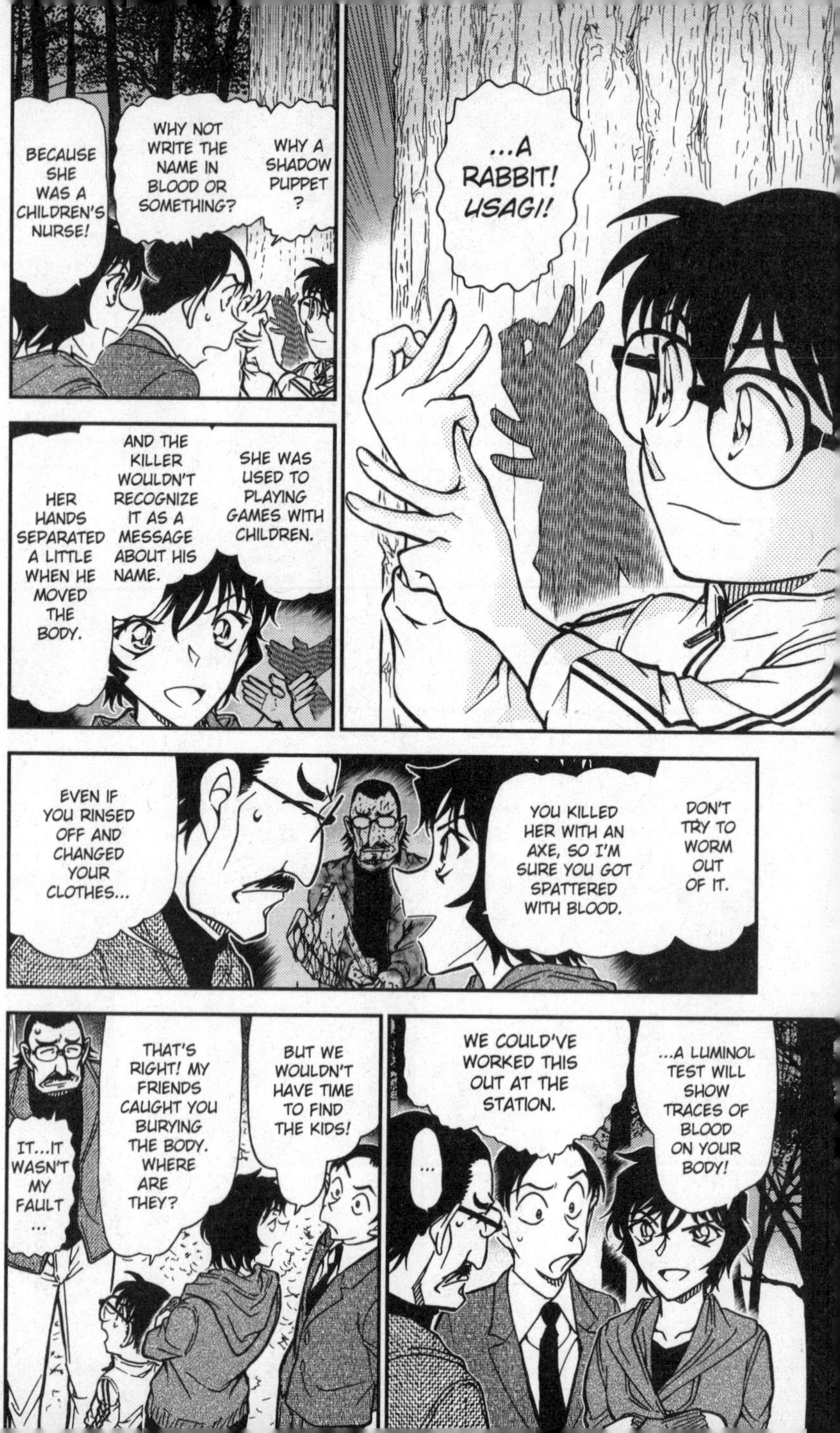
...A RABBIT! USAGI!
WHY A SHADOW PUPPET?
WHY NOT WRITE THE NAME IN BLOOD OR SOMETHING?
BECAUSE SHE WAS A CHILDREN'S NURSE!
SHE WAS USED TO PLAYING GAMES WITH CHILDREN.
AND THE KILLER WOULDN'T RECOGNIZE IT AS A MESSAGE ABOUT HIS NAME.
HER HANDS SEPARATED A LITTLE WHEN HE MOVED THE BODY.
DON'T TRY TO WORM OUT OF IT.
YOU KILLED HER WITH AN AXE, SO I'M SURE YOU GOT SPATTERED WITH BLOOD.
EVEN IF YOU RINSED OFF AND CHANGED YOUR CLOTHES...
...A LUMINOL TEST WILL SHOW TRACES OF BLOOD ON YOUR BODY!
WE COULD'VE WORKED THIS OUT AT THE STATION.
...
BUT WE WOULDN'T HAVE TIME TO FIND THE KIDS!
THAT'S RIGHT! MY FRIENDS CAUGHT YOU BURYING THE BODY. WHERE ARE THEY?
IT...IT WASN'T MY FAULT...

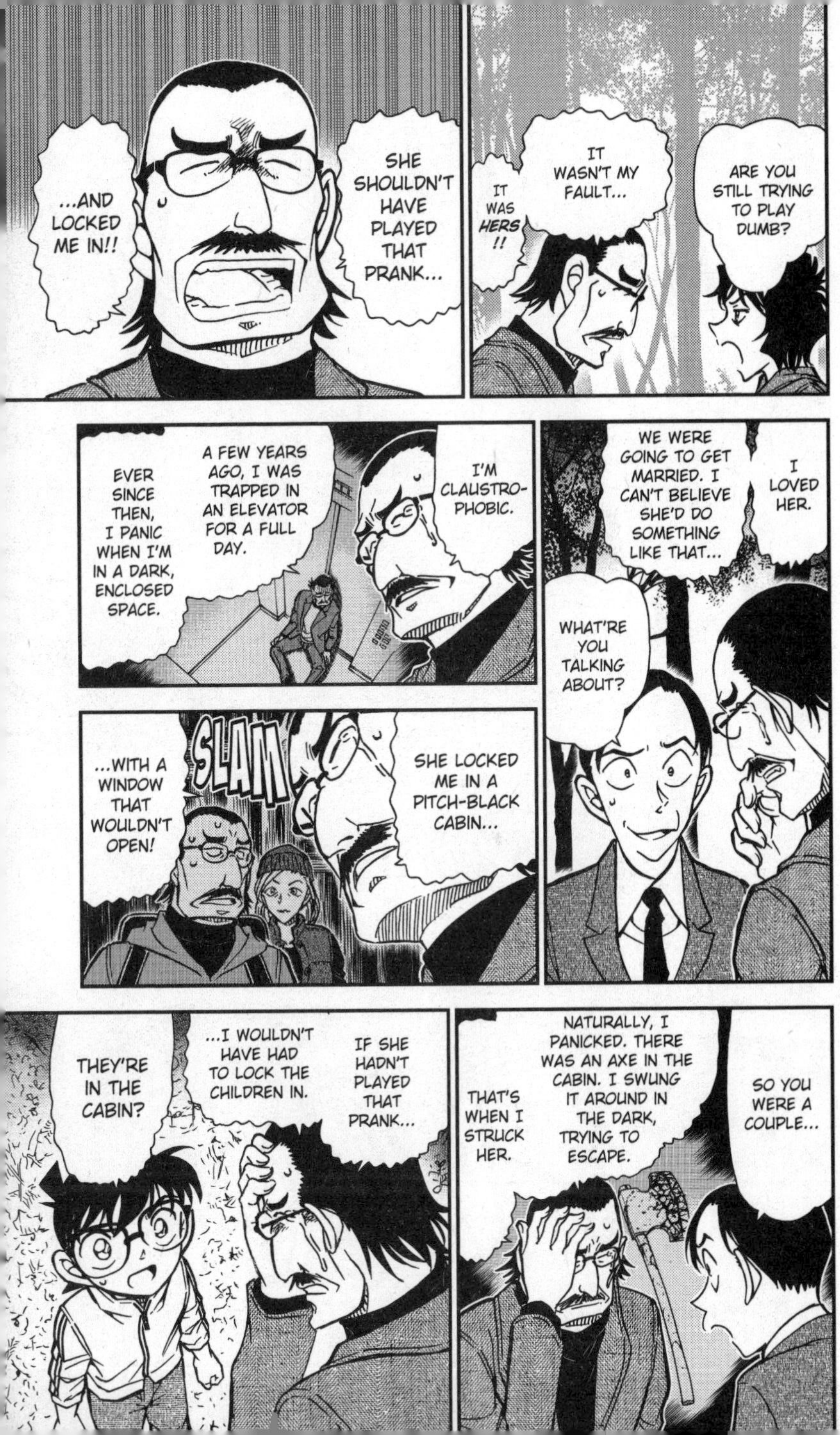
ARE YOU STILL TRYING TO PLAY DUMB?
IT WASN'T MY FAULT...
IT WAS *HERS*!!
SHE SHOULDN'T HAVE PLAYED THAT PRANK...
...AND LOCKED ME IN!!
I LOVED HER.
WE WERE GOING TO GET MARRIED. I CAN'T BELIEVE SHE'D DO SOMETHING LIKE THAT...
WHAT'RE YOU TALKING ABOUT?
I'M CLAUSTROPHOBIC.
A FEW YEARS AGO, I WAS TRAPPED IN AN ELEVATOR FOR A FULL DAY.
EVER SINCE THEN, I PANIC WHEN I'M IN A DARK, ENCLOSED SPACE.
SHE LOCKED ME IN A PITCH-BLACK CABIN...
SLAM
...WITH A WINDOW THAT WOULDN'T OPEN!
SO YOU WERE A COUPLE...
NATURALLY, I PANICKED. THERE WAS AN AXE IN THE CABIN. I SWUNG IT AROUND IN THE DARK, TRYING TO ESCAPE.
THAT'S WHEN I STRUCK HER.
IF SHE HADN'T PLAYED THAT PRANK...
...I WOULDN'T HAVE HAD TO LOCK THE CHILDREN IN.
THEY'RE IN THE CABIN?

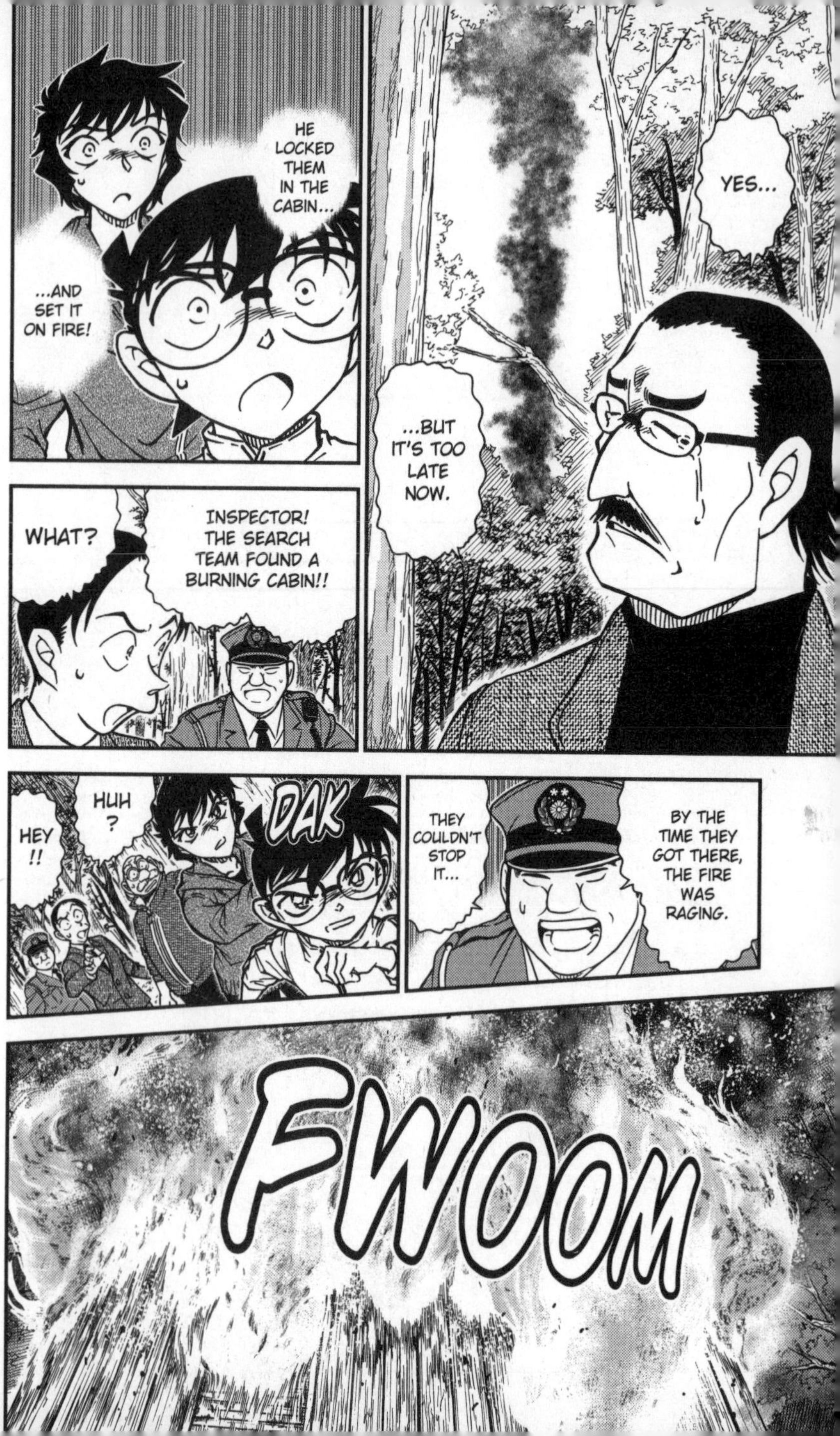
YES...
...BUT IT'S TOO LATE NOW.
HE LOCKED THEM IN THE CABIN...
...AND SET IT ON FIRE!
INSPECTOR! THE SEARCH TEAM FOUND A BURNING CABIN!!
WHAT?
BY THE TIME THEY GOT THERE, THE FIRE WAS RAGING.
THEY COULDN'T STOP IT...
DAK
HUH?
HEY!!
FWOOM

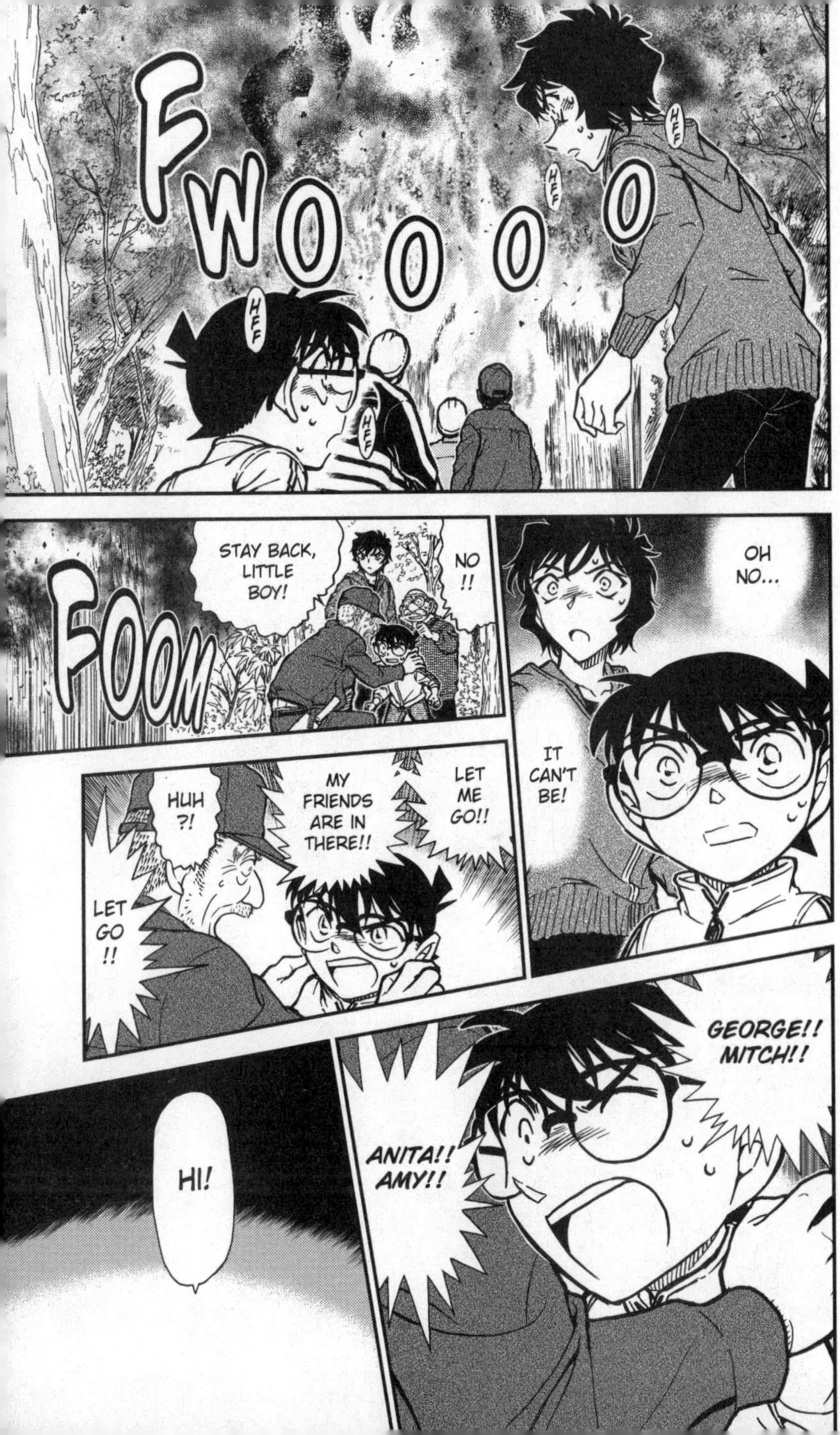
FWOOOO
HEFF HEFF
HEFF HEFF
OH NO...
IT CAN'T BE!
NO!!
STAY BACK, LITTLE BOY!
FOOM
LET ME GO!!
MY FRIENDS ARE IN THERE!!
HUH?!
LET GO!!
GEORGE!! MITCH!!
ANITA!! AMY!!
HI!

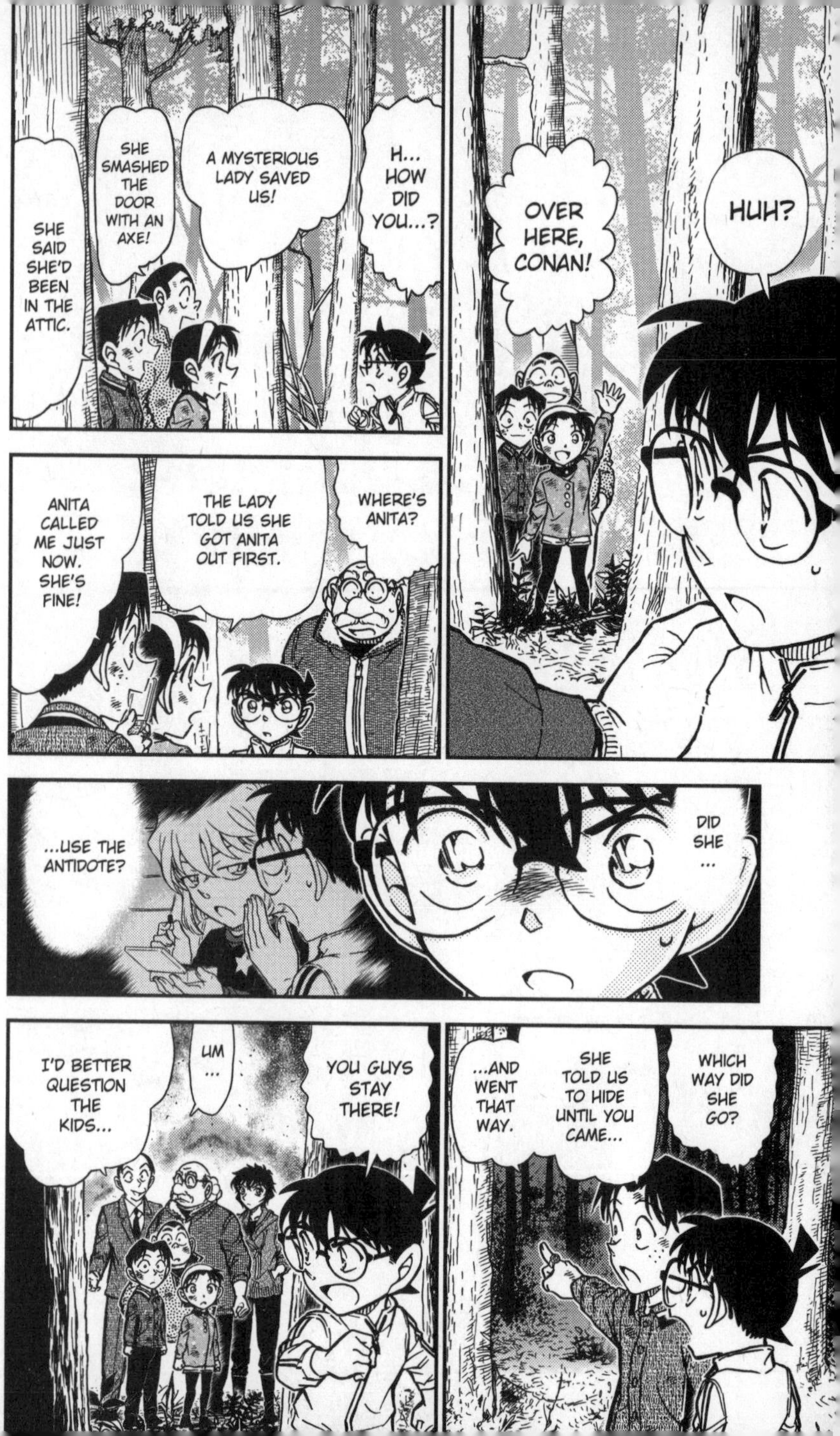
HUH?
OVER HERE, CONAN!
H... HOW DID YOU...?
A MYSTERIOUS LADY SAVED US!
SHE SMASHED THE DOOR WITH AN AXE!
SHE SAID SHE'D BEEN IN THE ATTIC.
WHERE'S ANITA?
THE LADY TOLD US SHE GOT ANITA OUT FIRST.
ANITA CALLED ME JUST NOW. SHE'S FINE!
DID SHE ...
...USE THE ANTIDOTE?
WHICH WAY DID SHE GO?
SHE TOLD US TO HIDE UNTIL YOU CAME...
...AND WENT THAT WAY.
YOU GUYS STAY THERE!
UM ...
I'D BETTER QUESTION THE KIDS...

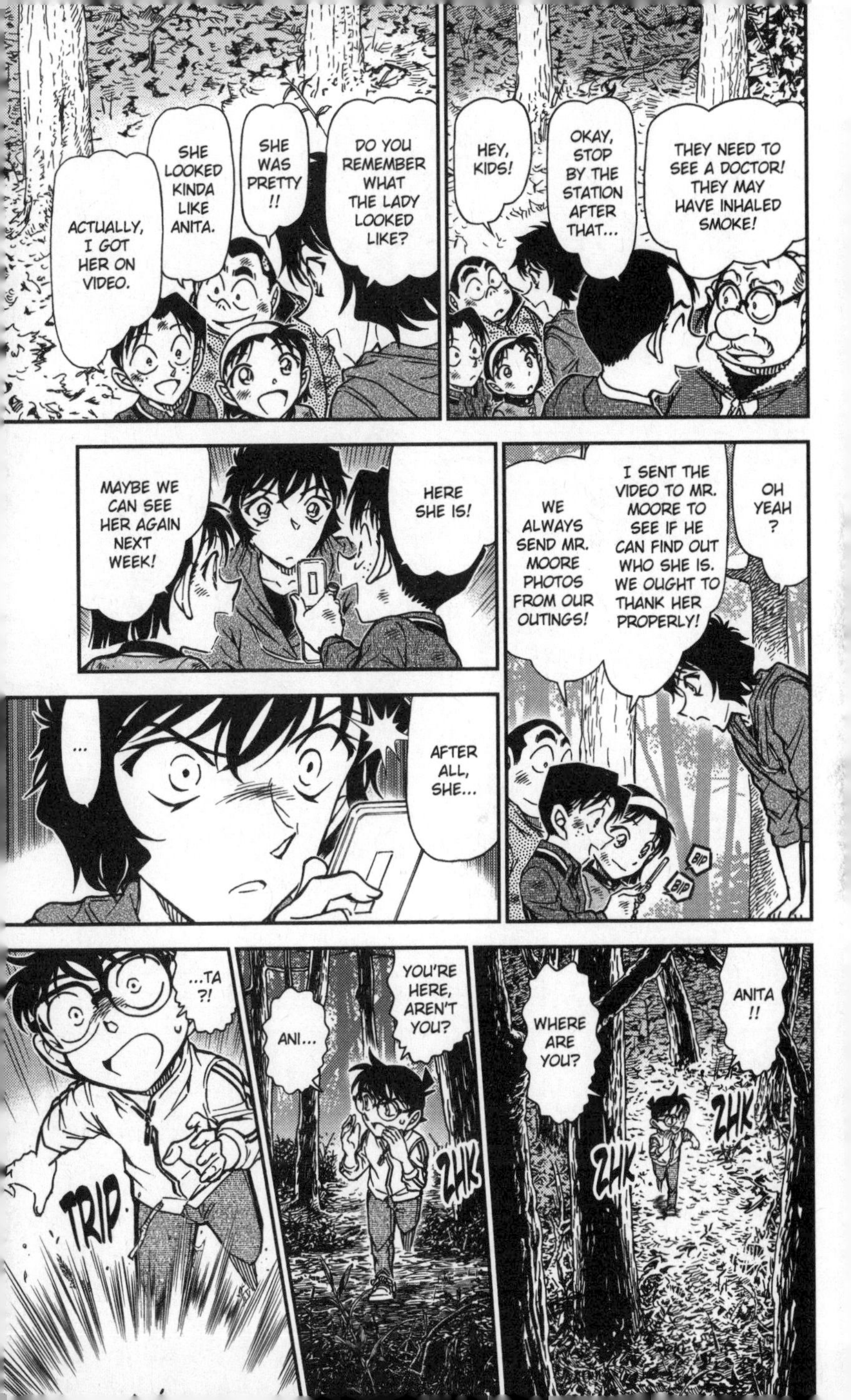
THEY NEED TO SEE A DOCTOR! THEY MAY HAVE INHALED SMOKE!
OKAY, STOP BY THE STATION AFTER THAT...
HEY, KIDS!
DO YOU REMEMBER WHAT THE LADY LOOKED LIKE?
SHE WAS PRETTY!!
SHE LOOKED KINDA LIKE ANITA.
ACTUALLY, I GOT HER ON VIDEO.
OH YEAH?
I SENT THE VIDEO TO MR. MOORE TO SEE IF HE CAN FIND OUT WHO SHE IS. WE OUGHT TO THANK HER PROPERLY!
WE ALWAYS SEND MR. MOORE PHOTOS FROM OUR OUTINGS!
BIP
BIP
HERE SHE IS!
MAYBE WE CAN SEE HER AGAIN NEXT WEEK!
AFTER ALL, SHE...
...
ANITA!!
WHERE ARE YOU?
ZHK
ZHK
YOU'RE HERE, AREN'T YOU?
ANI...
ZHK
...TA?!
TRIP

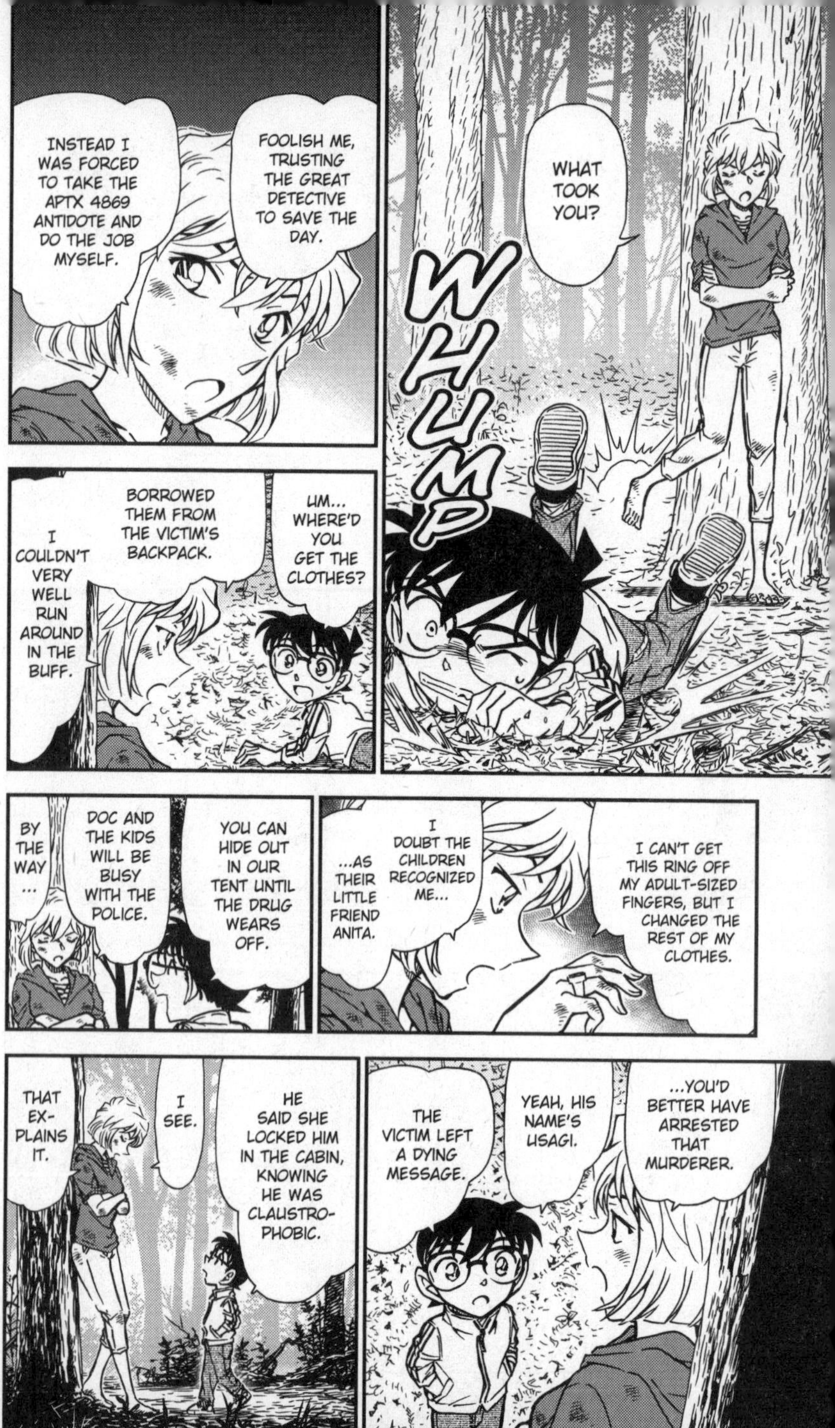

WHAT TOOK YOU?
WHUMP
FOOLISH ME, TRUSTING THE GREAT DETECTIVE TO SAVE THE DAY.
INSTEAD I WAS FORCED TO TAKE THE APTX 4869 ANTIDOTE AND DO THE JOB MYSELF.
UM... WHERE'D YOU GET THE CLOTHES?
BORROWED THEM FROM THE VICTIM'S BACKPACK.
I COULDN'T VERY WELL RUN AROUND IN THE BUFF.
I CAN'T GET THIS RING OFF MY ADULT-SIZED FINGERS, BUT I CHANGED THE REST OF MY CLOTHES.
I DOUBT THE CHILDREN RECOGNIZED ME...
...AS THEIR LITTLE FRIEND ANITA.
YOU CAN HIDE OUT IN OUR TENT UNTIL THE DRUG WEARS OFF.
DOC AND THE KIDS WILL BE BUSY WITH THE POLICE.
BY THE WAY...
...YOU'D BETTER HAVE ARRESTED THAT MURDERER.
YEAH, HIS NAME'S USAGI.
THE VICTIM LEFT A DYING MESSAGE.
HE SAID SHE LOCKED HIM IN THE CABIN, KNOWING HE WAS CLAUSTRO-PHOBIC.
I SEE.
THAT EX-PLAINS IT.

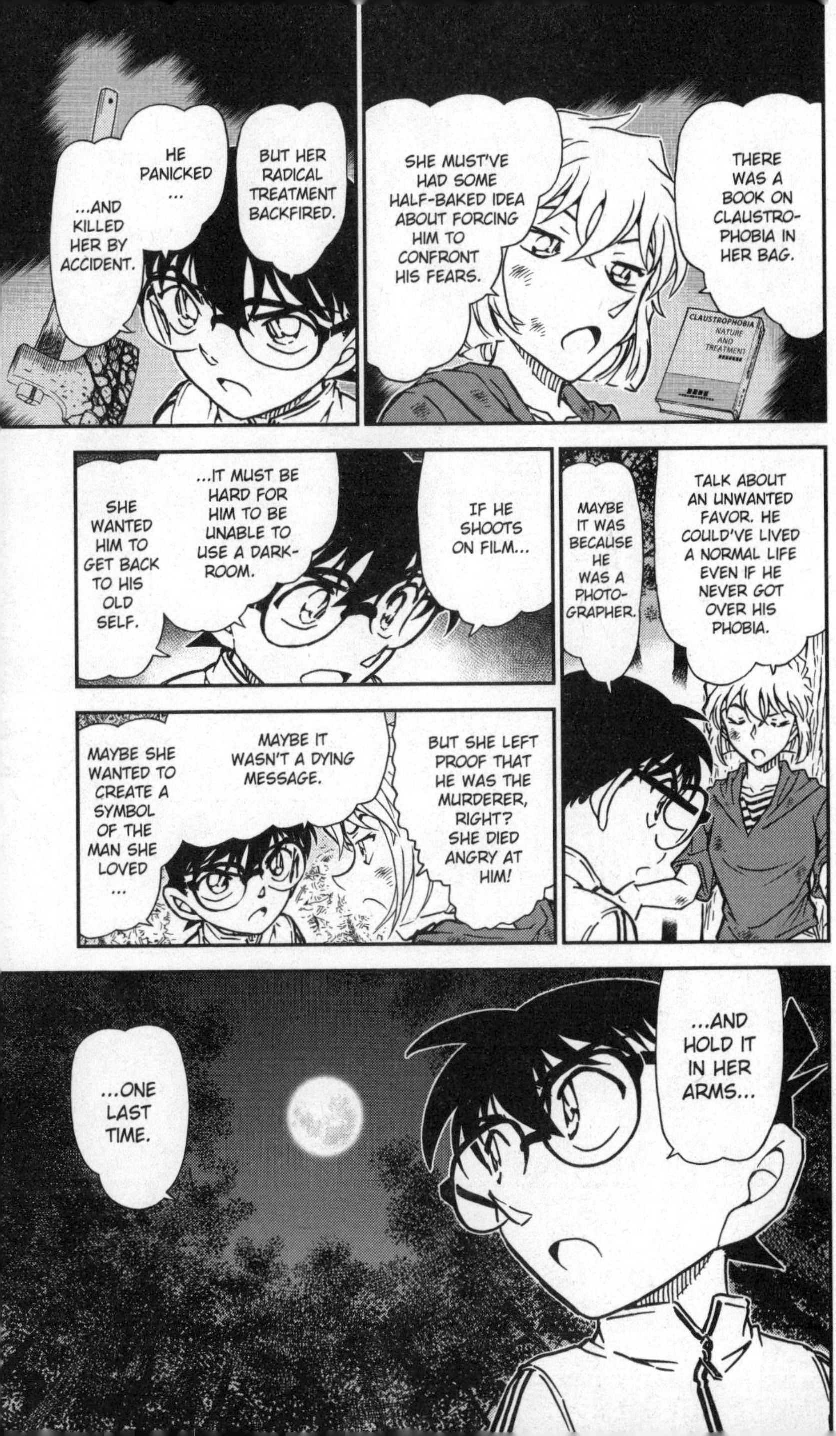
THERE WAS A BOOK ON CLAUSTRO-PHOBIA IN HER BAG.
CLAUSTROPHOBIA NATURE AND TREATMENT
SHE MUST'VE HAD SOME HALF-BAKED IDEA ABOUT FORCING HIM TO CONFRONT HIS FEARS.
BUT HER RADICAL TREATMENT BACKFIRED.
HE PANICKED ...
...AND KILLED HER BY ACCIDENT.
TALK ABOUT AN UNWANTED FAVOR. HE COULD'VE LIVED A NORMAL LIFE EVEN IF HE NEVER GOT OVER HIS PHOBIA.
MAYBE IT WAS BECAUSE HE WAS A PHOTO-GRAPHER.
IF HE SHOOTS ON FILM...
...IT MUST BE HARD FOR HIM TO BE UNABLE TO USE A DARK-ROOM.
SHE WANTED HIM TO GET BACK TO HIS OLD SELF.
BUT SHE LEFT PROOF THAT HE WAS THE MURDERER, RIGHT? SHE DIED ANGRY AT HIM!
MAYBE IT WASN'T A DYING MESSAGE.
MAYBE SHE WANTED TO CREATE A SYMBOL OF THE MAN SHE LOVED ...
...AND HOLD IT IN HER ARMS...
...ONE LAST TIME.

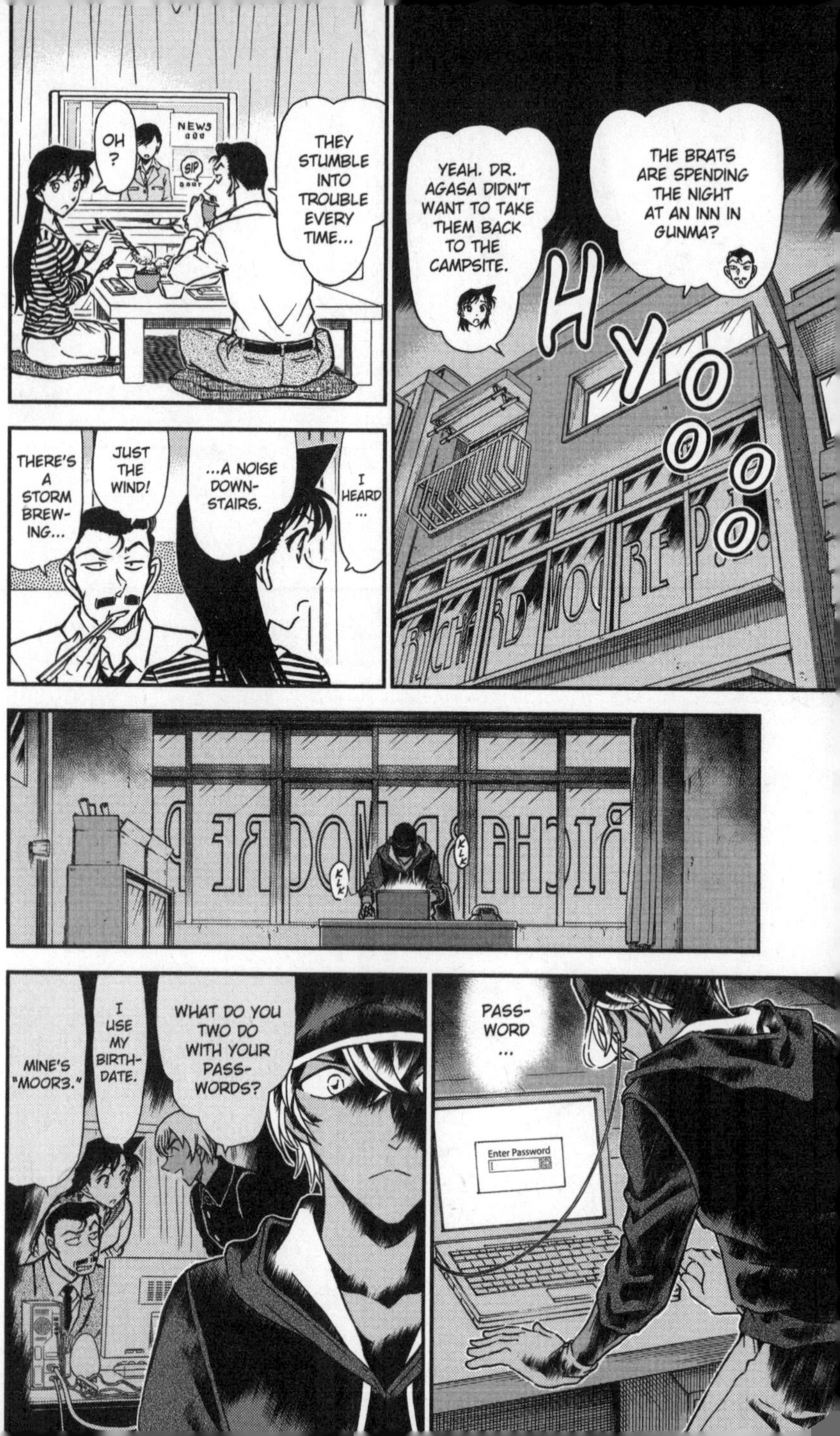
THE BRATS ARE SPENDING THE NIGHT AT AN INN IN GUNMA?
YEAH. DR. AGASA DIDN'T WANT TO TAKE THEM BACK TO THE CAMPSITE.
HYOOOOO
THEY STUMBLE INTO TROUBLE EVERY TIME...
OH?
NEWS
SIP
I HEARD...
...A NOISE DOWNSTAIRS.
JUST THE WIND!
THERE'S A STORM BREWING...
KLK
KLK
PASSWORD...
Enter Password
WHAT DO YOU TWO DO WITH YOUR PASSWORDS?
I USE MY BIRTHDATE.
MINE'S "MOOR3."

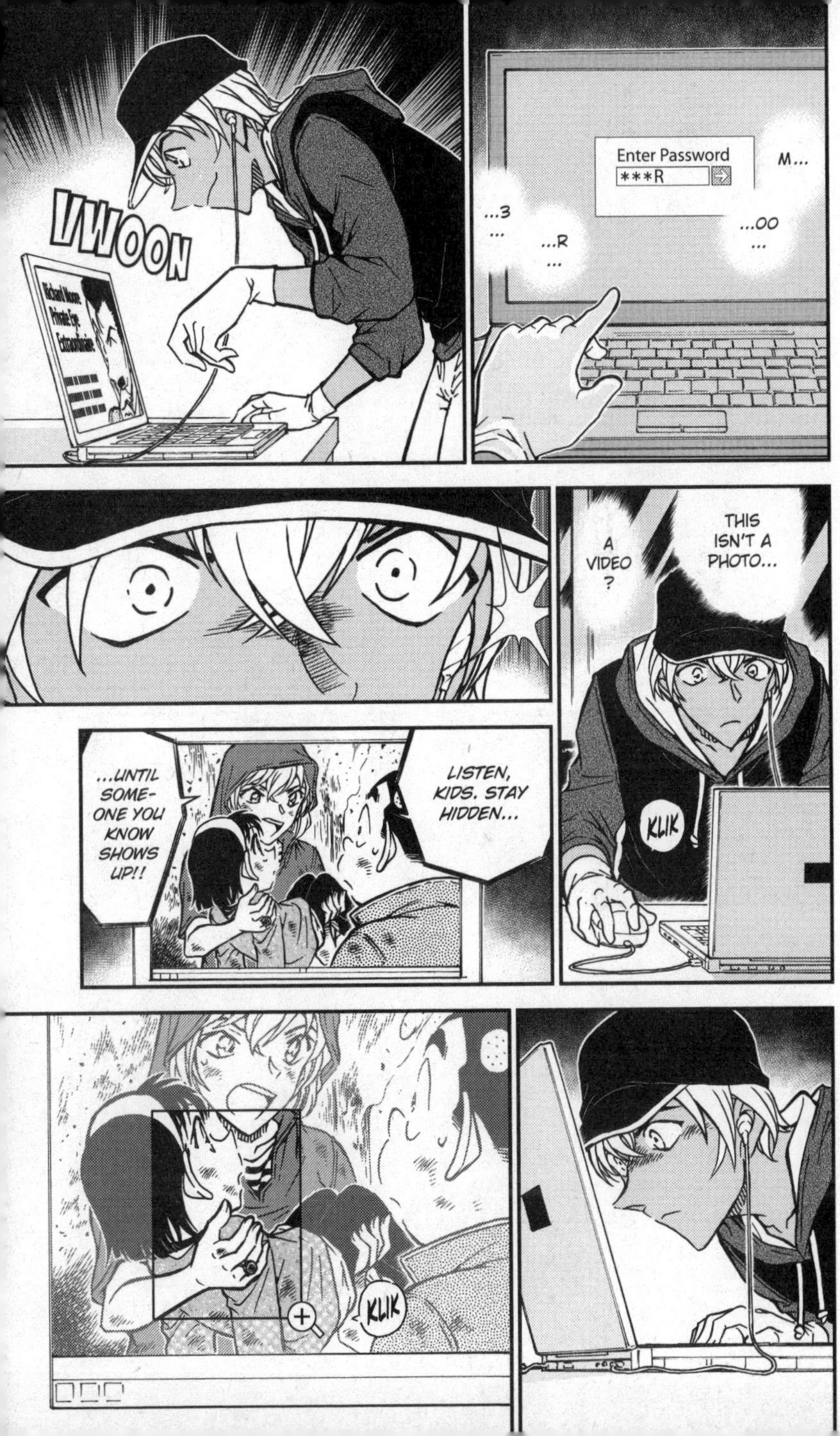
M...
...OO
...
Enter Password
***R
...R
...
...3
...
VWOON
Richard Moore
Private Eye
Extraordinaire
THIS ISN'T A PHOTO...
A VIDEO ?
KLIK
LISTEN, KIDS. STAY HIDDEN...
...UNTIL SOME-ONE YOU KNOW SHOWS UP!!
KLIK

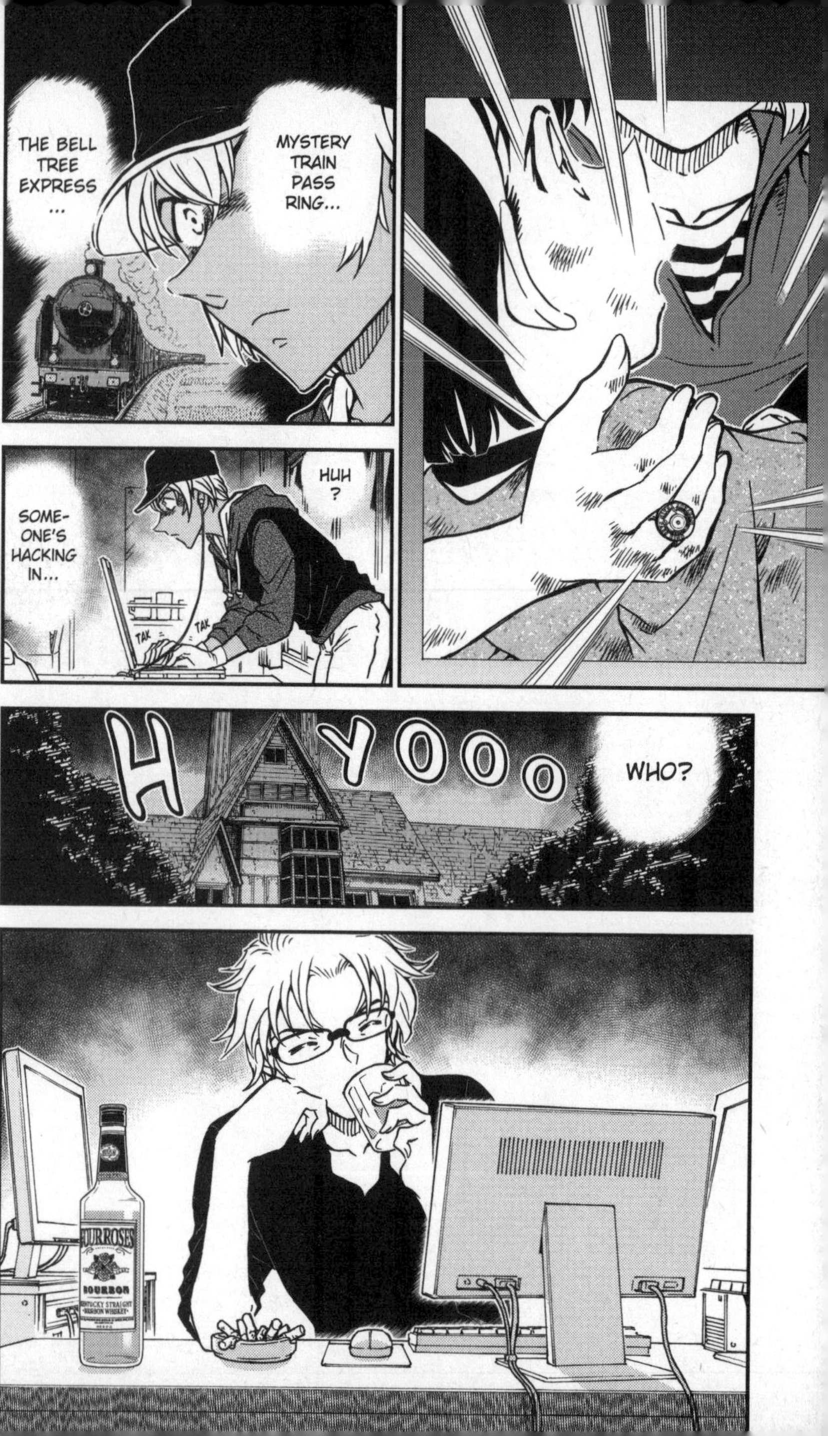
MYSTERY TRAIN PASS RING...
THE BELL TREE EXPRESS ...
HUH?
SOME-ONE'S HACKING IN...
TAK
TAK
HYOOO
WHO?
FOURROSES
BOURBON
KENTUCKY STRAIGHT BOURBON WHISKEY

Hello, Aoyama here!

Everyone was excited about the London Olympics* this summer, but I was already revved up before that. After all, my alma mater, Tottori Chuo Ikuei High School, made it to the finals in the Tottori baseball tournament! They lost 6 to 7 in a very close game, but I was just watching it on tape and got worked up all over again, even though I knew the outcome. *Heh*...Baseball is fun!

*The creator's commentary and the original Japanese volume 77 were written and published in the same year as the London Olympics.

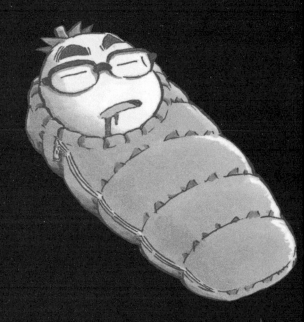

Gosho Aoyama's Mystery Library

77

KEI ENOMOTO

The perfect sleuth to solve an ironclad locked-room mystery is the professional of keys and locks, Kei Enomoto! Small and slender, he seems to be in his 20s or 30s but his age is unknown. He's a mysterious figure who calls himself a security consultant and specializes in locked-room murders. He never loses his calm, even in the most baffling situations, and masterfully solves seemingly impossible mysteries. He often displays an extraordinary knowledge of locks and security, which impresses his client, attorney Junko Aoto...but also leaves her suspicious, since Enomoto seems to have more experience in breaking than in preventing break-ins.

Author Yusuke Kishi decided to turn this concept into a series because he had too many locked room ideas to fit into one novel. I wish he'd share some ideas with me. *Heh.*

I recommend *The Glass Hammer*.

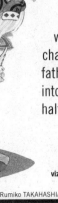